Lost Laughs of
'50s and '60s
Television

Lost Laughs of '50s and '60s Television

Thirty Sitcoms That Faded Off Screen

DAVID C. TUCKER

McFarland & Company, Inc., Publishers
Jefferson, North Carolina, and London

ALSO BY DAVID C. TUCKER
AND FROM MCFARLAND

Shirley Booth: A Biography and Career Record (2008)
The Women Who Made Television Funny: Ten Stars of 1950s Sitcoms (2007)

Frontispiece: Guest star Mickey Rooney (top) tries to knock some sense into Cara Williams in *Pete and Gladys*.

LIBRARY OF CONGRESS CATALOGUING-IN-PUBLICATION DATA

Tucker, David C., 1962–
    Lost laughs of '50s and '60s television : thirty sitcoms that faded off screen / David C. Tucker.
        p.   cm.
    Includes bibliographical references and index.

    ISBN 978-0-7864-4466-3
    softcover : 50# alkaline paper ∞

    1. Situation comedies (Television programs) — United States. 2. Television series — United States. I. Title.
PN1992.8.C66T82   2010
791.45'617 — dc22
                                          2010008154

British Library cataloguing data are available

©2010 David C. Tucker. All rights reserved

No part of this book may be reproduced or transmitted in any form or by any means, electronic or mechanical, including photocopying or recording, or by any information storage and retrieval system, without permission in writing from the publisher.

Front cover: *from top* Merry Anders, Lori Nelson and Barbara Eden in *How to Marry a Millionaire*, FOX TV Series 1957–1959 (Photofest); TV art ©2010 Shutterstock

Manufactured in the United States of America

McFarland & Company, Inc., Publishers
  Box 611, Jefferson, North Carolina 28640
    www.mcfarlandpub.com

For Ken,
who can always make me laugh

Acknowledgments

At the end of most sitcom episodes you'll see a list of several dozen people who were integral to the creation of that half-hour — Hollywood professionals who styled the stars' hair, operated the camera, edited the film, or otherwise played a role in putting the finished product on television. While this book didn't require as many writers as *Pete and Gladys,* and the only musical accompaniment came from my prized collection of Peggy Lee CDs, there were nonetheless quite a few people who deserve a credit line for help along the way. My thanks to:

Ken McCullers and Emile Worthy, advance readers who gave this book its first sampling and made a number of valuable suggestions.

My parents, Edward and Louise Tucker, who allowed me to watch my favorite sitcoms as a kid — but also encouraged me to read.

My writer friends who give their best efforts to documenting motion picture and television history — among them Lynn Kear, James Robert Parish, Hal Erickson, and the stalwarts of the McFarland Authors Discussion Board.

My friends and colleagues at the DeKalb County Public Library who have been supportive of my work — in particular my boss Magda Sossa, the fine folks of the Library Processing Center, and Vera Carswell, who isn't actually my publicist, but should be.

Gregg Oppenheimer, who added background information to my chapter on his dad's little-known show *Angel,* and John Eimen, who happily reminisced about his days as Cadet Monk Roberts on *McKeever and the Colonel.*

Most of all, of course, this book owes its existence to the talents on both sides of the camera who created the thirty shows featured herein. Their contribution is gratefully acknowledged.

Table of Contents

ACKNOWLEDGMENTS vi
INTRODUCTION 1

Angel 5
The Bill Dana Show 12
The Governor and J.J. 20
The Great Gildersleeve 27
Grindl 33
Happy 40
Hennesey 47
Hey, Jeannie! / The Jeannie Carson Show 54
How to Marry a Millionaire 61
Ichabod and Me 67
I'm Dickens ... He's Fenster 74
It's a Great Life 80
It's About Time 87
The Jim Backus Show: Hot Off the Wire 94
Love on a Rooftop 100
Margie 107
McKeever and the Colonel 113
Meet Mr. McNutley / The Ray Milland Show 120
The Mickey Rooney Show: Hey Mulligan 128
Mr. Adams and Eve 136
Mr. Terrific 143
Mrs. G. Goes to College / The Gertrude Berg Show 149
My Hero 157
O.K. Crackerby! 164
Occasional Wife 171

The People's Choice 178
Pete and Gladys 186
Peter Loves Mary 194
The Tom Ewell Show 202
Wendy and Me 208

APPENDIX: CHRONOLOGICAL LIST OF SHOWS 215
CHAPTER NOTES 217
BIBLIOGRAPHY 225
INDEX 227

Introduction

When we talk about television history, it is usually in terms of the shows that were the most popular, or the most fondly remembered — those believed in hindsight to have had the greatest impact. Yet for every *I Love Lucy* or *Twilight Zone*, there were a dozen other shows on the networks' schedules. And since the earliest days of network broadcasting, the half-hour situation comedy, or "sitcom," has been a genre that has never lost favor with programmers or viewers.

This book focuses on thirty half-hour situation comedies originally aired on network television or in first-run syndication during the 1950s and 1960s. Many of the shows covered here are little-known to today's television viewers. By and large, they are not the shows that won Emmys, nor the shows seen most often in reruns. Most of them have not had an official DVD release as of this writing, and quite possibly never will. In this book, each of these "lost" shows receives a full-length chapter that pieces together the limited information generally available about them, and puts them into perspective alongside their better-known peers.

It would be difficult to argue that most of the shows included in this book *deserve* to be as heralded or as studied in detail as *I Love Lucy, Bewitched,* or even *Gilligan's Island*. By and large, they don't. However, each was interesting to me in some way. At least a few were enjoyable enough that I happily watched all the episodes I could locate, and would have watched more if they had been available. In particular, I'm glad to have had the opportunity to take my first look at such shows as *Angel, The Governor and J.J., Love on a Rooftop,* and *Wendy and Me*. My favorite, though, was probably *Mrs. G. Goes to College*, a smart and warm comedy that made me an instant fan of leading lady Gertrude Berg.

Though these shows are not often seen today, this is not just a book about "sitcom flops." Some, like *The People's Choice*, were quite popular when they were on the air, and enjoyed a good run on network TV. It is also worth noting that, in the mid–1960s, Nielsen ratings estimated that approximately 30 to 32 million viewers watched prime time television every night, the vast majority tuning in to the shows aired by ABC, CBS, and NBC. In other words, a "flop" show was one that was watched only by, perhaps, seven or eight million people each week.

Other shows featured in this book played a role in the careers of some of Hollywood's best-known performers. You'll find the little-known sitcom work of Academy Award–winning actors Ray Milland and James Dunn, among others. You'll also read about some of the misfires of notable TV names like creator-producer Sherwood Schwartz, and *Burns and Allen* star-producer George Burns. *The Bill Dana Show* is fascinating to watch for the chance to see two well-known actors play early, embryonic versions of characters they would later make famous—Don Adams as a bumbling hotel detective who's practically a kissing cousin to Maxwell Smart (*Get Smart*), and Jonathan Harris, as the hotel manager, in a pre–*Lost in Space* role that strongly resembles his Dr. Zachary Smith.

Prior to the mid–1960s, it was comparatively rare for a television sitcom to run for less than a year, even if its ratings were low—most shows were bankrolled by no more than one or two sponsors and were typically sold for a full-season run. In several cases, the shows covered are interesting for the ways in which producers and/or sponsors tried to make adjustments midstream, when they realized that the shows weren't attracting large audiences. Some changed titles, added or dropped cast members, or replaced key staff in an effort to set the show on a smoother course.

Because these sitcoms were not the front-runners, nor widely seen in reruns, accurate information about them is scarce. Standard reference sources like Tim Brooks and Earle Marsh's *The Complete Directory to Prime Time Network and Cable TV Shows,* valuable as they are, typically contain only the briefest of entries on these shows. Since the shows themselves are difficult to see, and have been for many years, what little information appears in reference books, or on various websites, is not always reliable. Details such as the full names of the next-door neighbors on *Angel,* or the role played by Leo Penn on *Mrs. G. Goes to College,* are often missing or incorrectly stated in other sources. Most sources that discuss *Margie,* a sitcom set in the 1920s, repeat a bit of misinformation concerning the show's use of silent film-style titles between scenes.

My foremost source for the information in this book was screening the shows themselves. As a ground rule, if I could not obtain a minimum of three or four episodes of a show to view, I did not include the show in this book. In most cases, I was able to watch a dozen or more episodes, and in some instances virtually the entire series. Additional information came from contemporary coverage in newspapers and industry publications like *Variety,* as well as sources such as actors' memoirs whenever possible.

All of the shows in this book are, just to be clear, 30-minute situation comedies that aired on U.S. broadcast TV (usually on one of the three major networks of the time, although a couple were instead seen in first-run syndication). The earliest one featured is *My Hero,* which premiered in the fall of 1952; the most recent one is *The Governor and J.J.,* a new entry on CBS' fall 1969 schedule. Another book certainly could (and perhaps will) be written about shows from the early 1970s forward, in the post–*All in the Family* era, but they are not the focus here.

For each show covered in this book, I have provided a synopsis of its storyline, setting, and major characters, along with quotes and dialogue excerpts to give the reader a sense of the type of humor it used. The show's production history is covered in some detail as well. There is also a sampling of critical response it received, as well as some biographical data about major players in front of and behind the camera.

Each chapter begins with a cast and crew list, substantially more detailed than those found in other sources and as complete as I could make it. Some of the shows used the same directors and scriptwriters each week, while others relied heavily on freelancers. So, for example, the listing for *Pete and Gladys,* which was largely written by freelancers, contains the names of more than two dozen writers who contributed at least one script to the series. The book's index will help the reader track those individuals who were affiliated with multiple shows covered here.

Although it's sometimes fun to laugh at "bad" TV, it is not the purpose of this book to jeer at these shows, or the people who made them. Some of them were failures, either artistically or financially. While I have tried to be truthful about the reasons why these shows went off the air, I do not wish to belittle them. You'll find a little critical commentary here and there, but I have shied away from overburdening the book with my own opinion. There is no three-, four-, or five-star scoring system employed in this book to "rate" the shows. I'll let readers judge for themselves.

I hope you will enjoy rummaging through this collection of surprisingly interesting shows that have been gathering dust in the overstuffed attic of television comedy. Given the genre under discussion here, I also trust that you might find a laugh or two within these pages.

Angel

Annie Fargé (*Angelique Smith*), Marshall Thompson (*John Smith*), Doris Singleton (*Susie Carpenter*), Don Keefer (*George Carpenter*)
Executive Producer–Creator: Jess Oppenheimer. *Producer*: Edward H. Feldman. *Writers*: Arthur Alsberg, Bill Davenport, Jack Elinson, Robert Fisher, Barbara Hammer, Alan Lipscott, Nate Monaster, Jess Oppenheimer, Louis Pelletier, Joe Quillan, Roswell Rogers, Henry Sharp, Charles Stewart. *Directors*: Lamont Johnson, James Sheldon, Ezra Stone. *Script Consultant*: Bill Davenport. *Associate Producer*: Jack Aldworth. *Production Supervisor*: W. Argyle Nelson. *Director of Photography*: Robert de Grasse. *Production Manager*: James Paisley. *Supervising Film Editor*: Bud Molin. *Art Directors*: Ralph Berger, Patricio Guzman. *Music*: Eliot Daniel. *Theme*: Eliot Daniel, Jess Oppenheimer. *Set Decorator*: Robert Priestley. *Casting*: Mercedes Manzanares. *Makeup Artist*: Lee Greenway. *Hair Stylist*: Irma Kusely. *Costumer*: Della Fox. *Property Master*: William Black. *Sound Engineer*: Cameron McCulloch. *Camera Coordinator*: James Niver. *Rerecording Supervisor*: Gene F. Martin. *Script Supervisor*: Dottie Larsen. Burlingame Productions, in association with CBS Films.
Aired Thursdays at 9 P.M. (through December 1960), then Thursdays at 8 P.M. (through April 1961), then Wednesdays at 9 P.M. on CBS-TV. First aired October 6, 1960; last aired September 20, 1961. 33 black-and-white episodes.

SUSIE: Annie, do you have any idea what's in store for you?
ANNIE (puzzled): What's in what store for me?

The 1960-61 television season would be the first in almost a decade that would offer no new product by the reigning queen of the sitcom, Lucille Ball. The anthology series *Desilu Playhouse,* which had included occasional hour-long Lucy-Desi segments for the past two seasons, was canceled in the spring of 1960, not long after Ball filed for divorce from husband and co-founder Desi Arnaz.

Nonetheless, all over the CBS schedule there were sitcoms a-plenty, some of them explicit reminders of the ongoing impact of *I Love Lucy*. Longtime *Lucy* writers Bob Carroll, Jr., and Madelyn Pugh Martin sold CBS a new sitcom, *The Tom Ewell Show* (q.v.). Another new entry that fall was *Pete and Gladys* (q.v.), starring red-haired Cara Williams as a character many found reminiscent of Lucy Ricardo. And *Lucy*'s original producer and head writer, Jess Oppenheimer, was represented with his new series *Angel,* which would inevitably be compared to *I Love Lucy*.

Whereas *I Love Lucy* had focused on a zany, impulsive American housewife married to a Cuban-born husband, *Angel* tells the story of an average American husband newly married to a young Frenchwoman. The show's comedy centers on the attempts of a newcomer to the U.S. to adapt to American ways, and settle into her daily existence as a housewife in a typical American suburb. *Angel* starred newcomer Annie Fargé and Marshall Thompson as the Smiths, a young California married couple. John, a successful architect in his early thirties, is married to 23-year-old, French-born Angelique Bouchard.

In the show's animated opening titles, Angel is seen hopping down from the Eiffel Tower, skipping across the ocean (with an umbrella), and running up to the Statue of Liberty. The Eiffel Tower becomes the *A* and Lady Liberty the *L* that spell out *Angel*. (Also seen is a cartoon of creator Jess Oppenheimer, bald-pated and with glasses, as his fingers fly furiously over typewriter keys.)

In the pilot, as we get our first glimpse of Fargé, John Smith (Thompson) explains via voiceover, "That is Angelique. I call her Angel, and she came all the way from France to marry me." A flashback sequence in a later episode, "The Wedding" (6/7/61), reveals that the Smiths were married hurriedly in the New York City hotel that John booked to serve as their honeymoon suite.

It's the women versus the men on *Angel*: Annie Fargé (Angelique) and Doris Singleton (Susie) face off against Marshall Thompson (John) and Don Keefer (George).

Because Angel misplaced her passport during the ocean voyage, she's initially refused entry into the U.S., and John has had a few drinks to console himself by the time the impromptu ceremony finally takes place.

Angel, still new to the U.S., is perfecting her English via classes. In a routine that would be familiar to *I Love Lucy* viewers, she vents her frustration over the confusing pronunciations of similarly spelled words like *through, bough,* and *cough*. Though not yet sure whether or not she completely understands the American way of life, Angel is deeply in love with John. Next-door neighbors George Carpenter, an insurance agent, and wife Susie are a slightly older couple who are more cynical about the ins and outs of married life, and amused by the starry-eyed Smiths.

The plot of the series opener centers on the Smiths' first dinner party, at which it becomes obvious that Angel is showing up her American counterparts. The men are charmed by her French accent, beauty, and Continental flair and enjoy her cooking. When she tells the other wives that she walked several miles across town to save five cents per pound on meat, their husbands are suitably impressed, and the women are appalled. Later, supposedly showing Angel how she is expected to act in America, they take her on an expensive shopping spree that results in the Smiths' first fight.

Susie takes it upon herself to provide Angel, whom she calls Annie, with "a little advice on the care and feeding of household pets, which includes dogs, cats, birds — and husbands." In "Happy Marriage" (1/26/61), Susie pays a morning visit decked out in her bathrobe and curlers, smoking a cigarette. She's taken aback to see that Annie is beautifully dressed and coiffed for her self-appointed morning task of fixing John's breakfast, which includes setting a rose on the table. In the show's second episode, Angel says that she and "Johnny," as she calls him, have been married for "five months, three weeks, four days, ten hours, and [checks her watch] twenty-six minutes."

Creator–executive producer Jess Oppenheimer didn't try to deny the parallels between *I Love Lucy* and *Angel*, but did point out a few distinctions. "Annie isn't a clown like Lucille," Oppenheimer said, "but she has a wonderful sense of comedy timing and I think her flair and her accent will go over big with viewers."[1] Indeed, the physical comedy at which Lucille Ball excelled would not play a substantial element in Oppenheimer's new show. The laughs in *Angel* would arise largely from the main character's impulsive, spitfire personality, and her puzzled reactions to American customs, phrases, and activities. (When John, refuting her point in an argument, retorts, "My foot!" Angel looks down at his feet uncomprehendingly.)

Angel's basic premise explored a number of American activities and habits with which its lead character was not familiar — income tax returns, elections, and the like — as well as providing a slightly new take on some old sitcom standbys. When John buys Angel a car, and she wants driving lessons, she calls a driving range. The first time that her mother-in-law comes to visit, Angel mistakes

Mrs. Smith for a maid John hired, and tells her to get busy washing the breakfast dishes.

In "The Trusting Wife" (11/24/60), John is asked to design a house for glamorous Hollywood star Lola Valdez. Warned by Susie that the actress has a well-deserved reputation as a home wrecker, Angel dismisses the matter until the Smiths attend a party at Valdez's home. After watching the star flirt shamelessly with John, Angel erupts at home, in her charmingly fractured English:

> ANGEL: That woman is a ... a ... house mover!
> JOHN: You mean a home wrecker.
> ANGEL: No, a house mover! She would like to move you from my house to her house!

Like some other sitcom stars of the day, Fargé and Thompson routinely appeared in commercials for their sponsors that were included in each week's episode. The weekly commercials were often written so as to coincide with the story, and play like a final scene in the show. Since Johnson Wax was a major sponsor of the show, the commercials often revolved around Angel's enthusiastic praise for the company's new furniture polish, Pledge.

At the time he developed the concept for *Angel*, Oppenheimer was intrigued with the idea of building the show around a young, beautiful, and charming Frenchwoman, but didn't have anyone particular in mind. Once his script was greenlighted by CBS in early 1960, he realized that finding the right actress to play Annie Smith would be more difficult than he'd anticipated. "I guess I interviewed every French actress in Hollywood," he later said.[2] He turned thumbs down on them all, and was at an impasse until someone told him about a little-known New York actress named Annie Fargé. At just over five feet tall and approximately 90 pounds, and herself a fairly recent immigrant to the United States, Fargé was perfect to play the role.

Born in 1936 as Annie Goldfarb, the future actress had a difficult childhood, growing up in a Jewish family just before World War II. She was shepherded out of France just in time to avoid Nazi occupation. As a teenager, she decided to become an actress, despite her mother's opposition. When Fargé auditioned for and was accepted by the prestigious *Conservatoire Nationale*, her mother consented, and her career grew from there. Married to ballet dancer-choreographer Dirk Sanders, whom she followed to New York City on a tour, she became the mother of a little girl shortly before *Angel* went into production. Producer-director Joshua Logan was credited with discovering Fargé and paying for her first lessons in English. Broadway producer David Merrick wanted to audition her for the lead role in a production of *Lili* he was mounting, but Fargé was then pregnant with her daughter, and spoke no English.

At the time *Angel* was being assembled, Fargé was understudying France Nuyen in the lead role of Broadway's *The World of Suzie Wong*. Her agent, learning that *Angel* was being cast, sent a photo to Oppenheimer, and the veteran producer arranged a telephone interview. In New York in December 1959, she met with CBS executive Robert Lewine, who called Oppenheimer on the West Coast and said, "Jess, I have your Angel here."[3] After a brief phone conversation, Oppenheimer agreed, and signed her to a contract without as much as a screen test.

Surprisingly, casting the role of Angel's nice-guy, straight-arrow American husband proved almost as difficult. At one point, Oppenheimer had his eye on up-and-coming comic actor Dick Van Dyke, but Van Dyke bypassed *Angel* in favor of a role in Broadway's *Bye Bye Birdie*. Oppenheimer arranged screen tests for five leading men, but once they'd tested opposite his leading lady, he deemed none of them satisfactory. Only days before the pilot went before the cameras did he identify and sign Marshall Thompson for the role.

This would be the first regular sitcom role for the 35-year-old actor, born James Marshall Thompson on November 27, 1925. Signed to an MGM contract in 1943, Thompson showed himself to be a clean-cut and likable young leading man, but did not emerge as a top star. In the early 1950s, when studios began releasing their contract players due to the increased competition from television, Thompson was cut loose. He had enough of a marquee name to win film roles as a freelancer, but as the decade progressed, they were increasingly of the ilk of *Cult of the Cobra* (1955) and *It! The Terror from Beyond Space* (1958). He began making guest appearances on live television dramatic anthologies, and starred in his first series, the ill-fated *World of Giants*, in 1959. Aside from his tenure in *Angel*, he is probably best-remembered for his later lead role as veterinarian Dr. Marsh Tracy in the African adventure series *Daktari* (CBS, 1966–69). As it happened, Thompson was near to signing with another producer when he was offered the role on *Angel*, but opted to accept Oppenheimer's offer instead.

Cast as Angel's new American best friend Susie was Doris Singleton (born September 28, 1919), familiar to *I Love Lucy* viewers for her recurring role as Lucy's rival Caroline Appleby. She and co-star Don Keefer, playing the Carpenters, would be the only other *Angel* regulars, with Singleton appearing more frequently, and prominently, than Keefer. Another *Lucy* veteran, actress Shirley Mitchell, was seen occasionally as Angel's other friend, Blanche. The ubiquitous Gale Gordon, who'd worked with Oppenheimer almost 15 years earlier in radio's *My Favorite Husband*, made a few guest appearances as Stanley Johnson, John's boss at the firm of Blake, Johnson, Corwin, and Nelson.

The shooting of the pilot took place during Fargé's pregnancy, requiring special camera angles to camouflage her condition. Oppenheimer saw this as a good omen, since Lucille Ball had also been with child when the audition episode of *I Love Lucy* was filmed. Once completed, however, *Angel* stirred little enthusiasm at CBS; despite its creator's comedic pedigree, executives rejected it. According to Oppenheimer's son Gregg, "Bob Lewine [head of CBS Films] took the pilot to General Foods and S.C. Johnson, who both liked it so much that they gave CBS an ultimatum: Put it on the network or we'll pull our sponsorship from all of our *other* CBS programs."⁴ Faced with the sponsors' insistence, network executives relented and placed the show on the fall 1960 schedule, but in a difficult time slot that would place it into direct competition with two other sitcoms.

Fargé relocated to Hollywood for the starring role in *Angel*. In April, she gave birth to daughter Leslie, and by June was shooting new episodes. Oppenheimer employed the same three-camera filming method that was originally perfected for *I Love Lucy* almost a decade earlier.

In the weeks before *Angel* premiered, Fargé and her new show were promoted with a gimmick in which postcards soaked in Chanel No. 5 were mailed to columnists with provocative messages like "I'll be seeing you" and "Hope you'll be nice to me when we meet." Only the final card was signed with the name of the actress, and urged them to watch her new show.

The premiere installment of *Angel* went over big with the industry trade paper *Variety* (10/12/60), which termed it "a truly funny show" and sang the praises of its star: "Miss Fargé is genuinely funny, a natural mimic and clown. When she's on, *Angel* is a comedy bulldozer, and she's on most of the time."

Others were slightly less enthusiastic. Critic Harriet Van Horne thought Fargé "a superb comedienne ... she moves like a humming-bird, never still, never silent, responding to life with passion and humor." There was only one small problem, the critic reported: She could not understand half or more of the lines that Fargé spoke, and said she would watch future episodes only if she had the services of a translator.⁵

Aside from writing the pilot that sold the series, Oppenheimer would not assume the bulk of the responsibility for *Angel* scripts, drawing on a cadre of thickly credited freelancers instead. However, according to Gregg Oppenheimer, his father "did at least a polish, and sometimes a full rewrite, on each of the scripts, but didn't take a writing credit for any of that work because he felt he'd attract better writers that way."⁶

Though she was pleased to be starring in her first major project, Fargé admitted that life in California didn't completely suit her. "It is wonderful for my daughter, who is eight months old, because of the sun. She is growing up so healthy. But for me, no. There is no theater, no night life, no intellectual life. After work, I rush home for the last glimpse of my baby. She gives me a smile and then, bang, she's asleep. And then I am there alone, with my TV set."⁷

Angel would be tried by CBS in three different time slots during the 1960-61 season. Initially outpointed by ABC's new family comedy *My Three Sons*, the first regular series for well-known film actor Fred MacMurray, *Angel* was moved at midseason to an earlier time period, and then to a different night of the week, but all to little avail. As Marshall Thompson would later note, "They kept changing the time slot until the standing joke was not if you'd seen *Angel*, but whether you knew where to look."⁸ In the spring of 1961, after a season of sluggish ratings, CBS canceled *Angel*. Also shown the door that spring was *The Tom Ewell Show*, the first major post–*Lucy* writing assignment for Madelyn Pugh Martin and Bob Carroll, Jr.

As Oppenheimer had admitted before *Angel* even premiered, a new TV series was always an uncertain thing. "You can't tell about shows because there's such an intermingling of things," he said. "There's one moment when the writing, directing, and the acting all have to click, and if they don't it just doesn't come off."⁹

Personally, Fargé was going through some changes as well. By the summer of 1961, her marriage to Sanders was kaput, and she had accepted an engagement ring from meat-packing heir George (Geordie) Hormel. Hormel had previously been married to actress Leslie Caron. In 1962, she starred in a touring production of *A Shot in the Dark*. She made television guest appearances on shows like *The Rifleman* (ABC, 1958–63) and *Perry Mason* (CBS, 1957–66) in the years following *Angel*, but eventually gave up her American career and returned to France.

Oppenheimer returned to CBS in 1963 with another female-centered sitcom, *Glynis,* starring British actress Glynis Johns as a mystery writer who becomes involved in real-life cases. That show had a shorter run than *Angel*. Always credited with knowing a thing or two about situation comedies starring funny ladies, Oppenheimer's last major production credit before retiring from the industry would be *The Debbie Reynolds Show* (NBC, 1969–70).

Though by no means a classic on the order of *I Love Lucy, Angel* is a charming and likable show that's reminiscent of *Lucy*, but enjoyable on its own terms. Under different circumstances, it could well have developed into a popular hit.

The Bill Dana Show

Bill Dana (*Jose Jimenez*), Jonathan Harris (*Jerome Phillips*), Gary Crosby (*Eddie*), Don Adams (*Byron Glick*), Maggie Peterson (*Susie*)
Executive Producer: Sheldon Leonard. *Producers*: Jack Elinson, Howard Leeds. *Writers*: Jerry Belson, Sam Bobrick, Dick Chevillat, Bill Dana, Iz Elinson, Jack Elinson, Bill Idelson, Sheldon Keller, Garry Marshall, Howard Merrill, Howard Ostroff, Ray Singer, Charles Stewart. *Directors*: Stan Cherry, Theodore J. Flicker, Sheldon Leonard, Al Lewis, Howard Morris, Jerry Paris, Coby Ruskin, Jay Sandrich, Danny Thomas. *Associate Producer–Production Supervisor*: Ronald Jacobs. *Director of Photography*: Henry Cronjager. *Art Director*: Kenneth A. Reid. *Story Consultants*: Jack Elinson, Norman Paul. *Production Manager*: Frank Myers. *Music*: Irving Szathmary. *"Jose" Theme*: Earle Hagen. *Set Decorator*: Ken Swartz. *Film Editors*: Robert Moore, Theodore Rich. *Makeup*: Tom Tuttle. *Hair Stylist*: Donna McDonough. *Costumes*: Stan Kufel. *Assistant Directors*: Stanley J. Brooks, Jay Sandrich, Don Torpin. *Casting*: Ruth Burch. *Camera Coordinator*: Robert Sousa. *Prop Masters*: Gene Gossert, Jerry McFarland. *Script Continuity*: Rosemary Dorsey, Gloria Morgan. *Rerecording Editors*: John Hall, Richard LeGrand, Robert Reeve. *Sound Engineer*: Cam McCulloch. Amigo Productions.
Aired Sundays at 7 P.M. (through September 1964), then Sundays at 8:30 P.M. on NBC-TV. First aired September 22, 1963; last aired January 17, 1965. 42 black-and-white episodes.

HOTEL GUEST (to Jose, who has just barged into his room): Didn't you see the "Do Not Disturb" sign?
JOSE (puzzled): I did not disturb the sign!

The naïve immigrant who comes to America with only a few dollars in his or her pocket, but a heart full of dreams—it's a staple of comedy that, with minor variations, could be seen in a number of popular shows—see, for example, *Angel* and *Hey, Jeannie!* (both q.v.). On radio, *Life with Luigi* became an enduring popular hit, and was briefly transferred to television. In the early 1960s, comedian Bill Dana became a favorite of television audiences playing a similar character, Jose Jimenez, in guest appearances on variety shows, and as a recurring character in *The Danny Thomas Show* (ABC and CBS, 1953–64). But *The Bill Dana Show,* which gave the likable character his own arena, enjoyed only a relatively short run, and soon fell victim to changing social attitudes about the appropriateness of American-born actors playing ethnic roles that some viewed as stereotypical.

Jose Jimenez is a young Mexican immigrant working as a bellhop in the exclusive Park Central Hotel in New York City. When off duty, he occupies a small room in the hotel basement. His best friend and fellow bellman, Eddie, is a young American who believes in getting by on as little work as possible. Eddie calls himself "the kid with the fast answers," relying on this rather than genuine effort to stay employed. Stuffy, sardonic Mr. Phillips, the hotel man-

Times change: The cast of *The Bill Dana Show* points out its second-season shift to a later time slot. Pictured (left to right): Don Adams (Byron), Maggie Peterson (Susie), Jonathan Harris (Mr. Phillips), and Bill Dana (Jose).

ager, regards both men with disdain but particularly chafes at the cheerful obtuseness of Jose. Not known for his kindness, patience, or generosity, Mr. Phillips is described by Eddie as "the man who roots for the wolf against Red Riding Hood."

In the first-season episode "The Hiring of Jose" (4/5/64), Eddie recalls how Jose landed his job at the Park Central. Just before his arrival, the hotel staff had been advised that a famous Latin American comedian had been booked by the Argentinean embassy for a stay. When Jose turns up to apply for the job of bellman, mentioning that "the Ambassador" sent him, he's mistaken for the celebrity in question. Jose is assured that he can sign a tab for anything he needs in the hotel, and given the best room in the house, lavish meals, and a new wardrobe. Told that the hotel's rates are $65 a day, Jose thinks this the salary he will earn as a bellman, and is deliriously happy. By the time the misunderstanding is cleared up, and Mr. Phillips learns that Jose is not an entertainer but a job applicant from the Ambassador Employment Agency, the manager is compelled to give him the job, since he has now has racked up a foot-high stack of bills for hotel goods and services.

Always well-intentioned, Jose nonetheless regularly puts himself in danger of losing his job. In "Honeymoon Suite" (11/10/63), he wants to give his cousin and her new husband a wedding present of a night in the Park Central's most luxurious and expensive unit, but can't afford the asking price ($50). Instead, he sneaks them into the unoccupied suite unbeknownst to Mr. Phillips, who then proceeds to rent the suite to some latecomers, creating havoc.

Fans of Dana's work, like writer Alan Ward, found the character of Jose endearing. "Jose Jimenez ... epitomizes all the gentle, slightly confused newcomers to our country whose misunderstanding of our language, and our mores and customs, lead them into linguistic and physical pratfalls. But who inevitably find a way out of a dilemma."[1] Other observers, however, would soon view Dana and his signature character less benignly.

Born October 5, 1924, as William Szathmary, Bill Dana broke into show business in the early 1950s, after graduating from Emerson College and relocating to New York City. Within a few years, he was beginning to enjoy some success as a comic actor, in shows like NBC's *The Martha Raye Show* (1955-56), when a mishap during a performance landed him in the hospital. He heeded his doctors' advice to find a safer way to earn a living, and took up comedy writing. Among his first clients was rising actor-comedian Don Adams, who would become his lifelong friend, and would later become an integral part of *The Bill Dana Show*.

In 1956, Steve Allen began his Sunday night prime time variety series on NBC, and Dana was hired as a writer. When his script readings made the star laugh, he was given the opportunity to participate in some of the show's sketches, including the "Man on the Street" segments that teamed him with

Allen regulars Don Knotts, Tom Poston, and Louis Nye. Combining his writing and performing skills, Dana eventually rose to the position of head writer on *The Steve Allen Show* by the time it ended its NBC run as a weekly series in 1960.

He would later recall that it was for a Steve Allen Christmas skit that he first tried out the character of Jose (whose name he, not surprisingly, spelled without any of the diacritics that would have made it more authentically Latin). The premise of the skit was a school for training prospective Santas. Dana and fellow writer Don Hinkley envisioned a Mexican Santa Claus who would pronounce "Ho, ho, ho!" as "Jo, jo, jo!" Eventually the character gave Dana a recurring role in CBS's popular *The Danny Thomas Show*, in which Jose worked as an elevator operator in the Williams' apartment building. The ongoing popularity of the character resulted in a book, *My Name Jose Jimenez: A Photographic Interview*, published by Pocket Books in 1961, as well as a series of comedy albums (*Jose Jimenez in Orbit*, *Jose Jimenez in Jollywood*, etc.).

The character of Jose met with such success that some viewers expected Dana, a Hungarian Jew, to be the same in person. "This is quite a phenomenon," Dana said. "Jose being considered a real person is possibly the reason for the looks of disappointment on the faces of people who stop me on the street to talk and I reply in fairly distinct English."[2]

The idea of making Jose a hotel bellhop, Dana explained, allowed the show's producers and writers the most latitude for the lead character to meet new people and participate in varied stories. Dana's business partners Danny Thomas and Sheldon Leonard entered into a deal with Bill Dana Productions to form Amigo Productions, a jointly owned company that would produce *The Bill Dana Show*.

He credited NBC executive Mort Werner with originating the idea for putting Jose Jimenez in his own series, and for placing the show on the network schedule without even the formality of a pilot. Given the involvement of the production team of Sheldon Leonard and Danny Thomas, then riding high with *The Andy Griffith Show* and *The Dick Van Dyke Show* aside from Thomas' own sitcom, Dana felt sure he was in good hands. Though the idea of *The Bill Dana Show* was percolating in the spring of 1962, it would be another year before the show made its NBC debut. In the meantime, Dana and his producing partners used his continuing guest appearances on *The Danny Thomas Show* to generate interest in the intended spinoff.

Though he had been uncertain about starring in a series, Dana eventually found himself, as Danny Thomas had been a decade earlier, tired of traveling and ready to settle down to a predictable routine. "I have a beautiful home here now, and if one can build a nest in an elm tree, why should he be flying all over the country? If God is good, the series will go into multiple years. Then I may say, 'Gee, I wish I could go on the road,' but right now I am happy."[3] Dana believed that his show improved the media image of bellhops. "Remember the old movie bellhops?" he said. "They were always sneaky little guys, peering through keyholes, trying to wangle big tips and sneaking bottles of bad booze up to the room."[4]

For today's viewer, *The Bill Dana Show* is probably most intriguing for the opportunity to see two future TV stars play prototypes of their later characterizations. Second-billed to Dana was actor Jonathan Harris (1914–2002) as Park Central Hotel manager Mr. Phillips. Harris, already a veteran of the syndicated spy drama *The Third Man* (1959–62), would become a TV icon with his role as cowardly Dr. Zachary Smith on the CBS science fiction adventure *Lost in Space* (1965–68).

With no robot in sight, Harris unleashes his insults instead on Dana's Jose, though he hasn't yet developed the knack for alliteration that will cause him to denote the Robot as a "bubble-headed booby." Instead, he calls Jimenez an "outrageous nincompoop," and informs him, "Of all the blundering numbskulls I've ever encountered, you're the absolute worst!" In virtually every episode, Jose's job is endangered, yet somehow he emerges victorious just in time for the closing credits.

A recurring guest star who quickly became one of the show's most popular players was Don Adams (1923–2005), playing the hotel's house detective Byron Glick ("150 pounds of ripping muscle," he says of himself). Not surprisingly to any fan of Adams' later hit series *Get Smart* (NBC and CBS, 1965–70), Byron was a woefully incompetent — though brashly confident — enforcer of the law. Byron was supposedly hired only because his father held the same job successfully for many years. The younger Glick is described by Mr. Phillips in one segment as the only hotel detective who couldn't prevent having his own wallet stolen by a pickpocket. For the show's second season, Adams became a regular, billed in the opening titles.

Adams credited Dana with originating what would become his signature line on *Get Smart*, "Would you believe...?" It was first conceived for a Bengal Lancers skit Dana wrote years earlier; Adams thought nothing much of the line and dropped it from that routine. It would later emerge from the mouth of Byron Glick a few times on *The Bill Dana Show*, though it wasn't yet a substantial part of Adams' shtick.

The other full-time regular during the series' first year was actor-singer Gary Crosby (son of Bing), who played Eddie, Jose's fellow bellhop. Seen occasionally was character actress Amzie Strickland as Mr. Phillips' devoted wife Cynthia. Like most of the output of producing partners Thomas and Leonard, *The Bill Dana Show* was filmed three-camera–style, before a live studio audience. Thomas and Leonard's house composer Earle Hagen, acclaimed for his themes for *The Andy Griffith Show* and *The Dick Van Dyke Show*, among others, contributed a bouncy, Latin-flavored theme to accompany *The Bill Dana Show*'s animated opening titles (in which Jose is depicted as a Don Quixote type). Surprisingly, given his background as a comedy writer, Dana apparently did not contribute strongly to the show's scripts, although he was credited with penning the second-season episode, "What Elephant?" (10/18/64).

In its first year, *The Bill Dana Show* aired at 7 P.M. on Sundays, leading into NBC's popular *Disney's Wonderful World of Color*. Though its only direct network competition in this time slot was CBS's *Lassie*, it was a time when children mostly dominated the television dial, and Dana's show pulled disappointing ratings, as another sitcom, *Ensign O'Toole*, had done the previous season. At the end of its first season, Dana's show was canceled — or so it seemed.

Unexpectedly, when NBC's quarrel with Screen Gems over *Grindl* (q.v.) reached a stalemate, *The Bill Dana Show* was unexpectedly revived, and offered the Sunday slot that Imogene Coca's show had previously occupied. Gary Crosby's character of Eddie was phased out for the second season. New for the show's sophomore year was Susie, a kindly waitress in the hotel coffee shop who, along with Byron Glick, becomes Jose's friend and confidante at work. Cast in that role was pretty blonde newcomer Maggie Peterson, today better known for her occasional appearances as Charlene Darling on *The Andy Griffith Show* (CBS, 1960–68). Dana also hoped to take stories outside the hotel a little more often, and incorporate more fantasy sequences. Indeed, most second-season episodes incorporated at least one lengthy scene done in the form of a skit. Usually these are worked into the show as a daydream that Jose is having. The skits gave Dana, his co-stars, and writers the opportunity to play a broader form of comedy more akin to a variety show.

Dana admitted that starring in a weekly show was tougher than he'd anticipated. "A weekly series is rough," he said as he was gearing up for the second season. "I found out that you can't watch *The Late, Late Show*, just the first two acts of Johnny Carson, and then turn out the light.... [U]nless you're careful and sensible, you end up by doing lots of shows feeling sick. I did. I caught everything that was going around, and I think a couple of the viruses were imported just for me."[5]

Midway through the 1964-65 season, NBC canceled *The Bill Dana Show*, for which co-stars Jonathan Harris and Don Adams should probably have sent network executives an effusive thank-you note. Within months, they would both land the major roles for which they are best remembered. In the fall of 1965, Harris began his unforgettable, three-year "special guest star" stint as Dr. Zachary Smith on *Lost in Space*, while Don Adams scored the lead in the Mel Brooks–Buck Henry spy spoof *Get Smart*. Gary Crosby went on to be a regular in the Jack Webb action series *Chase* (NBC, 1973-74) and *Adam-12* (NBC, 1968–74) but later became better known for his bitter 1982 memoir *Going My Own Way*, which painted a disturbing picture of the parenting skills of his famous father. He died of lung cancer on August 24, 1995.

Whether or not it was so designed, the show's forty-second and final episode, "The Court Jester" (1/17/65), scripted by Howard Ostroff, served as a fitting conclusion to *The Bill Dana Show*, as well as a response to some of its critics. In this segment, two businessmen staying at the Park Central get a kick out of Jose's personality and malapropisms, and offer him a job. The offer comes at an opportune moment for hapless Jose, who's in hot water as usual, for transgressions such as telling another guest he'd probably like the rooms at the hotel across the street better. The job opportunity allows him to stand up to his tyrannical boss for the first time. But when Mr. Phillips learns that the men only want to hire Jose because he'll be "the perfect company clown"—good for a few laughs around the company convention and elsewhere—he upbraids them: "Jose may have his shortcomings, but he's not someone you can show off as your personal clown.... Perhaps he's naïve and gullible, perhaps he doesn't have as much education as the rest of us, but he has more dignity and honor than you will have with all of your success."

Even after the series' cancellation, Dana continued to revive his Jose Jimenez character in guest appearances on the most popular variety shows of the mid- to late 1960s: *The Jackie Gleason Show* (CBS, 1962–70), *The Danny Kaye Show* (CBS, 1963–67), and *The Hollywood Palace* (ABC, 1964–70). On the heels of his sitcom's cancellation, Dana announced that he was preparing a cartoon show, tentatively titled *The Adventures of Uncle Jose*, but the series never materialized. In 1966, Dana served as producer of Milton Berle's short-lived comeback ABC variety show, on which he also appeared occasionally as Jose.

Within a few years, however, Hispanic-American advocacy groups were beginning to protest the stereotypical images of their culture seen on American television, and most of them no longer found Dana's act amusing, any more than they did Frito-Lay's commercial character "The Frito Bandito." In 1968, Dana's series of telephone company ads in which Jose promoted the "yellow pages" drew the ire of a group called IMAGE (Involvement of the Mexican-American in Gainful Endeavors).

Perhaps in response to the criticism, Dana involved himself in charitable activities that would benefit Hispanics. During his sitcom's original run, Dana established a scholarship for theater arts students at UCLA, giving first preference to students of Mexican-American heritage. Shortly after the show's cancellation, he awarded the first scholarship to student Jose Luis Gonzalez, a budding filmmaker. Still, as the sixties marched on, the feeling began to grow that Jose Jimenez had outlived his time, and before long Dana took the hint.

"After tonight, Jose Jimenez is dead," Dana told attendees of a Congress of Mexican-American Unity event in the spring of 1970. As recently as January of that year, he had done a Jimenez routine on CBS's *The Ed Sullivan Show*. While he had never intended to give offense with the characterization, and did not believe it was insulting, he understood that in changing times a different standard prevailed. He denied that he had given in to pressure groups, but told the *Los Angeles Times*' Cecil Smith, "[I]t was people from this country who would tell me 'Boy, I sure love it when you play that dumb Mexican!' that made me drop the character." There were other accents in his repertoire, Dana said, that he could unveil instead.[6]

Having abandoned his most famous character, however, Dana entered a relatively quiet period of his career in the 1970s, and was little seen on television. In 1970, he wrote and produced a variety special for Don Knotts that resulted in the comedian's 1970-71 NBC series. A 1974 booking as a standup comedian at the Playboy Club was received with only lukewarm enthusiasm. In 1980, he scripted *The Nude Bomb,* the feature film revival of *Get Smart,* and in 1983 had a featured role as Bernardo in CBS's short-lived sitcom *Zorro and Son.* Dana would surface occasionally on NBC's *The Golden Girls* (1985–92), a series for which Danny Thomas' son Tony served as co-executive producer. Seen in an early guest appearance as Sophia Petrillo's father, he later settled into a recurring character as Dorothy's goofy, lecherous Uncle Angelo. He subsequently retired.

Not until the 1990s, with the advent of ABC's *The George Lopez Show,* would a Mexican-American comedian have the opportunity to star in a sitcom as the non-stereotypical lead character. In today's more culturally sensitive environment, *The Bill Dana Show* seems unlikely to be revived, and perhaps that's best. It does, however, provide an opportunity to see a genuine comedic talent at work, and to assess some of the ways in which television has grown up in the past few decades.

The Governor and J.J.

Dan Dailey (*Gov. William R. Drinkwater*), Julie Sommars (*J.J. Drinkwater*), Neva Patterson (*Maggie McLeod*), James Callahan (*George Callison*), Nora Marlowe (*Sara Andrews*), Ed Platt (*Orrin Hacker*)

Executive Producer: Leonard Stern. *Creators*: Leonard Stern, Arne Sultan. *Producer*: Arne Sultan. *Writers*: Barbara Avedon, Earl Barret, Frank Red Benson, Chris Hayward, George Kirgo, Bill Manhoff, Douglas Morrow, Richard Powell, Burt Prelutsky, Roger Price, Leonard Stern, Arne Sultan, Jay Terry, Gene Thompson, Harry Winkler, Roland Wolpert. *Directors*: Earl Barret, Nicholas Colasanto, Dan Dailey, Lee Philips, Alan Rafkin, Jay Sandrich, Leonard Stern, George Tyne, Charles Walters. *Associate Producer*: Budd Cherry. *Director of Photography*: William T. Cline. *Art Director*: Perry Ferguson II. *Story Editor*: Earl Barret. *Production Executive*: Harry T. Sherman. *Music Composed and Conducted by* Jerry Fielding. *Set Decorator*: Don Sullivan. *Post-Production Supervisor*: Ted Rich. *Assistant Director*: Hap Weyman. *Supervising Music Editor*: Gene Feldman. *Music Supervisor*: Bruce Broughton. *Sound Mixer*: Cam McCulloch. *Camera Coordinator*: Gil Clasen. *Script Supervisor*: Hope Williams. *Makeup Artist*: Lon Bentley. *Hair Stylist*: Lynda Gurasich. *Women's Costumer*: Dorothy Rogers. *Men's Costumer*: Bob Harris, Jr. *Mr. Dailey's Wardrobe*: Worsted-Tex. *Title Visualization*: Reza S. Badiyi. Talent Associates/Norton Simon, Inc., in association with CBS-TV.

Aired Tuesdays at 9:30 P.M. (through September 1970), then Wednesdays at 8:30 P.M. on CBS-TV. First aired September 23, 1969; last aired December 30, 1970. 39 color episodes.

MAGGIE (the governor's secretary): Good news. Mayor Dutton called. He wanted you to know the strike is over.
GOVERNOR: Which one — transit, garbage, or teachers?
MAGGIE: I'll check — now that the phone strike's over.

The public and private life of a governor, his daughter, and his staff were the focus of this sitcom that served as a bridge between the fantasy-based, escapist shows of the 1960s, and the harder-edged, more realistic comedies that became all the rage in the 1970s.

In the pilot episode, 47-year-old Governor Bill Drinkwater, who presides over an unnamed Midwestern state, is still recovering from the recent death of his wife Mary. Prior to being elected to public office, he was a partner in a successful law firm. His 22-year-old daughter Jennifer Jo, known to all as J.J., has a job as assistant curator at a children's zoo. Needing someone to accompany him to a fundraiser, Drinkwater asks his daughter, despite the misgivings of his associates, including party leader Orrin Hacker, who classifies J.J. as "way out."

Though she's initially ill at ease, J.J. acquits herself well at the party. Afterwards, Drinkwater says, "I like having her with me. I need her. She's my first lady." According to a CBS press release, Governor Drinkwater "regards himself politically as a middle-of-the-roader who has a strong feeling for the underdog and often finds himself involved in social reforms." He welcomes J.J.'s role as his new first lady because she serves as "a necessary catalyst and bridge to the younger generation."[1]

Co-creator Arne Sultan described the governor's politics as being neither strictly right or left, though there was a slight leaning toward the liberal. Much

When the governor's away, J.J. will play (or so her father fears) — Julie Sommars with guest star Craig Stevens in *The Governor and J.J.*

of the show's comedy centered on the generation-gap conflicts between the middle-aged governor and his young daughter, who share an abiding affection and loyalty for each other even amidst any temporary disagreements.

Comprising the nucleus of the governor's loyal staff are motherly housekeeper Sara, his secretary Maggie, and his press secretary George. In later episodes, the Drinkwaters adopt a basset hound named Guv.

Star Dan Dailey was born Daniel James Dailey, Jr., on December 14, 1915. He'd been signed as an MGM contract player in 1940, following a successful Broadway run in *Babes in Arms*. A fixture in MGM musicals of the 1940s, he was later paired with Betty Grable at 20th Century–Fox in films like *Mother Wore Tights* (1947) and *When My Baby Smiles at Me* (1948), for which he received an Oscar nomination as Best Actor. When musicals went out of favor in the 1950s, Dailey's movie career slowed accordingly, coming to a dead stop after a role in a 1963 short, *Las Cuatro Noches de la Luna Llena* (a.k.a. *Four Nights of the Full Moon*). By then, he'd appeared in more than 50 films. Dailey's sister Irene was also an actress, known for her stage work (*The Subject Was Roses*) and roles on TV soap operas. During the run of *Governor*, she was a regular on CBS's daytime drama *The Edge of Night*, and later had a lengthy run as Liz Matthews on NBC's *Another World*.

Prior to *The Governor and J.J.*, Dailey's only experience with a continuing series role was the short-lived British adventure series *Four Just Men*, seen on England's ITV network during the 1959-60 season. As the title implied, Dailey, playing Paris-based American journalist Tim Collier, was one of a quartet of lead actors who took turns playing the lead role in the 39 segments filmed. His co-stars were Jack Hawkins, Richard Conte, and Vittorio de Sica.

When he was approached about the starring role in CBS's new sitcom, Dailey was occupying himself with touring productions of the hit Neil Simon comedies *The Odd Couple* (as Felix) and *Plaza Suite*. Initially told by his agent that he was being offered a sitcom, Dailey said no. He had invested his movie earnings carefully, was well-set financially, and hesitated to take on the burden of another series. But he met co-star Julie Sommars and liked her, and decided his career needed a new direction.

"There isn't any dancing any more ... they're not making the musical movies, and you can't do any real dancing on television. There's not enough scope or range, you can't move. TV is a closeup business. That's why it's a singer's business."[2] As for movies, Dailey cracked, "They wouldn't want me in the kind of pictures they make today anyhow because I don't look good in the nude."[3]

He played the role of Governor Drinkwater with a dry wit, investing the character with an intelligent, bemused persona that made him a far more credible (if idealized) political leader than the duly elected nitwits Governor James Gatling of *Benson* (ABC, 1979–86) and Mayor Randall Winston of *Spin City* (ABC, 1996–2002).

Despite Dailey's top billing, *The Governor and J.J.* had actually originated as a vehicle for second-billed Julie Sommars. She'd been under contract to Talent Associates to develop a show suited to her. The company's Leonard Stern had first spotted her making a guest appearance in *The Man from U.N.C.L.E.* (NBC, 1964–68), where her pretty face and distinctive speaking voice intrigued him. Talent Associates paired Sommars with future *Brady Bunch* star Robert Reed in a sitcom pilot that went nowhere before dreaming up *The Governor and J.J.* It was reportedly Sommars herself who urged executives to pursue Dan Dailey for the series role. "He *looked* like a governor — he had such dignity — but he was still so funny," she explained.[4]

Receiving co-star billing in the show's closing titles were Neva Patterson, as Maggie, and James Callahan as George. Of his longtime secretary, Maggie, the governor says, "That Maggie. She doesn't type, you can't read her handwriting, and when she files something you can't ever find it. If she wasn't such a good secretary, I'd get rid of her." Callahan, previously featured in *Wendy and Me* (q.v.), was cast as Governor Drinkwater's pragmatic press secretary. According to network publicity, Callahan did research for his role by working a day as press aide to Washington state Governor Dan Evans; he took part in a press conference and sat in on a meeting with foreign officials.

Ed Platt, who co-starred as the Chief in Stern and Sultan's hit series *Get Smart* (NBC and CBS, 1965–70), had a recurring role as the head of Governor Drinkwater's (unspecified) political party. Platt stepped into the role after a pre–*All in the Family* Carroll O'Connor, billed as "special guest star," played it in the series pilot. Gary Collins made a couple of appearances during the first season as young veterinarian Dr. Bob Livingston, a love interest for J.J. Another recurring character introduced during the show's first season was Governor Drinkwater's jet-setting mother Ella, played initially by veteran character actress Jessie Royce Landis and in later appearances by Linda Watkins. Kent Smith played Ella's long-ago beau, Frank Courtwright, a lobbyist who ultimately became her second husband. They continued to appear periodically until the series finale, "From Here to Maternity" (12/30/70), which focuses on the mistaken belief of the governor's 70-year-old mother and her husband that she is pregnant.

Early episodes also featured cameo appearances by some real-life governors, and it became a status symbol for the politicians who dropped in long enough to exchange a few lines with Dan Dailey's fictional counterpart. The gifted Jerry Fielding contributed an appropriately stirring theme. Unusually for this period in television, *The Governor and J.J.* was a three-camera show, filmed in front of a live audience. Along with another CBS show, *Here's Lucy* (1968–74), it was one of the few using this method, which was ill-suited to the fantasy sitcoms and rural comedies then so prevalent.

Julie Sommars was pleased by the decision to use a studio audience. "It's the only way you can really improve your craft and your comedy timing," she said. "I feel I'm really learning working before a live audience every week, and especially working with someone as great as Dan Dailey. He's one of the fine actors of our time."[5]

By the standards of late 1960s television comedy, *The Governor and J.J.* had a distinctly topical tone. The scripts allude to X-rated films, student protests, birth control, etc. There's also an occasional swipe at real-life figures like then–Governor Ronald Reagan. UPI's Rick Du Brow, well-known for despising earlier sitcoms like CBS's *Gilligan's Island* (1964–67), and saying so in no uncertain terms, found Dailey and Sommars' show more to his liking. He made no claims that the show was brilliant, but confessed that he enjoyed "watching professionals race through a weekly, frothy farce with style and good humor, and generally favorable results." Its regular players he deemed "a comedy cast that may well be the best and most attractive, from top to bottom, on television."[6]

Other critics concurred, and in February 1970, the show was one of the big winners at the annual Golden Globe Awards. *The Governor and J.J.* was awarded best musical or comedy on television, Dailey the best actor in that genre, and Sommars (tied with Carol Burnett) as best actress.

Though respected in the industry, *The Governor and J.J.* was not a breakout hit for CBS; its first-season ratings were only moderate opposite NBC's *Tuesday Night at the Movies* and the last half-hour of ABC's popular series of 90-minute made-for-TV features. According to Sultan, a network executive told him, "We're keeping you because the show did so well against the movies."[7] Initial plans were for the show to retain the same time slot, but a later round of schedule-juggling moved it to Wednesday's lineup.

A running theme throughout the show's second-season episodes was Governor Drinkwater's election campaign for a second term in office. The story arc, which was set to run through the first half of the 1970-71 season, began in the season opener, "And the World Begat the Bleep" (9/16/70), scripted by co-creators Stern and Sultan with story editor Earl Barret. In that episode, the governor and his daughter have been booked as guests on *The Joe Baxter Show*, a talk show whose confrontational host intends to challenge the governor on his decision to appoint his daughter to a state ecology commission. When Drinkwater comes down with laryngitis, he asks J.J. to do the interview without him. She reluctantly agrees to do so, and allows Joe Baxter to goad her into calling him an unprintable name on the air.

Mortified, J.J. later tries to defend herself to the governor's staff, saying the term she used isn't anything people haven't heard elsewhere.

> J.J.: George, what I said is really pretty common usage.... It's not all *that* shocking.
> GEORGE: Coming from a governor's daughter, it is. Now I know some people could use that language, it wouldn't raise an eyebrow.
> MAGGIE: What people?
> GEORGE: Philip Roth, Henry Miller....

Later, when J.J. is trying to explain to her father exactly what she said, George offers, "Governor, if it will help you at all, it's what you called Senator Ryan when he killed your welfare aid bill." The next day, Governor Drinkwater tells a colleague he's having second thoughts about seeking another term, concerned that J.J.'s *faux pas* will be rehashed during the campaign and cause her to feel responsible if he isn't re-elected. When J.J. gets wind of this, however, she tells her father she will feel much worse if he derails his political career because of her, and encourages him to run.

Later episodes identify the governor's opposition candidate as Larry "Buck" Bradbury, a former television western star whose long-running program, *Gunbarrel*, seems to have been something akin to *Bonanza*. (Cast in the role was actor Andrew Duggan, who'd just finished his run as the star of CBS's *Lancer*.) Bradbury is able to command endorsements from the likes of Doris Day (heard in a brief vocal cameo).

In "Fawcett Is Running" (10/28/70), the governor's running mate resigns abruptly, leaving him to consider various candidates for the post of lieutenant governor. Governor Drinkwater and his party chairman discuss one particular candidate:

GOVERNOR: Wasn't he involved in a gambling scandal once?
HACKER: That was a rumor, Bill. They never proved anything.
GOVERNOR: Oh, well I'm glad it wasn't true.
HACKER: Oh, it was true. They just never proved anything.

Though the show's scripts often featured some smart political humor, Dailey did not think the political elements were what made his sitcom appealing. "We're essentially a family show," he told a syndicated columnist in 1970, admitting that the scripts didn't really explore in depth the tough issues a man holding that office in real life would be facing. The scriptwriters would try to mine suspense from the ongoing story of Drinkwater's re-election campaign, but off-camera Dailey took a realistic stance on the outcome of the fictitious competition. "The only vote I need is from Bob Wood who is one of the network vice presidents and he's in charge of programming. As long as we get his vote we're re-elected."[8]

In fact, the show was more to Wood's taste than some of the other entries on CBS's schedule. Wood was among the younger executives at the network who saw no future in their long-running rural comedies *The Beverly Hillbillies* (1962–71) and *Mayberry R.F.D.* (1968–71), which appealed primarily to older audiences in smaller markets. Wood had begun working behind the scenes to persuade network founder William Paley to try out a new approach, resulting in CBS's choice not to return some old chestnuts like *Petticoat Junction* (1963–70) and *The Red Skelton Show* (a network fixture since 1953) to the fall 1970 schedule.

Unfortunately for the star, viewers also had a substantial vote, and second-season ratings for the show failed to live up to the first. For 1970-71, CBS slotted *The Governor and J.J.* in a new Wednesday time slot, where its lead-in was a bomb called *Storefront Lawyers*. Competing for viewers' attention on ABC was the second year of *Room 222* (1969–74). The 8:30 P.M. time slot was ill-suited to the adult comedy being offered in *The Governor and J.J.*, and by late 1970 the show had received its cancellation notice. CBS would revive the show briefly on Friday nights in the summer of 1972, showing reruns that were intended to seem timely while America made up its mind in the real-life race between Richard Nixon and George McGovern for president.

Having discovered that he enjoyed series work, Dailey went on to a starring role in *Faraday and Company*, a detective drama that made up one of the rotating elements of the *NBC Wednesday Mystery Movie* during the 1973-74 season. That show was dropped after its first season.

The last years of Dailey's life were far from placid. Thrice divorced, he also suffered the loss of his son by suicide in 1975. Not long afterwards, Dailey broke a hip when he fell onstage during a North Carolina production of *The Odd Couple*. "He had an artificial hip put in, then it became infected and he developed anemia," said the star's manager, Al Melnick. "We urged him to go to a hospital but he hated hospitals and refused to go."[9] Dailey died on October 16, 1978. His co-star Julie Sommars resurfaced in the late 1980s in a regular role as an assistant district attorney on NBC's *Matlock*. Right on the heels of her role in *The Governor and J.J.*, Neva Patterson was cast in a featured role in James Garner's *Nichols* (NBC, 1971-72), and continued her career as a busy character actress into the early 1990s. James Callahan was featured in Quinn Martin's action drama *The Runaways* (NBC, 1978-79), but may be most recognizable for his lengthy run on *Charles in Charge* during its late 1980s revival in first-run syndication.

Written and played for adults, *The Governor and J.J.* was a well-done show that deserves to be better-remembered than it is today. That it did not achieve a lengthy run seems more a result of scheduling choices than any inherent lack of quality. Coming onto network TV at a time when schedules were still filled with the likes of *The Beverly Hillbillies, My Three Sons,* and *The Brady Bunch*, it may also have been simply ahead of its time.

The Great Gildersleeve

Willard Waterman (*Throckmorton P. Gildersleeve*), Ronald Keith (*Leroy Forrester*), Lillian Randolph (*Birdie Lee Coggins*), Stephanie Griffin (*Marjorie Forrester*), Doris Singleton (*Lois Kimball*), Forrest Lewis (*J.W. Peavey*), Willis Bouchey (*Mayor Terwilliger*), Barbara Stuart (*Bessie*), Earle Ross (*Judge Hooker*)
Producer: Matthew Rapf. Writers: Richard Baer, Joseph Calvelli, John Elliotte, Andy White. Directors: Charles Barton, Robert S. Finkel. Director of Photography: Lothrop Worth. Film Editors: Frank Baldridge, Frank Sullivan. Production Supervisor: Sidney Van Keuren. Art Director: McClure Capps. Set Decorators: Rudy Butler, Hal Gausman. Assistant Director: Marty Moss. Photographic Effects: Jack R. Glass. Sound: Jack Goodrich, Frank McWhorter, Joel Moss, Dean Thomas. National Broadcasting Company; Hal Roach Studios.
Aired in first-run syndication, fall 1955–summer 1956. 39 black-and-white episodes.

While some of radio's most popular half-hour comedies would enjoy a prosperous reincarnation on television, the transition from hit radio sitcom to hit television sitcom had more pitfalls than might be imagined. A number of radio's top comedies—*Duffy's Tavern, Fibber McGee and Molly, Life with Luigi*—failed to duplicate that track record in their 1950s video adaptations. *The Great Gildersleeve*, which enjoyed a sixteen-year reign on radio, was among the unlucky ones that failed to make a successful transition, as evidenced by this early syndicated series.

Throckmorton P. Gildersleeve is quite the ladies' man, seeing a number of women simultaneously and always ready to meet a new one. He lives with his teenage niece Marjorie and her little brother Leroy, the children of Gildersleeve's late sister. Keeping order in the household is housekeeper Birdie, a patient and sensible woman who handles her boss' foibles calmly. Birdie is extremely loyal to her employer, but would like to see him settle down; "Every good man needs a good wife," she says. Gildersleeve is employed as the water commissioner in the small town of Springfield. Occasionally his busy love life makes for complications at City Hall, as in "Too Many Secretaries," when Gildy is caught entertaining a woman in his office late at night, and doesn't dare correct the mayor when he assumes the lady is his new secretary.

Among Gildy's steady dates is pretty Lois Kimball, proprietress of a local dress shop, Kimball Creations. Lois is fond of Throckmorton, but well aware he's fickle, describing herself as "Wednesday night Lois." Indeed, Gildy tends to take Lois for granted — until another man shows interest in her.

He's always ready for a new conquest, as in "Gildy, Bard of Summerfield," when he seeks to win the heart of Amy Miller, member of the local poetry society. Gildersleeve tries to dazzle his new lady friend by composing an original poem, but it's so awful that Leroy and Margie substitute an Elizabeth Barrett Browning poem in its place. The poem indeed impresses Miss Miller, who helps arrange for Throckmorton to give an evening-long reading of his work to her club members. Unable to prevent their uncle from making a fool of himself, Leroy and Marjorie watch in dismay as he reels off a steady stream of his doggerel. Surprisingly, the president of the poetry club likes his "primitive" style, and once again Gildersleeve somehow comes out on top in the end.

Leroy could deflate his uncle, as when he overhears Gildersleeve asking Birdie to sew a button on his coat:

LEROY: Puttin' on weight and bursting your buttons again, Unc?
GILDERSLEEVE: I caught it on the drawer of my desk when I got up too fast.
LEROY: The mayor walk in and catch you asleep?

Birdie, too, gets in her licks. When Gildy turns down a piece of cake to go with his after-dinner coffee, she wants to know why. "Well, in the first place," he says, "I'm getting a little too fat." Says Birdie cheerfully, "You're getting a little too fat in the second place too," cackling to herself as she walks away.

Willard Waterman is happy to be starring in the TV adaptation of radio's beloved *The Great Gildersleeve.* Maybe he hasn't read the reviews yet.

Town druggist Mr. Peavey, whose store Gildersleeve patronizes regularly, is a seemingly low-key, modest fellow who nonetheless keeps Gildy in line. His usual response to his pal's more outrageous statements is a mild-mannered, "Well, now, I wouldn't say that, Mr. Gildersleeve."

Though Gildersleeve has a healthy self-image ("For fourteen years, I've been the shining light of City Hall," he says in one episode), Mayor Terwilliger is not quite so enthusiastic. He doesn't think much of Gildersleeve, or of his minimally competent secretary Bessie, who often spends her day in the office trying to correct whatever work she bungled the day before. As critic Bob Foster pointed out on the eve of the televersion's debut, "Gildy represents a type of personality in just about every city and hamlet in the country ... the pompous, harmless, and bumbling small fry city official.... As long as there's a municipal government anywhere, there will be Gildersleeves."[1]

The Great Gildersleeve had been a favorite radio attraction since 1941, when it made its debut as a spinoff of *Fibber McGee and Molly*. The role of Gildersleeve was tailored specifically to the talents of actor Harold (Hal) Peary, who'd previously voiced various supporting roles on the show. Originally introduced as a friendly rival to McGee, Gildersleeve was judged strong enough to carry his own show. It was, as NBC publicity pointed out at the time, "believed to be the first time that a character role created on one radio program has been transplanted to become the star of a big-time show of his own."[2]

On the radio show, Gildersleeve's niece had grown up during the show's run, and eventually took a husband and began a family of her own. (By the mid–1950s, the radio Margie was the mother of twins with husband Bronco Thompson, and lived next door to the Gildersleeve house with her own family.) The television version, however, reverted to the days when Margie was a teenager. Stories that had already been played out on the radio show, like Gildy's courtship of the Widow Knickerbocker, sister of his pompous rival Rumson Bullard, were reprised on television.

The show's radio popularity resulted in a series of low-budget RKO films based on the *Gildersleeve* characters. Following a positive reception to *The Great Gildersleeve* (1942), the series continued with *Gildersleeve's Bad Day* and *Gildersleeve on Broadway* (both 1943), and wrapped after *Gildersleeve's Ghost* (1944).

Fans of the radio series still associated actor Harold Peary with the character, even though Waterman had taken his place in the show's later days. Waterman (born August 29, 1914) inherited the radio role in 1950, after Peary cut a lucrative deal to switch from NBC to CBS, one of many stars who participated in a talent raid between the rival networks just as television was coming into its own. Assuming his longtime sponsors would follow him, Peary was taken aback when they instead opted to stay with *The Great Gildersleeve*, recasting the lead role with another actor. Peary gave up his long-running role in favor of starring in a show he owned and produced, *Honest Harold*, which failed to catch on. Peary and his replacement had known each other for many years, as both had been radio performers in Chicago in the 1930s. Prior to assuming the role of Throckmorton P. Gildersleeve, Waterman had starred in the mid–1940s radio comedy *Those Websters*.

Not only were the two men vocally similar, they looked somewhat alike as well, though Waterman was taller and thinner than Peary. Waterman asserted that the producers of *The Great Gildersleeve* had never asked him to mimic Peary's performance to the letter, though the same could not be said of some fans. "They always come up to me and say, 'Laugh like Gildy,'" the actor reported. "Well, the old laugh — the one that starts high and gets lower — was a trick Peary used even before he played Gildersleeve. I don't use it. Frankly, I can't do it very well, and I wouldn't want to use another man's trademark."[3] The laugh aside, Waterman sounded so much like his predecessor that many listeners of the radio show apparently never noticed the casting change.

The television show was to be shot using the staff and facilities of the Hal Roach Studios, for NBC. Plans for the show got underway in 1954, though the show wouldn't reach the airwaves until the following year. According to publicity of the time, both Peary and Waterman were invited by NBC executives to audition for the television version, with Waterman winning out. One columnist reported, however, that "there is some speculation that NBC simply called in Peary to be polite, and perhaps even save itself some legal trouble later."[4]

The original series pilot, shot in the spring of 1954, received somewhat mixed reactions when it aired on NBC. Explained Waterman, "We tried not to make this a TV series that looked like a warmed-over radio show. We must have tried too hard, because the complaint was that the show wasn't typical Gildersleeve. But even with that comment, the response was good."[5]

That version didn't make the NBC schedule. In 1955, a second try was more favorably received, though it wasn't sold to a sponsor for network airing. Instead, NBC offered the show in first-run syndication, and sold it in more than 80 markets. Though there was less prestige involved in syndication, Waterman claimed he didn't mind. "Actually, it's a better deal for me," he asserted. "A successful syndicated series usually gets three years of filming and loads of reruns after that. So I stand to make more out of it this way than if it had been a network show."[6]

Waterman would continue to play his radio role while the filmed series was in production. After playing the character for so long on radio, Waterman was looking forward to being able to incorporate some movement into his performances, rather than being tied down to a microphone. At 6'4", Waterman towered over most other performers, forcing the producers of TV's *Gildersleeve* to take this into account in casting his co-stars.

Off-screen, Waterman, quieter than the character he played, lived with wife Maryanna and their two daughters in the San Fernando Valley. A founding member of the actors' union American Federation of Television and Radio Arts (AFTRA, changed from AFRA when television came along), Waterman continued to be active in union affairs during the course of his busy performing career. Near the end of his life, AFTRA officials awarded him a special honor in recognition of his "dedication to the welfare of performers everywhere."[7]

Held over from the radio cast was African-American actress Lillian Randolph (1898-1980) as Gildersleeve's housekeeper Birdie Coggins. Randolph and her elder sister Amanda were among the busiest black actresses of their day, with both having been featured in *Amos 'n' Andy* (CBS, 1951–53). Both had taken a turn at starring in *Beulah,* Lillian on radio and Amanda in both radio and television. Lillian Randolph would be the only actress to inhabit the role of Birdie, and by virtue of having also appeared in the films of the early 1940s, the only *Gildersleeve* player to appear in all three media incarnations of the property. Randolph later appeared in *The Bill Cosby Show* (NBC, 1969–71) and, near the end of her long career, played a featured role as Sister Sara in the acclaimed television miniseries *Roots* (ABC, 1977). Likewise, actor Forrest Lewis (1899–1977), heard for the past few years as Mr. Peavey on radio, was signed to reprise his role for the television version.

Other key roles, however, had to be recast. Versatile character actor Walter Tetley, who'd voiced nephew Leroy on the radio, was deemed unsuited to play the television role at the age of forty, giving way to child actor Ronald Keith, who'd already been featured in CBS's *Life with Father* series (1953–55). Pretty newcomer Stephanie Griffin, whose résumé mainly consisted of modeling jobs, won the role of Marjorie, played on the radio by Lurene Tuttle, Louise Erickson, and finally Mary Lee Robb.

Among the actresses playing Gildy's love interests in the television series were two who are quite familiar to *I Love Lucy* fans for their roles as members of the Wednesday Afternoon Fine Arts League. Doris Singleton, who played the recurring role of Caroline Appleby on *Lucy,* was cast as Lois Kimball, while Shirley Mitchell, veteran of numerous radio appearances before playing Lucy's pal Marion Strong in a handful of episodes, played Gildersleeve's Southern belle sweetheart Leila Ransom. Seen occasionally as his fumbling secretary was actress Barbara Stuart, probably best-remembered today for her recurring role as Sergeant Carter's lady friend Bunny Halper on *Gomer Pyle, U.S.M.C.* (CBS, 1964–68).

Feminine pulchritude was to be a regular feature of TV's *The Great Gildersleeve*, said Waterman. "Fortunately, I'll have a lot of pretty young ladies as love interests to keep the men occupied. You see, I'm quite a lady chaser, although quite timid, in the series."[8] Even in the show's opening titles, Gildersleeve cuts a dignified figure as he walks toward his office, stopping to pat a little boy on the head, but can't resist turning to gape at a pretty lady who saunters by.

Producer Matthew Rapf racked up a long string of credits during a career lasting more than thirty years, though comedy was not his usual genre. Rapf was credited as producer or executive producer on series as varied as *The Loretta Young Show* (NBC, 1953–61) and *Kojak* (CBS, 1973–78). The writing team of John Elliotte and Andy White, who had penned scripts for the radio *Gildersleeve*, took credit for the majority of the TV episodes.

Waterman marked the television series premiere by hosting a viewing party aboard a yacht in the Catalina channel, to which friends and reporters were invited. The series opener, "Practice What You Preach," failed to impress the reviewer from *Daily Variety* (9/19/55), who wrote, "In four words, 'Gildy' has had it. What was good family comedy a dozen years ago is warmed-over stew today. Waterman tries too hard to be funny...."

The TV version received a lukewarm response from both viewers and critics, most of whom found it inferior to the radio show to which they'd been loyal. Failing to attract a large audience, the TV sitcom was not renewed for a second year's worth of episodes, though the 39 segments filmed would continue to circulate in syndicated reruns.

In the fall of 1956, with the TV show kaput, Waterman resumed his radio performances as Gildersleeve. The radio show, falling victim to the medium's general decline in popularity, would not last much longer, winding down in 1958 after a series of reruns. The original Gildersleeve, Hal Peary, though never landing a starring role in his own TV sitcom, was a regular on NBC's 1957 *Blondie,* as well as the unsuccessful NBC adaptation of *Fibber McGee and Molly* which ran for one season in the 1959-60 season.

In the 1960s, Waterman enjoyed a long run as a featured player in the Broadway production of *Mame,* playing Mr. Upson. Though *The Great Gildersleeve* remained his sole starring role on series television, he continued to be in demand as a character actor. He had a recurring role on *Dennis the Menace* (CBS, 1959–63) and turned up in guest appearances on a number of other popular shows of the day (*Mister Ed, The Lucy Show, The Dick Van Dyke Show,* and others). He died on February 2, 1995, of bone marrow disease. His radio work is commemorated with a star on the Hollywood Walk of Fame.

Among aficionados of Old Time Radio, *The Great Gildersleeve* is still a fondly remembered classic, but even the most fervent fans of the audio version concede that little of its enduring magic came across on television. Perhaps, just as it was once said that children "should be seen but not heard," *Gildersleeve* was a show that should be heard, but not seen.

Grindl

Imogene Coca (*Grindl*), James Millhollin (*Anson Foster*)
Executive Producer: Harry Ackerman. *Creator*: David Swift. *Producers*: Bill Davenport, Winston O'Keefe. *Writers*: Joe Bigelow, Dick Chevillat, Bill Davenport, Paul David, Jerry Davis, Keith Fowler, John L. Greene, Budd Grossman, Lou Huston, Seaman Jacobs, Ed Jurist, Phil Leslie, Albert Lewin, Lee Loeb, John McGreevey, Bud Nye, George O'Hanlon, James O'Hanlon, Ray Singer, Burt Styler, David Swift. *Script Consultant*: Jay Sommers. *Directors*: Charles Barton, King Donovan, Sherman Marks, Paul Nickell, Christian Nyby, Stanley Prager, William D. Russell, Barry Shear, David Swift. *Associate Producer*: Charles Tannen. *Director of Photography*: Robert Wyckoff. *Art Directors*: Ross Bellah, Robert Peterson. *Film Editors*: Hugh Chaloupka, Jack Gleason, Aaron Nibley. *Set Decorator*: James M. Crowe. *Makeup Supervision*: Ben Lane. *Music*: Frank DeVol, Joseph Weiss. *Music Supervisor*: Ed Forsyth. *Sound Effects*: Sid Lubow. *Production Supervisor*: Seymour Friedman. *Post-Production Supervisor*: Lawrence Werner. *Assistant Directors*: Donald Gold, R. Robert Rosenbaum, Dave Silver. David Swift Productions; Screen Gems.

Aired Sundays at 8:30 P.M. on NBC-TV. First aired September 15, 1963; last aired September 13, 1964. 32 black-and-white episodes.

Imogene Coca, the beloved and acclaimed sketch comedienne from early television's *Your Show of Shows*, made her debut in a regular sitcom role with this little-remembered NBC series that cast her as a Jill-of-all-trades for a temporary employment agency.

Grindl (seemingly her only name) is a maid and housekeeper who works on temporary assignments through Mrs. Foster's Agency. Her long-suffering supervisor, Anson Foster, sends her out on a variety of assignments. When housekeeping work is not available, she tries working as a bank teller, a store clerk, babysitter, or whatever else someone is willing to hire a "Foster Girl" to do.

"Actually, she is a romantic dreamer — a Walter Mitty type of Harold Lloyd or Danny Kaye," Coca said of her character. "She's the sort of person who, if she saw windmills erected along Sunset Boulevard, would imagine herself Don Quixote and act accordingly. And, when she is thrust into the lives of those seeking her services, absolute chaos is the end result."[1]

Creator Swift described the series as "a modified anthology with a semi-confused maid as the central character."[2] It was entirely a vehicle for Coca, the only performer billed in the show's opening titles each week. The only other recurring role went to actor James Millhollin, featured for a few minutes as her supervisor at the beginning, and occasionally the end, of each episode.

In "Grindl, She-Wolf of Wall Street" (9/29/63), the temporary worker has been out of work for more than a week. Grindl is pleased to be hired as the telephone secretary to a young stockbroker who's under the thumb of his disapproving father-in-law. When she successfully uses numerology to predict winning stocks, her young boss thinks he has it made. But when a garbled telephone message causes him to invest a fortune in the wrong stock, Grindl finds herself talking her panicky boss off the ledge outside his office window. In "The Great Schultz" (12/15/63), Grindl is sent to work at the home of Professor Schultz, whom she is told is an important scientist conducting top secret research. He's actually a stage magician developing his latest illusion, "The Cosmic Regenerator," which purports to turn a woman into a rabbit. After seeing the magician and his wife rehearse this routine, Grindl contacts the police to report that her employer has murdered his wife, and plans to serve her remains as rabbit stew for dinner.

Coca claimed that her real-life misadventures were only slightly less wacky than those of the character. "I don't dare drop a dime into a coffee machine because invariably the paper cup will drop crookedly from its slot and miss the coffee completely.... All [the writers] have to do is follow me around and they've got the entire series written."[3]

Born November 18, 1908, in Philadelphia, as Imogene Fernandez de Coca, she came by her interest in show business naturally: She was the daughter of a bandleader and a dancer, and began pursuing a career by the time she was ten years old. Not fond of her birth name, the young Coca would try out various stage names early in her career — Donna Hart, Helen Gardiner, Jill Cameron — but eventually reverted to being Imogene. Never a classic beauty, she had this drummed into her head rudely at an early age. She never forgot the rejection she encountered at a dancing audition at which the casting director told her mother, "There's nothing wrong with her talent. It's the way she looks!"[4]

One of her first professional breakthroughs was in *New Faces of 1934*. Hired to dance, she made producer Leonard Sillman laugh during rehearsals, and was allowed to do a comedy routine that became one of the highlights of the show. Sillman subsequently cast Coca in six additional Broadway shows over the next several years. Among their collaborations was *Fools Rush In* (1935), where Coca met her first husband, actor-singer Robert Burton.

Coca was a regular television performer in the early days of the medium. In 1948, she was featured with comedian Jerry Bergen in ABC's *Buzzy Wuzzy*, a fifteen-minute comedy-variety show that lasted only four weeks. Only a year later, Coca became a familiar face to early television viewers in the live comedy show *The Admiral Broadway Revue*, simulcast on both NBC and the DuMont network. Though that show too was short-lived, it teamed her for the first time with Sid Caesar. From there it was just a short jump to their smash success as the stars of *Your Show of Shows*, a weekly 90-minute extravaganza that was the mainstay of NBC's Saturday night schedule from 1950 to 1954.

In her early forties, Coca became the darling of television viewers, and an Emmy winner, as the leading lady of *Your Show of Shows*, giving her a showcase the likes of which she would never find again. Though the husband-and wife sketches in which Caesar and Coca played Charlie and Doris Hickenlooper were particular favorites, she was versatile enough to play a wide array of characters. The rapport onstage between her and Caesar was so tangible that many viewers wrongly believed they were real-life husband and wife. A brilliant sketch comedienne, Coca would nonetheless never be able to recapture the magic of that early classic show. Her

Good help is hard to find, even after you've hired *Grindl* (Imogene Coca).

own *Imogene Coca Show*, which aired during the 1954-55 season on NBC, was not a success, and ABC's 1958 *Sid Caesar Presents*, which reunited her with her favorite leading man, went under after only a half-season run.

Coca was widowed in 1955 after twenty years of marriage to Robert Burton; in 1960, she married actor King Donovan, with whom she'd appeared in the Broadway comedy *The Girls in 509*. Though she was still a favorite of TV viewers, she largely eschewed guest shots in the early 1960s. "It takes a while for me to get to know people," Coca explained in 1962. "The first few days on a show, when you're a guest star, are always slightly embarrassing for me. I'm just getting to know the cast and crew when it's all over. I much prefer touring with a show — or a series, of course."[5]

After spending several years on the road doing theater, Coca and husband Donovan were receptive to the idea of settling down for a while. It was in Boston, while the couple was co-starring in a production of *A Thurber Carnival*, that she accepted the offer from Screen Gems' William Dozier to play the title role in *Grindl*. "It just seemed the right time for me to return to a steady television series," she explained. "I hadn't been looking for a series really, but now seemed the time to accept one. I believe there is a time for everything — and this is the time for *Grindl*."[6] Donovan served as director for a number of *Grindl* segments.

Coca had worked with creator David Swift in the movie comedy *Under the Yum Yum Tree* (1963), in which she played the maid to Jack Lemmon's character. Swift was able to persuade Screen Gems to resuscitate a project he had originally done in 1961, when *Grindl* was a pilot starring Mary Grace Canfield (later to be best-known as lady carpenter Ralph Monroe on *Green Acres*). Swift reportedly adapted the lead character's odd name from his visit to a Swiss town, Grindwald. Since Swift had first pitched the show, *Hazel,* in which Oscar winner Shirley Booth played a maid, had become a major prime time hit for Screen Gems, making it that much easier to persuade NBC that lightning could strike again with *Grindl.*

Seen as Grindl's long-suffering boss was stage and film actor James Millhollin (1915–93). A highly respected character player who specialized in playing jittery, ineffectual types, he racked up guest appearances on most of the major TV shows from the mid–1950s through the late 1960s, including *The Twilight Zone, Perry Mason, That Girl, The Man from U.N.C.L.E.,* and others. His pained reactions to Grindl's antics provide a nice counterpoint to Coca's energetic performances. NBC's initial announcement of *Grindl,* in March 1963, said that wrestler-turned-actor Henry Kulky, veteran of the sitcom *Hennesey* (q.v.), would also be a regular in the series, but this did not pan out.

Like his star, series creator David Swift was a veteran of early TV who'd concentrated his energies elsewhere in recent years. Originator of the classic live sitcom *Mr. Peepers* (NBC, 1952–55) with Wally Cox, Swift had gone on to write screenplays for the hit Disney films *Pollyanna* (1960) and *The Parent Trap* (1961). Now, with filmed TV shows, and the residuals they often paid, providing a better financial incentive, Swift was ready to work in the broadcast medium again. "Grindl will earn me more this year than all the movies I've directed," he explained.[7] After *Grindl,* he would create and produce *Camp Runamuck* (NBC, 1965-66).

The *Los Angeles Times'* Hal Humphrey was quite impressed when he screened the *Grindl* pilot that summer, declaring it "twice as funny as most of the shows currently passing for situation comedy on TV," but worried that subsequent episodes wouldn't be able to maintain the standard. He reported that series creator Swift, after writing the pilot episode that sold the program, had had little to no involvement in the production of later installments.[8] Instead, Jay Sommers, whose credits went back to radio comedy, was installed as head writer, and would also pen a number of episodes. (Sommers had more lasting success as the creator and chief scriptwriter of TV's *Green Acres.*)

There would be plenty of physical comedy on *Grindl.* In the pilot, Telly Savalas (*Kojak*), playing a possibly murderous husband, was to chase Coca with an ax. At the crew's urging, he told the nervous star that, as a method actor, it might not have been a good idea to equip him with a real ax for the scene. "Believe me, in that chase scene, I really ran," said the jittery star.[9] Later episodes found the star plunging into a bathroom full of soap suds, or wielding a paint sprayer that spatters everyone and everything in sight.

In "There's No Such Thing as a Bad Barracuda" (4/19/64), Mr. Foster has donated Grindl's services for one week as a prize in a police fundraiser, and the winners are the Strunks, a family residing in a rough neighborhood. Mr. and Mrs. Strunk take the opportunity to enjoy a rare vacation from their rambunctious kids, leaving Grindl to not only babysit, but reform the oldest boy, who's become a member of a gang called the Barracudas. In her own bumbling way, Grindl is, of course, equal to the task of taking on the gang.

Once several episodes of the show were in the can, Coca went on a personal appearance tour to promote its forthcoming debut. In the course of one week, the shy performer gamely promoted her show in Chicago, Minneapolis, St. Louis, Cleveland, Washington, Boston, and New York. She found the trip nerve-wracking. "So far on this trip, I've lost my credit cards, my shoes, and my checkbook. Before I left Hollywood, the crew gave me a big going-away party. They gave me all sorts of things to lose on my trip, all tagged with my name and address. They even had a tag for *me*. It read, 'I am Grindl. If lost, please return to Screen Gems.' Now I don't even know where *that* is."[10]

Swift was pleased with NBC's decision to slot *Grindl* at 8:30 P.M. on Sundays, the same time slot that had once played host to his beloved *Mr. Peepers*. More recently, it had been in the possession of the Nat Hiken sitcom *Car 54, Where Are You?* (1961–63), causing a bit of resentment among that show's cult following when *Grindl* took its place.

Though Coca played a woman who worked as a cook, the actress confessed that her real-life kitchen skills were limited. "I used to cook a little bit, but King can't stand my cooking. His attitude completely demoralized me, so now we have a sleep-in maid who does all the cooking."[11]

Coca admitted that the working methods of a sitcom forced her to abandon some of the techniques she had used doing sketch comedy with Caesar. On *Your Show of Shows*, the cast members had been free to tinker with scenes up until the moment they went out on the air live. The mechanics of a one-camera sitcom, as well as the logistics of this series, forced her to adopt a more stringent way of working: "Since the format of *Grindl* calls for me to act with a new group of performers who study their scripts in advance, any changes at shooting time would simply create havoc."[12] She also revealed that the daytime shooting hours of a television sitcom, unlike her stage work, forced her to give up her viewing of TV soap operas.

The show's anthology-like format, while giving its writers wide latitude in creating varied stories and situations, deprived viewers of some of the sense of continuity that helped make viewing of a situation comedy series a habit. One week, the show might be taking place backstage at a theater, the next in a grocery store or a hospital.

According to Coca, network executives put her through the wringer for much of the spring, as they contemplated whether to renew *Grindl* or another first-season entry, *The Bill Dana Show* (q.v.). "It was like being in the middle of a war," she said. "Every few days, there were new communiqués from the front lines. First, we were being renewed. Then we were off. Then we were back in.... Trying to get a straight answer from the people in charge was impossible. They just patted me on the head, and told me to keep doing a 'great job' and not to worry."[13]

In January 1964, the *Los Angeles Times*' Cecil Smith reported that NBC would drop both Coca's and Dana's shows, with *Grindl* to give way to a new sitcom starring comedian Paul Lynde. Over the next few weeks, however, indecision reigned. Most likely, there were some strings being pulled behind the scenes on behalf of Dana's show, a product of the successful Sheldon Leonard–Danny Thomas partnership that had generated *The Andy Griffith Show* (1960–68) and *The Dick Van Dyke Show* (1961–66) for rival CBS and sponsor Procter & Gamble.

Coca later said that *Grindl* failed to begin a second season despite the fact that ratings were good, and that the sponsor had agreed to continue. She blamed the show's demise on a disagreement between NBC and Screen Gems, whose executives were demanding an increased license fee for the new year.

All in all, it had been a rough year for new shows featuring even the most established stars; Phil Silvers, Judy Garland, and Jerry Lewis were among the stars licking their wounds in the aftermath of a quick cancellation. Also among those whose new shows fell by the wayside was none other than Coca's longtime partner Sid Caesar, whose self-named ABC variety show failed to deliver strong ratings on Thursday nights.

Even after the ax had fallen, Coca remained wistfully hopeful that her series could somehow be revived. A stock engagement during the summer of 1964 with her husband, King, left Coca taken aback by the new name recognition her TV sitcom had brought. "Wherever we went, people didn't call me Imogene or Miss Coca. It was always 'How are you, Grindl?' or 'We watch you on television, Grindl.' Especially the kids. They didn't know I wasn't Grindl any more. But I knew. And every time I heard the name, it was like a little slap in the face."[14]

During the 1964-65 season, Coca appeared occasionally on CBS' *The Danny Kaye Show* (1963–67), and in 1966 accepted an offer from Sherwood Schwartz to appear in his caveman sitcom *It's About Time* (q.v.), her last regular series role. The baby boomer generation would know her best from guest appearances in shows like *Bewitched* (ABC, 1964–72), playing a burned-out Tooth Fairy, and *The Brady Bunch* (ABC, 1969–74), as eccentric Aunt Jenny.

She slowed her work activities after being injured in a 1973 traffic accident, which resulted in the loss of her vision in one eye. Around the same time, a new audience had the opportunity to see some of her best comedy via the feature film *Ten from Your Show of Shows* (ten skits from the vintage series). She later joined Sid Caesar for a touring stage show in which they delighted audiences with the chemistry they still shared after so many years. However, moviegoers of the 1980s would know Coca primarily from her appearance as addled Aunt Edna, who suffers a grim but hilarious fate, in the hit comedy *National Lampoon's Vacation* (1983). Widowed for the second time in 1987, Coca died on June 2, 2001, at the age of 92. She had been suffering for some time with Alzheimer's disease.

A comedienne of rare talent, Coca may not have found her ideal role in *Grindl*, but the series makes it easy to see why she endeared herself to TV viewers. It's our loss that neither this show nor her second sitcom venture, *It's About Time* (q.v.), gave her the showcase her gifts merited.

Happy

Lloyd Corrigan (*Charlie Dooley*), Ronnie Burns (*Christopher Hapgood Day*), Yvonne Lime (*Sally Day*), Doris Packer (*Clara Mason*), David and Steven Born (*Christopher Hapgood Day, Jr.*), Leone Ledoux (*Voice of Happy*)

Executive Producer: Alvin Cooperman. *Producer*: E.J. Rosenberg. *Creators–Associate Producers*: G. Carleton Brown, Frank Gill, Jr. *Writers*: G. Carleton Brown, Dick Conway, Iz Elinson, Margaret Fitts, Fred S. Fox, Frank Gill, Jr., Roland MacLane. *Directors*: Hy Averback, Robert Butler, Norman McLeod. *Production Manager*: George Tobin. *Production Supervisor*: W. Argyle Nelson. *Production Executive*: Burt Nodella. *Directors of Photography*: Wilfrid M. Cline, Ed Fitzgerald. *Art Directors*: Rolland M. Brooks, Edward Ilou, Charles F. Pyke. *Set Decorators*: Mac Mulcahy, Kenneth Swartz. *Assistant Directors*: Vernon Keays, Gil Mandelik. *Costume Supervisor*: Richard James. *Costumer*: Neva Rames. *Editorial Supervisor*: Bill Heath. *Film Editors*: Archie Dattelbaum, John Mick, Dan Nathan. *Property Masters*: James Trepeck, Fred Turk. *Script Supervisors*: Marie Kenney, William E. Orr. *Music Supervisor*: Irving Friedman. *Music Editor*: Igo Kantor. *Sound Effects Editors*: James Nelson, Roy Siegel. *Sound Mixer*: Victor B. Appel. *Makeup*: Gene Roemer. *Hair Stylist*: Anna Malin. Roncom Video Films, Inc.

Aired Wednesdays at 9 P.M. (June–September 1960), then Fridays at 7:30 P.M. (January–September 1961) on NBC-TV. First aired June 8, 1960; last aired September 8, 1961. 26 black-and-white episodes.

Decades before the hit movie comedy *Look Who's Talking* (1989) and its TV spinoff *Baby Talk* (ABC, 1991-92), *Happy* introduced television audiences to a talking baby. Happy, in this case, was not just an adjective, but a proper noun — the nickname of the show's infant lead character. Happy himself introduces each episode with a voiceover, saying, "Hi, folks! This is Christopher Hapgood Day, Jr. But my friends call me Happy." When the adults have gotten themselves into another situation, he's likely to remark, "Grownups! They're so childish." Throughout each episode, he makes wry asides to the audience that belie his years. His special talent is not made apparent to his parents or any other observers.

The series opener, "Wedding Anniversary" (6/8/60), establishes that young Chris and Sally Day have been married for three years. They first came to the Desert Palms Hotel on their wedding night, when Chris booked Room 7 for their stay. While registered as guests, they accept an offer from owner Clara Mason to stay on and manage the resort in exchange for a piece of ownership. (In the pilot, they have just paid off a note that makes them 10 percent owners of the resort.)

Also taking up residence at the hotel is Sally's Uncle Charlie, a well-intended bumbler who does his best to be of assistance, but usually just mucks things up. When profits aren't what they should be, it's often because Charlie forgot to turn off the "No Vacancy" sign, or misadjusted the heater in the swimming pool and brought the water to a boil. Charlie occasionally has his head turned by the pretty women in swimsuits who populate the resort's swimming pool (as does Happy, who watches one pass by and remarks, "One of these days!")

In "Wedding Anniversary," Chris, having forgotten the noteworthy day, tries to make amends to his wife by booking Room 7 for a romantic evening, complete with the roses, gardenias, and three-tiered wedding cake that she remembers from their wedding night.

> CHRIS: I want everything to be the same as it was three years ago.
> HAPPY: That lets me out!

The scheme is complicated when Sally simultaneously rents out the unit to a traveling businessman (played by *The Andy Griffith Show*'s Howard McNear), whom Charlie tries to displace while the young couple is out to dinner.

A number of observers found *Happy* similar to *The People's Choice* (q.v.), which had employed a dog in a similar device during its 1955–58 run on NBC. The two shows in fact shared some behind-the-scenes talent. *Happy* was created by G. Carleton Brown and Frank Gill, Jr., who had been integral to the success of Gale Storm's 1950s sitcom *My Little Margie* (CBS and NBC, 1952–55),

Ronnie Burns (left) and Yvonne Lime (right) were the young leads, though not the top-billed stars, of *Happy*.

as well as to *The People's Choice*. Brown and Gill also served as associate producers of *Happy*.

Just as *Happy* was arriving on the television scene in the summer of 1960, some American theaters were screening Shirley Jones' British-made comedy *Bobbikins* (released in the U.K. in 1959). This modest comedy concerned a 14-month-old who not only liked to make conversation, but was able to give surprisingly accurate tips on the stock market to his befuddled father (comedian Max Bygraves). The tagline for the film in some theaters was, "Who Ever Heard of a Talking Baby???" Luckily for Miss Jones, far more theaters were playing her acclaimed performance in *Elmer Gantry*, for which she would take home a Best Supporting Actress Oscar the following spring.

Interestingly, *Happy* too boasted a cast member with Oscar credentials, though not for his acting. Lloyd Corrigan, playing Uncle Charlie, was the show's top-billed star despite his basically supporting role in the series. (Unusually for the period, *Happy*'s cast members were billed only in the show's closing titles.) Corrigan (1900–69) took precedence over young leads Ronnie Burns and Yvonne Lime, who shared a secondary billing card and took turns as to whose name appeared at left or right each week. The veteran character actor, who also worked as a director, was born in San Francisco to a family of actors. Corrigan studied dramatics at the University of California, Berkeley, receiving a degree in 1922. He proceeded to work in stock companies and then broke into the movies as a comedy writer for Paramount in the late 1920s. By the mid–1930s, he was directing, and his 1934 comedy short *La Cucaracha* won an Oscar as Best Short Subject. He went on to direct Boris Karloff in Universal's *Night Key* (1937), among other assignments, but from the 1930s forward he was primarily busy as an actor in dozens of films.

Born July 9, 1935, in Evanston, Illinois, Ronald John Burns was adopted by Mr. and Mrs. George Burns from a local orphanage called The Cradle, as was his sister Sandra. Initially a sickly child, Ronnie grew into a handsome, healthy and active teenager. At his parents' suggestion, he enrolled in dramatic classes at the Pasadena Playhouse. After his graduation performance in the Playhouse production of *Picnic*, George hired his son as a regular on *The George Burns and Gracie Allen Show*, playing himself. Joining the show in the fall of 1955, Ronnie continued for the remainder of its run, attracting a stronger teen following to the long-running sitcom. After his mother's retirement in 1958 laid *The George Burns and Gracie Allen Show* to rest, he spent another year co-starring with his father in NBC's *The George Burns Show* (1958-59). He had a brief stint as a singer, and scored roles in films like *Bernardine* (1957), with Pat Boone, and *Anatomy of a Psycho* (1961). Said his proud father in 1958, "Maybe I'm too much of a father to give an unbiased opinion of Ronnie Burns, but I've been in show business too long not to know that he's got a future as an actor."[1]

Said Ronnie upon his casting in *Happy*, "Personally, I enjoy doing comedy much more than drama. You go to see a picture like *Suddenly, Last Sum-*

mer and after a while you get ... well ... sick. I think it's better to entertain people, to make them laugh." Asked how his parents had reacted to the news that he had been signed to a lead role in a weekly series, he said dryly, "They were very pleased that I was going to work."[2]

The young actor knew that playing the leading man in the series meant more pressure than he'd been used to on *Burns and Allen*. "I gotta go it alone, and I've gotta be good," he acknowledged. "To make the show a success, I'll have to work my hardest the whole time." Despite the added responsibility, Burns welcomed the opportunity that *Happy* provided him to move on from teenager roles in his mid-twenties. "This series breaks my connection with being the oldest teenager in Hollywood," he said.[3]

Pretty blond Yvonne Lime, born April 7, 1938, was Burns' leading lady. According to the actress, Lime was not a stage name but her birth name. Adding to the fruity flavor of her life, her mother's maiden name had been Lemon, and her telephone number was in the Citrus exchange. As a girl, Lime had been shy, and was sent to dramatic school as a means of overcoming her timidity with strangers, but found that she liked acting well enough to pursue it professionally. She'd had a recurring role as Betty's pal Dotty Snow on *Father Knows Best* (CBS and NBC, 1954–60), as well as being featured opposite Michael Landon in *I Was a Teenage Werewolf* (1957).

One-year-old twins David and Steven Born had the series' title role. Because of California laws limiting child performers to four hours of work per day, broken up into small blocks, casting twins was the norm for such a role. Series executive producer Alvin Cooperman, himself a parent to twins, found the Born boys through a local "Mothers of Twins Club." After acting in a few episodes, both boys had learned the significance of the word "Cut" on a television set, and would visibly relax and unwind once they'd heard it. Catching on to this, the show's directors eventually learned to keep the camera rolling even after the magic word had been said, in the interests of getting some spontaneous footage of the two stars. Should the series turn into a long-running hit, producers said, they would simply allow the Day twins to age naturally along with their portrayers.

Voicing Happy was Leone Ledoux (1911–87), a veteran "child impersonator" who had voiced moppet roles in numerous radio shows, including *Blondie* (playing both Baby Dumpling and Cookie) and *Baby Snooks* (as Robespierre).

Doris Packer (1904–79), cast in the recurring role of hotel owner Clara Mason, was a veteran Broadway and television actress. Not seen in every episode, she alternated her *Happy* appearances with the role of wealthy snob Mrs. Chatsworth Osborne on *The Many Loves of Dobie Gillis* (CBS, 1959–63). The widow of Broadway producer Rowland Edwards, Packer credited her Hollywood career to actor Larry Keating, of *Burns and Allen* fame, who persuaded her not to retire after Edwards' death in 1953 and helped her find work in television. Friendly with George Burns and Gracie Allen, on whose show she made several appearances, Packer considered herself a mother figure to Ronnie Burns, whom she thought talented but in need of discipline and guidance from his elders. "And I give it to him, good," she boasted with a laugh.[4]

Happy joined the NBC schedule as a temporary replacement for Perry Como, whose popular variety show was being supplanted for the summer by the new sitcom and a half-hour Western drama, *Tate*. Como filmed an intro for affiliate stations in which he called the two new entries "shows of quality that entitle them to be programmed alongside of the best in TV." His enthusiasm for the shows was no doubt increased by the fact that both were produced under the auspices of the star's Roncom Productions. The popularity of the crooner's longtime show had allowed him to negotiate a deal with NBC and sponsor Kraft that funded not only his regular series, but also its summer replacements. NBC promoted *Happy* upon its June debut: "Baby-talk was never funnier than in this laugh-packed series." (*Tate* was ballyhooed with the rather tasteless line, "He had only one arm — but that's all it takes to draw a forty-five!")

The *Los Angeles Times*' Cecil Smith thought *Happy* pleasant but unremarkable, with the exception of its central gimmick, and the joke lines given to its young stars. Smith admitted, "Some of these are very funny coupled to the remarkable expressions that cross the infant's face."[5]

One viewer who got no pleasure whatsoever from *Happy* was syndicated columnist Bill Fiset, who claimed that the mere sight of the program's name in the TV listings threw him into a state of depression. He termed it "such a classic example of situation comedy pap that everyone should experience an episode at least once. One will be enough. It's like watching a hanging — see one and you're against capital punishment."[6] Critic Jay Fredericks likewise despised both *Happy* and its follow-up *Tate*, calling them "two horrors" that comprised a good argument for preferring summer reruns to new shows. He complained, "The laugh track goes wild at the slightest line. Let someone say, 'Hello, dear,' and the laugh track almost busts a gut."[7]

Even *TV Guide*, which featured the Born twins in a photo spread that summer, couldn't resist getting in a few licks. The uncredited author of the accompanying article clearly wasn't impressed by *Happy*, and thought it "unlikely" that the show he considered mediocre at best would catch on, but noted that creators Brown and Gill's previous effort *My Little Margie* had survived similar critical disdain to become a long-running popular hit.[8]

Happy was booked for a thirteen-week run that summer, with the hopes that its ratings would justify continuing it during the regular season. In fact, the show did perform fairly well. In November 1960, columnist Hedda Hopper reported that *Happy* was back in production with a new slate of episodes, due to return to the air in early 1961.

In the time since the first season episodes had been shot, Yvonne Lime had played a secretary in a guest appearance on the CBS sitcom *Bringing Up Buddy*

(1960-61), causing one viewer to write her an indignant letter, asking, "Why did you leave your nice husband and lovely baby to go to work in an office?"[9] For a time, there had been discussion about using Lime as a recurring love interest for star Frank Aletter in *Bringing Up Buddy,* but those plans fell by the wayside when NBC exercised its option to put *Happy* back on the schedule as a mid-season replacement.

According to the Associated Press' Cynthia Lowry, producers of *Happy* were doing "all sorts of remodeling work" to spruce up a show that "was not, quite frankly, received with wide critical acclaim even as a summer replacement."[10] While the show had initially been shot on the 20th Century–Fox lot, filming of the show's second season episodes took place on the soundstages at Desilu. Seen in recurring roles during the second season were the Days' friends Joe and Terry Brigham, played by Burt Metcalfe and Wanda Shannon. Returning to the NBC schedule in January, *Happy* was paired with a new situation comedy, *One Happy Family*, starring Dick Sargent and Jody Warner as newlyweds forced to live with her parents. The two sitcoms took the place of *Dan Raven*, a cop show set in Hollywood starring Skip Homeier; NBC consigned it to the wastebasket after only a brief run.

Among the show's more noteworthy second-season episodes was the April 7, 1961, installment featuring a guest appearance by Lime's friend Sara Buckner. Friends since they had appeared together in *Dragstrip Riot* (1957), the two young women had been sent to Japan on a personal appearance tour that opened a surprising new chapter in their lives. "We found tiny homeless children wandering the streets. We collected some of them and fed them rice but our rooms were too small to keep them so we tried to place them in orphanages," Lime told columnist Hedda Hopper.[11] Back home, the two young women founded a charitable organization in an effort to address the situation. The organization, at that time called International Orphans, Inc., eventually grew into the well-respected ChildHelp USA, still in existence today.

Ratings for *Happy* were not high enough to justify renewal for the 1961-62 season, and the saga of Christopher Hapgood Day, Jr., and family came to an end after 26 episodes.

Yvonne Lime retired from acting in the late 1960s, not long after marrying TV producer Don Fedderson (*My Three Sons, Family Affair*). She is still active today with her charity, ChildHelp USA. Not long after *Happy* finished its run, Ronnie Burns brought his acting career to a close. Having concluded that he would be happier in a more down-to-earth occupation than show business, Burns busied himself in later years with real estate investments and raising Arabian horses. Burns died of cancer on November 14, 2007, at his home in Pacific Palisades, California, survived by wife Janice and three sons.

In the early 1990s, the popularity of *Look Who's Talking*, starring John Travolta and Kirstie Alley, led not only to a sequel, but encouraged ABC to air a sitcom version called *Baby Talk*. The notoriously troubled production, which lasted from 1991 to 1992 amidst low ratings and critical derision, went through a succession of leading ladies—Connie Sellecca (*Hotel*) walked out before the show premiered, was replaced by Julia Duffy (*Newhart*), and finally by Mary Page Keller (*Duet*). Thirty years after *Happy*, it appeared that the talking-baby sitcom was still an idea whose time had yet to come.

Hennesey

Jackie Cooper (*Lt. Charles W. Hennesey*), Roscoe Karns (*Captain Walter A. Shafer*), Abby Dalton (*Lt. Martha Hale*), James Komack (*Harvey Spencer Blair III*), Henry Kulky (*Max Bronski*), Arte Johnson (*Seaman Shatz*)

Creator-Producer: Don McGuire. *Producer*: Jackie Cooper. *Writers*: Richard Baer, Hugh King, James Komack, Don McGuire. *Directors*: Hy Averback, Robert Butler, Jackie Cooper, Don McGuire, Gene Reynolds. *Director of Photography*: Harry Wolf. *Assistant Directors*: Joseph Depew, George King. *Associate Producer*: E.W. Swackhamer. *Film Editors*: Larry Heath, William Shea. *Set Designer*: Archie Bacon. *Set Decorator*: Dorcy Howard. *Art Director*: Walter McKeegan. *Property Master*: Joe Montenaro. *Costumer*: Robert Dawson. *Chief Set Electrician*: Ray Wostak. *Sound Mixers*: Hugh McDowell, Lloyd Wiler. *Script Supervisors*: Frank Kowalski, Richard Michaels. *Casting*: Stalmaster-Lister Co. *Makeup*: Ernie Young. *Hair Stylist*: Lillian Hokom. *Music Composer-Arranger-Conductor*: Sonny Burke. *Music Editor*: William Martin. *Sound Editor*: Bernard F. Pincus. *Assistant Editors*: Bill Garst, Lynn McCallon. *Key Grip*: Arvard Wooden. *Production Supervised by* King Production Service. The Hennesey Company; Jackie Cooper Productions.

Aired Mondays at 10 P.M. on CBS-TV. First aired September 28, 1959; last aired September 17, 1962. 96 black-and-white episodes.

Jackie Cooper returned to series television after his three-year run in *The People's Choice* (q.v.) with this comedy-drama about the life of a peacetime physician in the U.S. Navy. A forerunner to *M*A*S*H* (CBS, 1972–83), *Hennesey* blended laughs with more serious moments, though it lacked that show's cynical tone.

In the pilot, young Dr. Hennesey arrives at the U.S. Naval Base in San Diego, ready to assume his post as physician. He's dropped off by a cargo plane, whose crew member announces him as, "Brand spanking new, and ready to take over the Navy!"

At the infirmary, Hennesey meets the coolly beautiful Lt. Martha Hale, who will serve as his chief nurse. His superior officer, Captain Walter Shafer, is a 24-year Navy veteran fiercely dedicated to the Navy, and a strict believer in by-the-book practices. When his first patient as base doctor proves to be a monkey (the pet of an officer's wife), Hennesey wonders what he has gotten himself into. In the climactic scene, however, Hennesey's skills are put to the test when he is called to an emergency involving a terrified young sailor whose arm has been caught in a piece of machinery. Overriding the instructions of his superior officer, Hennesey manages, with help from the hulking Max, to free the sailor's trapped arm.

Actor-turned-screenwriter Don McGuire, who collaborated with Cooper in developing *Hennesey,* said he drew inspiration from a real-life acquaintance. "I knew a Navy doctor who was the closest I've seen to a dedicated man,"

Jackie Cooper (Chick) takes Abby Dalton (Martha) for a ride in *Hennesey.*

McGuire told *TV Guide* in 1959. "And without being square about it. I couldn't get him out of my mind. He had wonderful humor, did not pretend to be infallible, admitted to feeling nervous and confused at times during his career. Always he was a human being trying his best — with extraordinary results."[1]

According to the biography that creator McGuire developed for his lead character, Charles "Chick" Hennesey was born in Redlands, California, son of a pharmacist and a music teacher. Joining the army during World War II, he eventually became a medic, serving two years in the South Pacific before being discharged as a technician, fifth grade. Chick returned to civilian life, tried clerking in his father's drugstore and playing drums with local bands, but eventually decided to enroll in college under the G.I. Bill. He went on to medical school at UCLA, and then enlisted as an officer in the U.S. Navy upon his graduation.

What producer-star Jackie Cooper and partner McGuire were after was a show that mixed elements of comedy and drama. As Cooper explained, "Like any normal person, Dr. Charles W. Hennesey is neither funny nor serious all the time.... His normalcy and intelligence prevent him from ever becoming a completely comic character.... But, at the same time, the very nature of life in a hospital lends itself to both serious and humorous situations."[2]

Actor Roscoe Karns (1891–1970), cast as the gruff but basically kind Captain Shafer, had a long list of film credits stretching back to his debut in a 1924 silent film. He was already a veteran of a television cop show, *Rocky King, Inside Detective*, one of the few successful series on the DuMont network. The cheaply produced drama ran from 1950 to 1954, winding down largely because the network itself was on its last legs. After the grind of that live weekly broadcast, Karns, known to his friends as Rocky, intended to retire and enjoy his hobbies (notably going to the racetrack) but accepted a small role in the film *Onionhead* (1958) and a guest appearance on *December Bride* before being approached about the role of Shafer. "I wouldn't have gone," Karns claimed of the job interview, "but when they suggested a morning appointment so I wouldn't have to miss the first race, they had me. I loved the role and I'm really having a great time."[3] Captain Shafer would be promoted to the rank of admiral during the run of *Hennesey*.

Hennesey was the first continuing series role for beautiful young Abby Dalton, cast as Chick's nurse Martha. The 24-year-old Dalton (born Marlene Wasden in Las Vegas, Nevada) already had to her credit roles in a few low-budget Roger Corman films, notably the memorably titled *The Saga of the Viking Women and Their Voyage to the Waters of the Great Sea Serpent* (1957). Dalton made her television debut in an episode of *Schlitz Playhouse*, cast as the Old West outlaw Belle Starr. She'd also made a guest appearance on *Maverick* (ABC, 1957–62), which was where she caught the eye of Cooper and McGuire. "We do not expect her to be unknown very long," said Cooper.[4]

"I'll admit I was rather timid and unsure in the beginning," Dalton said of her stint on *Hennesey*. "I used to have a tendency to roll my eyeballs and deliver all the good jokes away from the camera.... But you know it's surprising how much technique you can pick up just being around this business."[5] As her talents developed, so did her role in the series: Cooper and McGuire expanded the role of Martha beyond what had originally been planned. In 1961, she received a Best Supporting Actress Emmy nomination for her work.

Seen as Max was professional wrestler-turned-actor Henry Kulky (born Henry Kulkovich). Kulky, in real life a World War II Navy veteran, had turned to acting in the late 1940s, appearing in a number of notable films. In the 1950s, he worked often in television, notably playing the recurring role of Otto Schmidlap on *The Life of Riley* (NBC, 1953–58). After *Hennesey*, Kulky went on to be a regular player in early episodes of *Voyage to the Bottom of the Sea* (ABC, 1964–68) before his untimely death of a heart attack in 1965. Admittedly not a trained thespian, Kulky's approach to his work was refreshingly simple: "Whatever I do, I guess it just comes natural. They tell me what to do and I do it. If it's wrong, I do it again until it's what they want. Then I go home."[6] Actor-comedian Arte Johnson, who would achieve his real fame as one of the ensemble players on *Rowan and Martin's Laugh-In* (NBC, 1968–73), made some early television appearances in *Hennesey* as another enlisted man, Seaman Shatz.

A recurring guest star was actor-comedian James Komack, seen as Chick's eccentric pal Harvey Blair. Komack's character was introduced in the series' third episode, "Hennesey Meets Harvey Spencer Blair III" (10/12/59). Martha tells Chick (and viewers) that Harvey is the eldest son of a deceased millionaire. Harvey's father, who had once been saved from a great deal of pain by a gifted dentist, had taken a vow that his first-born son would take up the profession. When Harvey proved reluctant, his father stipulated in his will that he would not inherit the sizable family fortune until he had been a practicing dentist for ten years. Harvey's dental skills are less than impressive to his friends and colleagues; Martha calls him "The Mad Butcher of Novocaine Row."

Komack, who'd been seen in both the Broadway and film version of *Damn Yankees*, also had a middling career as a standup comic. Auditioning for the role of Harvey, Komack impressed creator-producer McGuire and was called back to meet Cooper. When Cooper's only objection to casting Komack proved to be the actor's protruding ears, some tape was employed to pin them back and the part was his. Eventually Komack contributed scripts to *Hennesey*. In the 1970s, after playing another best-friend-of-the-star role in *The Courtship of Eddie's Father* (ABC, 1969–72), Komack entered television production, bringing forward such hit shows as *Chico and the Man* (NBC, 1974–78) and *Welcome Back, Kotter* (ABC, 1975–79).

Other guest stars who popped up in the series included singer Bobby Darin, who made his television dramatic debut in "Hennesey Meets Honeyboy," the show's second aired episode (10/5/59). Sammy Davis, Jr., portrayed a Navy frogman injured in an accident in "Tight Quarters" (1/29/62), while TV comedian Soupy Sales was at the center of a slapsticky episode that saw Cooper, among others, hit with a pie.

The resulting show appealed to Cooper much more than had his previous effort, *The People's Choice* (q.v.), which had found him largely playing straight man to a talking dog. Contributing to the show's ambience was its jazzy theme by former big band leader Sonny Burke, who also composed the hit song "Black Coffee" that was immortalized by Peggy Lee.

CBS placed the show in an unusual time slot for a sitcom, Mondays at 10 P.M., where it would compete with Steve Allen's NBC variety hour and the second half of ABC's *Adventures in Paradise* (1959–62). The show's mixture of comedic and dramatic elements seemed to please its alternate sponsors. According to Cooper, executives at Kent cigarettes liked the more serious segments, while those that hewed closer to sitcom seemed better suited to selling Jell-O.

Variety's reviewer (9/30/59) termed *Hennesey* "a lightweight in the laugh department," saying the series' serious moments came off more effectively than the comedy. Comparing it to the much-beloved *The Phil Silvers Show* (1955–59), which had just exited the CBS schedule, the *Variety* review found Cooper's vehicle wanting. Viewers, however, warmed to the show, and Cooper found himself busy with his second successful television series.

In "Hail to the Chief" (10/3/60), the second season opener, Chick encourages Max to apply for a promotion to chief petty officer, but his assistant tells him he's happy with things as they are. Captain Shafer and Martha also want to see Max promoted, and put the pressure on Chick to make it happen. On Martha's advice, Chick tries criticizing Max more, and giving him tiresome duties, hoping it will make him apply for the new position. When that doesn't work, Chick tries to shame Max by giving all his duties to the inept Seaman Shatz. Finally, his pride hurt, Max agrees to take the promotional exam and scores well. He's relieved to learn that his boss was only trying to get him the promotion, and both he and Chick are happy to learn that he'll remain as the doctor's assistant despite his new title.

In "The Annapolis Man" (2/22/60), Captain Shafer orders Chick to find an enlisted man bright enough to put forward as a candidate for officer training at Annapolis. Young sailor Bobby Williams (guest star James Franciscus), with his IQ of 149, seems the perfect candidate, but refuses to take the examination. Quite by accident, Dr. Hennesey discovers that the glasses Bobby wears contain miniature hearing aids, designed to cover up the fact that his hearing is not up to Navy standards after a teenage bout with the mumps. Captain Shafer reluctantly orders the young sailor discharged, until Chick and Martha persuade him to arrange surgery that may correct his hearing loss.

The show's respectful and positive depiction of the Navy won star-producer Cooper friends in military circles. The episode "Remember Pearl Harbor" (12/4/61), commemorating the 20th anniversary of the historic attack, and the Navy men who lost their lives there, won Cooper a commendation from the national Pearl Harbor Survivors Association.

One of the show's most frequent directors was Gene Reynolds, a former child actor like Cooper. In the 1930s, the two had worked together at MGM. In 1959, when the *Hennesey* pilot was shot, Cooper and McGuire cast Reynolds in a guest role as the sailor whose arm was trapped in machinery. Offered the chance to direct, Reynolds resigned from his post as NBC's Hollywood casting director in order to assume his duties on *Hennesey*. More than a decade later, Reynolds began a long association with another CBS show about military doctors that mixed comedy and drama, the long-running and critically acclaimed *M*A*S*H*. Though the two shows aren't really that similar, they do share a like typography used in their opening titles, designed to look like stenciling.

Cooper himself also directed a number of episodes of the series, presenting some logistical challenges. His stand-in Barney Elmore took his place onstage while director Cooper blocked scenes.

In the third-season finale, Hennesey finally wed Lt. Martha Hale. Cooper explained, "In the past year or two we've been getting a lot of mail from viewers, especially young persons and church people, wondering when Hennesey and his girl friend are going to get married." Having concluded that the scriptwriters had largely exhausted the story possibilities of a dating couple, Cooper said, "It was time to get a new dimension."[7] He promised, however, that the marriage would not convert *Hennesey* into a typical domestic sitcom.

Much to Cooper's disappointment, *Hennesey* was canceled at the end of its third season, with just under 100 episodes in the can. CBS proposed to give the Monday night slot where Cooper's show had reigned since 1959 to *The New Loretta Young Show* (1962–63), the star's sitcom follow-up to her long-running dramatic anthology series.

Once *Hennesey* closed up shop, Dalton was signed to play Ellie Barnes, the star's love interest on NBC's *The Joey Bishop Show* (1961–65), added to the cast after the show had struggled through its first season. A frequent celebrity panelist in the early years of *The Hollywood Squares*, as well as a regular sketch player on *The Jonathan Winters Show* (CBS, 1967–69), she returned to prime time television in the 1980s playing a featured role as Julia Cumson in the popular prime time soap opera *Falcon Crest* (CBS, 1981–90).

Initially, Cooper continued to pursue his acting career. His unsuccessful efforts to pitch a comeback show called *Calhoun* to CBS president James Aubrey were covered in *Only You, Dick Daring!*, the book by Merle Miller. In 1964, he accepted an executive position at Screen Gems. In the 1970s he alternated between acting and directing, his most visible acting credit coming when he stepped into the role of Perry White in the hit film *Superman* (1978) as a last-minute replacement, later reprising it in two sequels. As a director, he won two Emmys for his work on *M*A*S*H* and the pilot episode that sold the series *The White Shadow* (CBS, 1978–81).

Though it enjoyed a longer run than the majority of shows featured in this book, and did have an afterlife in syndication, *Hennesey* is rarely seen today. It's not meant as an insult to say that *Hennesey* may be the least funny show listed in this book. Creators Cooper and McGuire seem to have anticipated by almost thirty years the trend that would be briefly popular on television in the late 1980s with shows like John Ritter's *Hooperman* (ABC, 1987–89), and Mary Tyler Moore's *Annie McGuire* (CBS, 1988) — the blending of dramatic and comedic elements in a 30-minute format that critics and producers termed the "warmedy."

Hey, Jeannie! / *The Jeannie Carson Show*

Jeannie Carson (*Jeannie MacLennan*), Allen Jenkins (*Al Murray*), Jane Dulo (*Liz Murray*), Jack Kirkwood (*Charlie O'Connell*), Vera Vague (*Mabel Jones*), William Schallert (*Herbert*)

Executive Producer–Creator: Charles Isaacs. *Producer*: William Harmon. *Writers*: Jack Elinson, Fred Fox, Charles Isaacs, William Manhoff, Nate Monaster, Maurice Richlin, Stanley Shapiro, Curt Siodmak, Charles Stewart. *Directors*: Rod Amateau, Les Goodwins, Paul Landres, Chris Nyby, William Redmond, John Rich, Don Taylor. *Associate Producer*: William Redmond. *Editorial Supervisor*: Bernard Burton. *Supervising Art Director*: Bill Ross. *Art Directors*: Charles Clarke, Duncan Cramer, Al Goodman, Frank Smith, Jan M. Van Tamelin. *Directors of Photography*: Joe Biroc, George E. Diskant, William Margulies, Nick Musuraca, Frank Redman, Guy Roe. *Production Supervisor*: Lloyd Richards. *Production Executive*: Frank Baur. *Editors*: Samuel E. Beetley, Roland Gross, Arthur D. Hilton, Desmond Marquette. *Assistant Directors*: Frank Baur, Grayson Rogers, Jack Sonntag. *Makeup Artist*: Karl Herlinger. *Set Dresser*: Budd S. Friend. *Set Decorators*: Armor E. Goetten, Ralph Hurst. *Draperies*: William R. Garrett. *Music Supervisor*: Harry King. *Music*: Frank DeVol. *Wardrobe*: Robert B. Harris, Agnes Henry. *Sound Effects*: Norval Crutcher, Jr. *Casting*: Betty Martin, Marjory McKay. Four Star Films/Jeannie Productions.

Aired Saturdays at 9:30 P.M. on CBS-TV. First aired September 8, 1956; last aired May 4, 1957. In first-run syndication in 1959. 32 black-and-white episodes.

Though not a familiar name to most of today's American TV viewers, musical comedy star Jeannie Carson was an established star in England, and well on her way to fame in America when she accepted an offer to star in this CBS sitcom. The program's format, a hybrid of sitcom and musical variety, was slow to catch on, and its brief run represented a career setback for its leading lady.

The series pilot, "Jeannie's Here," scripted by creator Charles Isaacs, aired as the show's fifth episode. It shows 24-year-old Jeannie MacLennan newly arrived in New York City from Scotland. Though her parents were Irish, Jeannie was born in Scotland. Born in industrialist Andrew Carnegie's hometown of Dunfernline, Jeannie takes inspiration from his success, and has decided to immigrate to America to seek her own fortune. She has done so, however, as a complete stranger to America, having made no definite plans for how she will support herself.

She's dismayed to learn from the immigration official (played by Jack Albertson) that gaining her U.S. citizenship papers will take as long as six months. In the meantime, the Immigration Service insists that she have a sponsor who will sign an affidavit taking financial responsibility for the young immigrant, and insure that she does not become a public charge. The old family friend she planned to look up upon her arrival turns out to be on relief himself, and unable to help her out.

Strolling down the sidewalk as she thinks through her situation, Jeannie is offered a ride by plain-spoken taxi driver Al Murray. She asks him to show her the George Washington Bridge, a sight she finds awe-inspiring:

JEANNIE: Look at that view! It's Heaven.
AL: That ain't Heaven, lady. That's New Jersey!

Jeannie can't resist standing on the state line between New York and New Jersey. She bursts into a rendition of "I Feel a Song Comin' On" as traffic on the bridge comes to a halt, and angry commuters lay on their horns. A scuffle breaks out, and the police are summoned, with officers from both states arguing over who will get to take her in and charge her with disorderly conduct. Now branded a troublemaker, she's in danger of being deported, and softhearted Al wants to help.

Al's down-to-earth sister Liz, summoned to the Immigration office, can't understand her brother's sudden readiness to take Jeannie in. "We've got hungry relatives all over the place, but you gotta be fancy," Liz says. "You gotta *import* extra mouths to feed!"

Despite Liz's misgivings, the Murrays take Jeannie home to their residence at 132 East 24th Street in Brooklyn. In subsequent episodes, Jeannie tries to adjust to American life and customs, and launch her career with odd jobs such as making doughnuts in the window of a store on Times Square. Almost every episode provided an opportunity for the star to warble a song or two, whether incorporated into the action of the story or featured in a dream or fantasy sequence, and frequently to dance as well.

In "Jeannie's Income Tax" (2/9/57), Jeannie figures she has earned a gross income of $1300.15 during her first several months in America, with her combined earnings from cab driving, doughnut making, and waitressing, plus the fifteen cents she won playing pinochle with Al. Thanks to Al's creative deductions, Jeannie winds up owing only $62 in tax, but decides to make it an even $100 as her way of thanking the United States for its hospitality to her. The $38 "tip" confounds the employees of Brooklyn's Department of Internal Revenue office, who try in vain to return it to the insistent Miss MacLennan. The resulting confusion, in which both Al and Jeannie fear they may be jailed for falsifying her taxes, comes to a happy conclusion once the Scottish lass promises to take pity on the local IRS men and file her return in the Bronx next year.

Though Jeannie Carson convincingly adopted a Scottish burr to play the role, it wasn't the way the actress spoke in real life. "Oh, no, I'm not really Scottish," Carson said in 1957. "My mother was born in Scotland, but I grew up in England."[1] Born Jean Shufflebottom on May 23, 1928, she came by her interest in show business naturally, being the daughter of vaudeville performers. Though she received no professional schooling in singing, dancing, or acting, she had ample opportunity to learn by observation, and eventually by doing. By the age of twelve, she had had her first professional engagement. During World War II, as a teenager, Carson entertained troops with Ensa, the British equivalent of the USO, an experience she later termed "the finest and most thrilling graduate school any hopeful entertainer could have attended."[2] In 1947, she made a splash in London with her role in Noël Coward's *Ace of Clubs*.

On the London musical comedy stage, where she was a ticket-selling attraction, Carson showed off everything from an Irish brogue to an American Southern drawl. In England, she was known to her fans as Jean Carson. When she arrived in the U.S., however, Actors' Equity already had someone registered by that name (the blonde actress perhaps best known as one of the "Fun Girls" on *The Andy Griffith Show*), so the newcomer adopted Jeannie Carson as her professional name stateside.

Producer Max Liebman (*Your Show of Shows*) had introduced Carson to American audiences with his television specials. Most notably, he cast her in the lead of his production of *Heidi*. The success of that October 1955 broadcast led NBC to sign her to a contract, and inspired veteran radio and television comedy writer and producer Charles Isaacs to pitch her a weekly series. By the

Back and forth between England and America was the norm in the 1950s for musical comedy star Jeannie Carson, star of *Hey, Jeannie!*

time she signed to star in *Hey, Jeannie!* she was said to be the second highest paid female performer in England, bested only by Vivien Leigh.

Carson allowed herself to be persuaded that the next logical step in her American career was to star in her own weekly series. As she explained, "Years ago, if you were going places in this business, you did a Broadway musical and then went to Hollywood to do a big musical picture. But they're not making these big musicals any more. Now we must think in terms of TV series and specials."[3] Isaacs, with Carson's input, assembled a series format that would somewhat parallel the actress' own experience as a relative newcomer to America. While gearing up for *Hey, Jeannie!,* Carson said she saw little distinction between American comedy and what she had known overseas, "except we have to clean up English comedy a bit when we bring it over here."[4]

Aside from Carson, the only performer to be billed in the show's opening titles was the veteran character actor Allen Jenkins (1900–74), who played Al Murray. A longtime Warner Brothers contract player, Jenkins was doing his second television series for creator-producer Charles Isaacs, having previously worked with him in *The Duke* (NBC, 1954), a short-lived sitcom about a professional boxer. As Jenkins himself readily admitted, "Typecasting has been my bread and butter since I got started in this business.... I've played nothing but mugs—a few sympathetic sorts, but always mugs.... I've been enough different taxi drivers in movies and on TV to man a whole New York cab fleet."[5]

Actress-singer Jane Dulo (1917–94) was cast in the role of Al's sister Liz. Born Bernice Dewlow in Baltimore, the comic actress first attracted widespread attention for her featured role in the mid–1940s Broadway musical comedy *Are You With It?* Previously billed as Jane Dillon, she adopted Dulo so as to avoid confusion with another singer of the time.

Hey, Jeannie! was a co-production between Four Star Films, headed by Dick Powell, and the star's own production company. Filming took place at the RKO-Pathé lot in Culver City. Carson's husband William Redmond, also her manager, was credited as associate producer on the series. She was simultaneously under contract to the J. Arthur Rank company in Great Britain for a yearly film role. Contractually obliged to shoot a film in England in early 1957, Carson had to complete shooting for the entire 1956-57 season of *Jeannie!* by Christmastime.

Settling into a rented home in Beverly Hills while *Hey, Jeannie!* was in production, Carson and Redmond adjusted to a way of life different than what they had known overseas. "No fog, rain, snow; autos with power steering, seats, windows, automatic shifts; pizza pie, five-and-dime stores, supermarkets—I could go on and on," she said of the differences."[6] Sharing the house with Carson and her husband was the actress' longtime friend and stand-in, June Berryman.

Though she tried to make light of it, Carson well knew that the success or failure of *Hey, Jeannie!* would have a profound effect on her American career.

As she told her husband, if the show tanked, "Well, ducky, it's back to the chorus line for me."[7]

The format developed for *Hey, Jeannie!* was an unusual one, attempting to meld her success in musical comedy with a sitcom structure. Although the premiere drew some good reviews ("a delightful time for those of us who enjoy light musical fare and comedy," wrote Bob Foster on September 12, 1956), the initial ratings were discouraging. She was fighting competition from some long-time American favorites, Lawrence Welk on ABC and Sid Caesar on NBC. Acting as her lead-in was *The Gale Storm Show: Oh! Susanna* (1956–60), Storm's second TV sitcom after *My Little Margie*.

Asked to describe his wife's appeal as a leading lady, Redmond said thoughtfully, "Well, she's not a Martha Raye or Lucille Ball type of comedienne. She's not raucous, you know. She's light and fluffy. As a matter of fact, she's a rather quiet girl. I think all this makes for a good deal of charm."[8]

Though most reviewers found Carson herself captivating, they were less enchanted with her sitcom. *Variety* (9/12/56) thought the star "cute as a button and deserves a better fate in the scheme of TV things," suggesting that Allen Jenkins' cab driver character should try to "pick up some good writers" while on the road.

By October, syndicated columnist Bob Foster, who'd loved the series opener, wrote that *Hey, Jeannie!* was headed in the wrong direction. According to Foster, network executives had clamored to have the series done live, which would have allowed for fine-tuning as the weeks progressed. "Unfortunately nothing can be done because 13 of the shows already are completed and in the vaults, mistakes and all."[9]

The format was also a little different from what had become the sitcom norm by the mid–1950s. "We've tried to make each show different," the star explained. "By that I don't mean that we've changed the characters each episode. But, we don't have the same type program every week. I guess it is working out all right. I don't think our audience is bored."[10] The show was well-received in her native England, where it aired on the BBC, despite some concern from Carson that viewers there might not appreciate its lead character's relentless praise for America.

Though Carson said she enjoyed the energy of live TV performances—she was booked in February to sing on *The Ed Sullivan Show*—she thought putting *Hey, Jeannie!* on film gave the show an advantage. "This way we can bring in many locales. We'll never be limited in our production plans."[11]

By late January, cast and crew were on tenterhooks, waiting to see if *Hey, Jeannie!* would be picked up for a second year. "We won't know until March," Carson told a reporter, "but it looks very favorable. The ratings have been climbing all the time, and the sponsors appear to be very happy with it. However, they never make a decision one way or the other until March."[12] In late March, Carson and her colleagues received the encouraging news that they had begun winning the ratings race against Welk, drawing a 29.4 rating as opposed to Welk's 27.4 on ABC. Sid Caesar was running a distant third, at 16.7. Feeling optimistic, Carson and husband Redmond had begun the process to apply for American citizenship.

Much to the surprise and displeasure of not only Carson, but Four Star's Dick Powell, CBS canceled the series despite recent signs that the show had turned a corner. Powell, by then a hardened veteran of the television wars, thought he knew why.

"I don't have the money to do it, but if I did I'd fight CBS on a restraint-of-trade charge," Powell angrily told the press. Although the show's original sponsor had dropped out, ratings for *Hey, Jeannie!* had been on the rise. Said Powell, "Wouldn't you think CBS would try to find another sponsor? But, no, they're being piggy again, and want their own show in there instead of an outside package. The network is making no effort to re-sell *Jeannie*."[13]

When Four Star Films was unable to interest a sponsor into bankrolling a second year, *Hey, Jeannie!* was laid to rest. By summertime, Carson was busy with a guest appearance on *Goodyear TV Playhouse* (NBC, 1951–60). Some observers, with the benefit of 20-20 hindsight, thought that occasional specials and guest shots presented Carson in a better light than her brief series had ever done. "The point, I should think," opined columnist Eve Starr, "is that Jeannie Carson, and a lot of other female stars, would more profitably enhance their careers by sticking to freelancing and avoiding series as the plagues."[14]

As it turned out, though, CBS's cancellation of *Hey, Jeannie!* was not the end of the story. In early 1958, plans were announced to revive Carson's show, with a change in format. "We were placed in a peculiar position with *Hey, Jeannie!*," Carson explained, "because the public liked the character, but the sponsors thought we were getting into a bind with the story lines, which we really intended to change after the first season anyway."[15] A year or so later, the show was back in production for ABC.

The revamped version would be known as *The Jeannie Carson Show*. The star would still be playing Jeannie MacLennan, but the entire supporting cast from the show's 1956–57 run on CBS had been dropped. The new episodes found Jeannie working as an airline stewardess. Radio comedienne Vera Vague, aka Barbara Jo Allen (1906–74), was cast as Jeannie's best friend and supervisor, chief stewardess Mabel Jones. Jack Kirkwood (1894–1964) played Charlie O'Connell, owner of the apartment building in which both women lived when not flying the friendly skies. William Schallert (born July 6, 1922), at the beginning of what would be a long and successful television career (*The Patty Duke Show*, *The Nancy Drew Mysteries*, etc.), was cast as the airline flight engineer, who also served as a sometime romantic interest for Jeannie.

Only a handful of episodes in the new format were produced, and Carson's show failed to win an ongoing slot on ABC. Instead, the show was sold in syndication. In 1960, ABC filled a summer slot with reruns of Carson's show, seen on the network's Thursday night schedule. Network publicity advertised the summer run, which included episodes from both versions, "a delightful new situation comedy." Carson herself was on Broadway in May and early June, playing the lead role of Sharon in a revival of *Finian's Rainbow*. It was there that she met actor Biff McGuire, who would become her second husband in November 1960.

Though mainstream American stardom largely escaped her, Carson continued to work on television and on stage, often in conjunction with McGuire. In 1962, she replaced Mary Martin in the Broadway company of *The Sound of Music* and then successfully took the show on tour. In the 1960s, she had a brief run on the CBS soap opera *Search for Tomorrow* (1951–86). Carson and McGuire continued to tour through most of the 1960s, in shows like *Cactus Flower, 110 in the Shade,* and *Camelot,* living in a Manhattan apartment when not on the road. They later had a long association with the distinguished Seattle Repertory Theatre, where they teamed for acclaimed shows including *Inspecting Carol.* Along the way, in 1965, Carson finally became an American citizen.

Jeannie McLennan would have been proud.

How to Marry a Millionaire

Lori Nelson (*Greta Hanson*), Merry Anders (*Mike McCall*), Barbara Eden (*Loco Jones*), Lisa Gaye (*Gwen Kirby*), James Cross (*Jesse*)
Executive Producer: Nat Perrin. *Producers*: Ben Feiner, Jr., Paul Jones. *Writers*: Jess Carneol, Dick Conway, Karen De Wolf, Bill Derman, Lou Derman, Bernard Drew, Everett Greenbaum, John L. Greene, Seaman Jacobs, John Kohn, Howard Leeds, Kay Lenard, Roland MacLane, William Manhoff, Laurence Marks, Harvey Orkin, Milton Pascal, Martin Ragaway, Si Rose, Margaret Schneider, Paul Schneider, Leo Solomon. *Based on a Screenplay by* Nunnally Johnson *and a Play by* Dale Eunson, Katherine Albert. *Directors*: Danny Dare, Lester Vail, Bernard Wiesen. *Director of Photography*: Lloyd Ahern. *Art Directors*: Lewis Creber, Edward Ilou, Lyle Wheeler. *Assistant Directors*: John C. Chulay, Maxwell Henry. *Editorial Supervisor*: Art Seid. *Film Editors*: Richard Cahoon, Roy V. Livingston, Otto W. Meyer, Paul Weatherwax. *Set Decorators*: Mac Mulcahy, Walter M. Scott, Charles Q. Vassar. *Properties*: Eddie Applegate, Clem R. Widrig. *Sound Recorders*: Alfred Bruzlin, Woodruff H. Clarke, Roy Meadows. *Wardrobe Supervisor*: Dick James. *Makeup*: Mel Berns, Richard Hamilton. *Hair Stylists*: Annabel, Helene Parrish. *Sound Editor*: Gene Eliot. *Script Supervisors*: Gana Jones, Diana Loomis, Mai Mohr. *Music Supervisor*: Alec Compinsky. *Music*: Leon Klatzkin. *Wardrobe*: Mr. Mort. 20th Century–Fox Television Productions; National Telefilm Associates.

Aired in first-run syndication from 1957 to 1959. 52 black-and-white episodes.

MIKE: You know, Loco, when the three of us figured out a budget so we could afford this penthouse, I'm afraid we left out a few items.
LOCO: What?
MIKE: Breakfast, lunch and dinner.

Three beautiful young women hoping to snare wealthy husbands set up housekeeping in a swank New York apartment they can barely afford in *How to Marry a Millionaire*. The show was one of the first TV sitcoms to be adapted from a hit movie, a practice that would eventually become quite commonplace. CBS had already tried *That's My Boy* (1954-55), based on the Jerry Lewis film. Just as that series, though, had not featured Jerry Lewis reprising his original role, *How to Marry a Millionaire* tried to emulate the success of the 1953 film without enlisting the services of original stars Lauren Bacall, Betty Grable, and Marilyn Monroe.

How to Marry a Millionaire, with a screenplay by Nunnally Johnson, was in fact a remake of an earlier film, *The Greeks Had a Word for Them* (1932). Credited alongside the scriptwriters for each TV segment, along with Johnson, were Katharine and Dale Eunson, whose play *Loco* had run only briefly on Broadway in 1946 but was also used as source material for the series.

In the TV *Millionaire*, savvy Mike works in a stockbroker's office, while Greta is employed as a hostess on a *$64,000 Question*–type television quiz show called *Go for Broke*, seen on the United Telecasters network, and Loco is pursuing a modeling career. Without her glasses, beautiful Loco is so nearsighted that she can't distinguish between the elevator button and the fire alarm, and reads the girls' bank balance as $1038 when it's actually $10.38. Still, she instinctively takes them off upon hearing a man's voice, even if it's only on the phone.

Each segment opens with a bit of stock footage depicting some glamorous, exotic, or exclusive setting, as an off-screen male narrator engages in a dialogue with one of the show's leading ladies. Over footage of the Sphinx in one episode:

> MALE: Isn't that an interesting expression on her face? Almost makes you wonder what she's thinking about.
> FEMALE: Same thing every woman thinks about ... *How to Marry a Millionaire.*

Our first view of the threesome comes as we see them engrossed in their favorite reading material: Mike is perusing a thick Dun and Bradstreet report, Greta is paging through *Who's Who in America,* and empty-headed Loco is captivated by her comic book. As in the original film, *How to Marry a Millionaire* depicts three young women who pool all available resources in order to pay the rent on a swanky penthouse, figuring that it will make the proper setting in which to attract rich husbands. Only Barbara Eden's Loco character was named the same as her movie counterpart, though the last name changed.

In the series opener, "The Penthouse," they have been living in Apartment G for several weeks, but haven't seen much return on their investment. Pragmatic Mike reminds her friends that they were disappointed with the caliber of men they dated while at their previous residence, a walkup on Amsterdam Avenue. They aspire to a better class of boyfriends than the "gas pump jockeys" they've met in the past.

When Greta and Mike meet a new man, they immediately sum up his prospects and rate him accordingly. A distinguished-looking older man they meet in the hallway of their apartment house mentions the country house where he's recently been, causing the girls to envision a money bag, hear the ka-ching of a cash register, and place a million-dollar value on his head. When he goes on, however, to clarify that he's only the butler in said country house, suddenly he rings up as NO SALE.

Loco, on the other hand, is a kindhearted and naïve soul who tends to meet nice men in places like public parks, and bring them home for a good meal that the girls can scarcely afford. When she meets a man she likes, she enters him in her address book under "L" for "eligible." Not the brightest soul, Loco reacts indignantly when someone is called a kleptomaniac, saying, "Please! Let's not drag religion into this!"

Judging from this series, New York City in the 1950s was teeming with attractive young millionaires. But when the three friends meet millionaires, as they do in almost every episode, they invariably manage to queer the pitch in one way or another. Usually it's because they don't recognize them as wealthy — because he's dressed casually, or in costume at a masquerade party, or temporarily working an entry-level job at the family business. In "A Call to Arms," Loco has attracted the interest of Roger Sutton (Ted Knight), but her friends mistakenly think she's enlisted in the Army after a quarrel with them. By the time they learn Loco was just at the recruiting center to do a modeling job, Sutton has signed up for a three-year hitch himself, in hopes of getting closer to Loco. In "The Utterly Perfect Man," Mike catches the eye of a handsome young widower, but a misunderstood reference to his racehorse Bluebeard, and confusion between him and his thrice-married father lead Loco and Greta to conclude that Mike's new man is a real lady-killer.

Always short on money, the girls sometimes find that they can charm store owners into extending their credit. From time to time they develop a new scheme to stay afloat, as in the episode "Subletting the Apartment," where the girls rent daytime access to their penthouse to a trio of musicians playing nighttime gigs at a local club. Nonetheless, they remain eternally one step ahead of financial ruin, and their disgruntled landlord:

MIKE: Did you get our check for the three months' back rent?
LANDLORD: Why, did you send it?
MIKE (sighing): No, I just thought we might get lucky.

Top-billed Lori Nelson, born August 15, 1933, was a Universal Studios contract player in the early to mid–1950s, where she'd taken part in the Ma and Pa Kettle and Francis the Talking Mule pictures that were the studio's bread and butter, as well as films like *Revenge of the Creature* (1955). Once her stint with Universal wound down, Nelson made low-budget horror and action films for Roger Corman and others, before making the switch to television.

Red-haired Merry Anders, born May 22, 1932, was already a television veteran with two previous sitcoms under her belt. She'd played teenage daughter Joyce in late episodes of ABC's *The Stu Erwin Show* (1950–55), and went on to a featured role as roommate and friend to star Janis Paige in CBS's unsuccessful sitcom *It's Always Jan* (1955-56). Anders had previously played a minor role in the film version of *Millionaire*. In 1959, Anders told syndicated beauty columnist Lydia Lane that she had learned a thing or two from her *Millionaire* alter ego. "I've played Mike McCall on TV now for two years, and she is a woman who always sees the funny side of every calamity. This point of view has rubbed off on me and it certainly has made life easier. I don't let trifles get under my skin the way they used to. When I stopped worrying, I found I felt better in every way."[1]

This was the first regular series role for up-and-coming starlet Barbara

Eden, who would become famous as the star of *I Dream of Jeannie* (NBC, 1965–70). Born Barbara Jean Moorhead on August 23, 1934, she originally intended to pursue a career as a singer. At the suggestion of her mother, the aspiring vocalist studied acting, with the intent of putting more feeling into her singing style. Instead, Eden, who didn't find a life of touring nightclubs congenial anyway, decided to switch gears and become an actress.

Eden had one of her first breaks when she auditioned for a bit on *The Johnny Carson Show* (the mid-fifties version). Reading for the part of a nitwit, she was deemed wrong for the role at first, until the producer decided, "She looks smart enough to do a good job of acting dumb."[2] She made another noteworthy early appearance in one of the last original episodes of *I Love Lucy*, "Country Club Dance" (4/22/57), playing a visiting knockout who arouses the jealousy of Lucy and Ethel. Earning an unimpressive $200 a week to co-star in *Millionaire*, Eden also made appearances in a few Fox films between shooting scenes. She reportedly shared Loco's poor vision.

Eden, the only one of the three leading ladies married off-screen, had already landed actor Michael Ansara, star of TV's *Broken Arrow* (ABC, 1956–58). In 1955, Merry Anders had married casting agent John Stephens, but the couple separated only a few months later. On camera, of course, marriage was to be an elusive goal. "No matter how long the series lasts," Nelson said, "none of us can ever actually marry a millionaire without spoiling the whole plot."[3]

Actor Dabbs Greer appeared in some early episodes as Mr. Blandish, the girls' landlord. Later, Joseph Kearns (*Dennis the Menace*) played the recurring role of Augustus P. Tobey, the apartment manager. Jesse, the elevator operator, was seen occasionally as well.

The version of *How to Marry a Millionaire* that made its TV debut in the fall of 1958 had undergone some changes. In the original pilot, shot in the spring of 1957, Lori Nelson's co-stars were Charlotte Austin and Doe Avedon, both brunettes. Fox executives had reportedly tested around seventy actresses before signing the three ultimately chosen. Avedon, whose real name was Dorcas Nowell, had been married to the noted photographer Richard Avedon until their 1949 divorce. She was cast in the Marilyn Monroe role of Loco. Austin, the daughter of singer Gene Austin, is today best remembered for two campily awful horror films in which she starred; the Edward D. Wood, Jr.–scripted *The Bride and the Beast* and *Frankenstein 1970*, both unleashed in 1958.

Not sold to one of the Big Three networks, *How to Marry a Millionaire* was instead distributed to independent stations by National Telefilm Associates, of which 20th Century–Fox was part owner. Stations subscribing to NTA's plan received a night of original programming that included the Desilu sitcom *This Is Alice*, the Western drama *Man Without a Gun*, and a package of first-run feature films. Serving as *Millionaire*'s executive producer was former screenwriter Nat Perrin, who'd penned funny vehicles for the Marx Brothers, Lucille

Ball, Abbott and Costello, and Red Skelton, among others. The original cast of *Millionaire* filmed 39 episodes to be aired during the 1957-58 season.

More than one contemporary critic commented that a show starring three beautiful women, whatever its other merits, would be a welcome change from the countless Westerns then occupying network schedules. Merry Anders agreed. "As the saying goes, 'It's a man's world,'" she sighed. "TV is a man's industry. What chance have women against westerns and detective shows? We can't fight, shoot, or take brutal beatings every week. But I think the trend will slowly change to where comedy will be popular again, and women will have chances for major roles."[4]

Though the show's premise centered on the desirability of snaring a rich husband, off-camera all three leading ladies professed that a man's bank balance was no reason to choose him. "At first it sounds wonderful," said Lori Nelson. "Everything in the world you'd possibly want. But you must realize a millionaire is too busy making money. He'd have no time for me!" Merry Anders concurred: "I don't honestly believe there'd be much home life with a man always trying to make more and more millions."[5]

A moderate success during its initial run, the show was renewed to return for an abbreviated second season, but did so without Lori Nelson, who quit in a huff. Much later she explained, "I felt that I was the biggest of the three

The golddigging beauties of *How to Marry a Millionaire* (left to right): Lori Nelson (Greta), Merry Anders (Mike), and Barbara Eden (Loco).

actresses in terms of star status ... I felt that I needed to move on. I didn't need to be stuck in that little series that was in syndication."[6]

In the spring of 1959, it was announced that Lisa Gaye, sister of movie leading lady Debra Paget, would join the cast with the 40th episode. Gaye's credits included a recurring role as beautiful model Colette DuBois on *The Bob Cummings Show* (NBC and CBS, 1955–59). With the cast change, Barbara Eden went from third to first billing, leapfrogging somehow over second-billed Anders. The new cast filmed only 13 episodes, however, before the series was laid to rest.

Lisa Gaye's character of Gwen Kirby was introduced in the episode "Cherchez la Roommate." As the segment opens, Loco and Mike are just returning home from attending the wedding of their former roommate Greta. Though she didn't land a millionaire, she has married the owner of a gas station and will be relocating to California. Building manager Mr. Tobey thinks this is the perfect opportunity to move out the girls in Apartment G, who are perpetually late with their rent. Under the gun, Loco and Mike decide to take out a newspaper ad seeking a new roommate. Instead, thanks to Loco's nearsightedness (Mike calls her "Miss Magoo"), and the resulting mix-up at the newspaper office, their ad instead leads readers to believe they are in need of a trained monkey. Fussy Mr. Tobey, finding the upstairs hallway teeming with monkeys and their trainers, is on the verge of showing Mike and Loco the door. Just then, the newspaper clerk shows up with Gwen, who's new in town and needs a place to stay. Mike and Loco happily take her in, teaching her the pledge by which they live: "On my honor, I promise to do my best to help one of us marry a millionaire. All for one, and one for all, so help us, Fort Knox!"

Of the three leading ladies, it would be Barbara Eden, of course, who enjoyed enduring television fame. After *Jeannie*, she starred in NBC's briefly popular *Harper Valley P.T.A.* (1981-82), its title shortened to *Harper Valley* after the first season. Merry Anders continued acting into the early 1970s before making a career change out of show business, as did Lisa Gaye. Lori Nelson would add few credits to her résumé after leaving the show.

Years later, after catching a rerun of the original film, NBC honcho Brandon Tartikoff wondered if there was once again a TV series to be made from *How to Marry a Millionaire*. At first, his idea was coldly received, the general feeling being that the premise of husband-hunting gold diggers was distasteful in the 1980s. After much rethinking, his idea eventually led to *The Golden Girls* (NBC, 1985–92), which would become one of the biggest comedy hits of its era. The three leading ladies of that show, all in their fifties and sixties, were called Dorothy, Blanche, and Rose. All three (played by Bea Arthur, Rue McClanahan, and Betty White, respectively) were single, one of them divorced and the other two widowed. None of them, according to *The Golden Girls*' backstory, had occupied a swanky New York apartment as young women in the 1950s. Yet it wasn't such a stretch to imagine that, thirty years previously, they'd been going by the names of Greta, Mike, and Loco.

Ichabod and Me

Robert Sterling (*Bob Major*), George Chandler (*Ichabod Adams*), Christine White (*Abigail Adams*), Jimmy Mathers (*Benjie Major*), Reta Shaw (*Lavinia*), Guy Raymond (*Martin Perkins*), Forrest Lewis (*Colby*), Jimmy Hawkins (*Jonathan Baylor*), Burt Mustin (*Olaf Olson*)

Executive Producers: Joe Connelly, Bob Mosher. *Producer*: Irving Paley. *Writers*: Joe Connelly, Gene L. Coon, Joseph Hoffman, Joanna Lee, Allan Manings, Bob Mosher, Leo Rifkin, Bob Ross, Don Stanford, Mel Tolkin. *Directors*: Norman Abbott, Sidney Lanfield. *Associate Producer*: Jon Zimmer. *Director of Photography*: Jack MacKenzie. *Art Director*: John Meehan. *Editorial Department Head*: David J. O'Connell. *Music Score*: Pete Rugolo. *Film Editors*: Joseph Harrison, Bud S. Isaacs. *Music Supervisor*: Stanley Wilson. *Music Editor*: Frank E. Morriss, Jr. *Sound*: William Lynch. *Sound Effects Editor*: George Ohanian. *Assistant Directors*: Les Berke, John Clarke Bowman, James H. Brown, Chuck Colean. *Set Decorators*: John McCarthy, James S. Redd. *Costume Supervisor*: Vincent Dee. *Makeup*: Jack Barron, Robert Dawn. *Hair Stylist*: Florence Bush. Kayro-JaM Productions, in association with CBS-TV.

Aired Tuesdays at 9:30 P.M. on CBS-TV. First aired September 26, 1961; last aired September 18, 1962. 36 black-and-white episodes.

ABBY: Father, why is it that the people in this town make so much of little things?
ICHABOD: Well, when nothing ever happens, you gotta make the most out of what does.

One of two sitcoms in this book to mine comedy from the world of newspapers and journalists—see also *The Jim Backus Show: Hot Off the Wire*—*Ichabod and Me* was a little-known effort from the typewriters of Joe Connelly and Bob Mosher, better known as the writer-creators of *Leave It to Beaver* (CBS and ABC, 1957–63) and their subsequent baby boomer favorite *The Munsters* (CBS, 1964–66). But while Backus' show explored the world of journalism in the metropolis, *Ichabod and Me* takes place in a small New England town.

The *Me* in *Ichabod and Me* is Bob Major, a widowed newspaperman who grows weary of the New York rat race (he was employed by the *New York Times*) and decides he wants to raise his five-year-old son in a different environment. He buys the *Phippsboro Bulletin*, a rural weekly in New Hampshire, from its longtime owner-editor, Ichabod Adams, and takes over as editor. The sixtyish Adams is also the mayor of Phippsboro, a post he has held for 28 years, and

Ichabod Adams (George Chandler) shares a book with young Benjie Major (Jimmy Mathers) in *Ichabod and Me.* Looking over their shoulders is Benjie's dad Bob Major (Robert Sterling), otherwise known as *Me* (Photofest).

shares his home with his beautiful adult daughter Abby. Adams regards the younger Major with bemusement.

Bob's struggles with the small-town ways of Phippsboro (population approximately 3000) often put him into conflict with his neighbors, especially when he writes inflammatory editorials for the *Bulletin* designed to stimulate progress in the sleepy community. Ichabod, who's become friendly with the younger man, offers some fatherly wisdom when Bob's affairs go awry. Abby initially professes disdain for Bob, but seems to warm to him as the series progresses.

Other longtime residents who look on Bob and his activities with suspicion include Martin Perkins, proprietor of the local hardware store, and his buddy Colby, who operates Colby's Seed and Fertilizer. Like Ichabod, both men are members of the city council. Bob's only regular employee at the newspaper is wide-eyed high school student Jonathan. Keeping house for Bob and Benjie is stern-visaged but basically soft-hearted Lavinia. The party line gets quite a workout in Phippsboro—Martin and Colby in particular monitor it closely—explaining why Bob says keeping a secret there "is like trying to hide a mole on Brigitte Bardot."

The show's humor arose from the conflict between the younger, more impulsive man's clashes with the New England climate. *Ichabod and Me* played on the archetypal image of the New Englander—spare with words as well as money, suspicious of strangers, and not easily convinced to change his ways.

In "The Old Stowe Road" (1/23/62), Bob is appalled by the broken-down condition of the road that leads from Phippsboro to Dover, and launches a campaign to build a new thoroughfare. Ichabod admits the Old Stowe Road, named after Harriet Beecher Stowe, is in poor shape, but reminds him that the people of Phippsboro don't always welcome change. "Not too long ago, indoor plumbing was considered the handiwork of the Devil," he says. Bob's stirring editorial, emphasizing the new business that a better road could bring to town, prompts the city council to approve his idea, especially since the county is willing to foot the bill. But when Abby finds out that the new road will require the Old Stowe Road to be bulldozed, she lines up the women of Phippsboro in protest, and Bob finds himself trying to resolve the dispute without becoming the pariah of Phippsboro.

In "The Barter System" (12/5/61), Bob vows to make good on more than $600 in delinquent accounts at the newspaper. With help from his accountant friend in New York, he sends sternly worded collection letters to more than thirty Phippsboro residents who owe money. Ichabod cautions him that this isn't the way things are done in a small New England town—"Up here, everything's personal"—and sure enough the letters do nothing but offend Bob's neighbors. One of the paper's debtors, retired lawyer Caleb Cunningham, resolves his $14 debt to the paper by presenting Bob with a live pig, citing an 18th century law still on the books that allows residents to pay their debts in barter. Word spreads, and soon Bob has an office full of livestock ("Looks like

Walter Brennan's living room," he cracks) and still no cash. Finally, at an auction, Cunningham urges his friends and neighbors to pay their debts to the newspaper, and Bob collects enough money to keep afloat.

Ichabod and Me had its origins in two segments of the long-running anthology series *Robert Montgomery Presents* (NBC, 1950–57), in which George Chandler created the role of Ichabod Adams. The first, aired in 1956, was called "Good-Bye, Gray Flannel," and co-starred Lee Bowman as Mr. Major. That show was so well-received that Chandler was invited back to reprise the role in "One Smart Apple" a year later.

In 1960, producers Connelly and Mosher made a pilot called *Adams' Apples*, signing George Chandler to reprise his lead role. Fred Beir co-starred as Mr. Major, whose first name here was Terry, and Christine White played Abby. Seen as Terry's housekeeper Livvy Perkins in the pilot was Dorothy Neumann, while Leon Ames played Major's former boss, who travels to Phippsboro in hopes of luring Terry back to his job in New York. In the pilot, scripted by George Tibbles from a story by J. Harvey Howells, Terry is a New York advertising man who decides to retire to New Hampshire and take up life as a gentleman farmer. There's no mention of the newspaper in this version of the show, which pits Major against Adams in a battle of wits over a business deal concerning apple crops. That version of the pilot didn't sell, though it aired as an episode of *General Electric Theater* (CBS, 1953–62) in 1960.

Chandler took personal credit for getting *Ichabod and Me* on the air despite the bumps along the way. "I took the bull by the horns and said here was a show I wanted to do. And, by God, I'm doing it! ... This is the first time I've ever felt strongly enough to want to package a show.... Actors generally wait for someone to call them. I followed the other route. I loved this show and I did something about it."[1] His partners in the project included creator-producers Connelly and Mosher, as well as comedian Jack Benny, whose J & M Productions put up much of the funding. By late 1960, *Variety* reported that *Ichabod and Me* had been "firmed" for a 26-week run on CBS, with Kellogg signed on as an alternate week sponsor. The trade paper noted that Chandler and leading lady White were set for the show but that the male lead had yet to be selected, although production was expected to be underway by late January.

CBS's enthusiasm for the show may have been due in part to the popularity of *The Andy Griffith Show* (CBS, 1960–68), one of the few successful shows launched amidst a flood of new sitcoms in 1960-61. Some saw similarities to another CBS newcomer, *Window on Main Street* (1961-62), which marked Robert Young's return to series television after putting *Father Knows Best* to rest a year earlier.

Star Robert Sterling, who'd been a busy movie actor as a contract player at Columbia Pictures and then MGM, had been an early convert to television. Born November 13, 1917, in New Castle, Pennsylvania, as William Sterling Hart, the actor made his film debut in 1939 and stayed busy in films for the next several years, interrupted only by his World War II service as a flight instructor. He came to *Ichabod and Me* already a veteran of the popular, much-rerun sitcom *Topper* (CBS, 1953–55), in which he played ghostly George Kerby, the role originated by Cary Grant in the 1937 film. When that show ran its course, he made a comeback with the short-lived sitcom *Love That Jill* (ABC, 1958), which cast Sterling as the owner of a modeling agency. Both of those shows had co-starred him opposite real-life wife Anne Jeffreys, whom he'd married after his divorce from actress Ann Sothern. He was still sufficiently boyish-looking at 43 to play young leading man roles.

Second-billed George Chandler (1898–1985) had a long list of film credits dating back to silent pictures in the late 1920s, and continued acting into the late 1970s. Prior to *Ichabod*, Chandler had spent the 1958-59 television season as a regular on CBS's *Lassie* (1954–71), playing Uncle Petrie Martin. At the time *Ichabod and Me* began, the busy actor was also serving as president of the Screen Actors Guild, a post he held from 1960 to 1963.

Character actress Reta Shaw (1912–82), who played Livvy, would have a more substantial role as a sitcom housekeeper in *The Ghost and Mrs. Muir* (NBC and ABC, 1968–70), and also made frequent guest appearances on *Bewitched* (ABC, 1964–72). Born of Maine stock herself, Shaw took no offense at the many matronly roles she was offered in the course of her television career. "There are lots of roles for mature, sexless females in television. And I'm delighted to play them."[2] Prior to *Ichabod*, she had already added to her bulging résumé continuing roles in *The Ann Sothern Show* (CBS, 1958–61), *The Tab Hunter Show* (NBC, 1960-61), and *Mr. Peepers*, and was also seen in Disney films like *Pollyanna* (1960) and *Mary Poppins* (1964). Among the actress' other credits, Shaw appeared on Broadway in the hit musical comedy *The Pajama Game*.

Cast as Sterling's love interest in the series was actress Christine White, who had made her first big splash playing a drug addict in Broadway's *A Hatful of Rain*. As an aspiring actress in New York, she'd palled around with fellow newcomer James Dean, of whom she later said, "We were just little street urchins running around with holes in our shoes looking for a way of life, our pockets loaded with faith. He'd say, 'Can you lend me five till the end of the week?' I'd say, 'I was just going to ask you the same thing.' That was our relationship."[3] In 1976, when writer William Bast adapted his memories of James Dean into an NBC telemovie, Candy Clark played the young Christine White onscreen, while White herself had a cameo role as a secretary.

Jimmy Mathers, who played Bob's six-year-old son Benjie in the series, was the lookalike little brother of *Leave It to Beaver* star Jerry Mathers, making his acting debut. Jimmy's role would be relatively minor, however, as few stories revolved around his character. In fact, Benjie and housekeeper Livvy would not even appear in a number of episodes.

The show was set to air at 9:30 P.M. Tuesdays, with *The Red Skelton Show* as its lead-in. Since Skelton not only enjoyed high ratings but was known to attract a sizable rural audience, this would seem to be a propitious placement for the new sitcom.

Early reviews, however, suggested that the show was in for a rough time, regardless of what time it aired. *Variety* (10/4/61) termed the series opener "just another run-of-the-mill situation comedy, typically innocuous in content and wholly bland in its approach.... [T]here were no surprises and few laughs on the first outing." The Associated Press' Cynthia Lowry (9/27/61) was similarly unenthusiastic, calling the series "a pretty tired, clumsy effort." She considered the show's portrayal of New Englanders more likely to offend residents of that region than charm them. For sheer dislike of the show, however, it's likely that few reviewers topped Harriet Van Horne. In her syndicated column, Van Horne (9/27/61) opined, "A network that would buy *Ichabod* for prime evening time would buy the Brooklyn Bridge from a tavern drunk — and pay cash."

Ichabod's most notable guest star was *Twilight Zone* creator Rod Serling, making what was billed as his dramatic debut in a March 1962 episode. Serling played reclusive writer Eugene Hollenfield (author of such opuses as *Picture in the Cornfield* and *Life with Louie*), who moves to Phippsboro to work in seclusion, but from whom Bob Major is determined to get an exclusive interview. Bob and Abby disguise themselves as beatniks in order to crash a party being held at the novelist's house. The episode gained *Ichabod* some welcome publicity, but didn't result in an ongoing rise in viewership. Serling, ill at ease in front of the cameras for more than his usual narrator role, was none too happy with the result of his venture into the sitcom world, complaining, "I never had a line that resembled the English language."[4]

By April, star Robert Sterling cheerfully admitted in an interview that his show's chances of seeing a second season were minimal at best. Saying that CBS had failed to adequately promote the show, Sterling professed himself bewildered by the rules of the current television game. "Show business has always been a gamble," Sterling said, "but with TV, gambling skill — as far as the actor is concerned — has been eliminated. A man could go crazy trying to figure out how a series he turned down, because he sincerely thought it was terrible, becomes a hit, and how a series he accepted because it had all the successful ingredients is a failure."[5]

In the years since he had appeared in *Topper*, Sterling said, sponsors had grown increasingly jittery about the rising costs of sponsoring a show, and were all too anxiously watching for signs of weakness from its first weeks on the air. Indeed, with ratings unimpressive, CBS canceled the show at the end of its first season.

Privately, according to wife Anne Jeffreys, Sterling was even more vocal about his dissatisfaction with *Ichabod and Me*. "He'd get up in the morning and say, 'God, I'd give anything not to have to do this crap,'" she remembered years later. "It was torture for him." Once the ax fell, according to Jeffreys, her husband said, "That's it! I'm getting out of this business."[6]

Having grown weary of the vagaries of show business, Sterling did in fact leave it altogether not long after his show ended. At midlife, he gave up performing for the business world, carving out a successful career in the emerging software industry and also marketing a line of Sterling Club golf equipment. From that point forward, he would act only occasionally, usually when he was offered an opportunity to work with his wife Anne Jeffreys. Sterling died on May 30, 2006, at the age of 89, after several years of declining health.

With an appealing cast and a viable premise, *Ichabod and Me* should have been a more enjoyable show. Scriptwriter Bob Ross, who would later write and produce for both *The Andy Griffith Show* (CBS, 1960–68) and its spinoff, *Mayberry R.F.D.* (CBS, 1968–71), seemed to have a particular affinity for writing about small-town life, and his *Ichabod* scripts are among the more effective ones. With a little luck, the show could have been a keeper, and not tossed away like last week's issue of the *Phippsboro Bulletin*.

I'm Dickens ... He's Fenster

John Astin (*Harry Dickens*), Marty Ingels (*Arch Fenster*), Emmaline Henry (*Kate Dickens*), Dave Ketchum (*Mel Warshaw*), Frank DeVol (*Myron Bannister*), Henry Beckman (*Bob Mulligan*)

Creator-Producer: Leonard Stern. *Writers*: Arthur Alsberg, Barry Blitzer, Dick Chevillat, Jerry Davis, Mel Diamond, Bob Fisher, Frank Fox, Fred Freeman, Don Hinkley, Sheldon Keller, Walter Kempley, Howard Merrill, Garry Marshall, Marty Roth, Ray Singer, Leonard Stern, Mel Tolkin. *Directors*: Norman Abbott, Claudio Guzman, Arthur Hiller, Leonard Stern. *Associate Producer*: Don Hinkley. *Story Editor*: Mel Tolkin. *Production Manager*: George Tobin. *Director of Photography*: Maury Gertsman. *Assistant Director*: Paul Wurtzel. *Art Directors*: Rolland M. Brooks, Claudio Guzman, Walter McKeegan. *Film Editors*: Marshall Neilan, Jr., Theodore Rich. *Editorial Supervisor*: Bill Heath. *Music Composer–Conductor*: Irving Szathmary. *Set Decorators*: Stuart Reiss, Frank Tuttle. *Sound Engineer*: Frank Webster. *Special Effects*: Perzy High. *Casting*: Mercedes Manzanares. *Makeup*: Harry Thomas. *Sound*: Glen Glenn Sound. Heyday Productions.

Aired Fridays at 9 P.M. on ABC-TV. First aired September 28, 1962; last aired September 13, 1963. 32 black-and-white episodes.

Real, old-fashioned slapstick comedy was largely absent from prime time TV in the early 1960s, until *I'm Dickens ... He's Fenster* came along. Creator-producer Leonard Stern, who'd previously written for Steve Allen and Jackie Gleason, as well as for *The Honeymooners,* believed that the show would fill a void on television. "We're going after the big laugh, but we're going to motivate it logically," he explained.[1] His original working title for the new series, reflecting the blue-collar employment of the lead characters, was "The Workers."

Like the characters of Ralph Kramden and Ed Norton on *The Honeymooners,* Harry Dickens and Arch Fenster are best friends working at an everyday job. The pilot episode, "A Small Matter of Being Fired," which aired as the series opener on September 28, 1962, establishes that Harry and Arch have been working as carpenters for the McKendrick Construction Company for the past nine years. Arch is single, but always falling for a different woman; Harry is happily married to sensible Kate. Chief among Harry and Arch's pals at work are Mel Warshaw, a devoted family man who works to support his eleven kids, and henpecked Bob Mulligan, whose conversation often revolves around his relationship with his wife Eloise.

Harry is thrilled when Mr. Bannister offers him the job of foreman, until he learns that his first official managerial duty will be to fire his pal Arch, who has acquired a reputation as a troublemaker. Arch, learning that the ax is about to fall, loyally tells Mr. Bannister that Harry fired him as instructed; Harry persuades him that the rumors about Arch are false, and saves his pal's job.

Producer Stern had originally envisioned his characters as being in early

TV newcomers Marty Ingels (left) and John Astin teamed up for the sitcom *I'm Dickens ... He's Fenster.*

middle age, but when he began to cast the show found two younger men suitable for the roles. It was while working with Steve Allen that Stern first met comedian Marty Ingels, and hired him to play a few small roles. Ingels, born Martin Ingerman on March 9, 1936, had from his youth a rubbery face that inspired laughter, so it wasn't surprising that he eventually gravitated toward performing. Stern followed Ingels' career for the next several years while the basic idea for what would become *I'm Dickens ... He's Fenster* germinated.

Signed to co-star with Ingels in the new sitcom was actor John Astin. Like Ingels, he wasn't yet well-known to television audiences. However, at the age of 32, Astin already had several Broadway shows under his belt, as well as a featured role in the Cary Grant–Doris Day comedy *That Touch of Mink* (1962). Born March 30, 1930, he relocated from New York to Hollywood in the early 1960s at the suggestion of actor Tony Randall, who was impressed by his performance in a Broadway show. Bemused to be termed a "discovery" when *Dickens ... Fenster* began, Astin did hasten to point out that he had in fact been a working professional for quite some time. "It's like I was discovered on an amateur hour and given my first professional opportunity," Astin said with a touch of asperity of the publicity surrounding the show. "Of course, this series may prove to be the best thing that's happened to me in my career — and I hope it will be — but it's certainly not the first thing by a long shot."[2]

The two stars became friends despite some initial hesitancy from both sides. "That first day," Ingels later said, "we worked together for 10 or 12 hours and we both felt it just wouldn't come off. We had different approaches." Brooklyn-born Ingels, with his background in comedy — some found him reminiscent of the young Red Skelton — tended to look for the sight gags and jokes in the script, and play those to the hilt. Astin, trained as an actor, had a different stance. "I look at a script," he said, "and I'm trying to find the honesty of the situation and the sincerity of the characters."[3]

Leonard Stern, however, thought the men perfectly suited to play off each other, and eventually his stars saw it too. They developed an amiable working relationship largely devoid of jealousy. Rather than argue over billing, both men readily agreed to alternate being top-billed in the show's opening titles. The determined effort at even-handedness extended to signage on the show's soundstage, according to *TV Guide*: A poster on one wall read "Marty Ingels and John Astin," while the opposite wall trumpeted "John Astin and Marty Ingels."

The series also provided the first major television exposure for 35-year-old actress-singer Emmaline Henry, cast as Harry's patient wife Kate and given "with" billing in the show's opening titles. A native of Philadelphia, she acted upon her gift for performing early, and had her own local radio show by the time she was twelve years old. She arrived in New York to pursue her career with less than $200 in her purse. "There was nothing waiting for me in New York," she recalled. "I worked as an usherette and in an office where I'm sure

I loused up the files for years to come. Eight months later I got a job in the chorus of *Gentlemen Prefer Blondes*."⁴ She went on to work opposite Phil Silvers in the Broadway hit *Top Banana* and in the film *Lucky Me* (1954). Other shows were less triumphant; Henry recalled a celebration at Sardi's on the opening night of the musical revue *Vintage '60*. When the first reviews came in, she watched producer David Merrick's face as he scanned them, and advised her colleagues, "Hurry up and eat. The food may not get paid for."⁵ Indeed, the show closed in less than a week.

She came to *Dickens* on the recommendation of co-star Ingels, who'd worked with her several years earlier in a revue at a New York hotel. "What talent!" Ingels raved. "She could act, sing, mug. She had comedy sense. She was beautiful, and a fine girl. You don't forget somebody like that."⁶ The two actors had dated for a time, which Henry admitted made it a little odd for her to play Astin's wife on the show, rather than Ingels'. Not abandoning her training as a singer, she sometimes sang for studio audiences as part of the warm-up each week before a new episode was filmed. Henry's singing voice was captured on film when she sang "Camptown Races" in the episode "Carpenters Four" (1/18/63), in which a young newcomer billed as James Nabors also appears.

After *Dickens*, she spent the 1964-65 season playing yet another understanding wife, to Mickey Rooney in his unsuccessful ABC sitcom *Mickey*. But it is probably her recurring role as strong-willed Amanda Bellows, wife of the base psychiatrist, in the long-running hit *I Dream of Jeannie* (NBC, 1965–70) for which Emmaline Henry remains best known. After *Jeannie*, she was seen in guest appearances on *The Bob Newhart Show* (CBS, 1972–77) and *Three's Company* (ABC, 1977–84) before her untimely death from brain disease in 1979.

Featured in the ranks of Dickens and Fenster's co-workers were Frank DeVol (1911–99), better known for his musical contributions to a host of popular movies (including *Pillow Talk*, *Guess Who's Coming to Dinner*, and *Cat Ballou*) as well as his themes for TV shows like *The Brady Bunch* (ABC, 1969–74). Henry Beckman, seen as Bob Mulligan, would go on to a featured role in *Here Come the Brides* (ABC, 1968–70).

An unusually high number of freelance writers were employed to develop scripts. Most of the better-known sitcom scribes of the early 1960s took at least one stab at this show. Frequently in the director's chair, beginning with the series pilot, was Arthur Hiller, who would go on to helm major motion pictures like *The Americanization of Emily* (1964), *Love Story* (1970), and *Outrageous Fortune* (1987).

At producer Stern's insistence, the show was filmed before a live audience, in three-camera style, not commonplace for sitcoms in the early 1960s. He rented facilities at Desilu, where newly installed president Lucille Ball was simultaneously gearing up for a three-camera sitcom of her own to be called *The Lucy Show* (CBS, 1962–68). "I think comedians work better when they hear the reaction of real people," Stern explained. "And I loathe laugh tracks."⁷

The show brought off some impressively timed and executed slapstick scenes, especially given the presence of a studio audience. Split-second timing earns a big laugh in the opening scene of "Senior Citizen Charlie" (2/22/63), when Astin (as Dickens) bends to tie his shoe just as a giant wrecking ball comes hurtling across the set, smashing the wall just inches over Astin's head. However, there could be a downside to shooting in front of a live studio audience, too, as demonstrated by a scene in "The Bet" (3/1/63). A sight gag involving a dust cloth gets a big laugh from the audience when Ingels, as Arch, unfurls it and spews dust all over the set. Good thing it's the climax of the scene, since the audience can be heard not only laughing, but coughing.

ABC executives thought highly enough of *Dickens* to place it in a time slot where the competition was formidable. Seen on Friday nights, the show did battle with the second half-hour of two established hits—*Route 66* (1960–65) on CBS and *Sing Along with Mitch* (1961–65) on NBC. Serving as lead-in to *Dickens* was the popular prime time cartoon *The Flintstones* (1960–66).

Early ratings reports for ABC's new sitcom were neither wonderful nor terrible. Not conclusively established as a hit, *Dickens* nevertheless was doing well enough by February 1963 that *TV Guide* reported that its sponsor would keep it going for the remainder of the season. Not numbered among its fans, however, was *TV Guide* critic Gilbert Seldes, who after watching most of the early episodes reported (2/8/63), "At the beginning I thought I couldn't tell the characters apart because I wasn't interested in them. After three months I'm pretty sure the reason is that I don't like them." On the other hand, *Time* (1/4/63) declared it "the best new TV comedy in several years."

In May, while on a national promotional tour to stimulate interest in the series, Emmaline Henry told a journalist that the *Dickens* cast and crew was still awaiting word on whether the show would be invited back for a second year on ABC. "We're in limbo now," Henry said. "We haven't been cancelled, and we haven't been renewed yet."[8] Meanwhile, the syndicated *TV Key* column (5/24/63) was urging viewers who'd missed the show earlier in the season to check it out in reruns, saying, "Everything an unpretentious farce should have is here, including pratfalls, wild sight gags, and general nonsense." Given the show's propensity for physical comedy, it had a following among children as well as adults, though this audience was somewhat restricted by the show's 9 P.M. time slot.

All indications were that the show's following was growing—and then ABC canceled the series. Ingels would later claim that he'd heard the news in a particularly odd way: After spending the morning filming scenes on a Desilu soundstage, he headed for lunch at the studio commissary, where he enjoyed ordering the Marty Ingels sandwich. "Everybody there [on the Desilu lot] had a sandwich named after him," Ingels explained. "You could order a Danny Thomas, a Mary Tyler Moore, a Dick Van Dyke, a Marty Ingels or a John Astin."

But when Ingels looked over the menu, the Marty Ingels, a pastrami on rye sandwich, had been crossed off the list. The nonplussed waiter, not knowing what to say to his celebrity customer, left it to the cook to break the news: "Mr. Ingels, I don't know how to tell you this, but your sandwich has been canceled."[9]

Though he'd been denied a long run in *Dickens,* the exposure from that series led John Astin to his starring role as Gomez Addams in another ABC sitcom, *The Addams Family,* which premiered in the fall of 1964. As it turned out, *The Addams Family* lasted only two seasons on ABC, but nonetheless became a cult favorite that played for years in reruns. Astin returned to ABC for a series of guest appearances on *The Phyllis Diller Show* (1967) and ten years later as the star of the military sitcom *Operation Petticoat* (1977-78). Behind the camera, he wrote and directed a short subject called *Prelude* (1968) that was nominated for an Oscar. In 1972, he married Oscar-winning actress Patty Duke, a union that lasted until the mid–1980s and produced sons Sean and Mackenzie.

Less fortunate was his co-star Marty Ingels. Once *Dickens* shut down, the comedian shot a pilot for a new sitcom to be called *Duncan, Be Careful.* Reassured by others that he was on the fast track to major stardom, Ingels bought an expensive Hollywood home on credit, and then found himself in deep trouble when the highly touted comedy pilot failed to sell, and work offers dried up. In 1977, he married Oscar-winning actress-singer Shirley Jones, in what struck many outsiders as an odd match of temperaments and personalities, becoming stepfather to her sons Shaun, Ryan, and Patrick. In later years, Ingels would work infrequently as an actor, but dabbled in other occupations, among them a thriving business in which he lined up celebrities to do television commercial endorsements.

Though *I'm Dickens ... He's Fenster* enjoyed only a short life on ABC, it's still remembered by a band of loyal fans. If the show lacked something that would have made it appealing to a wider audience, it may have been a sense of anything being at stake for the characters. Harry and Arch are nice guys who seem content with their jobs. Harry has a loving wife, while Arch is enjoying his freedom as a bachelor. There's no particular sense that the men are striving to achieve any goals, or overcome any real obstacles. If comedy is indeed a man in trouble, the nature of the trouble in most episodes of *I'm Dickens ... He's Fenster* was so slight and transitory as to be nearly invisible to viewers.

It's a Great Life

Michael O'Shea (*Denny Davis*), William Bishop (*Steve Connors*), James Dunn (*Earl Morgan*), Frances Bavier (*Amy Morgan*), Barbara Bates (*Kathy Morgan*)
Creators-Producers: Dick Chevillat, Ray Singer. *Writers*: Harrison A. Baker, Dick Chevillat, Bernard Ederer, Leonard Gershe, Joel Kane, Ray Singer, Robert White. *Director*: Christian Nyby. *Production Supervisor*: Sidney Van Keuren. *Directors of Photography*: Lucien Andriot, Nicholas Musuraca. *Associate Producers*: Thomas Greenhow, Sidney A. Singer. *Supervising Film Editor*: Frank Capacchione. *Film Editor*: Newell P. Kimlin. *Music Composed and Conducted by* David Rose. *Assistant Directors*: Thomas F. Kelly, Arthur Lueker. *Art Director*: McClure Capps. *Photographic Effects*: Jack R. Glass. *Set Decorations*: Rudy Butler. *Sound*: Joel Moss, Elmer Raguse, William Russell. *Gowns*: Robert Link. Raydic Productions.

Aired Tuesdays at 10:30 P.M. (through September 1955), then Sundays at 7 P.M. on NBC-TV. First aired September 7, 1954; last aired June 3, 1956. 78 black-and-white episodes.

DOCTOR (lecturing fun-loving Denny on the importance of a virtuous lifestyle): I lead a clean, normal, healthy life. I don't smoke, I don't drink, I don't run around with women. I go to bed every night at nine o'clock, and at six o'clock the next morning, I get up.
DENNY: Why?

In 1946, the acclaimed film *The Best Years of Our Lives* told the stories of American soldiers returning from World War II, and seeing what life in postwar America would be like. Several years later, a similar theme was at the center of *It's a Great Life,* and perhaps it was intentional that the title of this mid-fifties sitcom was not unlike that of the film.

In the pilot, widowed Amy Morgan, who lives in a Los Angeles suburb with her brother Earl and adult daughter Kathy, has decided to raise some needed money by renting out the upstairs bedroom previously occupied by Earl. She shows the room to a middle-aged married couple, Eddie and Stella Garson (played by Richard Wessel and Vivi Janiss) who promptly agree to take it. When Amy leaves the house to help the Garsons pick up their bags, Kathy opens the door to Denny and Steve, two ex–Army men recently arrived in Hollywood. The two best friends are Korean War veterans who have recently relocated from New York in order to make a fresh start. They agree to rent the room for $12 a week, and eventually emerge victorious over their "competition" the Garsons.

Denny Davis is a lazy, wisecracking, scheming guy, prone to hitting on every attractive woman he meets, while Steve Connors is the handsome straight arrow who immediately attracts the interest of Mrs. Morgan's pretty daughter Kathy. According to the first-season episode "Friendship" (2/8/55), the guys have been friends for the past ten years, and originally met standing in line at the draft board. Both Denny and Steve quickly become fond of the Morgans, and soon they both address Amy as "Mom." In the show's stories, Denny and Steve try to find their niche in postwar America, trying various jobs and schemes in order to better themselves. Their longest-lasting gig is a job selling Handy Dandy vacuum cleaners door to door, though they aren't terribly successful at it. In other episodes, they try their hands at opening a restaurant, working in retail, and even booking Steve as a prizefighter.

Uncle Earl is an incurable loafer whose only gainful employment is his annual gig as a department store Santa. When someone suggests he consider getting a steady job, his response is, "Who made that awful crack?" He tells sis-

Top-billed Michael O'Shea (Denny, far right) seems to be telling guest player Nancy Kulp that *It's a Great Life* when you have your own sitcom. William Bishop (Steve, center) probably wouldn't disagree.

ter Amy that going to work in the morning would interfere with his afterbreakfast nap.

In the episode "B-Day for Earl" (10/9/55), Amy, Steve, and Danny decide to observe Uncle Earl's forty-seventh birthday by inviting all of his high school friends over for a reunion styled after TV's *This Is Your Life*. Unfortunately, as the guests begin to reminisce, it becomes clear that Earl's accomplishments were few—he took eight years to complete high school, is described by the school coach as the worst football player ever on his team, and is still blamed by one of his friends for an incident that caused him to lose the girl he loved.

The show's top-billed star was comic actor Michael O'Shea (1906–73). O'Shea made his film debut opposite Barbara Stanwyck in *Lady of Burlesque* (UA, 1943). While playing the title role in UA's *Jack London* (also 1943), he met a newcomer named Virginia Mayo, cast in a small role. O'Shea and Mayo were married in 1947 and continued to pursue their film careers into the 1950s.

O'Shea's co-star, actor William Bishop, born July 16, 1918, first came to attention playing Lov Bensey in the Broadway production of *Tobacco Road*. Relocating to Hollywood in the early 1940s, Bishop had more than thirty films on his résumé by the time he was signed for *It's a Great Life,* though he had yet to attain top stardom. Bishop hoped to use his television exposure to further his film career. His role on the comedy series reportedly attracted the interest of more than one Hollywood studio. However, he said, "You can bet I won't be signing any contract that takes me out of this series. After all, it's easy to see that TV was solely responsible for the rebirth of interest in my career."[1]

For both leading men, there was occasional overlap between their TV characters and their own lives. In "A Visit from Steve's Mother" (10/26/54), O'Shea played a dual role, appearing as himself in addition to his regular role as Denny. The episode referenced O'Shea's real-life marriage to Virginia Mayo, though she did not appear. For that same episode, the producers enlisted actor Bishop's own mother Helen, who happened to be visiting her son at the time, to step into the role on-screen as well.

Featured as kindly Amy Morgan was Frances Bavier, well-known to a later generation of TV viewers as *The Andy Griffith Show*'s Aunt Bee (CBS, 1960–68), a role for which she would win an Emmy as Best Supporting Actress in 1967. Her role here was somewhat similar, as she served as surrogate mother to Steve and Denny. Though the actress was only in her early fifties, Bavier's character in *It's a Great Life* is occasionally described in the show's dialogue as "an old lady."

The bulk of the show's comedy, however, revolved around its three leads, as played by Bishop, O'Shea, and James Dunn. "We pretty much play ourselves," claimed O'Shea in an interview with United Press' Vernon Scott, who noted that the three stars ad-libbed a good many lines and actions during filming. The statement drew a friendly rebuke from Dunn, who asserted, "That's not so. You guys are always saying that. It takes work to play a bum."[2]

Dunn, born November 2, 1901, had a film career that dated back to the late 1920s. Some older viewers remembered him as a romantic leading man in pictures like *Bad Girl* (1931), or playing paternal roles opposite Shirley Temple in no less than three 1934 releases: *Baby Take a Bow, Bright Eyes,* and *Stand Up and Cheer.* In the late 1930s, Dunn was the real-life husband of starlet Frances Gifford, but by then his career was slowing. A few years later, however, he won a Best Supporting Actor Oscar for his role as the alcoholic father in *A Tree Grows in Brooklyn* (1945).

After winning the Oscar, Dunn hoped for a resurgence of his film career, but was mostly doomed to disappointment. He left 20th Century–Fox after squabbling with management over the scripts he was being offered, and lost a substantial amount of his own money investing in a Broadway show that flopped. "One day, when things looked the blackest, I looked at the mantel and the Oscar was gone. I asked [my wife] Edna about it. She said she had hid it and wasn't going to tell me where it was." When an offer to co-star in *It's a Great Life* came down the pike, Dunn decided his prized Academy Award was nothing but a jinx. "I don't care if I never see it again."[3]

The show was the creation of comedy writers Ray Singer and Dick Chevillat, who had been writing as a team since radio's *The Sealtest Village Store* in the early 1940s. They had worked on the Phil Harris–Alice Faye radio comedy, and scripted the Esther Williams musical comedy *Neptune's Daughter* (1949). "This is our first crack at television," said Chevillat of *It's a Great Life*. "And it's a lot tougher than radio or movies. In pictures they expected only two or three pages of script a day. Now we turn out 40 pages a week."[4] Although Singer and Chevillat continued to take a prominent "written by" credit in the show's opening titles every week, by the second season other writers were credited as well. Several episodes were credited as "based on a teleplay by" other writers. Singer and Chevillat went on to collaborate on *The Jim Backus Show: Hot Off the Wire* (q.v.) before going their separate ways in the early 1960s. Later Chevillat would be one of the main writers of *Green Acres* (CBS, 1965–71) while Singer contributed scripts to *The Lucy Show* (CBS, 1962–68), among others.

The show's regular director was Christian Nyby, best-known for directing (or not directing, depending on whom you ask) the 1951 film classic *The Thing from Another World*. Actress Barbara Logan originated the role of Kathy Morgan in the series pilot, but did not appear in the regular series. The producers wrote around the character for the next few weeks, until Barbara Bates took over the role in the show's fourth episode. *It's a Great Life* was filmed at the Hal Roach Studios, using some of the same personnel who worked on series like *The Amos 'n' Andy Show* (CBS, 1951–53) and *My Little Margie* (CBS/NBC, 1952–55). The show was under the sponsorship of Chrysler Plymouth, whose jovial announcer Ron Rawson reminded viewers at the end of each episode that it would always be a *Great Life* when one owned one of the company's cars.

The fourth episode, "Objective: Moon" (9/28/54), introduced Bates as

Kathy, an aspiring actress; several early episodes depicted her efforts to get a career break in show business. Bates was signed to a contract by Warner Brothers in 1947, while still in her early twenties, but never hit the heights. Today she is probably best remembered for her minor role as Phoebe in the closing reel of *All About Eve* (1950); she was also featured in films like *Cheaper by the Dozen* (1950).

Variety (9/15/54) was noncommittal about the series at first look, seemingly reserving judgment. "[Singer and Chevillat] have come through with funnybone material that depends on some stock but laff-raising situations for its effect. However, the playing and timing thrust the opener into a position to command future attention." Syndicated columnist Jack O'Brian (9/9/54) termed it "a shallow skimover of familiar situations in a trifling script held at arm's length by some good performers."

Though the show was not filmed in front of a live audience, the laugh track was reported to be genuine, the result of showing completed episodes to a preview audience. Syndicated columnist Erskine Johnson reported that the show's three stars enjoyed attending these previews, where they laughed it up at their own antics and encouraged audience members to do likewise.

In the early episodes, Steve and Denny are consigned to the attic, where they share a double bed with the similarly displaced Uncle Earl. The Garsons continue for the next few episodes to stake their claim for the bedroom, until they move out in the eleventh episode. (An interesting commentary on 1950s TV censorship: Steve and Denny, whose relationship is obviously meant to be platonic, frequently share a double bed in early episodes, while the actors playing the married couple the Garsons are forbidden to do so, and play their bedroom scenes in separate beds.)

That spring, while first-season episodes were still in production, Erskine Johnson reported in his column that Barbara Bates was being written out of the series, though no reason was specified. Bates made her final appearance in an episode aptly titled "Kathy Goes to New York" (3/22/55), which depicted her character relocating in order to accept a stage acting job. In truth, Bates' role in the series had always been pretty inconsequential, and her final episode was no different. Most of the script revolved around the shenanigans that arise after Uncle Earl loses the money Amy gave him to buy Kathy's ticket. Though Steve is saddened that "my girl" is leaving town, the writers don't even give the couple a final scene together, and the details of Kathy's big break are sloughed off with Denny's vague line that she "was offered that good role in that play." Upon leaving the show, Bates was signed to a British movie contract by the J. Arthur Rank company, but their association proved short-lived. By the late 1950s, having developed a reputation for instability, she found her career options dwindling and left the business. Bates committed suicide in 1969, at the age of 43.

It's a Great Life failed to draw high ratings during its first season. Some blamed the 10:30 P.M. time slot, not an ideal placement for a half-hour sitcom. As the first season progressed, ratings gradually rose, winning out over competing programs though its overall numbers didn't keep pace with shows aired earlier in prime time.

In 1955, the show received some welcome attention when O'Shea won an Emmy as Most Outstanding New Personality, and the sponsor was persuaded to give the series a second chance. For the 1955-56 season, it would air in an early Sunday evening slot, competing with CBS's *Lassie* and ABC's long-running audience participation show *You Asked for It* (1950–59). New opening titles for the second season gave O'Shea, Bishop, and Dunn separate billing cards, with featured billing for Frances Bavier as well.

For an episode revolving around a retired movie star, Singer and Chevillat persuaded silent era leading lady Laura La Plante to play herself, after almost a quarter-century in retirement. In "The Movie Star" (11/13/55), the actress' maid quits abruptly, Denny and Steve find Miss La Plante cleaning up the maid's cottage and assume she is destitute. If the plot sounds familiar, it may be because writer Ray Singer recycled it more than a decade later for an infamous 1968 episode of *The Lucy Show* that starred Joan Crawford.

O'Shea found it stressful to shoot 39 episodes a year in which he played a leading role and did a substantial amount of physical comedy. "Nowadays," he said in 1956, "if you see a man hobbling down the street, bent over and just barely making it, either there's a tack in his shoe or he's on TV!"[5] An accomplished worrier, O'Shea said, "Comedy can be tragedy to the TV comedian who must try to top himself every week. You rack your brain for new gestures, ad libs and comedy gimmicks. But after a couple of seasons of doing a show every week, you've had it."[6]

The trio of stars was reportedly responsible for the odd ending to "Smog Gets in Your Eyes" (2/5/56). The episode depicts the confusion that results when Denny, Steve, and Earl unwittingly dilate their eyes just before Amy's dinner party, causing them to disrupt the evening so badly that she thinks her men are drunk. The last scene called for Bavier, as Amy, to lock her three co-stars in the downstairs coat closet, telling them to "sleep it off." O'Shea, Bishop, and Dunn ad-libbed a new ending in which, only seconds after they go into the "closet" and offstage, they bound down the living room stairs to confront a startled Amy. The three men thought it was a hoot, and persuaded the producers to let them do it in the final episode. Only after the show received a good many letters from confused viewers did they realize that the surrealistic finale might not have been such a good idea.

Second-season ratings for the show were not strong enough to earn it a renewal for the 1956-57 season. Of the show's leading players, Bavier would go on to do the most extensive television work. Prior to landing her signature role as Aunt Bee, she spent a year as a regular on *The Eve Arden Show* (CBS, 1957-58). After *The Andy Griffith Show*, she played Aunt Bee for two more years on its spinoff *Mayberry R.F.D.* (CBS, 1968–71). Bavier died in 1989, after spending her last several years retired in the real Siler City, North Carolina.

James Dunn, prior to his death in 1967, stayed busy with guest appearances in shows like *Ben Casey* (ABC, 1961–66) and *The Virginian* (NBC, 1962–70), and made a few more films. William Bishop died of cancer in 1959, at the age of 41, without ever reaching the level to which he'd aspired. The nephew of famed playwright Charles MacArthur, Bishop had continued to work as an actor, most recently in the western film *The Oregon Trail*, which was in general release at the time of his death. He was survived by his wife Shirley, whom he had married near the end of his run in *It's a Great Life*.

O'Shea grew disenchanted with show business and worked rarely as an actor after *It's a Great Life*. In 1957, with his show bringing in residuals, O'Shea said, "Today they want these people with long sideburns who play guitars and I'm afraid I can't do that."[7] In 1969, after being out of the public eye for several years, O'Shea was found working as a sheriff's deputy in Ventura County, where he lived with his wife and daughter. Over the age of sixty, he was fulfilling a lifelong dream that had run aground in his youth, when the New York Police Department rejected him for being too small. He died in 1973 while accompanying wife Virginia Mayo on a road company production of *40 Carats*. The 67-year-old actor was found dead in the apartment his wife had rented, the victim of a heart attack.

With 78 episodes available, the show went into syndication, for a time having been retitled *The Bachelors*. Rarely seen today, *It's a Great Life* offers an interesting look backward at the hopes and dreams of ordinary Americans in the new, post–World War II era.

It's About Time

Frank Aletter (*Captain Mac MacKenzie*), Jack Mullaney (*Lt. Hector Canfield*), Imogene Coca (*Shad*), Joe E. Ross (*Gronk*), Cliff Norton (*Boss*), Mike Mazurki (*Clon*), Pat Cardi (*Breer*), Mary Grace (*Mlor*), Alan DeWitt (*Mr. Tyler*), Frank Wilcox (*General J.P. Morley*)

Executive Producer–Creator: Sherwood Schwartz. *Producer*: George Cahan. *Writers*: Jerry Adelman, Alan Dinehart, Herbert Finn, Bill Freedman, Ben Gershman, Budd Grossman, David P. Harmon, Bruce Howard, Joel Kane, Albert E. Lewin, Sam Locke, Roland MacLane, Michael Morris, Brad Radnitz, Joel Rapp, Marty Roth, Elroy Schwartz, Sherwood Schwartz, Burt Styler. *Directors*: Jack Arnold, George Cahan, Dick Darley, Richard Donner, Leslie Goodwins, Jerry Hopper, Hal March, David McDearmon, Jack Shea. *Story Consultant*: Joel Kane. *Associate Producer*: Robert L. Rosen. *Directors of Photography*: Neal Beckner, Richard L. Rawlings. *Theme*: Gerald Fried, Sherwood Schwartz, George Wyle. *Production Manager*: Don Guest. *Unit Production Manager*: Claude Binyon, Jr. *Art Director*: Craig Smith. *Film Editors*: Frank Cappachione, Ben Marmon. *Music Composed and Conducted by* Gerald Fried. *Assistant Directors*: Wilbur D'Arcy, Major Roup. *Casting*: Pam Polifroni. *Set Decorators*: John Lamphear, Herman Schoenbrun, Donald E. Webb. *Special Film Material*: Jack H. Harris. Redwood Productions, in association with Gladysa Productions.

Aired Sundays at 7:30 P.M. on CBS-TV. First aired September 11, 1966; last aired August 27, 1967. 26 color episodes.

Though most TV viewers associate writer-producer Sherwood Schwartz with his two Baby Boomer favorites, *Gilligan's Island* (CBS, 1964–67) and *The Brady Bunch* (ABC, 1969–74), he was also responsible for this single-season CBS sitcom revolving around the adventures of two astronauts who were transported to one million B.C. Similar in feel and style to *Gilligan*, and intended to be similarly attractive to the kids who made up much of the early-evening viewing audience, *It's About Time* nonetheless failed to catch fire.

At least it began somewhat more promisingly. Schwartz had lost a battle with CBS executives two years earlier when *Gilligan* was launched, unable to persuade them that the show's premiere episode should depict how the castaways came to be shipwrecked on the island. This time, with experience on his side, he was able to open *It's About Time* with a pilot that set up the basic premise. As with *Gilligan*, he incorporated a theme song that would provide the back story in subsequent airings, accompanied here by animation. (The show's title is usually spelled on screen as the incorrect *Its About Time*, minus the apostrophe.)

In "And Then I Wrote Happy Birthday to You" (9/11/66), scripted by creator Schwartz with Elroy Schwartz and David P. Harmon, U.S. astronauts "Mac" MacKenzie and his second-in-command, Hector, make a crash landing in their spaceship. Uncertain where they've landed, they soon see cavemen in the distance, and a dinosaur. They realize they have "broken the time barrier" and been transported back to prehistoric Earth.

The first of the cave people they meet is Breer, a young boy who's been sent out in the jungle to hunt wildlife as a coming-of-age ritual to prove his manhood. Stalked by a dinosaur, Breer is grateful to be rescued by the astronauts, and takes them back to his village. Breer's father Gronk and mother Shad, along with his beautiful teenaged sister, blonde Mlor, welcome the strange visitors. (In the pilot, the mother's name is Shag. In the series, she will be Shad.) The astronauts' new friends help them hide when they incur the wrath of the tribal chief, a diminutive, petty tyrant known simply as Boss. Boss' henchman and sidekick is bulky, dimwitted Clon, whom Hector describes as the "man with the over-anxious club." Returning the favor, the astronauts save Breer from having to fulfill his dangerous mission by convincing the tribe members

Mike Mazurki (Clon) and Cliff Norton (Boss) had featured roles in *It's About Time*—until low ratings led to a mid-season overhaul.

to replace their longstanding ritual with a more modern one — the birthday party.

It's About Time sold to CBS in the wake of Schwartz's success with the critically maligned — but popular — *Gilligan's Island*, which had been doing well on the network since its 1964 debut. Viewers familiar with the adventures of Gilligan and his fellow castaways surely felt a nagging sense of *déjà vu* watching Schwartz's new show, which not only featured a similar type of kid-friendly humor but also used the device of a small group of people living apart from modern civilization in an isolated setting. Others, however, saw *It's About Time* as a live-action version of *The Flintstones* (ABC, 1960–66), the long-running Hanna-Barbera cartoon about "a modern Stone Age family."

Like *Gilligan*, Schwarz's new sitcom had a fairly large ensemble cast, though only four of them — astronauts Frank Aletter and Jack Mullaney, and prehistoric parents Imogene Coca and Joe E. Ross — received star billing in the show's opening titles. Aletter and Mullaney alternated top billing from week to week. As with Schwartz's previous series, a major investor was Gladysa Productions, the company owned by actor Phil Silvers of *Bilko* fame. Though his own *The New Phil Silvers Show* (CBS, 1963-64) had not been a success, Silvers' production company had turned quite a tidy profit from investing in *Gilligan's Island*, and readily provided funding for the new project.

Schwartz packed his cast with experienced sitcom players. Leading man Frank Aletter (1926–2009) had previously starred in two short-lived CBS sitcoms, *Bringing Up Buddy* (1960-61) and *The Cara Williams Show* (1964-65). Aletter was prior to his television work a Broadway stalwart in shows like *Bells Are Ringing*. In 1958, he married actress and former Miss America Lee Meriwether. Aletter would later admit that working on Williams' show had been a trying experience, giving him migraine headaches from the on-set tension. After shooting the *It's About Time* pilot in September 1965, Aletter had bided his time, assured by Schwartz that the series was a definite go for the fall 1966 schedule.

Interviewed a few weeks before the show's premiere, the star admitted that he couldn't quite tell what was in store yet. "Given this kind of premise and cast," he said frankly, "the show could either be terrible or great."[1] Aletter and then-wife Lee Meriwether had an unusual distinction in that both spouses were starring in new fall series — she in the Irwin Allen adventure *The Time Tunnel* (ABC, 1966-67) — and both shows were about time travel.

Jack Mullaney (1929–1982) played the more comedic role of Hector. Most recently a veteran of *My Living Doll* (CBS, 1964-65), he had been introduced to sitcom audiences with a recurring role as the bellboy in *The Ann Sothern Show* (CBS, 1958–61), and also had a continuing role in *Ensign O'Toole* (NBC, 1962-63). A native of Cincinnati, Mullaney broke into show business while on a visit to New York, when he befriended producer Fred Coe. Mullaney got one of his first jobs in television as an audience shill for the 1950s sitcom

Mr. Peepers, paid ten dollars a week for his ability to prime the studio audience for hearty laughter during the live broadcasts. Aside from his television work, he had roles in the Elvis Presley vehicles *Tickle Me* (1965) and *Spinout* (1966).

Mullaney told columnist Joan Crosby he had a difficult time deciding just how much comedy to inject into his role as Lt. Hector Canfield, without completely sacrificing believability. "In the pilot everyone was trying too hard to be funny," he said. "I was terrible.... There has to be a basis for reality, because I am playing an astronaut. But if you see a dinosaur, even if you're an astronaut, you scream, don't you?"[2]

The show represented the second sitcom venture for the gifted sketch comedienne Imogene Coca, whose own vehicle *Grindl* (q.v.) had lasted for only a year on NBC. Offered the chance to play Shad, Coca took a meeting with creator-producer Schwartz, whom she'd never previously met, and said yes. She enjoyed making the pilot, but doubted it would sell. "I would guess the critics will hate the show because it isn't intellectual," Coca predicted. "But I think the public will like it because it seems very funny to me."[3]

Cast as Coca's husband Gronk was actor Joe E. Ross, best-known for co-starring with Fred Gwynne in the critically acclaimed but relatively short-lived *Car 54, Where Are You?* (NBC, 1961–63). On that show, one of Ross' gimmicks as the slow-witted New York City police officer Gunther Toody had been an excited exclamation, "Ooh! Ooh!" According to Ross, a meeting was held to discuss whether or not the actor should use his trademark exclamatory in the new series. The result? "Sherwood ... said I should keep it, because cavemen made sounds like that. So I'm using it. Imagine—a conference about ooh! ooh!"[4]

Co-star Cliff Norton (1918–2003) was a longtime utility player on television, who had his own comedy show, *The Public Life of Cliff Norton,* in the early days of the medium. Alongside Norton as Boss, Kathleen Freeman made a few appearances in early episodes as his wife, Mrs. Boss. Wrestler-turned-actor Mike Mazurki (1907–90), featured as Clon, stood 6'5" and had been a hulking presence in scores of films since the early 1940s. Billed in the ring as "Iron Mike" Mazurki, he debuted with a minor role in *The Shanghai Gesture* (1941), and went on to make more than two dozen films, notably *Murder, My Sweet* (1944) and *Night and the City* (1950). He had previously appeared on *Gilligan's Island*, and would later be a regular on another short-lived sitcom, *The Chicago Teddy Bears* (CBS, 1971).

Completing the regular cast were young actors Pat Cardi and Mary Grace, as Breer and Mlor. Cardi had previously played a recurring role on *Hazel* during its 1965-66 season, while 21-year-old starlet Grace was a veteran of the short-lived soap opera *Never Too Young* (ABC, 1965-66).

Schwartz completed the first 13 segments of *Gilligan's Island* for the 1966-67 season before jumping into production with *It's About Time* that summer. He would enlist the aid of many of the same writers and directors to work on both shows. Even some of the same musical cues can be heard. Film producer Jack H. Harris, who'd produced the 1960 stop-motion adventure *Dinosaurus!*, was credited each week for "special" footage used in *It's About Time* (the rather unconvincing footage of dinosaurs that was seen occasionally).

The show's Sunday 7:30 P.M. time slot, occupied for the past three years by *My Favorite Martian* (1963–66), seemed an ideal placement for a sitcom with strong kid appeal. However, the other networks were actively pursuing a similar audience, ABC with the Irwin Allen adventure *Voyage to the Bottom of the Sea* (1964–68), and NBC with *Walt Disney's Wonderful World of Color*.

Safely ensconced between two long-running hits—*Lassie* and *The Ed Sullivan Show*—Schwartz's new sitcom was heavily sampled by viewers in its early weeks on the air, and showed signs of possibly becoming a success in its own right (to the dismay of several critics). But as the season wore on, it became clear that the audience was drifting away from *It's About Time*.

Critic Bob MacKenzie claimed that an eight-year-old of his acquaintance had termed the show "dumb." MacKenzie's main objection to the show, however, was, "[W]hy let Imogene Coca, one of the world's funniest women, go to waste in a miserable turkey like *It's About Time*? She deserves better. So do eight-year-olds."[5]

By January, major changes were in store for *It's About Time*, which was posting disappointing ratings. By the mid–1960s, networks no longer let a lagging show play out an entire year, having introduced the concept of the "second season"—shows that premiered in January to supplant those that had done poorly in the fall. Determined to save his show from this fate, Schwartz set up emergency meetings with CBS executives to propose radical changes in the next batch of *It's About Time* episodes.

"We're the first show to replace itself on the second season," Schwartz said good-naturedly in a United Press International interview. He acknowledged that story possibilities in the prehistoric setting were limited, and thought there was more fun to be had with bringing his caveman characters to modern-day America. "This change will give the series a new lift. It was a little drab what with caves and people running around in furs. Now there will be more colorful surroundings."[6] He'd also come to realize that viewers found it wearying to hear almost all the show's dialogue spoken in broken English ("Gronk hungry!").

The revamped format meant that co-stars Cliff Norton (Boss) and Mike Mazurki (Clon) would be dropped from the cast. (Norton, who'd been unhappy working on the show, later told TV historian Wesley Hyatt that his reaction to the news was "Thank God!"[7]) New to the cast in recurring roles were Alan DeWitt (1921–76) and Frank Wilcox (1907–74).

In the show's twentieth episode, "20th Century, Here We Come" (1/22/67), scripted by Elroy Schwartz, the new concept is introduced. Mac and Hector have finished repairing their spaceship, thanks to some diamonds that Shad and

Gronk provided. Ready to take off, they learn that Boss intends to have Gronk and his family killed for giving away gems from a precious idol. Mac decides the best way to repay their debt, and keep their friends safe, is to take them back home to the 20th century. Since Mac and Hector have never told the cave dwellers that they are from another century, Shad, Gronk, Mlor, and Breer believe they are traveling to "the other side of the hill."

The astronauts and their passengers arrive back in modern-day Los Angeles safely, but it soon becomes clear that Shad, Gronk, and the children will suffer a serious case of culture shock. Seeing an approaching Volkswagen driven by a little old lady, Gronk mistakes it for a marauding beast and attacks the car with his club. Other city dwellers don't quite know what to make of the cave people either, mistaking them for refugees from a masquerade party, or just urban oddballs. ("You beatniks belong in a coffee house," says one clean-cut passerby.)

Arriving at the apartment that the two astronauts share, Shad is impressed: "Mac and Hec have nice cave!" Mac tries to break the news of their stowaways to the astronaut's superior officer, General J.P. Morley. The general, however, refuses to believe his men's story, and simply assumes they are hallucinating after suffering a "terrible ordeal" in space. He sends them to the Air Force psychiatrist (shades of *I Dream of Jeannie*!), who does his best to deprogram them. Meanwhile, left on their own in the apartment, Gronk and his family proceed to wreak havoc — bashing the kitchen faucet with a club and flooding the apartment, smashing the television set when they see an oncoming train onscreen, running in terror from the vacuum cleaner, and "hunting" dinner from the dining room of the apartment across the way.

Living directly downstairs from Mac and Hec is the building manager, fussy Mr. Tyler, who learns of the new arrivals when they bash a hole in his ceiling so as to drain the water from the "cave." Over the next few weeks, the astronauts think up a variety of excuses to explain the presence of the cave people, telling their landlord at one point that they are distinguished guests from the country of Nordania ("west of Siberia and east of Alaska"). Subsequent episodes deal with Breer's experiences attending public school, and the difficulties that ensue when Shad and Gronk fall victim to door-to-door salespeople.

The show's revised concept also required Schwartz to alter the show's theme song and opening titles to explain the new circumstances, depicting a move forward in time rather than the reverse. Schwartz and his staff were given only six episodes to sell the audience on the new and improved *It's About Time*. By March, the show's cancellation notice had been posted, to no one's great surprise. (*Gilligan's Island* also received the ax, reportedly due to CBS honcho William Paley's last-minute demand that his programmers reinstate the due-to-be-canceled *Gunsmoke*.)

In the series' next-to-last aired episode, "Our Brothers' Keepers" (3/5/67), Mac and Hec take one last stab at convincing General Morley that they brought back cave people from prehistoric times. Just as Shad and Gronk's examination by a physician is beginning to convince the general, Mac and Hec realize that, if he's convinced, the cave people will be taken into military custody. Instead, they talk their way out of the situation and, once back at home, are relieved:

> HEC: Now those cave people can live with us for the rest of their lives!
> MAC: Happily ever after.

Mac opens the kitchen door and walks into a flood of soapy water — Shad and Gronk have caused the dishwasher to overflow again. Sighing, a soaking wet Mac walks back out into the living room and sits down next to Hec. "Happily ever after," he repeats wearily at the fadeout of what should have been the series finale.

Not lacking for work, Coca went almost immediately into a reunion special with former co-stars Sid Caesar, Carl Reiner, and Howard Morris. Nonetheless, she was disappointed by the failure of her sitcom. "The management of the show and the cast were wonderful to work with; nobody sluffed [sic] it off.... There was only one trouble: the audience didn't seem to like the show."[8]

The Jim Backus Show: Hot Off the Wire

Jim Backus (*John Michael O'Toole*), Nita Talbot (*Dora Miles*), Bobs Watson (*Sidney*), William McLean (*Dave*)
Producers: Dick Chevillat, Ray Singer. *Writers*: Dick Chevillat, Stanley Davis, John L. Greene, Mannie Manheim, Arthur Marx, Elon Packard, Joe Quillan, Phillip Shuken, Ray Singer. *Directors*: Johnny Florea, Jerry Hopper, Christian Nyby, Gene Reynolds. *Based on an Idea by* Robert A. Cinader. *Associate Producers*: Richard A. Larson, Milt Trager. *Directors of Photography*: Henry Cronjager, Paul Ivano. *Production Supervisor*: W. Argyle Nelson. *Production Manager*: James Paisley. *Assistant Directors*: Tom Kelly, Maurice Vaccarino. *Art Directors*: Ralph Berger, Leroy Coleman, George W. Davis. *Casting Supervisor*: Ralph Acton. *Theme Music*: David Rose. *Music Supervisor*: Marlin Skiles. *Set Decorators*: Budd Friend, Ross Dowd, Henry Grace. *Property Master*: Lou Wildley. *Special Effects*: Joe Lombardi. *Film Editors*: Harry Knapp, Bill Lewis. *Editorial Supervisor*: Bill Heath. *Recording Supervisor*: Franklyn Milton. *Sound Mixer*: Stan Cooley. California National Productions.

Aired in first-run syndication from 1960 to 1961. 39 black-and-white episodes.

The adventures of a motley crew of second-rate newspapermen working for a two-bit New York wire service were seen in the syndicated *The Jim Backus Show: Hot Off the Wire,* one of the least-known television ventures for the actor fondly remembered as the voice of Mr. Magoo, and as bombastic Thurston Howell III on *Gilligan's Island* (CBS, 1964–67).

Based in New York City, Worldwide Press Service provides copy to more than 100 weekly newspapers around the U.S., under the leadership of veteran newsman Mike O'Toole. The members of Mike's small staff take on various assignments—and pen names—to crank out the amount of copy required. When she's not acting as receptionist or stalling bill collectors, his assistant Dora Miles is apt to be found dutifully typing something along the lines of, "A Dozen Delightful Dinners for a Dollar, by Mary Morgan, WPS food authority." Hardly a stickler for journalistic accuracy, Mike likes colorful copy more than he likes facts. Complains Mike: "You know, today newsmen are all machines. There's no imagination, there's no drive."

The agency is perpetually hovering on the brink of bankruptcy. According to one episode, a small newspaper pays $150 per year for the privilege of being a subscriber. When a subscribing editor threatens to cancel, Mike blithely tells him the agency is about to release "the biggest story of the year," then hangs up the phone and tells his staff they'd best think up such a story post-haste.

Sidney is the reluctant copy boy who longs to be a reporter, but is mostly assigned to keep WPS's minimal equipment (primarily an ancient mimeograph

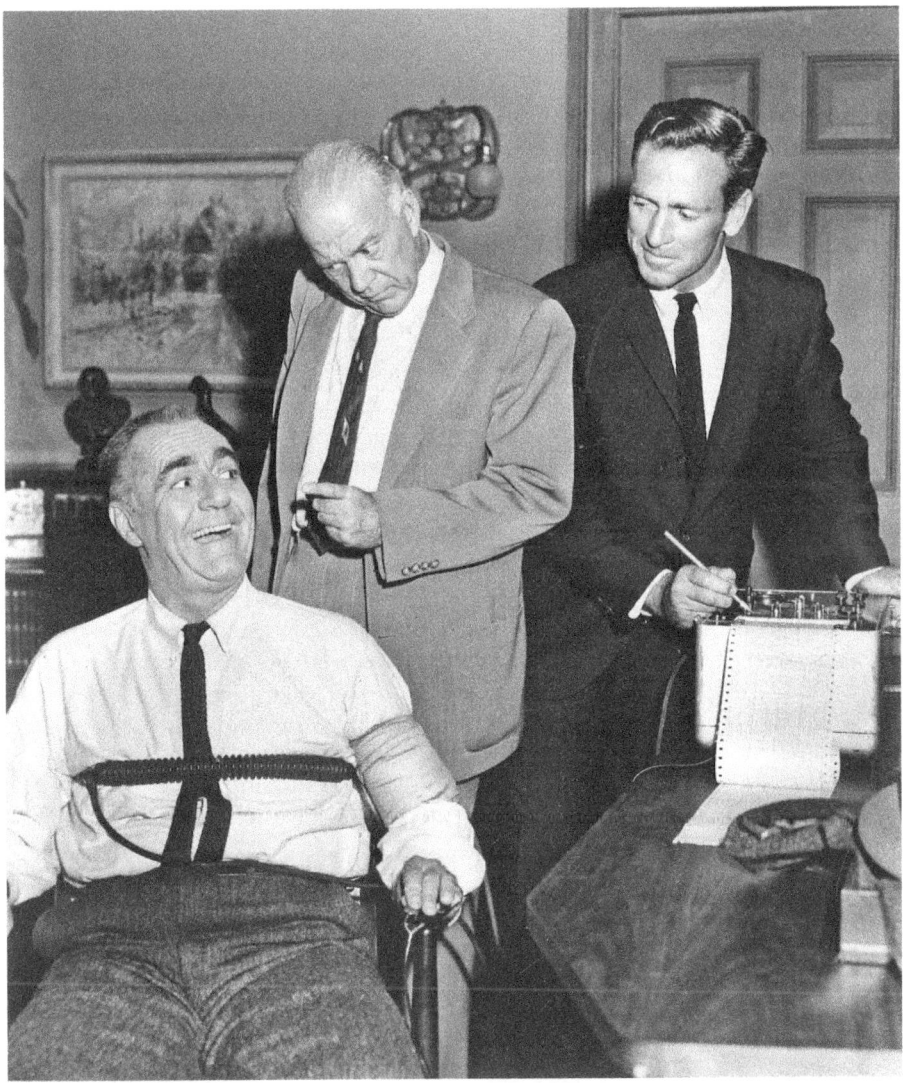

Would Mike O'Toole tell a lie? Guest star Willis Bouchey (center) puts Jim Backus (left) to the test in *The Jim Backus Show: Hot Off the Wire*. Also pictured: Bill McLean (Dave).

machine) in working order, and to run errands like taking out Mike's shoes to be resoled, or fetching coffee. When he threatens to quit, as he does periodically, Mike mollifies him by pretending to give him an assignment. However, wet-behind-the-ears Sidney is too ineffectual to carry most of them off, coming back from one outing bruised, battered, and with shoe prints clearly visible on his face.

Downstairs from the office is Heartless Harry's, a bar popular with newspaper people. Harry, well aware of the precarious financial status of Mike's operation, has a standing rule that no one from his staff is admitted "without a posted $10 deposit." Mike pays $100 a month to rent his office space from the Bagley Realty Company, but often has trouble producing the funds. His paychecks to his staff are sometimes erratic as well, and occasionally he attempts to borrow the money back.

In the pilot episode, Mike, longing to compete with the big players, wants WPS to solve New York City's hottest criminal spree of the moment — a bomber who targets police cars. The bomber in question is actually meek Otto Gunther (guest star William Kirshner), a quiet, mousey man whose grievance with the police centers on the fourteen traffic tickets he received since moving to New York a year ago. Mike's press service runs a series of articles on him, including one that purports to analyze the bomber's psychiatric shortcomings. Taking offense at the way he's characterized in the column, Otto drops by the Worldwide Press Service office and delivers a bomb, concealed in a parcel of books by Sigmund Freud. After a slapstick climax in which the bomb is tossed frantically from staff member to staff member, and Mike's pants fall down, the bomber is captured.

The attendant publicity calls attention to the fact that there's a better-known agency called Worldwide Press Service, whose owners threaten a lawsuit if O'Toole's outfit continues to use the name. Mike promptly renames his company Headline Press Service, as it will be known in the weekly series.

In "The Woman's Touch," Dora tells Mike that she could run the office in a more businesslike way than he has, resulting in a healthy profit. Accepting her challenge, Mike reverses roles with his assistant, putting her in charge. Dora proceeds to upgrade the office's dress code and to hire a slick-talking sales manager, Douglas Aldrich. In fact, he is "Love 'em and Leave 'em Anderson, the most notorious polygamist in America today." The clever con man plays up to Dora, while running up a hefty expense account, pocketing what few proceeds come in, and plotting to make her his 12th wife, until Mike exposes him as a fraud.

Producers Ray Singer and Dick Chevillat, who also contributed a good number of the show's scripts, had previously helmed *It's a Great Life* (q.v.). Composer David Rose contributed a snappy theme that effectively conveyed the rush and energy of the newspaper business. The show's basic concept was courtesy of Robert A. Cinader, who would go on to a long association with producer Jack Webb, producing and creating the long-running police drama *Adam-12* (NBC, 1968–75) and working on various action-adventure shows. Not sold to a network, *The Jim Backus Show* was instead released to individual stations in first-run syndication beginning in the fall of 1960.

Born February 25, 1913, Jim Backus was a former radio performer who made his television series debut as a regular ensemble player on a short-lived ABC comedy-variety show, *Hollywood House* (1949-50). He went on to a more visible assignment, spending three years as leading man to comedienne Joan Davis in the popular NBC sitcom *I Married Joan* (1952–55). Though his role as Judge Bradley Stevens, patient husband to a screwball wife, made him a well-known entity to television audiences, Backus regarded that raucous, slapstick-oriented series as a largely thankless assignment. He would later complain that he carried half the show while receiving substantially less pay than Davis, and billing that relegated him to a featured player. After *Joan* folded, he played a rare dramatic role as James Dean's father in *Rebel Without a Cause* (1955). Aside from his radio and television roles, he was instantly recognizable as the voice of the visually challenged cartoon character Mr. Quincy Magoo.

If not quite a top-rank star, Backus was a versatile actor who was always in demand. In the fall of 1957, he began a weekday daytime *Jim Backus Show* on ABC radio. At the time, he dismissed ideas of doing a TV sitcom again. "It's a frightening experience and I'd never do another one unless I could disappear for five years afterward." Surveying the video scene in the late 1950s, he bemoaned the trend that seemed to displace established comedic talents in favor of variety shows centered on musicians. "I feel the only people with talent — like Sid Caesar and Jackie Gleason — have been taken off. Now you have the relaxed school exemplified by Perry Como [who] gets the biggest hand when he forgets the lyrics or can't read the idiot board."[1]

Backus' leading lady was actress Nita Talbot. In 1955, having finished a run in the CBS daytime soap opera *Search for Tomorrow* (1951–82), she starred in the short-lived sitcom *Joe and Mabel*, playing the girlfriend of a commitment-shy New York City cab driver (played by Larry Blyden). Columnist Dick Kleiner said that Talbot, then in her twenties, had already become a favorite of many male viewers in her earlier TV guest appearances, "a tall, beautiful blonde with the lightest blue-gray eyes this side of the stratosphere." Born in the Bronx on August 8, 1930, Talbot used what she termed a "pidgin–Brooklyn accent" in most of her roles. From a child she aspired to perform. "My sister and her friend and I used to act out movies after we came home. And we'd put on shows. We had the biggest bargain in the Bronx — we got an old rocking-horse and we made lemonade and for a penny we'd give the kids a ride on the horse and some lemonade and the show."[2]

Columnist Vernon Scott claimed Talbot's track record as a performer was impeccable — but not in a good way. Describing her as "a tall, pretty girl with a highly developed sense of humor," the columnist described her first ventures into motion pictures—*Bundle of Joy* (1956), *I Married a Woman* (1958, opposite George Gobel), and *Once Upon a Horse...* (1958)—as "three consecutive bombs," saying that *Once* put RKO out of business altogether. On TV, she'd been a featured player in the second and last season of NBC's *The Thin Man* (1957–59). Scott predicted that she would bring about a similar fate for *The Jim Backus Show*.[3]

Featured as Sidney was former child star Bobs Watson, only one of a passel of Watson siblings who acted in the 1930s. Snagging his first acting assignment when he was only six months old, Watson came to prominence at the age of seven with his featured role as Pee Wee in *Boys Town* (MGM, 1938). The film's star, Spencer Tracy, subsequently won an Oscar for his performance as Father Flanagan, and dispatched a telegram to the Watson home that night, saying, "Thank you Bobby dear — half the statue belongs to you — Uncle Spencer." Over the next decade, Watson enjoyed a successful career that often pivoted on his ability to cry on cue. His role on *The Jim Backus Show*, when he was in his early thirties (though playing a character younger than that), was one of his last professional experiences before leaving show business for a second career as a Methodist minister.

The series pilot was shot on the Desilu lot, but when regular production got underway the show moved to MGM's studios. A few less-than-top rank guest stars passed through the show, limited no doubt by the budget of a syndicated show. Billed as "special guest stars" were actress Patricia Barry and Maurice Gosfield (Doberman from *The Phil Silvers Show*), as well as actor Charlie Ruggles. Some up-and-coming talents like Ken Berry were showcased as well.

Among the writers who sold a script for the show was Backus' wife Henny, who pitched the producer an idea based on a joke Jim had told her concerning a golf-playing gorilla. The only hitch, she reported, was the elite typeface on her typewriter, which rendered her final script the prescribed length of 36 pages, but so long that cuts had to be made. "I'd written a *Playhouse 90* and didn't know it!" she joked of her episode, which also included a role for herself as guest star.[4]

Critical reaction to *The Jim Backus Show* was lukewarm at best. Commented critic Bernice Ashby, "Newspaper editors the country over are, no doubt, moaning at the jibes this series deals them. We say Jim Backus deserves better material on a better theme."[5] Evidently viewers agreed, as the show's ratings did not justify continuing into a second season.

Despite the failure of his sitcom, Backus was hardly absent from TV. In 1962, he hosted CBS's *Talent Scouts,* a summer-replacement revival of Arthur Godfrey's popular variety show of the 1950s. In the wake of the cancellation, Backus was once again telling reporters he'd never undertake another series. In 1964, he accomplished the unthinkable, snagging lead roles in two series on two different networks. For NBC, he voiced the star role in *The Famous Adventures of Mr. Magoo,* but his better-known role came when he signed to play wealthy Thurston Howell III in *Gilligan's Island* for producer-creator Sherwood Schwartz, with whom he'd worked on *I Married Joan.* Not only did Backus find himself working for competing networks, but for a time in 1965 both shows were in direct competition on the Saturday night schedule. Despite a fearsome critical response, *Gilligan's Island* was mildly successful in its CBS run, lasting until 1967, and became a perennial Baby Boomer favorite in syndication. He followed that up with a role in CBS's brief revival of *Blondie,* playing Dagwood's grouchy boss Mr. Dithers, but the show was in and out in thirteen weeks on the 1968-69 schedule.

Nita Talbot went on to play a recurring role as a Russian spy in *Hogan's Heroes* (CBS, 1965–71), which netted her an Emmy nomination. In 1973, Talbot played the ex-wife of future *Dallas* star Larry Hagman in ABC's sitcom *Here We Go Again,* about a newly married couple constantly bedeviled by the interference of their respective ex-spouses. Talbot, by then twice divorced, knew a little something about the situation depicted in the series. It died a quick death opposite CBS's red-hot *All in the Family* (1971–79) on the Saturday schedule. Her 1979 series *Supertrain* was similarly short-lived. In the 1980s, at the height of the Luke-and-Laura craze, Talbot had a recurring role as dress shop owner Delfina on the daytime soap *General Hospital* (ABC, 1963–), and also played a featured role in the syndicated sitcom *Starting from Scratch* (1988-89).

A gifted comic actor and a genuinely funny man, Backus found little opportunity to display his talents in this series. He died on July 3, 1989, after a multi-year battle with Parkinson's disease and other ailments. On paper, at least, the newspaper business offered a promising setting for a sitcom. What emerged on *The Jim Backus Show,* too often, was a mediocre product with weak scripts and a lead character who lacked appeal.

Ironically, for a performer whose résumé bulged with sitcom roles, Backus was ambivalent about the genre, and regular television work in general, both before and after the series that bore his name. In 1969, with some half-a-dozen shows under his belt, Backus complained, "[A]gents love to put an actor in a series, 'cause you don't bother them for nine months. You're like the living dead. They throw you in in September and let you out in June. You live in a vacuum and come out asking who's president." Backus claimed he had formed a self-help group called Series Anonymous, designed to do an intervention when actors found themselves being offered a series role. "They call me up, bring over a bottle of booze, and I talk them out of it."[6]

Love on a Rooftop

Judy Carne (*Julie Willis*), Peter Deuel (*Dave Willis*), Rich Little (*Stan Parker*), Barbara Bostock (*Carol Parker*), Herbert Voland (*Fred Hammond*), Edith Atwater (*Phyllis Hammond*), Sandy Kenyon (*Jim Lucas*)

Executive Producer: Harry Ackerman. *Creators*: Harry Ackerman, Bernard Slade. *Producer*: E.W. Swackhamer. *Writers*: Barbara Avedon, Tom August, Helen August, Richard Baer, Dorothy Cooper Foote, James Henerson, Het Mannheim, Marty Roth, Bernard Slade. *Directors*: Jerry Bernstein, Mack Bing, Robert Ellenstein, Claudio Guzman, Richard Kinon, Russell Mayberry, Gene Reynolds, R. Robert Rosenbaum, E.W. Swackhamer. *Associate Producer*: Philip Rogers. *Post-Production Executive*: Lawrence Werner. *Music*: Mundell Lowe. *Music Supervision*: Ed Forsyth. *Music Consultant*: Don Kirshner. *Title Song*: Howard Greenfield, Jack Keller. *Art Directors*: Ross Bellah, Robert Purcell. *Film Editors*: Howard Kunin, Eda Warren. *Set Decorators*: Louis Diage, Anthony Mondello. *Assistant Director*: Marvin Miller. *Makeup Supervisor*: Ben Lane. *Sound Effects*: Fred J. Brown. Screen Gems.

Aired Tuesdays at 9:30 P.M. (through January 1967), then Thursdays at 9:00 P.M. (through April 1967), then Thursdays at 9:30 P.M. on ABC-TV. First aired September 6, 1966; last aired August 31, 1967. 30 color episodes.

Rich girl meets poor boy and both fall instantly in love in this appealing ABC sitcom depicting a newlywed couple who set up housekeeping in an oddball apartment high atop San Francisco.

Julie Hammond is a pretty, free-spirited 21-year-old art student. Dave Willis, a more down-to-earth type, is an apprentice architect with the firm of Bennington and Associates, earning a salary of $85.37 per week. They meet when his sandwich falls from the scaffold where he's having lunch, dropping into Julie's purse as she walks by. For both, it's love at first sight, and a whirlwind marriage is the result.

Julie's parents are wealthy — he owns nine used car lots — and drive a Rolls-Royce, but Dave hails from a far more modest background. After his parents died, Dave was raised by a succession of foster parents. He served a stint in the Army before studying architecture. Wanting to live within their means, Dave and Julie must find an affordable apartment in which to begin their life as newlyweds. As the narrator explains in the pilot, "They both agreed on the sort of place they wanted to live in—cheap, practical, charming, cheap. Something with atmosphere, and a view—and cheap."

The couple moves into a cramped apartment on the top floor of a commercial building that also houses the Loomis Gift Shop. The apartment, a converted storeroom, is so small that their bed is in the living room, and if they want to have a private conversation they squeeze into the tiny bathroom. Its main asset is the spectacular view of San Francisco that Julie and Dave have by climbing the interior stairs to the roof, which she insists on calling the patio. Since the apartment itself has no windows, Julie paints a mural to provide a view.

Not until after their wedding does Dave learn that his new wife comes from an affluent family, when he comes home one day to find his in-laws have returned from a trip to Europe. Trying to prevent Dave from being embarrassed, Julie's friend Carol and landlady Mrs. Loomis (seen only in the pilot) borrow furniture and fixtures from their own apartments to spruce up the Willises' drab place before the Hammonds arrive. Nonetheless, grouchy Fred Hammond is appalled when he sees how his daughter is living. Wife Phyllis, who's favorably impressed by Dave, reminds her husband that their first place was no better, having started their married life (during the Great Depression) with "a card table, two chairs, and a beat-up sofa." His wedding gift to the newlyweds is to have two windows cut in the brick walls of their apartment.

Many of the show's plots revolve around Dave and Julie's efforts to make ends meet without resorting to the assistance of her father, which Dave rejects. Because his daughter is living with so few amenities, Mr. Hammond terms it "a marriage of inconvenience." Julie and Dave quarrel occasionally when she spends their money on something whimsical, like Japanese lanterns to brighten up the apartment, rather than the bills.

Living downstairs from the Willises are their friends Stan and Carol Parker. (Stan's admiring wife describes him as "a freelance genius.") In various episodes, Stan works as a shoe salesman, an organizer of children's parties, and a dancing instructor. Among his ideas are Forever gum, a pack of which costs $25 and is guaranteed to last a lifetime, and a movie to which no one will be admitted in the first six minutes, because of the surprise beginning. He also tries to launch Drive-a-Drunk, a business in which he provides rides home to inebriated partygoers (at a time when this was considered whimsical rather than practical), a 24-hour-a-day Dial-a-Joke telephone service, and his program of Medicare for pets. Another recurring character, Jim Lucas, is Dave's slightly more cynical friend at work.

In "There's Got to Be Something Wrong With Her" (12/6/66), Julie has the opportunity to meet Dave's last girlfriend, stewardess Barbara Ames. Only weeks before impulsively marrying Julie, he broke up with this woman when he told her he wasn't ready to get married. Barbara (guest star Gayle Hunnicutt) is uncommonly beautiful, so Carol assures Julie that Dave must have found some other flaw in her; she must be dumb, or dull, or cold. In fact, she's none of these things, and ultimately Julie is heartened to realize that Dave had good reasons for preferring her to Barbara, giving her a new sense of security in her marriage.

"Dave's Night Out" (11/29/66) begins with a sitcom cliché: Dave's friends, who have been married longer than he has, advise him to insist Julie allow him a night out on his own every week. Dave finds his first night playing poker with the boys boring, and would rather be home with his wife, but is loath to admit this to Julie once he's taken a stand. Julie grows concerned when she hears that his nights out revolve around women named Brigitte and Lillian — not knowing that he's been attending a Brigitte Bardot film festival in the neighborhood, and hanging around a local Laundromat where he keeps frowsy, middle-aged Lillian and the other bored housewives company.

Credit for creating *Rooftop* was shared by writer Bernard Slade and Screen Gems executive Harry Ackerman. Slade, not that many years older than his lead characters, would later receive acclaim for his Broadway comedies *Same Time, Next Year* and *Romantic Comedy*. Under contract to Columbia, he had most recently served as script consultant on *Bewitched* (ABC, 1964–72). Aside from creating the show's concept, Slade also contributed a number of its first-season scripts. Running *Rooftop* on a day-to-day basis, under the supervision of executive producer Ackerman, was producer E.W. Swackhamer, who also directed a number of segments.

The genuine chemistry between co-stars Judy Carne (Julie) and Peter Deuel (Dave) made it easy to believe in *Love on a Rooftop*.

Leading lady Judy Carne, given top billing in the series, was born April 27, 1939, in Northampton, England, as Joyce Botterill. As a girl, she studied dance, and was enrolled in a theatrical school. While living in London in her early twenties, not yet firmly established as an actress, Carne was sent for an interview with producer Cy Howard, who was in England casting an American comedy series, *Fair Exchange* (CBS, 1962-63). Carne won the featured role of an English girl who comes to live with an American family. The hour-long Desilu sitcom was not a success, but launched Carne on an American television career nonetheless. During a CBS promotional tour for the series, she met actor Burt Reynolds, then playing the role of Quint Asper in *Gunsmoke* (CBS, 1955–75), and married him in June 1963. After *Fair Exchange*, she was cast in another single-season sitcom, *The Baileys of Balboa* (CBS, 1964-65). As *Rooftop* got underway, she was awaiting the finalization of her divorce from Reynolds (also the star of a new ABC series in the fall of 1966, the detective show *Hawk*). Though her agents didn't encourage her to spread the word, she was 27 at the time of her casting in the show. Since there was no reason for Julie Hammond to sport a British accent, Carne tried to minimize hers when shooting scenes. (It slipped through occasionally.)

Though he would later simplify his professional name to Pete Duel, Carne's leading man was at this time being billed as Peter Deuel. Born in Rochester, New York, on February 24, 1940, Deuel grew up in a family of doctors, but had no interest in following their footsteps. Arriving in Hollywood in 1963, he set a goal for himself of landing a series role within five years, but it took only two; Deuel spent a year playing a featured role in *Gidget,* and not long after its cancellation was offered the male lead in *Love on a Rooftop*.

Publicly, Deuel exuded self-confidence. Shortly before *Rooftop*'s debut, he told a journalist, "All the superficial ingredients are present to make me a star. I'm 26. I'm single. I'm good-looking. And I have a natural talent. At this point, I've really got what it takes."[1]

Though he and Carne were friendly, and worked well together, both actors readily admitted that their working relationship was marked by a certain combative spirit, in which the language flew freely. A *TV Guide* reporter profiling Carne was present on the set for one relatively mild exchange. Left waiting on the set while Deuel made a costume change, the leading lady greeted his return with the complaint, "Where the hell have you been? It's hot under these lights." To which her co-star responded, "Were you glued to the chair?"[2]

Of working with Carne, he would later say, "[We] were both kind of highstrung. We would fight—loud fights—but we understood each other. I imagine people who didn't know us well got nervous."[3] Both insisted that the fights cleared the air and left no resentment in their wake. In fact, Carne later said in her memoirs that she and Deuel had an affair during the show's run, conducted mostly during the trips they took to San Francisco every few weeks to shoot exterior footage for episodes.

Rooftop also gave Canadian-born impressionist Rich Little, cast as Dave and Julie's friend and downstairs neighbor Stan, some of his first nationwide exposure. Born November 26, 1938, Little previously made an impression (so to speak) with a guest appearance on *The Judy Garland Show* (CBS, 1963-64). His repertoire included more than 130 celebrities he could impersonate, Jack Benny being a particular favorite. The sitcom role made little use of his talent for mimicry, though in "Shotgun Honeymoon" (2/9/67) he does snare a hotel reservation for Dave and Julie by impersonating John Wayne when he calls the manager.

Edith Atwater (1911–86), who played Julie's patrician but sensible mother, was a Broadway veteran who later appeared as Aunt Gertrude in early episodes of TV's *The Hardy Boys Mysteries* (ABC, 1977–79). Atwater played a far more fearsome mother-in-law than Dave Willis' in William Castle's *Strait-Jacket* (1964), going *mano-a-mano* with Joan Crawford as the chilly society matron who doesn't want her precious son marrying the daughter of a convicted ax murderess. Herbert Voland (1918–81), cast as Julie's father, was a busy character actor with an extremely recognizable face, though most TV and movie fans would have a difficult time naming more than one or two of his credits. Like Atwater, he too turned up occasionally on *The Hardy Boys Mysteries,* playing Bayport Police Chief Collig.

Love on a Rooftop was yet another product from the busy Screen Gems arm of Columbia Pictures. Screen Gems was in its heyday during the 1960s, as was executive producer Harry Ackerman, with long-running hits *The Donna Reed Show* (ABC, 1958–66), *Bewitched* (ABC, 1964–72), and *Hazel* (NBC and CBS, 1961–66) among its prolific and profitable output.

More than one journalist noted a similarity to the Broadway hit *Barefoot in the Park,* though series creator Bernard Slade pointed out that the romantic comedy genre had existed long before that show. Even Carne freely admitted the resemblance to the hit Neil Simon comedy, the film adaptation of which went into general release while *Rooftop* was in its first season.

TV writer Rick du Brow found the series opener promising: "[A]lthough it is almost inevitable for situation comedy writers to fall back eventually on gimmicks when the well of real ideas runs dry, *Love on a Rooftop* could continue to be most charming if only all hands connected with it remember — as the premiere did — that the best comedy is drawn from the little human truths."[4] *TV Key* (9/6/66) found it "a notch or two above the expected groove, thanks to the two personable young leading players.... This handsome couple adds a great deal of charm to the otherwise familiar plot...." The *New York Times*' Jack Gould also liked the lead players, but thought the series opener "burdened with an excess of strained antics."[5]

The time slot found it playing opposite CBS's *Petticoat Junction* and NBC's Tuesday night movie. ABC spent substantial money that fall promoting its new shows in color, still something of a novelty in 1966. Long-running black-and-white shows like *The Donna Reed Show* (1958–66) and *The Patty Duke Show* (1963–66) had been retired. Also new was *The Pruitts of Southampton*, marking the sitcom debut of comedienne Phyllis Diller. *Rooftop* and the other shows new to ABC's Tuesday schedule were among the first fall premieres of the season, while NBC's movie series was still in summer reruns. *TV Guide* editors thought highly enough of the show's prospects to spotlight Carne and Deuel on the magazine's cover in October.

Said Carne of her show, "Naturally, I am hoping that our series hits it big, but whether it does or not, I feel the public is ready for the 'charming' type of show. It has had its bellyful of horses, doctors, nurses, patients with brain tumors, detectives, spies, ghouls, and people with supernatural powers. The new drift may be toward warm, natural comedy."[6]

At midseason, ABC moved *Rooftop* to Thursday nights, where it would serve as lead-in to another first-season sitcom, Marlo Thomas' *That Girl* (1966–71). Though the two shows made a compatible pair, and even earned similar ratings, ABC renewed Thomas's show for a second year while declining to do the same for *Rooftop*.

Despite the premature cancellation, both of the show's appealing stars found further work in television. In 1968, Carne was one of the original ensemble cast members of *Rowan and Martin's Laugh-In*, an innovative show that quickly became a popular hit for NBC. Often bikini-clad, she familiarized the phrase "Sock it to me!" with American audiences. She left the show after only two years, but would never again find a hit series or film, despite her obvious talent. By the mid–1970s, her American career was winding down, and she was struggling with substance abuse problems. Carne subsequently returned to her native England.

In the late 1960s, Deuel simplified his stage name to Pete Duel when he was cast opposite Kim Darby in the feature film *Generation* (1969). In 1970, he was signed to co-star with Ben Murphy in ABC's youth-oriented Western *Alias Smith and Jones*. As Hannibal Heyes, Deuel played one of two former outlaws trying to go straight in a lighthearted show that appealed to viewers who had liked *Butch Cassidy and the Sundance Kid* (1969).

During the summer of 1971, with his new show *Alias Smith and Jones* gaining in popularity, ABC scheduled reruns of *Rooftop*. In retrospect, Duel said of his short-lived sitcom, "It was a fine series. It was sentimental without being maudlin, although every once in a while it got a little sticky. I don't usually like to watch gooey sentimentality myself, but sometimes it's a release."[7]

Though *Alias Smith and Jones* proved popular with audiences, Duel seemed to take little pleasure in his TV success, and struck his co-workers as a complicated and somewhat troubled man. On December 31, 1971, the actor died of a self-inflicted gunshot wound at the age of 31. With some reluctance, his colleagues on *Alias* resumed production on the series in January, having hurriedly recast his role with actor Roger Davis, who'd previously served as the show's narrator. The chemistry between Duel and Murphy, however, had been the key element in the show's success, and without that it soon wound down, being canceled in early 1973.

Love on a Rooftop holds up well today, though there's a certain poignancy in watching reruns forty-odd years later, knowing how life turned out for both its likable young stars. Nonetheless, it's a charming, likable comedy that should have enjoyed a longer run.

Margie

Cynthia Pepper (*Margie Clayton*), Dave Willock (*Harvey Clayton*), Wesley Marie Tackitt (*Nora Clayton*), Penney Parker (*Maybelle Jackson*), Tommy Ivo (*Heywood Botts*), Hollis Irving (*Phoebe Gibson*), Johnny Bangert (*Cornell Clayton*), Richard Gering (*Johnny Green*)

Executive Producer: William Self. *Producers*: Hal Goodman, Larry Klein. *Writers*: John Bradford, Ray Brenner, Robert Fisher, Benedict Freedman, Ralph Goodman, Barbara Hammer, Arnold Horwitt, Albert E. Lewin, Alan Lipscott, Milton Pascal, Larry Rhine, Leo Rifkin, Burt Styler, Mel Tolkin, Robert Van Scoyk, Alan Woods. *Directors*: Rod Amateau, Jack Donohue, Gene Reynolds, Don Richardson, James Sheldon, Jack Sher. *Developed for Television by* Hal Goodman, Larry Klein. *Director of Photography*: Richard L. Rawlings. *Costume Design*: Adele Balkan. *Music Score*: Warren Barker. *Music*: Cyril J. Mockridge. *Music Supervised and Conducted by* Lionel Newman. *Art Directors*: Edward Ilou, Jack Martin Smith. *Film Editors*: Michael Luciano, Dan Nathan, Gerard J. Wilson. *Assistant Director*: Wilbur L. D'Arcy. *Set Decorators*: Chester Bayhi, Walter M. Scott. *Music Editor*: Donn Cambern. *Sound Effects Editor*: James M. Miller. *Production Manager*: Gaston Glass. *Post-Production Manager*: James Moore. 20th Century—Fox Television.

Aired Thursdays at 9:30 P.M. (through April 1962), then Fridays at 7:30 P.M. on ABC-TV. First aired October 12, 1961; last aired August 31, 1962. 26 black-and-white episodes.

One of TV's infrequent sitcoms not set in the present day, *Margie* tells the story of a typical teenager growing up in a small town during the 1920s. Margie Clayton is a pretty, spirited 17-year-old, living at home with her parents Harvey and Nora and her little brother Cornell, in the town of Madison, in this predecessor to shows like *Happy Days* (ABC, 1974–83).

Margie is a junior at Madison High School. Her father works as a loan officer at the Great Eastern Savings Bank, where his boss is Mr. Yates. Mother Nora is a homemaker. Margie's best friend and classmate is Maybelle Jackson, a more worldly and sophisticated girl who lives next door. Maybelle's boyfriend is Johnny Green, Madison High's star football player, whom she coyly calls "Johnnikins." Margie's steady date is brainy Heywood Botts, who is devoted to her, but doesn't always live up to her romantic ideals. Margie regularly develops crushes on more exciting men (she confesses to her diary that she is in love with movie heartthrob Ramon Novarro), and takes Heywood somewhat for granted. After school, the kids hang out at Crawford's Ice Cream Parlor. Margie is the editor-in-chief of the school newspaper, the *Madison Bugle*, a job she temporarily loses when Maybelle contributes phony and inflammatory items to Margie's gossip column, "Thru the Keyhole."

Margie's father, who fancies himself an inventor, likes to spend his spare time tinkering in his cellar workshop. Most of his inventions don't work out. His portable radio is so heavy he can barely lift it, and his wife scoffs at his idea of a motor in the sink that grinds up garbage.

Living with the Claytons is Margie's free-wheeling Aunt Phoebe. An attractive single woman in her thirties, Phoebe has an active social life, but Margie's mother thinks Phoebe should find a "steady and reliable" man and settle down before she becomes a "lonely old maid."

Aside from the superficial trappings that tie the show to an earlier era, it was basically a standard-issue family sitcom, with episodes about dating, family misunderstandings, parent-child disagreements, etc. In "Flaming Youth" (2/1/62), Margie's parents see a movie about reckless teenagers, causing them to become overly concerned that their own daughter will get into trouble. Margie realizes it's not the moment to let them see that Maybelle has just raised the hems on all of Margie's dresses, befitting the latest style that calls for hemlines above the knees. A series of misunderstandings results in Mr. and Mrs. Clayton wrongly concluding that Margie has eloped with Heywood.

Margie would not be the only ABC show of the time to capitalize on public interest in the 1920s. Two hour-long dramatic series, *The Untouchables* (1959–63) and *The Roaring Twenties* (1960–62), were doing well enough, though their view of the period was undeniably harsher. The sitcom's writers occasionally offer a joke that draws on our knowledge of how the world has changed since that time, as when Margie's father, listening to a politician's speech on the radio, muses, "You know, it's a shame you couldn't be

Cynthia Pepper is named a Promising Female Star of Tomorrow for her title role as a 1920s teenager in the sitcom *Margie*.

seeing him at the same time you're hearing him. Impossible!" When Harvey opens the monthly bills, and finds they're paying $1.65 for gas, and $2.80 for electric, he moans, "What are we running here, a power plant?"

The series was adapted from the successful 1946 Fox film *Margie* which had starred Jeanne Crain and, in his film debut, Alan Young. Fox had been a relatively late convert to television, but by the late 1950s was eager to become a major player in the medium. The studio had successfully launched *The Many Loves of Dobie Gillis* (CBS, 1959–63) and *Adventures in Paradise* (ABC, 1959–62). While preparations for *Margie* were underway in the spring of 1961, Fox was also preparing *Bus Stop*, as well as a pilot for a Ginger Rogers sitcom in which the actress would play twins. (Coincidentally, Rogers was the ex-wife of star Cynthia Pepper's father.) Former *Maverick* producer Roy Huggins was in charge of the studio's television ventures for 1961.

As co-producer Klein readily admitted, the series was only loosely based on the film. "The movie Margie was quite delightful," he said. "But we have preferred to create our own family and situations rather than rely on fixed characters created by someone else."[1] In the film, set in 1928, Margie's mother died when she was a little girl. Because her father, a mortician, is busy with his career, Margie lives with her grandmother, a former suffragette who hopes the teenager will one day be America's first female president. There's a character similar to Maybelle, though her name is Marybelle. As in the series, Marybelle is the most popular girl in school, and calls her boyfriend Johnnikins. The film largely revolves around Margie's crush on the new high school French teacher, Mr. Fontayne (played by Glenn Langan).

Though they received no credit in the TV version of *Margie*, the film was based on stories by Ruth McKenney, of *My Sister Eileen* fame, which she adapted into a screen treatment with her husband Richard Bransten. The screenplay was credited to veteran screenwriter F. Hugh Herbert, whose credits (stretching all the way back to the silent era) included *The Moon Is Blue* (1953) and the Corliss Archer character that would become the basis of a popular radio and television show.

Born September 4, 1940, Cynthia Pepper was in fact 21 years old (and already married) at the time she was cast as Margie Clayton. The daughter of character actor and former vaudevillian Jack Pepper and his ex-dancer wife Dawn, Pepper had been groomed for stardom from an early age. She made her acting debut at the tender age of four, appearing in a Broadway show, *It's a Gift*, which starred Julie Harris. That gig lasted only as long as it took for her employment to come to the attention of New York's child welfare authorities.

Having never reached stardom himself, Jack Pepper wanted to see his daughter attain the heights that had eluded him. At the age of fourteen, she began working part-time jobs to pay for her singing and dancing lessons. Upon her graduation from Hollywood High School, where she had appeared in several student productions, Pepper began to seriously pursue a show business career. On Easter Sunday 1960, she became the wife of Mervyn (Buck) Edwards.

During the first season of the long-running comedy *My Three Sons* (ABC and CBS, 1960–72), Pepper had a recurring role as Jean Pearson, and that's where the producers of *Margie* spotted her. What they were looking for, according to Hal Goodman, was "a girl as identifiable as Mary Pickford was in her day. America's sweetheart — the girl next door."[2] Initially, Pepper didn't take the possible job on *Margie* seriously. She had recently auditioned for the lead role in a Desilu pilot called *Sweet Sixteen*, and felt sure she was perfect for that part. One of about two dozen actresses invited to do a screen test for the role in *Margie*, Pepper was surprised when she was offered the job.

Once she'd landed the role, she turned to her father for help with learning about life in the 1920s, including the popular music of the era, and how to dance the Charleston. The show offered her an opportunity to sing in the episode "The Jazz Band" (11/30/61), which deals with the efforts of Margie and her friends to form a musical troupe.

Before starring in *Margie*, Wesley Marie Tackitt, who played Nora Clayton, had worked as a society reporter and editor for a Santa Barbara newspaper, then began appearing in local theater productions and summer stock. A native of Clinton, Oklahoma, she grew up in San Gabriel, California. She was married in 1960 to a New York–based architect and would have a long-distance marriage for the duration of *Margie*'s run. Only thirty-five years old when she won the role of Nora, Tackitt was young to be playing the mother of a teenage girl, though this is partially disguised by her drab costuming.

Dave Willock (1909–90), seen as Margie's father, broke into motion pictures playing minor roles, including Frank Capra's classic *Mr. Smith Goes to Washington* (1939). He eventually racked up dozens of movie credits as a reliable supporting actor, among them a larger-than-usual role in the unforgettable *Queen of Outer Space* (1958). Somewhat typecast, he played a bellhop so many times that eventually he acquired his own set of uniforms to wear in these roles. For a time, he was teamed with actor-comedian Jack Carson in a vaudeville act, and in 1952 teamed with actor-comedian Cliff Arquette (playing his "Charley Weaver" character) for NBC's early daytime comedy-talk show *Dave and Charley*. Playing the father of a daughter was no big stretch for Willock, who had five of his own at home ranging from ages eight to twenty-six. He also brought to the role his own experience, having been a teenager in the 1920s.

Tommy Ivo, cast as Margie's boyfriend, was a former child actor who still, well into his twenties, could believably play teenagers. His film credits included *I Remember Mama* (1948), *Belles on Their Toes* (1952), and *Plymouth Adventure* (1952).

Penney Parker, who played Maybelle, previously spent a year playing the daughter on *The Danny Thomas Show* (ABC and CBS, 1953–64). Born Jacqueline Francine Kerner, Parker began her career as a teenager in the mid–1950s.

After enrolling in a professional children's school, Parker appeared in the Broadway show *Anniversary Waltz*, and by the age of eighteen was singing in a New York club. She came to Hollywood in 1959, given a month-long vacation there by her parents as a high school graduation present. Spotted by an agent, she found herself playing a role on *Dobie Gillis*. Later that year, she was cast as Danny Thomas' daughter Terry on *The Danny Thomas Show*, putting on hold her plans to attend college. Onscreen, she married Pat Harrington, Jr., but both characters were written out a year or so later. Though she was playing a high school student in *Margie*, Parker was married during the show's run, a union that ended in divorce less than a year later.

Raymond Bailey, better known for playing another banker in *The Beverly Hillbillies* (CBS, 1962–71), made a couple of appearances as Mr. Clayton's boss, bank president Mr. Yates.

Among the show's fans was songwriter Benny Davis, who wrote the lyrics for the song "Margie" in 1920, inspired by his infatuation with a young lady he met on a San Francisco cable car. Set to music by Con Conrad and J. Russel Robinson, "Margie" tells the story of a young man who promises his girl a wedding ring and a home. The song was popularized with audiences by Eddie Cantor, who included it in a successful revue called *The Midnight Rounders*. "Eddie told me later he was halfway through the number before he realized he was singing one of the most popular songs of his career," Davis recalled. "He liked it so much he sang three encores."[3] It would be heard behind the show's opening titles each week.

ABC slotted *Margie* at the tail end of an evening full of popular sitcoms (*The Adventures of Ozzie and Harriet*, *The Donna Reed Show*, *The Real McCoys*, and *My Three Sons*). *Margie* would be in direct competition with another brand-new sitcom, NBC's *Hazel* (1961–66), starring Oscar winner Shirley Booth.

The show premiered with an episode titled "The Vamp," in which Margie tries to emulate her best friend Maybelle's more flirtatious personality and success with boys. *Variety* (10/18/61), reviewing the series opener, called Pepper "a real find.... Besides being a doll, she also appears to have talent and enthusiasm...."

The critic of the syndicated "TV Scout" column (10/12/61) wrote of the opening installment, "It's a well-made show, but it is hard to see what age group it appeals to—it's too unsophisticated for today's teenagers, yet not quite nostalgic enough for the older folks." Clearly, slotting the show at 9:30 P.M., ABC executives didn't expect young viewers to make up the show's primary audience.

Nonetheless, an ABC press release announcing the show said, "Margie, a series designed for viewing by the entire family, will tell stories of a young girl and her friends caught in the timeless, tragic-humorous dilemmas of youth.... Its stories, set against a background of jazz time rhythms, raccoon coats, and Stutz Bearcats, will stress the carefree, happy side of the '20s, when America itself was in the throes of growing up. A mixture of light-hearted comedy and nostalgia, Margie will draw on Twentieth Century–Fox's reserve of period props, sets, and costumes for an authentic recreation of 'The Era of Wonderful Nonsense.'"[4]

More than one contemporary source reports that episodes of *Margie* regularly featured slides interspersed between scenes as in silent films, with slogans like "Please Pay Attention" or "The Plot Thickens." This element did figure into the series pilot, and was commented upon by several reviewers, but none of the subsequent episodes screened contains the device.

As early as November, syndicated columnist Harriet Van Horne listed *Margie* among the shows that were on the critical list, ratings-wise. At midseason, *Margie* switched to an early evening time slot on Fridays, opening it to the possibility of attracting a younger audience, but the change did not result in a notable ratings bump. At least one source reported in the spring of 1962 that *Margie* had been renewed for a second season, but this proved to be incorrect.

Pepper went on to play a featured role in *Take Her, She's Mine* (1963), and, most notably, to appear opposite Elvis Presley as Corporal Midge Riley in *Kissin' Cousins* (1964). Though she never returned to TV with another regular role, she appeared in three pilots for series after *Margie*. In 1965, she teamed with Gary Lockwood for *Sally and Sam,* a CBS pilot about a young working woman's relationship with a medical student, a show she later described wistfully as "*Love on a Rooftop* [q.v.] too soon."[5] For writer-producer Hal Kanter, she also starred in a pilot adapted from the 1954 film *Three Coins in the Fountain,* and played a schoolteacher in an episode of *Julia* (NBC, 1968–71).

Though *Margie* did not emerge as a hit series, ABC would have greater success a year or so later with *The Patty Duke Show* (1963–66), which did similar stories in modern-day dress. *Margie* also has parallels with a later ABC hit, *Happy Days* (1974–84), which also traded on viewers' nostalgia for an earlier, supposedly simpler era (in this case, the 1950s). Like Margie Clayton, that show's Richie Cunningham (Ron Howard) had a businessman father, a homemaking mother, a likably bratty younger sibling, and a worldlier friend. Unlike *Margie,* however, it became a ratings blockbuster and enjoyed a lengthy run.

McKeever and the Colonel

Allyn Joslyn (*Col. Harvey T. Blackwell*), Scott Lane (*Cadet Gary McKeever*), Jackie Coogan (*Sgt. Claude Barnes*), Elisabeth Fraser (*Frances Warner*), John Eimen (*Cadet Monk Roberts*), Keith Taylor (*Cadet Tubby Anderson*)
Producer: Tom McKnight. *Creators*: Harvey Bullock, R. Allen Saffian. *Writers*: Ray Allen, Barry Blitzer, John Bradford, Lou Derman, Bob Fisher, Harvey Helm, Austin Kalish, Al Lewin, Sam Locke, Allan Manings, Arthur Marx, Bob Marcus, Joel Rapp, Dean Riesner, Leo Rifkin, Elroy Schwartz, Jerry Seelin, Burt Styler, Max Wilk. *Story Consultant*: Arthur Marx. *Directors*: Norman Abbott, Stanley Z. Cherry, Jeffrey Hayden, Christian Nyby, Don Weis. *Associate Producer*: Bill Harmon. *Producer's Assistant*: Bud Otto. *Production Supervisor*: Jack Sonntag. *Editorial Supervisor*: Bernard Burton. *Music Composer-Supervisor*: Herschel Burke Gilbert. *Music Scoring*: Joseph Mullendore. *Directors of Photography*: Chas E. Burke, Wilfrid M. Cline. *Supervising Art Director*: Bill Ross. *Art Director*: J.M. Van Tamelen. *Production Manager*: Barry Crane. *Assistant Director*: Bob White. *Sound*: Woodruff Clarke. *Set Decorator*: Andy Nealis. *Editors*: Norman Colbert, Les Orlebeck, Stanley E. Johnson. *Makeup Artist*: Carlie Taylor. *Wardrobe*: Robert B. Harris. *Music Editor*: Harry King. *Sound Effects*: Mandine Rogne, Kay Rose. *Casting*: Betty Martin. Four Star–Harlen Productions.
Aired Sundays at 6:30 P.M. on NBC-TV. First aired September 23, 1962; last aired June 16, 1963. 26 black-and-white episodes.

The comic adventures of three mischievous boys attending military school were the focus of this kid-appeal sitcom, which had a one-year run on NBC but played in syndicated reruns for years afterward. To some observers, the show represented "Dennis the Menace in military school," while others saw the lead character as an adolescent version of Phil Silvers' Sergeant Bilko.

The series takes place at Westfield Military Academy, a California boys' school led by long-suffering Colonel Harvey Blackwell. Ten-year-old cadet Gary McKeever, himself the son of an Air Force officer, is the bane of Colonel Blackwell's existence, and the ringleader of a trio of troublemakers. Gary is a handsome boy whose face is the epitome of wide-eyed, clean-cut innocence, but whose life and soul are dedicated to the planning and execution of practical jokes. He routinely maintains a supply of firecrackers in his locker, saving them for just the right moments, and has been known to put goldfish in the water cooler. Cadet McKeever's two best friends are Monk and Tubby, his roommates, who are willing accessories to all of his shenanigans. Tubby (even his parents call him this) is the prototypical fat kid, whose main concern is raiding the school refrigerator for snacks after lights out.

When he's in a charitable mood, the colonel will say that Gary and his buddies are just mischievous. On the other hand, he considers Gary McKeever to have "one of the great evil minds of the century." Though Col. Blackwell often ends up the hapless victim of the boys' pranks and schemes, this isn't usually intentional on their part. He just happens to be standing under their dorm room window when McKeever's pet frog jumps out and lands on his coat, or looking out his office window just as the boys are spray-painting the building.

As an NBC press release put it, "Colonel Blackwell finds that the daily tensions of being father, mother, counselor, sergeant-at-arms, nurse-maid and molder-of-men to 212 boys, ranging in age from 10 to 17, produce nostalgic recollections of even his toughest experiences during 19 years of active Army duty."[1]

The colonel's loyal, though not particularly capable, assistant is chunky, baldheaded Sergeant Claude Barnes. Blackwell and Barnes have been friends since they were stationed in France together during World War II. Miss Warner is the school dietician, who acts as something of a surrogate mother to the boys, as well as accompanying Barnes to dinner or the movies occasionally.

The cadets of Westfield Academy monkey around with a newcomer. Pictured (left to right) with the simian guest star are *McKeever and the Colonel*'s Scott Lane (Gary), Keith Taylor (Tubby), and John Eimen (Monk) (courtesy John Eimen).

Blackwell, who has been in charge of the school for the past ten years, knows the boys who attend the academy tend to refer to him as "Old Knucklehead." Sgt. Barnes gently corrects him: "That was last year, sir. This year it's Old Ratchetface."

Col. Blackwell often tries to keep McKeever out of trouble by assigning him extra shifts of KP or guard duty. Though he spends much of his time trying to keep McKeever and his pals in line, he is actually fond of the boys, and will even offer to get Tubby a scholarship when it seems that his parents may be unable to afford the school's tuition. Likewise, the boys want to help when they believe that either Blackwell or Barnes will lose his job, and even take up a collection on one occasion to honor the colonel with a bust of himself.

McKeever and the Colonel was created by comedy writers Ray Allen and Harvey Bullock, whose credits included episodes of *The Andy Griffith Show* (CBS, 1960–68) and *The Many Loves of Dobie Gillis* (CBS, 1959–63). They would later serve as writer-producers on *Love, American Style* (ABC, 1969–74), as well as writing numerous segments for *The Love Boat* (ABC, 1977–86). The show's opening titles depict a pair of toy soldiers on sentry duty in front of a mockup of the school.

Oddly, the three lead cadets interact in the show almost exclusively with adults. Other students at Westfield Academy are little seen, beyond the sparing use of extras and bit players (one of them a young Tim Matheson). Exteriors representing the school campus were shot at the old Republic studios. The production schedule called for a day to read through the script, followed by three days of shooting, during which the young featured actors received three hours of studio schooling daily.

Top-billed Allyn Joslyn, the old pro who held the show together, was a veteran of more than forty movies, including such notable films as *Heaven Can Wait* (1943) and *Titanic* (1953, playing a passenger who dresses in drag to obtain a prime seat in a lifeboat). Born July 21, 1901, in Milford, Pennsylvania, Joslyn was himself an alumnus of a military school, Philadelphia's Chestnut Hill Academy. His Broadway credits dated back to the late 1910s and included a lengthy run as Mortimer Brewster in the original production of *Arsenic and Old Lace*. Joslyn made his film debut playing a hard-edged reporter in *They Won't Forget* (Warners, 1937), a role he essayed so believably that he would become somewhat typecast playing gentlemen of the press. He began working extensively in television in the 1950s, where he was featured in the 1953-54 CBS sitcom *Where's Raymond?* (subsequently retitled *The Ray Bolger Show*) before spending a year as leading man of *The Eve Arden Show* (CBS, 1957-58). His gift for slapstick comedy would receive quite a workout in *McKeever*, as he was routinely sprayed with hoses, splattered with paint, and the like.

For Joslyn, a working actor for nearly fifty years, a series role was welcome. "As a matter of fact," Joslyn said, "a performer is very lucky to land a regular part in a television series. Sure, there's more work around now than there ever has been because of all the television. But a lot of it is just for one day or for a week."[2]

Scott Lane, cast as Gary McKeever, was eleven years old when the series began, and earned a salary of $750 a week. Prior to winning this role, he had been seen in a guest appearance on NBC's *Hazel*. According to network publicity, he'd taken up acting at the suggestion of his Sunday school teacher. He was the son of composer-conductor Ivan Lane.

Given co-star billing in the show's opening titles were Jackie Coogan and Elisabeth Fraser. The role of Sergeant Barnes provided a comeback opportunity for Coogan, better known for his later role as Uncle Fester on *The Addams Family* (ABC, 1964–66). A popular and highly paid child actor in the early 1920s, Coogan would see little of the money he earned for starring in movies like Charlie Chaplin's *The Kid* and *Peck's Bad Boy* (both 1921). Eventually his situation, and that of other child actors, led to the passage of legislation (commonly known as the Coogan Act) requiring parents or guardians to keep a portion of a child actor's salary in trust for the performer to receive upon reaching adulthood. His adult career had been decidedly spotty, including a mad scientist role in the low-budget *Mesa of Lost Women* (1953), though his fortunes took a step up when he became a favorite of producer-director Albert Zugsmith in the late 1950s (*High School Confidential!*, *Sex Kittens Go to College*), giving him regular paychecks if not cinematic prestige. Now bald and stocky, the middle-aged Coogan's expressive face brought him work as a character actor.

Having learned a few tricks about working with child actors in the course of his long career, Coogan told an interviewer he gave no slack to the boys featured in *McKeever and the Colonel*. "The very first day, I said to 'em, 'Look, call me anything as long as it's Mr. Coogan.... Once in a while one of the kids will pop up during rehearsal and say, 'Mr. Coogan, don't you think it would be funnier if...?,' and I stop him right there by shouting, 'No!'"[3] John Eimen, featured as Monk, doesn't dispute Coogan's belief in discipline on the set, but notes that he also helped the boys in the series with some of the requirements of playing military cadets. "He was the one who taught us how to do our ties correctly," Eimen says. "He went through the drills with us."[4]

Elisabeth Fraser, seen as Miss Warner, had previously had a recurring role as Sergeant Bilko's love interest Sgt. Joan Hogan on *The Phil Silvers Show* (CBS, 1955–59), and been featured in the short-lived sitcom *One Happy Family* (NBC, 1961). Born January 8, 1920, Fraser was a stage veteran whose Broadway credits included roles in *There Shall Be No Night*, *Winged Victory*, and *Great Day in the Morning*. She reprised her stage role in *The Tunnel of Love* in the 1958 film version that starred Doris Day. A native of Brooklyn, Fraser was supposedly discovered and given her first stage role by legendary Broadway star Alfred Lunt.

Pretty, blonde, and slightly plump, Fraser was divorced from actor-singer Ray McDonald, and the mother of three daughters. She admitted her own children had snickered at the idea of her playing a dietician in the series, given her fondness for chocolate and other sweets. "Ever since they've been born all they've heard me say is, 'I've got to go on a diet,'" the actress said ruefully. "Actually, I do go on a diet about every three weeks—it doesn't last very long. But I get snappish and I have to go back to eating for the good of the group."[5]

The last of the three juvenile actors cast in the series was John Eimen, chosen for the role of Monk. Not from a show business family, young Eimen had an unexpected entrée into the business thanks to his first-grade teacher, whose best friend was a Hollywood talent agent. The agent, visiting her friend's classroom, took note of red-haired, freckled Johnny, who had an outgoing personality, and signed him as a client. One of Eimen's early roles was a much-replayed commercial for the then-new Alpha-Bits cereal, which earned him several thousand dollars in residuals. He also played small roles in episodes of *Leave It to Beaver* (CBS and ABC, 1957–63) and made a guest appearance on *The Twilight Zone* (CBS, 1959–64) prior to being cast in *McKeever*. He and Keith Taylor were paid $400 a week by Four Star for their featured roles.

For such a light comedy, *McKeever* was a surprisingly long time being born. Joslyn first starred in the series pilot in 1960, but that version didn't sell. By the time NBC was ready to greenlight the show two years later, the child actor originally cast to play Gary McKeever had outgrown the role, and had to be replaced. At that time, NBC announced that the supporting cast would consist of "David Kent as Don McKeever, Gary's older brother; Kipp Hamilton as Nancy Lewis, the school nurse, and John Gabriel as Coach Hopper, whose thoughts often stray from intramural athletics to Miss Lewis." Max Wilk was credited with writing the pilot episode, with Billy Friedberg producing and Gene Nelson directing.

In the summer of 1962, however, producer Tom McKnight announced that Jackie Coogan and Elisabeth Fraser had been signed. Regular production of the series' first-season episodes began in August 1962, just weeks before the premiere was scheduled to air on NBC.

The show's scheduling at 6:30 P.M. on Sundays placed it just outside the official beginning of prime time. CBS programmed this same time slot for much of the early sixties with a show with similarly strong kid appeal, *Mister Ed* (1961–66). *McKeever* was the lead-in to another new military sitcom, *Ensign O'Toole*, which starred Dean Jones. Both were products of the busy Four Star factory headed by Dick Powell.

McKeever drew lukewarm reviews upon its September 1962 debut, though mostly from critics far outside the age range at which it was targeted. The Associated Press' Cynthia Lowry (9/24/62) complained that the series opener offered "one of the most raucous laugh tracks heard in recent seasons, as well as the fewest laughs." Many critics seemed to prefer to ignore the show, seeing not much reason why an adult would tune in. *Time*, however, allowed (10/12/62) that the show might be "good amusement for little boys," while *Variety*

(9/25/62) thought it an "early evening fun show for the tyke monopoly on the home sets," and reported that both Joslyn and Lane did well with their lead roles. Columnist Harvey Pack commented that his six-year-old daughter didn't especially like the show itself, but had fallen instantly in love with star Scott Lane and hoped to marry him.

Though many child actors would later have conflicting feelings about their time in front of the cameras, John Eimen has only positive memories of his career, and *McKeever* in particular. While the starring role of Gary McKeever represented a significant responsibility for a young performer ("I think Scott had a big weight on his shoulders," Eimen says today), Eimen's featured part as Monk was not overly demanding. "I had a life outside the studio," he says. "I got to be a kid too." Four Star established fan clubs for Eimen and the other two boy actors, and they were recipients of a goodly amount of fan mail, in Eimen's case often from young girls.

A few guest stars turned up in the series, especially as the season progressed and ratings were less than anticipated. Ann B. Davis played tough-as-nails Sergeant Maxine Groover in "Too Many Sergeants" (1/6/63), while Jim Backus appeared as "The Neighbor" (1/27/63), who blames his insomnia on the school's daily 6 A.M. reveille. In "The Old Grad" (3/3/63), Soupy Sales was cast as a former Westfield cadet whom Col. Blackwell thought the most polite, respectful boy who ever attended the school—until he comes back for a visit and flawlessly pulls off a series of pranks that impresses even McKeever, who's wrongly blamed for them. Character actor David White (later to play Darrin's boss Larry Tate on *Bewitched*) made a few appearances as Henry Carlson, head of the school's Board of Trustees, while Peter Hansen (*General Hospital*) was seen once or twice as Gary McKeever's father.

According to John Eimen, the guest player who made the biggest impression on his juvenile co-stars was wrestler-turned-actor Mike Mazurki, later featured in *It's About Time* (q.v.). "All of us were really into professional wrestling," Eimen explains. He also remembers meeting the great voice artist Mel Blanc, who read the lines of a talking parrot in one segment.

Probably the most adults who ever saw the show were reluctant witnesses to the mid-June rerun of "Love Comes to Westfield." NBC abruptly cut off coverage of the Thunderbird golf championship in its final moments so as to switch over to the sitcom, angering most adult viewers. It was *McKeever*'s final broadcast.

For a brief time in 1963, there was also a Dell Comics adaptation of *McKeever and the Colonel*, but it faded from sight just as the TV show did. Though *Ensign O'Toole* drew better critical response than *McKeever*, neither was renewed for a second year. The show's cancellation came as a distinct surprise to some cast members. "We were just floored when it wasn't picked up," John Eimen recalls of himself, Scott Lane, and Keith Taylor.

Once *McKeever* was canceled, little would be seen of the three on television, though Eimen went almost immediately into a guest appearance on *The Lloyd Bridges Show* (CBS, 1962-63). Taylor had perhaps the most noteworthy career of the trio, making guest appearances on Irwin Allen's *Lost in Space* (CBS, 1965–68) and *Land of the Giants* (ABC, 1968–70), as well as appearing in an early episode of *Star Trek* (NBC, 1966–69). Lane made a few appearances as well, but his acting career didn't last much past adolescence. Today, Eimen works as a flight attendant and continues to pursue his lifelong interest in music.

Though *McKeever and the Colonel* provided him with steady employment for only a year, Jackie Coogan had reason to be grateful for even a brief run. He was spotted on the show by producer David Levy, who thought him perfect for the role of Uncle Fester in *The Addams Family*. As it happened, Coogan and Allyn Joslyn worked together again in *The Addams Family*. Joslyn played a truant officer in the series pilot, the first of many visitors to be comically unnerved by a visit to the Addams manse, and reprised the role in later episodes.

Joslyn died on January 21, 1981, while a resident at the Motion Picture and Television Country Home and Hospital in Woodland Hills, California. Coogan continued to work until shortly before his death on March 1, 1984. Elisabeth Fraser died May 5, 2005 in Los Angeles, after a career that had spanned forty years.

For kids in the 1960s, the pleasures of *McKeever and the Colonel* most likely centered on the freedom its youthful protagonists enjoyed. Despite the limited number of episodes available, *McKeever* reruns were popular enough to play on local stations well into the 1970s. For older viewers who encounter the show today, its strongest asset may be the polished performances of its adult players, comic pros all of them.

Meet Mr. McNutley / The Ray Milland Show

Ray Milland (*Prof. Ray McNutley/McNulty*), Phyllis Avery (*Peggy McNutley/McNulty*), Minerva Urecal (*Dean Josephine Bradley*), Gordon Jones (*Pete Thompson*)
Creators: Joseph Connelly, Bob Mosher. *Producers*: Joe Connelly, Bob Mosher, Harry Tugend. *Writers*: Russell Bender, Ardelle Brebner, Lou Breslow, Kitty Buhler, Joe Connelly, Nathaniel Curtis, Morris Freedman, Siegfried Herzig, Charles Hoffman, Jack Jacobs, Albert E. Lewin, Larry Marks, Bob Mosher, Milton Pascal, Irving Phillips, George Savage, Ben Starr, Burt Styler, Rik Vollaerts, Malvin Wald. *Directors*: Rod Amateau, Charles Barton, Jules Bricken, James Neilson, Ted Post, Sidney Salkow, William Seiter. *Directors of Photography*: John MacBurnie, John L. Russell. *Art Director*: Martin Obzina. *Music Supervisor*: Stanley Wilson. *Set Decorator*: James S. Redd. *Film Editors*: Michael R. McAdam, Daniel A. Nathan. *Makeup*: Jack Barron. *Assistant Directors*: Richard Birnie, Jack Corrick, James Hogan, Willard Sheldon. *Editorial Supervisors*: Richard Currier, Richard G. Wray. *Sound*: Earl Crain, Sr., William Lynch, Perc Townsend. *Miss Avery's Dresses*: McKettrick. *Miss Avery's Wardrobe*: Amelia Gray, Beverly Hills. Revue Productions.

Aired Thursdays at 8 P.M. (through June 1955), then Fridays at 9:30 P.M. on CBS-TV. 78 black-and-white episodes.

One of television's most notable trends in 1953 was the number of movie stars who were ready to take the plunge into regular video work. In February, Ann Sothern launched her successful sitcom *Private Secretary* (1953–57). That fall, Loretta Young began her long-running anthology series, originally titled *A Letter to Loretta*. Not only ladies were signing TV contracts, however; the 1953-54 season also marked the series debut of actor Ray Milland, who'd taken home an Oscar for Best Actor of 1945 for his performance as alcoholic Don Birnam in Billy Wilder's *The Lost Weekend*. Milland's new vehicle was originally titled *Meet Mr. McNutley,* the deal calling for not only a weekly television program, but also a concurrent radio series.

Ray McNutley is a professor of English literature at Lynnhaven College for Women in New England. His wife is a pretty blonde named Peggy, whom he married after completing his military service in World War II. The McNutleys live on suburban Maple Drive. Ray's brash best friend, who calls him "Rayboy," is Pete Thompson, whom Ray has known since they served in the Army together. Pete is a happy-go-lucky bachelor whose lady friends are so plentiful that he sometimes has trouble remembering their full names when introducing them. Ray's supervisor is Dean Josephine Bradley, a stuffy older woman who's a 30-year veteran of the school, and who in turn reports to Dr. Peabody, chair of the Board of Trustees.

The show's original creators and producers were Joe Connelly and Bob

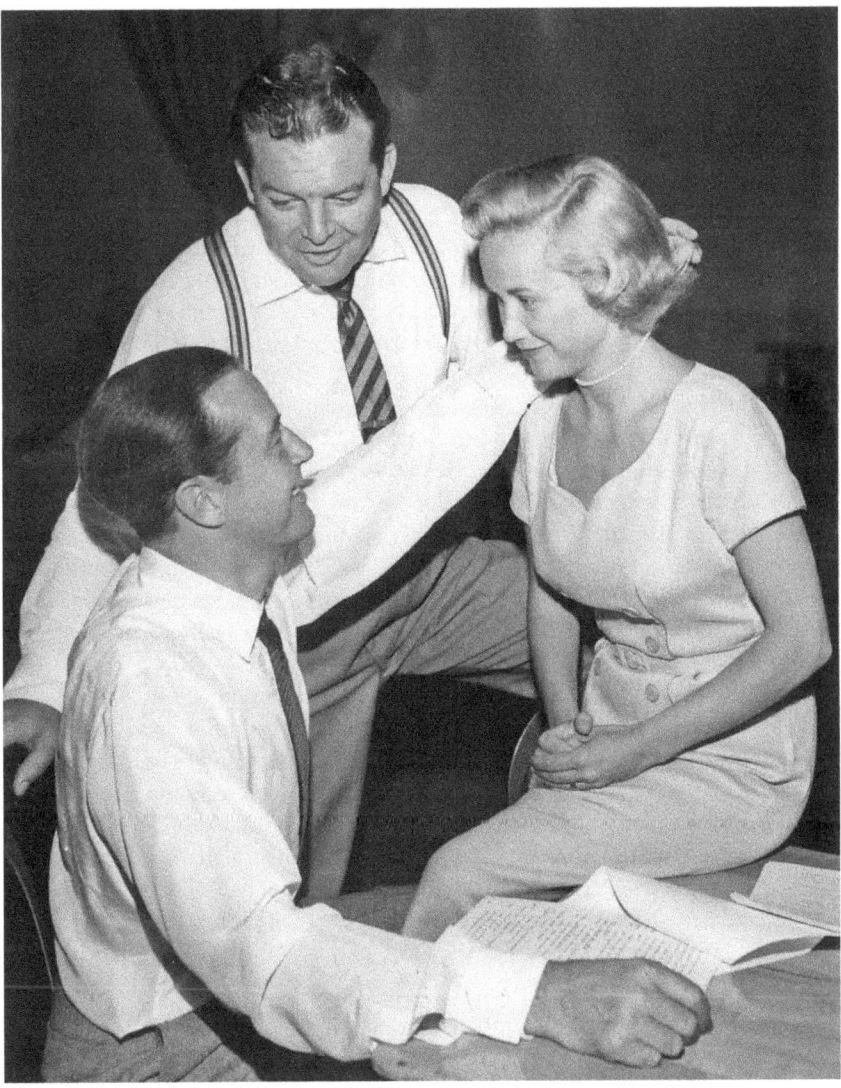

Ray Milland (left) rehearses with co-stars Gordon Jones (Pete) and Phyllis Avery (Peggy) for the radio broadcast of *Meet Mr. McNutley*. The trio also starred in the TV version.

Mosher, whose TV sitcom fame rests largely on two shows that came later in their careers, *Leave It to Beaver* (CBS and ABC, 1957–63) and *The Munsters* (CBS, 1964–66). At this time they were better known for contributing scripts to TV's *Amos 'n' Andy* (CBS, 1951–53). Milland would later tell reporters that his agent at MCA had basically tricked him into making a pilot film for the series, though it's difficult to imagine how he could have failed to grasp the purpose of shooting such a film. Unlike some of the film actors who made an early jump into TV, Milland was still in demand with movie producers. In fact, he interrupted filming of his first-season segments to play the top-billed role in Alfred Hitchcock's *Dial M for Murder,* opposite Grace Kelly and another once-and-future sitcom star, Bob Cummings.

During that first season, Milland learned first-hand what a grind TV could be. "I've got to turn out 14 in a row, take a recess, then turn out 14 more," he told the Associated Press' Bob Thomas. "I haven't got time for anything else."[1] He told Thomas that his television commitment cost him a co-starring role opposite Shirley Booth in Paramount's *About Mrs. Leslie* (1954).

As he readily admitted, his motive for accepting a filmed TV sitcom was largely financial. "There are a hundred or so TV markets now," Milland told Thomas. "There are supposed to be around 1,000 in five years. They'll need a lot of film to fill up all that air time with." Offered a healthy share of profit participation in the series, Milland readily signed on. *Meet Mr. McNutley* was set for a September premiere on both radio and television, under the sponsorship of General Electric, which had already made a splash on TV with its anthology series *General Electric Theater* (CBS, 1953–62). Tying the new sitcom to its already established show, the sponsor would have early episodes introduced as "The General Electric Comedy Theater presents Ray Milland in *Meet Mr. McNutley.*"

An early *TV Guide* blurb concerning the forthcoming show (5/1/53) said that Milland would play "a high school teacher who doubles as basketball coach." In the format that finally emerged, the movie actor was cast as the prototype of the absent-minded professor. In the pilot episode, he is said to be writing a book called "The Key to a Perfect Memory," though he cannot remember that he invited a fellow faculty member to dinner. Milland was ill-suited to play a character described in a CBS press release as "slightly pixilated," though the network's PR men tried to make the case otherwise, calling him "the kind of actor whose extreme sensitivity to people and wide experience make possible this unusual virtuosity."[2]

Born January 3, 1905, in Wales, as Reginald Truscott-Jones, the future Ray Milland played his first film roles in the late 1920s in England. Relocating to Hollywood a few years later, he graduated from bit parts to young leading man status in the mid–1930s, and settled in for a long stint as a Paramount contract player. Milland was versatile enough to carry lead roles in a variety of genres— comedies, historical epics, and finally his memorable Oscar performance in *The*

Lost Weekend. He had made more than 80 films by the time he accepted the lead role in *Meet Mr. McNutley*.

Leading lady Phyllis Avery, born November 14, 1924, was a veteran of eight Broadway shows, having appeared most successfully in a 1940-41 revival of *Charley's Aunt* and in Moss Hart's wartime musical *Winged Victory* (1943-44). The daughter of screenwriter Steven Morehouse Avery (*The Male Animal, Deep Valley*), the actress was not yet thirty when *Meet Mr. McNutley* premiered, a bit young to be paired with the 46-year-old Milland. Minerva Urecal (1894–1966), featured as Dean Bradley, would go on to play the title role in the syndicated *Adventures of Tugboat Annie* (1957) before settling into the featured role of "Mother" on *Peter Gunn* (NBC and ABC, 1958–61). Gordon Jones (1911–63), seen as Ray's friend Pete, was a veteran movie and TV character actor who'd previously played a recurring role as Mike the Cop in the syndicated *The Abbott and Costello Show*. Actress D.J. Thompson appeared occasionally during the first year as Peggy's friend Gwen Harrison, another English instructor at Lynnhaven.

Meet Mr. McNutley was added to CBS' Thursday night schedule. Its 8 P.M. time slot placed it in direct competition with Groucho Marx's *You Bet Your Life* on NBC, then one of television's top five shows. As the season got underway, CBS executives had high hopes that Milland's star power could put the brakes on the runaway popularity of Groucho's quiz show.

The pilot episode struck most viewers as unnecessarily weighted down with slapstick, hardly Milland's specialty. Critics thought the series opener, which called for Milland to fall out of a rowboat and lose his pants, beneath the star. Others found it a distaff version of *Our Miss Brooks* (CBS, 1952–56), the better-written vehicle of movie character actress Eve Arden.

Influential New York critic John Crosby (9/30/53) termed the series opener "an unqualified disaster," complaining, "The comic strips progressed way beyond this level of humor a good many years ago and it does seem a shame that television, which has become very big business, has to go through it all over again." Noting that Connelly and Mosher both produced and wrote the show, he suggested that they needed to be replaced in at least one of those capacities, and possibly both. The radio version received a similar reaction, with one critic noting, "Unfortunately, Mr. Milland does little to help this series — and the series is doing plenty to harm him. Milland's fine ability for comedy is smothered here by slapstick and overall bad writing."[3] *TV Guide* (10/30/53) also panned the show, but did like Phyllis Avery's work as Peggy. Avery, the reviewer thought, was "one of the show's brighter notes, making the most of a role which calls for her mainly to smile lovingly at the scrapes into which her husband's memory lapses lead him."

Made more than a year prior to the series' debut, the pilot was different from the weekly episodes, which did not lean so heavily on slapstick. Still, the prevailing opinion among the show's staff seemed to be that star power was all that was needed to insure the success of even the most mediocre show. It didn't take long for the bubble to burst. Although ratings scores weren't available quickly in those days, it soon became apparent to CBS, Milland, his sponsor, and MCA that television success wasn't going to fall into his lap as readily as they might have assumed. By late September, *Variety* noted that *Meet Mr. McNutley,* which had been "taken over the critical coals," was shaping up as a disappointment. "The days when a client could afford to play around with a show in the hopes of building it into a click no longer exist," the trade paper warned, in an article titled "Sponsors Want Quick Clicks."

Not long after the series got underway, it attracted some unwelcome publicity when reporters learned that the real-life marriages of Milland and his TV wife were experiencing more serious problems than the McNutleys' lightweight shenanigans. In November, Milland was separated from his real-life wife, reportedly due to his extramarital affair with his movie leading lady Grace Kelly. Avery had also recently split from her real-life husband, actor Don Taylor.

Meet Mr. McNutley also came under attack for its excessive laugh track. Though filmed sitcoms were commonplace by 1953, many of them, like *I Love Lucy,* were being shot three-camera style, in front of a live audience. Though there might have been some "sweetening" of the laughter, much of the audience reaction was genuine. That wasn't the case with one-camera sitcoms like *McNutley,* which relied upon the producers' judgment to keep the simulated reactions at a reasonable level. Judging from an October article in *Variety,* Connelly and Mosher weren't hitting the mark: The trade paper listed Milland's show, along with others like Paul Hartman's *Pride of the Family* and Danny Thomas' *Make Room for Daddy,* as ones where "the questionable guffaws are getting completely out of hand." (The latter show was, in fact, filmed in front of a live studio audience, though it's possible their reactions were being electronically augmented.)

Those first-season episodes seemed to have been devised under the principle that there was no such thing as a plotline too inconsequential — or too implausible — for TV sitcom fans. In "The Egg and Ray" (3/4/54), Ray and Peggy adopt a pet parakeet, and are thrilled to find that it has laid an egg. When the bird proves unwilling to hatch the egg, however, Ray takes it upon himself to help the process along. For the next several days, he neglects his work duties to stay home, where he's attempting to incubate the egg using the warmth from their basement furnace. His devotion to the bird somehow wins favorable publicity for the professor and for Lynnhaven College as this supposedly erudite scholar gamely babysits an egg. Then, as if the proceeding scenes haven't made Milland look sufficiently foolish, there's a surprise ending in which he's told that the "egg" he's been nurturing is actually a piece of candy that a neighbor boy left in the bird's cage. "What a shock!" Milland exclaims. "To think that, for the past ten days, I've been expectant father to a jellybean!" The laugh track roars.

In "The Tree" (3/11/54), Ray and Peggy decide to spend a tax refund check on a shade tree for their yard. Pete, who sells them an insurance policy for the tree, tells them a covenant in their neighborhood prevents them from planting it in the spot Peggy has chosen. Once he's moved it, Ray learns that an exception to the rule has been made, and he can plant it there after all. He moves it back, but Pete sees it and moves it again. Finally it ends up in the yard of Ray and Peggy's new neighbors Mr. and Mrs. Adams. The newcomers, seeing the tree moved back and forth, accuse Ray of stealing the tree from their lot.

Connelly and Mosher were shown the door following the show's unsuccessful first season, though they would retain a "created by" credit for the remainder of the show's run. Syndicated columnist Erskine Johnson reported in April 1954 that Milland had been making noise about bolting from the show altogether after the painful first season. But he was still under contract to General Electric, and that summer production began on a substantially revamped vehicle that would carry the title *The Ray Milland Show*.

Helming the second season would be veteran writer-producer Harry Tugend, whose résumé included a 1940s stint at Paramount Pictures, where he produced Milland's 1947 film *Golden Earrings*. A network press release practically apologized for the first season, but promised better things ahead, gushing, "With this outstanding producer and the new creative talent he has available, *The Ray Milland Show* can't miss being outstanding entertainment."[4]

Among the second-season changes were a new setting, and the dropping of supporting players Minerva Urecal and Gordon Jones. In Tugend's revamped version, Milland would be employed at co-educational Comstock University, and would teach dramatics instead of English literature. The name of Milland's character also underwent a slight but meaningful change, from McNutley to McNulty. In the star's view, the original name had a goofy connotation that led viewers to expect pratfalls. The change was one way of letting them know that a different take on the show was in store for year two.

Tugend's overhaul of Milland's sitcom earned plaudits from most reviewers. *Variety* (9/22/54) called the difference "so vast the series is scarcely recognizable.... [T]he series [has] a new polish and sophistication, and Milland consequently comes over much better." The Associated Press' Wayne Oliver (11/23/54) also thought the show markedly improved in its second year. "It's more believable and more in keeping with the very literate Milland's talent for subtle wit. It's a refreshing change from the burlesque of last year, although part of the effect is lost because of the overly loud laughter for some of the milder humor that would rate only a smile at best."

Second-season episodes provided slightly more adult storylines than had been the norm under the show's initial regime. In "Field Trip" (12/2/54), Peggy is unable to accompany Ray to New York, where he is to deliver a lecture at a theatrical conference. En route, Ray meets a beautiful and notorious actress (guest star Osa Massen) who decides he'll do nicely when her press agent advises her to link her name romantically with a mature and presentable man.

Though most sitcoms in the early days of television were scripted by a small, in-house staff, season two scripts for *The Ray Milland Show* came from a variety of freelancers. Once production was underway, the star told a reporter that he was well pleased with the majority of the scripts he'd seen thus far. As for the others, "You just can't get 39 good stories a year," Milland said philosophically.[5] The show's production schedule for a one-camera show called for two days of rehearsals, followed by two days of shooting.

One key change that *didn't* happen was a new time slot for the ratings-plagued sitcom. Only during its final cycle of summer reruns was the show tried in a different placement, Fridays at 9:30 P.M. It was a much more suitable time slot for an adult comedy, but by then the boat had sailed.

At the end of the show's second season, sponsor General Electric pulled the plug on *The Ray Milland Show*, but the star shed no tears. "I'm the happiest man in the world," he told AP's Bob Thomas that June. Asked whether another venture into series television lay in his future, Milland snapped, "I should say not." When news of the cancellation broke, Milland was already at work on his next picture, playing Stanford White in Fox's *The Girl in the Red Velvet Swing* (1955) opposite leading lady Joan Collins.

Though the series had been less than a success, there were enough episodes in the hopper to make syndication feasible, and television stations were hungry enough for filmed programming in 1955 to give it replays. In reruns, the series would be known only as *The Ray Milland Show*, with a new set of animated opening titles. In order to lessen the confusion about the two locales, reruns would frequently open with an establishing shot of the school in question, labeled "Comstock University" or "Lynnhaven College for Women."

Though he'd sworn off television series work in the wake of this unhappy, experience it would be only a few years before he debuted in his second weekly series. Milland accepted the lead in the half-hour detective drama *Markham*, which premiered on CBS in the spring of 1959. By the end of the 1959-60 season, however, that show too was a goner, having enjoyed an even shorter run than Milland's sitcom. His leading lady Phyllis Avery resurfaced briefly as a featured player on *The George Gobel Show* during the 1958-59 season (Avery replaced Jeff Donnell as Gobel's wife Alice in a recurring sketch), and later had a continuing role as a faculty member in the high school drama *Mr. Novak* (NBC, 1963–65).

In 1962, Milland directed and starred in AIP's *Panic in Year Zero!*, a cheaply made but interesting film about a suburban family's struggle for existence after a nuclear holocaust. In the 1970s, he would be a frequent player in made-for-TV movies, and was featured in *Love Story* (1970). In what was perhaps his career low point, he and former football player Rosey Grier each played half the title role in *The Thing with Two Heads* (AIP, 1972). Milland died of lung cancer on March 10, 1986.

Seen more than five decades after it was made, *The Ray Milland Show* is little more than a curio. That its star took on such a project at a time when he was making films with the likes of Alfred Hitchcock is mildly astonishing. That it failed to capture the favor of TV viewers is substantially less so.

The Mickey Rooney Show: Hey Mulligan

Mickey Rooney (*Mickey Mulligan*), Claire Carleton (*Nell Mulligan*), Regis Toomey (*Sgt. Joe Mulligan*), Joey Forman (*Freddy Devlin*), Carla Balenda (*Pat Harding*), John Hubbard (*Charles Brown*)

Executive Producers: Mickey Rooney, Maurice Duke. *Producer*: Joseph Santley. *Writers*: Benedict Freedman, John Fenton Murray. *Directors*: Leslie H. Martinson, Richard Quine (pilot). *Based on Characters Created by* Blake Edwards, Richard Quine. *Directors of Photography*: Joseph F. Biroc, Ray June, James Van Trees. *Art Directors*: Stephen Goosson, Jerome Pycha, Jr. *Set Decorators*: James Crowe, Jack Mills. *Production Supervisor*: Dewey Starkey. *Costumes*: Lon Anthony. *Property Master*: Josef Bernay. *Sound*: Hugh McDowell. *Makeup Supervisor*: Robert Schiffer. *Assistant Directors*: Frank Bauer, Ralph Black, Leonard Katzman. *Music Composed and Conducted by* Van Alexander. *Supervising Editor*: Marvin J. Coil. *Production Manager*: Eddie Saeta. *Assistant to Producer*: Tony Roberts. *Script Clerks*: Dorothy Aldrin, Marie Messinger, Gloria Morgan. *Mr. Rooney's Clothes*: Damico. Mickey Rooney Enterprises; Volcano Pictures, Inc.

Aired Saturdays at 8 P.M. on NBC-TV. First aired August 28, 1954; last aired June 4, 1955. 33 black-and-white episodes.

He's too small to be a wrestler, and too big to be a puppet.—IBC-TV executive Mr. Brown, on why Mickey Mulligan has no future in television

Between 1952 and 1954, a number of Hollywood film actors followed in the footsteps of pioneering Lucille Ball and made the leap from the silver screen to television, often in the burgeoning sitcom genre. Also ready to make such a transition was Oscar-winning former child star Mickey Rooney, whose career had sunk quite a few notches from his heyday as the highly paid star of MGM's *Andy Hardy* series. Since leaving his full-time employment with MGM in 1948, Rooney's career had been floundering, and he was only too happy to accept NBC's offer to develop a situation comedy show under the banner of his own production company, Mickey Rooney Enterprises.

Mickey Mulligan is an ambitious, well-intended, but bumbling young man working as a page at the studios of the fictitious International Broadcasting Company (IBC) while awaiting his big break as an actor. Mickey, who's paid $47.62 a week for his services, lives at home with his parents; father Joe is a 29-year-veteran of the police force, and mother Nell is a former burlesque dancer (as Rooney's real-life mother had been) whom his father first met when he arrested her. He has a love interest in Pat, who works as the secretary to studio program director Mr. Brown, and his best friend since childhood is Freddy, a fellow page at IBC. Each week the show opens with an off-screen voice yelling the show's title, *Hey Mulligan,* causing the star to drop a huge pile of scripts, spill the contents of the office water cooler, or trip on a skateboard.

Mickey Rooney makes friends with an imposing co-star in "Lion Hunt," an early episode of *The Mickey Rooney Show: Hey Mulligan* (Photofest).

In the series pilot, Mickey is studying acting at the Jonathan Swift Academy of Drama and Theater Arts. (Some reference sources wrongly credit actor Alan Mowbray, who guest stars in the pilot show as Jonathan Swift, as a series regular.) Mickey has been chosen to understudy leading man David Lambert (played by guest star Robert Clarke) in the Swift Academy's newest production, "Tomorrow Begins September," written by pretentious aspiring playwright Rogerson P. Hammerstine (William Bakewell). When Lambert falls victim to laryngitis the night before the show is to open, Mickey is promoted to leading man, and invites Mr. Brown to see his debut.

Just before the curtain rises, Lambert's voice returns, but Mickey's father tricks the actor into gluing his mouth shut so that Mickey will have his chance to be seen. Unfortunately, the play is a slapstick disaster. The next day, Pat's boss Mr. Brown tells Mickey not to feel so bad, that the play as written was hopelessly terrible and at least he was funny.

In subsequent episodes, Mickey abandons his work with the acting school, but not his dreams of getting a show business break at IBC, where he is occasionally given gigs such as a late-night disc jockey show. Meanwhile, his job is constantly in jeopardy thanks to incidents such as the one in which Milton Berle (in a cameo appearance) approaches Mickey and asks where his dressing room is, to which the hapless page replies, "I'm sorry, I don't know, Mr. Hope."

The show's most effective episodes revolved around Mickey's efforts to further his career at the TV network. (Though the network depicted on *Hey Mulligan* was a fictitious one, IBC's offices and corridors are decorated with publicity photos of then-current NBC stars like Gale Storm and Charles Farrell of *My Little Margie,* and Groucho Marx of *You Bet Your Life.*) "Fan Mail" (12/25/54) finds Mr. Brown in hot water because a new IBC television show he personally championed, *Everybody's Hour,* is a ratings disappointment. He hopes to demonstrate the show's viability with an on-air plea for viewers who like the show to write the network. Mickey and Freddy try to help out by personally writing more than 400 letters, but find themselves hoist by their own petard when the show's sponsor insists on meeting some of the viewers who have written in. In "The Average Man" (2/26/55), Mickey is found to have a unexpected knack for predicting audience reaction to new IBC shows like *True-to-Life Tim,* "the only comedy show on the air that makes you cry."

"Seven Days to Live" (2/5/55) begins as Mickey and Freddy take the free physical examinations offered to IBC employees. Though Mickey's report shows that he's in perfect health, a distracted nurse mistakenly types up the wrong diagnosis, giving Mickey the same rare disease suffered by the leading lady in IBC's medical drama *Young Dr. Pierce Probes Life.* Believing that he has only a week to live, Mickey buys expensive presents for his parents, encourages girlfriend Pat to find a new man, and volunteers to defuse a bomb that's been planted at the studio. Future *Zorro* and *Lost in Space* star Guy Williams makes an early TV appearance as the dashing star of *Young Dr. Pierce.*

The Mickey Rooney Show

Rooney seemed a natural to have his own TV sitcom, despite the setbacks that had afflicted his career in recent years. Various explanations were offered for why Rooney's popularity was on the downslide in the early 1950s. Some blamed it on the fact that, having passed the age of thirty, he no longer had the boyish appeal that had made him an audience favorite in the *Andy Hardy* series. Others, including the star himself, thought negative publicity had hurt his career. "There was a campaign for a while there against me — no more Rooney," Rooney told a reporter. "I guess it was because of my unfortunate marriages."[1] (By the early 1950s, those included his stormy unions with actresses Ava Gardner and Martha Vickers, as well as beauty queen Betty Jane Rase. His then-current spouse, Elaine, was not an actress. What no one knew was that, when it came to tying the knot, Mickey was just getting warmed up.)

Rooney had recently been making low-budget pictures at Columbia, and enlisted the help of his film colleagues Richard Quine and Blake Edwards to develop his sitcom format. Quine, a former child actor and longtime friend of the star, had directed Rooney's recent Columbia comedies *Sound Off* (1952) and *All Ashore* (1953, which Quine co-authored with Edwards). The original title for the TV series was to be *For the Love of Mike*, but this proved to have been registered already, and creators Edwards and Quine had to regroup.

Carla Balenda had previously acted under the name Sally Bliss, but studio executives at RKO, where she was a contract player, decided the name was too cute for her. Her role in *Hey Mulligan* almost ended before it started: In the summer of 1954, weeks before the show premiered, syndicated columnist Erskine Johnson wrote that the actress had become entangled in "a grim contract hassle"[2] with the show's producers. The stalemate, reported to be about salary as well as Balenda's ability to do work outside the NBC-TV show, eventually had to be settled with the assistance of the Screen Actors Guild. Balenda replaced actress Pat Walker, who played the role of Pat in the pilot episode.

Not seen in the pilot, but featured prominently in the weekly series, was Mickey Mulligan's best friend and fellow page, Freddy. Twenty-four-year-old actor-comedian Joey Forman was signed for this role. Veteran character actor Regis Toomey filled the role of Mickey's father. Hillary Brooke, who had recurring roles on several popular shows of the 1950s, mostly notably *My Little Margie* (CBS and NBC, 1952–55) and the syndicated *The Abbott and Costello Show* (1952–53), made a couple of appearances as Mr. Brown's wife Alice.

In June, the *Washington Post* reported that six episodes of Rooney's new show had been committed to film, and had pleased the sponsors enough to order a full season's worth. NBC executives were apparently quite taken with the pilot film as well, and *The Mickey Rooney Show: Hey Mulligan* was awarded a spot on the network's fall 1954 schedule. However, that particular time slot — Saturdays at 8 P.M.— was home to CBS's top-rated *The Jackie Gleason Show*. (ABC, barely considered a major player at this point, had scheduled an odd musical show featuring a performer named Dotty Mack whose specialty was lip-syncing to other singers' records. It was, presumably, at least an inexpensive show to throw away in that time slot.)

Although the show's Saturday evening time slot was a difficult one, competing with *The Jackie Gleason Show* for viewer attention, Rooney's manager Maurice Duke predicted big things. "I think we can knock off Gleason," Duke said confidently in a July interview, before the season got underway. "The kids used to like Gleason because of the crazy characters he did. But lately he's been concentrating on the man-and-wife skits. The kids don't like that so much. And Mickey has always been a kids' favorite."[3]

The star himself professed more modest goals. "I don't want to knock off anybody," Rooney said. "All I want to do is put on a nice, funny show that people will like." His involvement in the show touched almost every aspect, according to Aline Mosby: "Rooney not only produces *Hey, Mulligan* and stars in it, but he writes the music, discusses gags with the director and shakes hands with visitors on the set."[4] The result was a show that NBC executives reputedly thought had the potential to become a big hit.

Rooney's television ambitions also extended to programs he hoped to produce beside his own. According to press reports, Mickey Rooney Enterprises had two more programs in the works, *The Magic Lantern*, starring the Indian actor Sabu, and *Date Line Tokyo* with Dane Clark.

Critical response to *Hey Mulligan* was mixed. Most observers thought the 34-year-old star had outgrown the type of roles he'd played in his younger years. Commenting on an early episode in which Mickey played an amateur boxer in the Police Athletic League, the *New York Times*' Jack Gould said (11/15/54): "A stalwart of the P.A.L. somehow loses a trace of his buoyant and boyish charm when the hairline has begun to recede. Similarly, a close-up becomes disconcerting when the firmness of flesh is creased by telltale lines and the youthfully mischievous grin is framed in a 5 o'clock shadow." The contrast was made even more striking when he played scenes with actor-comedian Joey Forman (Freddy), who at 24 was at least within spitting distance of the same age as his character. (Though many early reviewers believed Rooney's character, who still lived at home with his parents, was meant to be a teenager, later episodes established the age of Rooney's character at about 23 years old, with mention made of his prior military service.)

Said syndicated columnist Hal Humphrey, "There seems to be a constant temptation for anyone writing or producing a Mickey Rooney opus to lard it too heavily with slapstick. Rooney is a master at this form of comedy, but in this case he is asked to go slightly overboard with it. His success as Andy Hardy stemmed in great part from a certain amount of naturalness and believability. Mike Mulligan doesn't have to take too many pratfalls to ingratiate himself with audiences, and the producers will be making a mistake if they let him."[5]

Added John Crosby, "I'm afraid the time has come for Mr. Rooney to face up to the fact that he's grown up. While it is not explicitly stated that he's a teenager, he certainly acts like one, lives at home with his parents, has a girl friend, and romps gaily through what may easily be the most delayed adolescence of our time. This is the sort of thing he used to do with Judy Garland in the movies more years ago than I care to think about. I have unbounded admiration for Mr. Rooney as a mugger with a great sense of timing and a certain animal ferocity, but I don't think he looks 19 any more and I can't understand his reluctance to grow up." On a more positive note, Crosby applauded the show's efforts to differentiate itself from the many other sitcoms that had joined the network schedules in the wake of *I Love Lucy*. "The shenanigans of a broadcasting network are certainly a wonderful starting point for light comedy and also fairly original. It's also a refreshing change from the husband and wife situation comedies that are clogging the air waves."[6]

Oddly, the second aired episode of *Hey Mulligan* paid little attention to the format established so carefully in the series pilot, being devoted instead to a far-out plot about Mickey and Freddy's efforts to build a rocket ship so that they can fly to the moon! In "Moon or Bust" (9/4/54), taking inspiration from the space comics he so avidly reads, Mickey assembles a rocket ship in his parents' garage and blasts off with Freddy, taking along beads to offer the natives they expect to encounter. Unfortunately, the journey takes them only as far as Glendale, where a suspicious farmer and his wife (played by Roscoe Ates and Ellen Corby) believe they are moon men. With plots like these, it's not surprising that many critics didn't realize Rooney's character was intended to be an adult.

Within weeks of the show's debut, it was evident that Duke's predictions of outperforming *The Jackie Gleason Show* were overly optimistic. Having gotten Rooney's show off to an early start with its late August debut, NBC didn't have the chance to see what would really happen once Gleason returned. Gleason's season premiere on September 25, 1954, opposite the fifth aired episode of *Hey Mulligan*, blew the competition out of the water. Gleason's season opener, which devoted almost its entire hour to a *Honeymooners* sketch, was the most-watched television show of the weekend on any network, seen by more than five times the number of viewers who tuned into Rooney's sitcom. By season's end, *The Jackie Gleason Show* would be ranked second only to *I Love Lucy* in household ratings.

In December, *The Washington Post*'s Laurence Laurent named *Hey Mulligan* to a list of ten shows he hoped to see disappear in 1955. "The pity is that Rooney does have a fine talent for comedy and is capable of giving pleasure to an audience. Next time, maybe he'll begin by crediting the public with taste, intelligence, and discrimination."[7]

Ratings for *Hey Mulligan* continued to be disappointing, though it remained on the network schedule into 1955. Columnist Erskine Johnson reported in May that the show would undergo some fine-tuning: Mickey Mulligan would receive a promotion at work, become a junior executive, and give up his steady girl in favor of "a flock of girl friends." In fact, Balenda's role in the show as Pat had never really been developed to any great extent, and by the time this announcement appeared, Rooney's chances of being picked up for the 1955-56 season were somewhere between slim and none.

By then, it seemed that Rooney had basically thrown in the towel on his debut TV series. Maurice Duke later told Rooney biographer Arthur Marx that Rooney was prone to some less-than-professional behavior once he had lost interest in a project. Noting that the star could sometimes be spotted on a nearby golf course after calling in sick to the *Hey Mulligan* set, Duke commented, "I could tell by just reading the script when Mickey was going to play hookey."[8]

Onscreen, Rooney played the humble and gracious star, appearing out of character in a brief coda each week to thank the show's sponsor. After hours, though, his relationship with the sponsor proved rockier. Midway through the production season, Rooney was among the guests at a party thrown by the show's alternate-week sponsor, Pillsbury. Late in the evening, after a fair amount of liquor had flowed, a member of the Pillsbury clan urged Rooney to get up and perform for the guests. Adding insult to injury, Mr. Pillsbury couldn't seem to remember the star's name, repeatedly addressing him as "Charlie." Whether he politely declined (Rooney's version) or stomped off in a huff (Duke's account), it was clear that he had displayed a show of independence that a man with low ratings could ill afford.

When NBC's fall 1955 schedule was announced that spring, Rooney's show was not on it. Not that the show's demise left Rooney out of work. Ironically, one of Rooney's first gigs upon laying his TV sitcom to rest was a well-paid stint at Las Vegas' Dunes Hotel, where he was rushed in as an emergency replacement for Wally Cox, who despite his own television success with *Mr. Peepers* (NBC, 1952–55) was a huge flop with his nightclub act. By June 1955, Rooney had reported to Republic Studios, where he was cast as a minister in *The Twinkle in God's Eye*, which also featured his *Mulligan* co-star Joey Forman. His business relationship with Maurice Duke, however, seemed to have been a casualty of the TV debacle. Only a few months after *Hey Mulligan* bit the dust, columnist Erskine Johnson reported (10/4/55) that the partnership of Rooney and his manager–co-executive producer "have called it a day after some choice name calling."

Rooney would make two more attempts to star in a television sitcom during the course of his lengthy career. In 1964, ABC signed him for *Mickey*, which cast him as the owner of a seaside hotel. Unfortunately, his second sitcom venture suffered from almost exactly the same fate as his first. This series had the misfortune to air opposite the original *The Dick Van Dyke Show* (CBS, 1961–66) at the height of its popularity and acclaim; it struggled through one season and was not renewed.

In 1982, back in the spotlight because of his stage hit *Sugar Babies,* Rooney returned to regular TV with NBC's *One of the Boys,* playing an older man who moves into a college dorm with his grandson and another student. Though this, too, was short-lived, one can at least, in retrospect, admire the casting director's eye for little-known talent: Playing the grandson was Nathan Lane, his roommate was Dana Carvey, pre–*Saturday Night Live,* and Carvey's girlfriend was a young Meg Ryan.

It's a puzzler that Mickey Rooney's considerable talent was unable to find proper expression in a TV comedy series, not just once but in three separate tries. He's not alone, however, as the list of box office stars whose TV shows were failures is a fairly long one, encompassing Jimmy Stewart, Jean Arthur, Glenn Ford, Anthony Quinn, and easily a dozen more.

Mr. Adams and Eve

Ida Lupino (*Eve Drake*), Howard Duff (*Howard Adams*), Hayden Rorke (*Steve*), Lee Patrick (*Connie Drake*), Olive Carey (*Elsie*), Alan Reed (*J.B. Hafter*)
Producer: Frederick de Cordova. *Writers*: Bernard Ederer, James Fritzell, Charles Lederer, Louella MacFarlane, Sol Saks, Robert White. *Based on Characters Created by* Collier Young. *Directors*: Frederick de Cordova, Richard Kinon, Don Weis. *Associate Producer*: Warner Taub, Jr. *Director of Photography*: George E. Diskant. *Editorial Supervisor*: Bernard Burton. *Art Directors*: Duncan Cramer, Bill Ross. *Production Supervisor*: Frank Baur. *Editors*: Samuel E. Beetley, Desmond Marquette. *Set Decorator*: Budd S. Friend. *Assistant Director–Production Manager*: James Anderson. *Music Supervisor*: Wilbur Hatch. *Theme*: David Rose. *Hairdresser*: Cherie Banks. *Script Supervisor*: Jane Ficker. *Wardrobe*: Robert Harris, Agnes Henry. Bridget Productions–Four Star Films, in association with CBS-TV.
Aired Fridays at 9 P.M. (through February 1958), then Tuesdays at 8 P.M. on CBS-TV. First aired January 4, 1957; last aired September 23, 1958. 66 black-and-white episodes.

Husband-and-wife movie stars played husband-and-wife movie stars in this CBS sitcom that was more sophisticated than most of its 1950s contemporaries. In the opening titles, the announcer explains, "This is Mr. Adams—and Eve. They play movie stars who are husband and wife. Starring Ida Lupino and Howard Duff—and in real life, they actually are husband and wife. It's *Mr. Adams and Eve*." As this is explained, animated figures of Duff and Lupino emerge from their dressing rooms.

Eve, born of a show business family, is full of drama off-screen as well as on, while Howard (a native of Seattle) is a down-to-earth guy who patiently indulges his wife's excesses. Elsie is their plain-spoken, down-to-earth housekeeper of twelve years' duration, while Steve is their friend and longtime agent. Eve and Howard are under contract to Consolidated Pictures, a studio whose boss is J.B. Hafter. Pragmatic J.B.'s primary motivation is to make profitable movies with titles like *Secret Love*. He reminds Eve and Howard that their pictures have to sound exciting enough to make little old ladies in Iowa go to the movies, instead of staying home to play Scrabble while watching television. In the series opener, guest star Gloria Talbott (*I Married a Monster from Outer Space*) plays a young newcomer given a small role in Eve and Howard's new film. The aspiring actress makes a play for Howard, in a riff on *All About Eve* (1950).

The stories in *Mr. Adams and Eve* often bore more than a passing resemblance to the events in its stars' life. In "This Is Your Life" (2/1/57), Eve's husband and friends conspire to make her the surprised guest on Ralph Edwards' popular show, but a series of misunderstandings leaves Mrs. Adams feeling abandoned and betrayed by her loved ones. Playing herself in this episode, as a friend of Lupino's character, is actress Mala Powers, who was a Lupino discovery and protégée. Not long afterwards, Lupino really was a guest on *This Is Your Life*, and excerpts from the episode were shown.

Lupino was probably the only leading lady on TV whose series concept was dreamed up by her ex-husband. Though she had divorced Collier Young in order to marry Duff, whose child she was carrying at the time they married in 1951, both insisted that there was no awkwardness involved in maintaining their professional collaboration. Young subsequently married actress Joan Fontaine (who made a guest appearance on *Mr. Adams and Eve*), and would later be best known for creating the successful Raymond Burr police drama *Ironside* (NBC, 1967–75).

The pilot episode, written by Young with Charles Lederer, showed Eve Drake and Howard Adams to be a loving couple who are nonetheless capable of spirited arguments. It opens with Howard and Eve attending the Academy Awards ceremony, where both have been nominated. En route to the theater by limousine, both assert firmly that the outcome of the awards will in no way affect their relationship. Eve is named Best Actress, while Howard loses out on Best Actor to a 12-year-old playing a juvenile delinquent. The resulting jealousy threatens to disrupt harmony in the Adams household, especially when Eve makes the mistake of offering some tips to Howard on his acting.

Husband-and-wife movie stars in real life, and on TV in *Mr. Adams and Eve*: Howard Duff and Ida Lupino.

Shortly after Eve's win, she and her husband are booked for an interview on *People to People* (with guest player Joseph Kearns as the Murrow-like interviewer Ned Darrow). The tension that has been rising in the Adams-Drake household comes to a boil in front of the live television audience. Says Howard of his wife's success, as she fumes:

"And she's worked so hard for it, Ned. Years and years! Why, I remember when I was in high school, I thought Eve should have won the award, not Janet Gaynor [thirty years previously, in 1927]. Of course, *Seventh Heaven* was a fine picture, but that job that Eve did in *Jungle Orchids* with that gorilla, mm-hmm!" Eve retaliates by inviting the interviewer into Howard's private den, showing off his collection of "first editions"—*Space Cadet, Prince Valiant,* and other comics.

At the fadeout, Eve and Howard kiss and make up, but there's definitely a sense that there will continue to be a rivalry. Rather than using the pilot as the series opener, CBS buried it midway through the first season, as the show's twelfth aired episode.

Born February 4, 1914, in London, Ida Lupino came from a venerable family of performers. Her father was actor-comedian Stanley Lupino, and from the beginning of her life Ida was exposed to the world of show business. From childhood, she and her sister Rita were appearing in plays staged in a mini-theater constructed by their father in their backyard. As a teenager, she attended the Royal Academy of Dramatic Arts, and not long afterward made her film debut. Arriving in the U.S. in 1933, she proceeded to build an impressive career, first as one of the best-known leading ladies of the 1940s, and later as a director. In the late 1940s, she and Collier Young founded their own film company, Filmakers, Inc. Lupino and Young's enterprise focused primarily on low-budget, realistic dramas like *Not Wanted* (1949), which focused on unwed motherhood, and *Outrage* (1950), controversial for the day in its treatment of the previously taboo screen subject of rape. Had the output of Filmakers been more commercially viable, Lupino might well have retired willingly from acting, but financial strains put the company out of business within a few years.

Lupino made her television series debut when she accepted an offer to join the rotating cast of CBS's *Four Star Playhouse* for the 1955-56 season. The only lead actress in the show's starring quartet that included Charles Boyer, David Niven, and Dick Powell, she appeared in eight series segments that season. The show offered her not only the opportunity to star in various roles, but also to contribute scripts.

Powell, who would increasingly take the reins behind the scenes at Four Star, recognized in Lupino a performer who could do high-caliber work on television, while remaining attuned to the new medium's schedule and budget limitations. He said, "A dame can stop to powder her nose at the wrong time and $3000 goes down the drain. 'Lupey' knows when to powder and when not to powder."[1] According to Four Star director Roy Kellino, she also routinely showed up on time, knowing her script cold, and on one occasion continued to work even after breaking an ankle.

Strong response to Lupino's appearances on that series inspired Four Star executives to place her in her own weekly series, as *Four Star Playhouse* wound down in the spring of 1956. Lupino, who would have happily given up acting in favor of directing by this time, agreed to take on a series for reasons both professional and personal.

Much like Lucille Ball had used *I Love Lucy* to promote the career of her lesser-known husband Desi Arnaz, Lupino wanted *Mr. Adams and Eve* to boost the stock of Howard Duff. Born November 24, 1913, Duff first came to attention as the star of radio's *The Adventures of Sam Spade* in the late 1940s. He had gone on to have a moderately successful film career, though it slowed considerably after he was listed as a suspected Communist sympathizer in *Red Channels*. On more than one occasion, he had played supporting roles in his wife's films. As with *I Love Lucy,* it was by design, not accident, that the title of the Lupino-Duff sitcom put his character ahead of hers, though Lupino (like Ball) retained top billing. The Duffs co-owned the show, produced under their production company named after daughter Bridget.

"You see, honey," Lupino told columnist Erskine Johnson, with tongue perhaps halfway in cheek, "we're *not* just like the people next door. We're movie stars and we live it and act it up like the public thinks movie stars do, and which they sometimes do. Why, even my nightgowns are trimmed with diamonds. All of my clothes are fabulous, and so are Howard's. We not only act like movie stars, but we dress like them."[2] Duff, however, took exception to the idea that he and his wife were playing themselves on TV—"[W]e're a little strange but not *that* strange."[3]

The Adams' house greatly resembled Lupino and Duff's own home. Part of the reason, Lupino told a reporter, was practicality—shooting had begun only two days after the show was sold, with little time available to dress sets. "We stripped the house of furniture, pictures, about everything, in fact, that was not nailed down, and used it all as set dressing," she said.[4]

Said head writer Sol Saks (later the creator of *Bewitched*), "We're trying to show life in Hollywood as it is today through two talented, humorous, energetic people. They are not the couple next door. But if you were lucky enough to live next door to a couple like this, I'd say these people you've got to meet."[5] Saks said the show was aiming for a type of sophisticated comedy exemplified by the 1930s films *My Man Godfrey* and *Nothing Sacred*. He spent time with the Duffs at their home, and drew on many of their own experiences, but chose to present their fictional counterparts more tenderly than the pilot script had done. Subsequent segments concerned the problems that arose when Eve was summoned for jury duty during production of a picture, or embarked on a strict diet to shape up for her next role.

Cast as Eve and Howard's agent Steve was Hayden Rorke (1910–87), known to baby boomer TV fans as Dr. Alfred Bellows on *I Dream of Jeannie* (NBC, 1965–70). Alan Reed (1907–77), seen as studio boss Hafter, was a veteran radio and television performer probably best known as the voice of the beloved cartoon character Fred Flintstone. Introduced in the fifth aired episode of *Mr. Adams and Eve* was Lee Patrick as Eve's mother Connie, also a performer. Patrick had previously played Henrietta on *Topper* (CBS, 1953–55), where she had amply demonstrated her ability to play vague, slightly misconnected women.

Even the Duffs' daughter Bridget got into the act with a brief appearance in the episode "The Ghosts of Consolidated" (5/20/58), playing a young Mary Pickford in a sequence about Eve and Howard's spooky overnight stay at the movie studio, where they are visited by the spirits and memories of prior productions. Another episode featured a cameo appearance by Four Star founder Dick Powell.

Though Lupino and Duff enjoyed the chance to work together, the leading lady inevitably had a longer day than her co-star. "We don't get to the job together because I have to be in makeup at 6:45 A.M.," Lupino explained with a sigh. "Howard lolls in bed until 7 and doesn't have to be on the set until 8:45 A.M."[6]

Serving as the show's producer was Frederick de Cordova, already a veteran of *The George Burns and Gracie Allen Show* (CBS, 1950–58), and later the longtime producer of Johnny Carson's *Tonight Show*. Looking back on his experience working with Lupino and Duff, he remembered mostly "tense and martini-filled weeks," saying that "very few of the comedic scripts were as convoluted as were the problems in getting the day's work done."[7]

Mr. Adams and Eve went into CBS's Friday night schedule as a midseason replacement for *The Crusader*, a drama series starring Brian Keith that had failed to attract an audience. Opening night critics were lukewarm to the Lupino-Duff effort, mostly liking the stars but not the script. Said columnist Hal Humphrey, "Ida's career in TV, and for that matter in the movies, has always had her cast as a woman suffering more than Bette Davis, yet tougher than Humphrey Bogart. It's a pleasure to see her in a comedy role and to discover that she is every bit as adept in that department."[8] Columnist Eve Starr called the series opener "as funny a show as I have seen in a long time, with Duff displaying a hitherto unrevealed knack for comedy that was just plain delightful."[9] Duff and Lupino were encouraged when the show's ratings climbed in subsequent broadcasts.

Though the series didn't crack the Top Ten during its first few months on the air, it performed well enough to be renewed for the 1957-58 season. Its competition going into Year Two would come from the new NBC police drama *M Squad*, starring Lee Marvin, and from Frank Sinatra's musical variety show on ABC. While the Sinatra show was a surprising failure, *M Squad* emerged as a popular series that undoubtedly cut into the audience for *Mr. Adams and Eve*.

In early 1958, CBS moved the show from Friday to Tuesday, where it was paired with the struggling first-season sitcom *The Eve Arden Show*. The explanation given to the stars was that a Tuesday berth would be more conducive to attracting a teenage audience. "Frankly, we didn't have teenagers in mind when we created the show," Duff said, puzzled by the logic.[10] In reality, the move came at the behest of Camel Cigarettes, which sponsored both *Eve* and the current occupant of that Tuesday night spot, *The Phil Silvers Show* (CBS, 1955–59). Silvers' ratings had taken a nosedive against competition from the popular ABC Western *Sugarfoot* and the NBC variety shows of George Gobel and Eddie Fisher.

By then, the bloom was off the rose for some viewers and critics anyway. United Press' William Ewald found *Mr. Adams and Eve* "peopled by phony characters involved in phony situations, all of it peppered with phony dialogue. It is a nonsense series and its 'fun' is ersatz."[11] However, the *Los Angeles Times'* Cecil Smith appreciated the show's efforts to bring sophisticated satire to television, and was sorry to see it take a nosedive with the move to Tuesday nights. Adapting an old show business truism, Smith noted, "Satire, in this case, closes soon — on Tuesday night."[12]

In fact, the move to an 8 P.M. time slot hurt the show, which had little kid appeal, and by early spring it was apparent that the move had been a tactical error where Duff and Lupino's show was concerned. "I think we're being thrown to the wolves," Duff told a columnist in the spring, after consulting the show's dismal ratings in its new time slot.[12] That spring, the falling ratings resulted in CBS canceling the show, as well as *The Eve Arden Show*.

In 1959, with the show already off the air for several months, Lupino was nominated for an Emmy as Best Actress in a Comedy Series, but lost to Jane Wyatt of *Father Knows Best*. Lupino had previously been nominated as Best Actress in a Drama Series for *Four Star Playhouse*. Duff and Lupino re-teamed in 1959 for a guest appearance on one of the hour-long *I Love Lucy* segments seen as a recurring feature in *Desilu Playhouse* (CBS, 1958–60).

While Duff would continue to be a busy actor, with continuing roles in *Dante* (NBC, 1960-61), *The Felony Squad* (ABC, 1966–69), and the prime-time soap opera *Flamingo Road* (NBC, 1981-82), Lupino began to scale back her performing activities in favor of directing. She had a particular fondness for horror and suspense shows, directing several episodes of *Thriller* (NBC, 1960–62), but also helmed episodes of everything from *The Virginian* (NBC, 1962–71) to *Gilligan's Island* (CBS, 1964–67). She also directed the Rosalind Russell film comedy *The Trouble with Angels* (1966).

Though Lupino and Duff would not dissolve their real-life marriage until the 1970s, their happy union was largely kaput by the early 1960s. She would later say that the period co-starring in their own television sitcom had been the happiest and most stable years of their marriage. She died August 3, 1995, having been out of public view for a number of years. By then, her pioneering work as a female director had won her substantial admiration. Duff died in 1990.

In 1999, a similar premise to *Mr. Adams and Eve* was seen in the WB Network's sitcom *Movie Stars*. Harry Hamlin (*L.A. Law*) and Jennifer Grant (daughter of Cary Grant and Dyan Cannon) played husband-and-wife performers, "the picture-perfect Hollywood power couple," as a network press release put it, living in a Malibu beach house with their three children. The show lasted a shorter time than its 1950s counterpart and was off the air by the summer of 2000.

While Lupino and Duff and their colleagues deserve credit for trying to raise the level of quality and sophistication on network TV, it is also probably true that *Mr. Adams and Eve* wasn't germane to many viewers. Nonetheless, this is a well-crafted show that might be better appreciated today than it was in 1958.

Mr. Terrific

Stephen Strimpell (*Stanley Beamish*), Dick Gautier (*Hal Walters*), John McGiver (*Barton J. Reed*), Paul Smith (*Harley Trent*), Bonnie Hughes (*Georgette*)
Executive Producer: Jack Arnold. *Producer*: Budd Grossman. *Writers*: R.S. Allen, Harvey Bulloch, Budd Grossman, David P. Harmon, William Raynor, Myles Wilder. *Directors*: Jack Arnold, Arthur Lubin, Tony Leader, Sidney Miller. *Associate Producer*: Byron Chudnow. *Directors of Photography*: Richard L. Rawlings, Walter Strenge. *Film Editor*: Tony Martinelli. *Sound*: Elbert W. Franklin. *Music*: Gerald Fried. *Assistant Directors*: Burt Astor, Henry Kline. *Editorial Supervisor*: Richard Belding. *Set Decorators*: John McCarthy, Ralph Sylos. *Musical Supervisor*: Stanley Wilson. *Hair Stylist*: Larry Germain. *Color Coordinator*: Robert Brower. Universal Studios.
Aired Mondays at 8 P.M. on CBS-TV. First aired January 9, 1967; last aired August 28, 1967. 17 color episodes.

For whatever reason, there appear to be times in Hollywood when two or more people bring forth basically the same idea. Perhaps the most famous example in sitcom-land was the two-year stretch from 1964 to 1966 in which ABC's *The Addams Family* vied for attention with CBS's *The Munsters*. Another such case involved the CBS superhero spoof *Mr. Terrific* and its NBC counterpart *Captain Nice*. Both shows premiered on the same day in January 1967, and aired for the last time on the same date in August, a few months later.

Mr. Terrific's hero is Stanley Beamish. Stanley and his best friend and roommate Hal are the proprietors of Hal and Stanley's Service Station in Washington, D.C. Hal is handsome, self-confident, a popular ladies' man, and has a busy social schedule. His best friend Stanley is a shy, gentle, nice guy who wishes women paid as much attention to him as they do to Hal.

The government's Bureau of Secret Projects has developed a pill that gives an ordinary man super-strength. For reasons unknown, however, the pill proved too potent for everyone else who tried it, but a computer identifies Stanley (described in the opening narration as "a weak and droopy daffodil") as the perfect candidate. Though Stanley has no experience with this type of work, and not a great deal of aptitude, he is quite pleased to be of service to the government, and readily volunteers to assume a secret identity as Mr. Terrific. From then on, a "Purple Alert" is issued whenever the Bureau has a crisis that calls for his assistance.

When it's time for Mr. Terrific to spring into action, Stanley dons a silver jacket and goggles. Swallowing a pill causes his face to turn a purplish tinge momentarily. Once he's popped a power pill, he can lift an entire house, and knock bad guys through walls with the force of his breath. He's forced to keep his second identity secret even from Hal.

Stanley is rationed to three pills per day, which are doled out to him by

It's a bird ... it's a plane ... it's a flop: Stephen Strimpell is *Mr. Terrific,* the superhero felled not by Kryptonite but by Nielsen ratings.

Mr. Reed's assistant Harley Trent. The first pill gives him an hour's worth of strength. After that, he can take two additional pills that are good for ten minutes each (provided he hasn't misplaced, dropped, or lost them, as is often the case). While fatherly Mr. Reed is happy to have Stanley help on top secret projects, cynical Harley, a former assistant district attorney, wishes they could find someone more competent. Though Stanley usually manages to botch each job he's assigned, ultimately the good guys always triumph in the climactic scene, and the unlikely superhero "comes out smelling like a rose," as Harley says grumpily.

In the pilot, Stanley is assigned to catch a speeding train en route so that he can rendezvous with a man who will sell the government an invention that stops any machine in action. Fumbling Stanley instead gives the $30,000 to a salesman for a doll that he mistakenly believes contains the weapon.

His later assignments include preventing a valuable jewel from being stolen at a foreign embassy's dinner party. In "Stanley the Jailbreaker" (3/6/67), Stanley goes undercover as a prison inmate, Slippery Sloane, so that he can help break out a notorious thief and recover the $2 million in loot that he hid somewhere on the outside before being jailed. In "Stanley the Fighter" (2/27/67), he impersonates a prizefighter so that he can infiltrate a ring of counterfeiters operating out of a local gymnasium.

As previously mentioned, *Mr. Terrific* was one of two superhero sitcoms that premiered on January 9, 1967. Thirty minutes after this show, NBC unveiled the first episode of *Captain Nice*, Buck Henry's sitcom about a mild-mannered chemist, Carter Nash, who discovers a secret formula. That show featured William Daniels (later the star of the critically acclaimed 1980s drama *St. Elsewhere*) as the hero, Ann Prentiss as his policewoman sidekick Candy Kane, and Alice Ghostley as his nagging mother, who wishes he'd named himself Wonderman or Musclehead.

The networks' enthusiasm for a comic take on superhero antics was no doubt fueled by the surprise success of ABC's *Batman*, which became a nationwide fad shortly after its debut in early 1966. The ongoing popularity of *Get Smart* (NBC and CBS, 1965–70) also seemed to show that there was an appetite for spoofs.

Mr. Terrific was originally intended to be a vehicle for actor Alan Young, who had recently finished his run as the star of *Mister Ed* (CBS, 1961–66). Young played Stanley in a pilot episode for producer Edward J. Montagne, known for *McHale's Navy* (ABC, 1962–66) and its less successful offshoot *Broadside* (ABC, 1964-65). The initial script was the work of writers George Balzer, Hal Goldman, Al Gordon, and Joel Kane, and was directed by Don Weis.

As played by Young, Stanley is a clumsy but well-intended shoe salesman at Finney's Department Store. His co-worker and girlfriend Gloria Dickinson (played by Sheilah Welles) is threatening to break off their engagement unless he asks tyrannical boss Mr. Finney (Jesse White) for a raise.

Having downed his first pill, Stanley instantly has highly intensified hearing (he says to a fly on the ground, "Will you stop that tramping up and down!") and super-strength. Tests prove that the pill remains potent for four hours and twelve minutes. In the pilot, Stanley is permitted to take a second pill only after a half hour has elapsed; otherwise, according to its inventor, "You'd explode."

Recruited to assist the Office of Special Assignments, Stanley springs into action when the Chief (Edward Andrews) is kidnapped by "an Iron Curtain ice skating troupe." The role was a physically demanding one for Young, then in his mid-forties.

The pilot was a candidate for CBS's fall 1966 schedule, and in February AP's Bob Thomas included it in a list of pilots that industry observers predicted would sell. However, when the network failed to give the green light to *Mr. Terrific*, it was substantially revamped, and re-staffed both in front of and behind the cameras. The producers, writers, and directors who had worked on Alan Young's *Mr. Terrific* were all replaced for the regular series.

Captain Nice creator Buck Henry was gracious when asked about similarities between his show and *Mr. Terrific*, and seemed quite content to believe that it was coincidence that had resulted in the two shows landing on the network schedules simultaneously. "But if I'd known about *Mr. Terrific*, I wouldn't have done *Captain Nice*," Henry admitted.[1] Executives at Universal Studios, however, were not pleased when they got their first look at *Captain Nice*, and complained loudly to NBC that their basic idea had been swiped.

As *Mr. Terrific* star Stephen Strimpell saw his character, "He is a total innocent, without any sense of evil, born not to recognize villains. It is the struggle of a very little man against the world."[2] In real life, Strimpell was a 26-year-old newcomer to television who'd earned a law degree at Columbia University before taking up an acting career. Born January 17, 1937, he was interested in acting from childhood, but discouraged from pursuing it by his parents. Something of a child prodigy, Strimpell finished high school shortly after his fifteenth birthday, whizzed through law school in three years, and was a duly acknowledged member of the New York bar at the age of 21.

Despite his burgeoning law career, Strimpell was still fascinated with the theater, and began making a name for himself in Off Broadway shows like *Dumbell People in a Barbell World*. Critics didn't always like the shows, but they noticed the young actor. Making his Broadway debut in a show called *The Sunday Man*, Strimpell was described by Dorothy Kilgallen in her syndicated column (5/14/64) as "someone for the talent scouts to catch. He's stopped the show at the previews." He was spotted by a television executive while appearing in a Broadway show called *The Exhaustion of Our Son's Love*. In Hollywood, some felt he resembled a young Red Buttons.

Ironically, Strimpell was brought west to read for the lead role in *Captain Nice*. He made a good test, but was passed over by producer Buck Henry in favor of the older William Daniels. (Strimpell later said that he was auditioned primarily as a studio ploy to keep Daniels' salary demands low.) But when executive producer Jack Arnold saw Strimpell's *Captain Nice* test, "I knew immediately I had my Mr. Terrific."[3] Since Strimpell was a newcomer to television, he was warmed up for his starring role by playing a guest appearance in *Run, Buddy, Run* (CBS, 1966-67).

Publicly, at least, the leading man's only complaint concerning his role in *Mr. Terrific* was the discomfort he sustained when shooting flying scenes. "They put me in a device," Strimpell said, "which must have been invented by Torquemada"[4]— the mechanical lift, known as "Jumping Jack" to the show's cast and crew, from which he was often suspended for several hours at a stretch. His usual workday began at 6 A.M. and continued until around 6 P.M. For the riskier action scenes, he had the assistance of stuntman Chuck Courtney.

Cast as Hal was Dick Gautier (born October 30, 1931), who'd enjoyed great success as Conrad Birdie in the Broadway hit *Bye Bye Birdie*. After moving to Hollywood, he'd done various TV guest shots, most notably several appearances as Hymie the robot on *Get Smart*. Not contracted as a regular on that series, he gave up the recurring gig temporarily for the steadier employment of *Mr. Terrific*. He later resurfaced as the leading man of *When Things Were Rotten*, Mel Brooks' short-lived 1975 ABC sitcom that parodied Robin Hood. Interviewed on the eve of the show's premiere, while shooting the eighth episode of *Mr. Terrific*, Gautier said cautiously, "So far I like it, but I'm really too close to judge. We'll just have to wait and see what it looks like on the small screen."[5]

John McGiver (1913–75), who played *Mr. Terrific*'s fatherly boss, was a familiar face to most TV viewers. He broke into the medium in the 1950s, playing roles in the better anthology dramas of the period (*Kraft Television Theatre, Studio One,* and others). In later years, he would drift more toward comedic roles. He played the star role in *Many Happy Returns,* a sitcom that ran to indifferent audience reaction during the 1964-65 season on CBS. After *Mr. Terrific*, he was a regular on *The Jimmy Stewart Show* (1971-72), as Dr. Luther Quince.

Paul Smith, featured as Barton Reed's cynical assistant Harley Trent, had been a regular on *Mrs. G. Goes to College* (q.v.) and went on to a featured role in *The Doris Day Show* (CBS, 1968–73). Added to the cast of *Mr. Terrific* in a recurring role after it got underway was newcomer Bonnie Hughes as George (full name Georgette), a pretty young lady hired by Hal to work as an attendant at the gas station.

Serving as the show's executive producer and principal director was Jack Arnold, best-known for directing popular 1950s Universal monster movies like *Creature from the Black Lagoon* (1954) and *The Incredible Shrinking Man* (1957). Arnold had also been associated with *Gilligan's Island* (CBS, 1964–67) before taking on *Mr. Terrific*. Some freelance writers contributed to the show, but writer-producer Budd Grossman, whose credits included *Dennis the Menace* (CBS, 1959–63), provided the bulk of the scripts.

Mr. Terrific went into the CBS lineup as a mid-season replacement for the low-rated sitcom *Run, Buddy, Run*, which had premiered the preceding September. Providing a lead-in the 7:30 P.M. spot was *Gilligan's Island*, enjoying solid ratings in its third season. Opening night ratings for *Mr. Terrific* were surprisingly strong according to Trendex surveys of larger TV markets, outpacing *I Dream of Jeannie* on NBC and the western drama *The Iron Horse* on ABC. *Captain Nice*, condemned to go head-to-head with CBS's *The Lucy Show* (1962–68), didn't fare so well, though some critics pegged it as "by far better plotted, fleshed out, sustained and produced" than its CBS counterpart.

At the time *Mr. Terrific* and *Captain Nice* made their bows, *Los Angeles Times* columnist Hal Humphrey reported wearily that TV fans "are in for more and more of this so-called spoofing of other series," noting that shows called *Walter of the Jungle* and *Alfred of the Amazon*, both seemingly parodies of *Tarzan*, were in development for future airing.[6]

Though viewers sampled the new show, they evidently didn't come back for more. By mid–February, after only a few episodes had aired, the Associated Press' Cynthia Lowry reported that *Mr. Terrific* was unlikely to be renewed for the 1967-68 season. A few weeks later, CBS officially canceled the show, as NBC likewise unloaded *Captain Nice*. The show's cancellation struck most observers as no great tragedy. Humphrey posthumously awarded *Mr. Terrific* his prize for Worst Situation Comedy of 1967, calling it an "asinine takeoff on Superman."[7] Universal would later try to recoup some of its losses by cobbling together footage from the series into the TV-movie *The Pill Caper*.

Strimpell continued to play occasional film and TV roles through the mid–1980s, taking particular pride in his role in the acclaimed indie *Hester Street* (1974), but was better-known in his later years as a respected acting teacher in New York. In an interview given to Mark Phillips, the actor looked back on *Mr. Terrific* with almost complete negativity and an abiding bitterness over his Hollywood experience. He had nothing good to say about any of his co-stars, calling John McGiver "a nasty, sullen, and arrogant old man," who on the first day of shooting, purportedly said to Strimpell's face, "Will someone tell this idiot New York method actor where the camera is?"[8] Paul Smith and Dick Gautier, according to Strimpell, resented their subsidiary roles in the series. Strimpell died on April 10, 2006.

Creatively, *Mr. Terrific* is, sad to say, almost a complete misfire. It's difficult to understand why CBS executives would have thought this version of the show any more viable than the Alan Young pilot, which was in many ways superior to the one they greenlighted. Though kids might have liked the special effects used in the show's action scenes, they were not frequent enough to keep them watching through the talky remainder of the show, which also had little appeal for adults.

Mrs. G. Goes to College / The Gertrude Berg Show

Gertrude Berg (*Sarah Green*), Cedric Hardwicke (*Professor W.W. Crayton*), Mary Wickes (*Winona Maxfield*), Skip Ward (*Joe Caldwell*), Paul Smith (*George Howell*), Aneta Corsaut (*Irma Howell*), Karyn Kupcinet (*Carol Martin*), Marion Ross (*Susan Benson*), Leo Penn (*Jerry Benson*)
Producer: Hy Averback. *Writers*: Cherney Berg, Gertrude Berg, Bill Davenport, Jim Fritzell, Everett Greenbaum, Howard Merrill, Arthur Stander. *Directors*: Hy Averback, Robert Butler, Marc Daniels, Richard Kinon. *Associate Producers*: Bob Claver, Bill Harmon. *Directors of Photography*: Howard Schwartz, Harry J. Wild. *Production Managers*: Lloyd Allen, Bruce Fowler, Jr., Norman Powell. *Assistant Director*: Don Torpin. *Supervising Art Director*: Bill Ross. *Art Directors*: Russell Forrest, Frank Hotaling. *Set Decorators*: Carl Biddiscombe, Andy Nealis. *Production Supervisor*: Jack Sonntag. *Editorial Supervisor*: Bernard Burton. *Editors*: Arthur D. Hilton, Chandler House, Thomas Neff. *Wardrobe*: Robert B. Harris. *Music Editors*: Harry King, Aubrey Lind. *Casting*: Marjory McKay. *Music Supervisor*: Herschel Burke Gilbert. *Music Scoring*: Rudy Schrager. *Sound*: Jack Solomon. *Sound Effects*: Monty Pearce, Kay Rose. *Makeup Artists*: Mel Berns, Burris Grimwood, Webster Phillips. Four Star–Jahfa Productions.
Aired Wednesdays at 9:30 P.M. (through December 1961), then Thursdays at 9:30 P.M. on CBS-TV. First aired October 4, 1961; last aired April 5, 1962. 26 black-and-white episodes.

One of the most successful and beloved stars of radio and early television, Gertrude Berg returned for one last bow in the endearing but overlooked CBS sitcom *Mrs. G. Goes to College*. Creator-star of the longtime family favorite *The Goldbergs* (originally, *The Rise of the Goldbergs*), Berg represented the prototypical loving Jewish mother to a generation of Americans. In *Mrs. G. Goes to College*, Berg cast herself as a sixtyish woman who fulfills her lifelong dream of completing her education. It was an ideal vehicle for the warm and gentle comedy she had spent a lifetime perfecting.

Born October 3, 1899, as Tillie Edelstein, the future Gertrude Berg had her first taste of performing in the Catskills resort hotel operated by her father, where she put on impromptu shows to entertain the guests. Married to Lewis Berg in 1918, Tillie eventually became the mother to daughter Harriet and son Cherney, but aspired to find an outlet for her writing gifts. In the early days of network radio, she persuaded NBC executives to give her a prime time slot for her gentle comedy-drama about the family life of a working-class Jewish clan called the Goldbergs. Over the next quarter-century, Molly Goldberg would become Berg's most enduring character, so much so that fans often drew little distinction between the character and the woman who created her. After a long run on radio, Berg adapted her characterizations into a successful Broadway show, *Me and Molly,* in 1948, and soon after invaded television.

Despite her radio success, Berg had something of a bumpy ride where TV was concerned. At first, neither CBS nor NBC had faith in a video adaptation of *The Goldbergs,* regardless of its previous track record, and it took a personal appeal to CBS honcho William Paley for Berg to get her shot at TV stardom. She soon proved herself worthy of his intervention. In the early days of television, urban audiences in New York and other cities made up much of the available viewing audience. Thanks to them, *The Goldbergs* was an enormous hit, selling untold numbers of cans of its sponsor's Sanka coffee, and netting its star an Emmy as Best Actress in 1951.

Not long after *The Goldbergs* launched a TV version, however, her leading man, actor Philip Loeb, found himself listed in *Red Channels* and publicly branded a suspected Communist. Under much pressure to fire Loeb and recast the role of her TV husband, Berg refused to do so, forcing her show off the air and damaging her career. By the late 1950s, after *The Goldbergs* had been revived for brief runs on the dying DuMont network, and as a filmed sitcom for first-run syndication, it appeared that her most famous creation had worn out its welcome. Since her radio and TV fans recognized Berg for no other role, it remained to be seen whether this meant the end of her career as well.

After *The Goldbergs,* Berg made some television appearances and played in summer stock productions, but wanted to do more. In 1959, she made a triumphant return to the Broadway stage, playing the tailor-made role of a Jewish widow in Leonard Spigelgass' comedy *A Majority of One.* Her unlikely leading man was the acclaimed classical actor Sir Cedric Hardwicke, playing a rather atypical romantic role (not to mention a native of Japan, which observers at the time insisted he did believably).

Because her performance was so good, many viewers assumed that the Broadway role was written with her in mind, but Berg was honest enough to shoot down that myth. "Oh, no," she said laughingly. "First they wanted Thelma Ritter, then Ruth Gordon."[1] The playwright and his producers apparently were leery of casting Berg, fearful that viewers would only see Molly Goldberg onstage. To which Berg's friend Garson Kanin responded, "So what's wrong with that? It might even sell a few tickets."[2]

It did. The show was a huge hit, both critically and commercially, earning Berg a Best Actress Tony the following year. Regardless, she was passed over for the film version in favor of Rosalind Russell, a casting decision that Berg learned of only when she read it in *The New York Times.* But the show's success reminded television executives that audiences adored Berg, and might welcome her return in a network series. In 1960, while in the midst of a national tour with *A Majority of One*, Berg was invited by Four Star Television, the successful production company helmed by Dick Powell, to star in a pilot for a new situation comedy. Rather than starring in a vehicle developed by someone else, Berg was given the opportunity to create a new sitcom format in collaboration with her writer son Cherney, who'd also co-authored her recent autobiography *Molly and Me*.

The Bergs developed a concept centering on a widow's late-in-life enrollment in college. The new show's working title was *Mother Was a Freshman* but this was changed, probably because of the similarity to *Mother Is a Freshman*, a 1949 Fox film comedy starring Loretta Young. From there, the title became *The Freshman*, but ultimately CBS placed Berg's new show on the schedule as *Mrs. G. Goes to College*. As one commentator noted, whatever the title onscreen, to most viewers it would be simply the Gertrude Berg show, anyway. Because she'd worked so well with Cedric Hardwicke in *A Majority of One*, Berg had a role for him in the new series as well, and insisted she would do the show only if he joined her.

In the pilot, "The First Day," which also aired as the series opener on October 4, 1961, sixtyish widow Sarah Green is arriving for her first day as a freshman student at Western University, accompanied by her married daughter Susie. After the camera pans past an anxious mother seeing her daughter off to school, and pinning her "Freshman" badge on her lapel, we see Susie and Sarah. The laugh track gives a chuckle when Berg, instead of her TV daughter, dons the "Freshman" badge. Wid-

Two unlikely college students: Gertrude Berg (Sarah) and guest star Fabian in *Mrs. G. Goes to College.*

owed after 31 years of marriage to Sam Green, a dressmaker whose specialty was "stylish stouts," Sarah is fulfilling her longtime dream of getting a college education. While raising her family, she completed her high school education at night school, though it took her twelve years. Now she's ready for college, but daughter Susie is dubious, and tries to persuade her mother to do something more suitable:

> SUSIE (coaxing): When you visited Aunt Dora in Florida last year, there was that nice Mr. Arnold. You could get married again.
> SARAH: Please...
> SUSIE: He'd still like to marry you.
> SARAH (smiling): Yeah, I'm afraid he'll have to wait. I don't think a girl should get married before she finishes school.

That scene, which concludes with Sarah walking up the steps into the classroom building to begin her new life, serves as a prologue leading into the show's opening titles. Unusual for the time, each episode of *Mrs. G. Goes to College* would go directly into the action, playing a brief scene before the music swelled and the words "Gertrude Berg" appeared onscreen. Sharing above-the-title billing with Hardwicke, Berg and her co-star's credits, along with the series title, would usually be flashed over the conclusion of the show's first scene, rather than featuring a separate titles sequence. The show's theme music, resembling a school band's marching song, helped set the mood, as did the exterior shots filmed on the University of Southern California campus.

Of her fellow students, the most prominently featured is freshman Joe Caldwell (Skip Ward), who befriends Mrs. G. on her first day at school, though he finds her hard to accept as a student at first glance. "Maybe it'll help if tomorrow I wear my saddle shoes?" she says with a smile. Joe arrives at college concerned mainly with identifying the "snap" classes, and earning good enough grades to avoid being drafted into military service. Under Mrs. G.'s influence, he develops a mother-son bond with Sarah Green, and together they team as lab partners in chemistry class (with guest star Peter Lorre as their professor). Actor Ward had previously played a young San Francisco police officer in the final season (1959-60) of Desilu's *The Lineup*.

Her adviser is Professor W.W. Crayton (Hardwicke), who is on exchange from Cambridge University. Initially, the hard-nosed Crayton is equally skeptical about this new student, whom he suspects of being "the type that thinks it would be just grand fun to go to college, and be a character, and draw attention to herself, instead of sitting in the quiet dignity of her parlor, as befits her years." Despite his initial rebuff, he will soon learn that, unlike many of his younger students, Sarah has a real respect for education. Like Berg, who in real life married husband Lewis partially because he respected her intellect, and promised to help her develop her gifts, Sarah values education for its own sake rather than the monetary rewards most of the young students seek.

The much-admired character actress Mary Wickes was featured in the series as Maxie, the pragmatic and salty-tongued widow who operates a boarding house for students called the Maxfield Apartments, and becomes a good friend to Sarah. Because her character is so down-to-earth and deglamorized, it will come as a slight surprise when we learn in a later episode that her given name is Winona. Wickes, a television veteran whose credits in the medium stretched back to the late 1940s, had one of her best showcases here.

Aside from Mrs. G. and Joe, Maxie's tenants included young psychology instructor George Howell (Paul Smith), his wife Irma (Aneta Corsaut), and their baby son Joey. Various young female residents had small speaking roles in early episodes as well, until Karyn Kupcinet, as Carol, became the most frequently seen.

Berg wrote the pilot script herself, in collaboration with her son Cherney and veteran sitcom writer Arthur Stander. Though she had written thousands of *Goldbergs* scripts over the course of the show's twenty-odd-year life, maintaining an extremely demanding schedule as producer, writer, and star, she did not propose to do the same with *Mrs. G. Goes to College*. While Cherney contributed several scripts, mostly co-authored with Howard Merrill, Mrs. Berg took no writing credit on episodes beyond the pilot. Instead, teams like Jim Fritzell and Everett Greenbaum, known for their work on character-driven comedy shows like *Mr. Peepers* (NBC, 1952–55) and *The Andy Griffith Show* (CBS, 1960–68), provided scripts.

Berg's contribution to the writing took the form of adding what she termed "raisins in the cake"— single lines of dialogue or bits of business that helped characterize and individualize Sarah Green. On *The Goldbergs,* she had been famous for her one-sided conversations out the kitchen window with her never-seen neighbor, Mrs. Bloom. The equivalent recurring bit on *Mrs. G. Goes to College* involved her regular telephone conversations with sister Dora, who lived in Florida, conducted from the pay phone in the hallway of Maxie's boarding house.

Because Berg was so fully identified with the Molly Goldberg type, some observers believed that she simply played herself onscreen, and thought her abilities as an actress limited. Hardwicke saw it differently. "I say versatility is not the greatest quality in an actress," Hardwicke told a *TV Guide* reporter in 1961. "When you look at a Reubens you don't have to be told who painted it. That's style, style, style. With it an actress can turn base metal into gold. And Mrs. Berg is an actress."[3]

But if viewers saw Sarah as merely an updated version of Molly Goldberg, the star felt no need to argue the point. In fact, one reporter said that she wanted the character to be Molly, several years later, and was disappointed when she was told the name could not be used.

Mrs. G. pleased critics like the Associated Press' Cynthia Lowry. "It is a funny show in the gentle and perceptive way which is a specialty of Miss Berg ... a warm, thoroughly nice show, well done and has— praise to the producer —

a discreet laugh track."[4] *Variety* (10/11/61) gave it "a tentative nod," liking the stars' chemistry and crediting it with some good laughs, though complaining that some clichés crept in along the way. The show offered relatively few overt jokes, but instead presented an engaging group of characters and a very pleasant atmosphere.

Not really a full-fledged regular in the series, actress Marion Ross (later Marion Cunningham on *Happy Days*) appeared in the pilot and a couple of later episodes as Sarah's married daughter Susie. Actor-director Leo Penn played Sarah's son-in-law Jerry (mistakenly identified as her son in some sources), while Mae Questel, known for her vocal renditions of Betty Boop and Olive Oyl, made a couple of appearances as Jerry's mother Jennie. Ross, then a fresh-faced all-American Midwestern type, seemed an odd choice to play the daughter of the show's obviously Jewish leading lady, and the character would be seen only a few times in the series. Instead, Mrs. G. became a surrogate mother to most of her fellow students at Maxie's.

While depicting challenges like her first chemistry test, *Mrs. G. Goes to College* largely presented an optimistic and positive view of college life, and a healthy respect for the privilege of education. Such stock elements as pep rallies, cheerleaders, and fraternity or sorority life played no significant role. Though the show never lost its charm and warmth, it was clear that Berg wanted to share with her viewers what she considered the more important aspects of college. "I'm a square," the star admitted in an interview upon the new show's debut. "I have faith and hope. Life has been very good to me, darling, and they haven't dropped the bomb yet, and I still believe we can have peace. Maybe that's what we have most in common, Molly and Mrs. Jacoby [from *A Majority of One*] and Mrs. G. and me, hope and faith."[5]

By mid-season, with ratings for *Mrs. G. Goes to College* less than stellar, CBS announced changes. In January 1962, the series was retitled *The Gertrude Berg Show* and moved from its Wednesday time slot to Thursday. There it would face competition primarily from NBC's new hit sitcom *Hazel* (1961–66), starring Oscar winner Shirley Booth as the goodhearted, busybody maid. This schedule change would make the 9:30 P.M. slot on Thursday completely dominated by sitcoms starring female characters, as ABC beamed *Margie* (q.v.) at the same time. Acting as Berg's lead-in on CBS would be *Tell It to Groucho*, the new quiz show that followed in the wake of Groucho Marx's long run with NBC's *You Bet Your Life* (1950–61). Replacing *Mrs. G. Goes to College* on CBS's Wednesday night schedule was another struggling first-year sitcom, *The Dick Van Dyke Show*, which had originally been inappropriately placed in an 8 P.M. slot not conducive to adult audiences.

"Maxie's Silent Partner," the show's thirteenth episode and the first to air under the new title, introduced a few new story elements as well. Finding herself in financial straits, Maxie sells a partial interest in her boarding house to Mrs. G. Joining the ranks of the tenants is none other than Professor Crayton.

Indications from the network were that subsequent episodes would focus more on the personal lives of the residents of the Maxfield Apartments, and less on the ins and outs of academic life.

Guest stars were worked into the show as well, particularly some who were expected to attract the younger generation to Berg's show. Subsequent episodes spotlighted the Kingston Trio, as well as pop singer Fabian, cast as a student at odds with his father over his desire to join the Peace Corps.

Throughout the bulk of the show's 26 segments, there had been no more than an occasional hint that the mutual admiration society developing between Sarah Green and Professor Crayton could possibly develop into a romance. However, toward the latter part of the season, there were moves in that direction. When Maxie and Sarah are making a list of eligible professors who might be matched with a student's widowed mother (guest star Arlene Francis) in "The Mother Affair" (2/1/62), Sarah balks at putting Professor Crayton on the list, though she won't say why. Finally, in "Curfew Shall Not Ring Tonight" (3/15/62), Mrs. G. accepts an invitation from her professor to accompany him to the opera. The following week, in "Gentleman Caller" (3/22/62), Crayton shows definite signs of jealousy when it appears that Mrs. G. has accepted a date with another man.

Though the move of *The Gertrude Berg Show* to Thursday nights provided enough competition to knock *Hazel* out of television's list of top ten shows, the show was not renewed for a second year. Berg was an Emmy nominee for Best Actress that spring, and her co-star Wickes was likewise nominated in the Supporting category.

The Gertrude Berg Show would be the last regular series role for both of its stars. In the spring of 1963, Berg returned to Broadway in the comedy *Dear Me, the Sky Is Falling,* which ran for a respectable 145 performances. It was the last major achievement of her career. On September 14, 1966, she died of heart failure. Her TV co-star, Sir Cedric Hardwicke, had passed away two years earlier. Even the young actress Karyn Kupcinet, featured as Carol Martin in Berg's sitcom, died not long after its cancellation. Kupcinet, the daughter of Chicago newspaper and television journalist Irv Kupcinet, was murdered on Thanksgiving Day 1963, a case that has remained one of Hollywood's unsolved mysteries ever since.

Others affiliated with the show went on to further success. Aneta Corsaut was soon cast in her most famous television role, as Helen Crump on *The Andy Griffith Show,* while Mary Wickes amassed hundreds of additional TV credits, including recurring roles in *Julia* (NBC, 1968–71) and *Doc* (CBS, 1975-76), and a co-starring role in *The Father Dowling Mysteries* (NBC and ABC, 1989–91), before her death in 1995 at the age of 85.

Thirty-five years after the premiere of *Mrs. G. Goes to College,* CBS launched a new sitcom with a very similar premise. *Pearl* cast Rhea Perlman, the Emmy-winning co-star of *Cheers* (NBC, 1982–93), as a widow fulfilling her longtime dream of attending college. But the resemblance to Berg's show went beyond the basic premise: Perlman's character, too, found herself under the tutelage of a rather snobbish and dismissive Britisher, played in this instance by Malcolm McDowell. Not a ratings hit, *Pearl* lasted for only the 1996-97 season and was then canceled.

In today's more cynical age, it's difficult to imagine a network offering viewers a show like *Mrs. G. Goes to College.* Nevertheless, viewed nearly fifty years after its creation, the show holds up well. Given the fact that so much of Gertrude Berg's work is lost to modern audiences, it's even more regrettable that so few contemporary viewers have an opportunity to see her second series.

My Hero

Robert Cummings (*Robert S. Beanblossom*), Julie Bishop (*Julie Marshall*), John Litel (*Willis Thackery*)
Producers: Edmund Beloin, Robert Cummings, Mort Greene. *Writers*: Dick Conway, Robert Cummings, Jack Elinson, Roland MacLane, Norman Paul, Maurice Richlin, Ben Starr, Rik Vollaerts. *Directors*: Harold Daniels, Leslie Goodwins, Oscar Rudolph. *Production Supervisor*: Ruby Rosenberg. *Director of Photography*: George E. Diskant. *Art Director*: Ralph Berger. *Set Decorator*: Glen Daniels. *Music Composed and Conducted by* Leon Klatzkin. *Editors*: Samuel E. Beetley, Frank Doyle, James E. Smith, Sherman Todd. *Assistant Director*: John Pommer. *Makeup Artist*: Karl Herlinger. *Miss Bishop's Clothes*: De De Johnson. Four Star Productions–Don Sharpe Enterprises.
Aired Saturdays at 7:30 P.M. (through April 1953), then Saturdays at 8 P.M. on NBC-TV. First aired November 8, 1952; last aired August 1, 1953. 33 black-and-white episodes.

A major sitcom star of the 1950s, Bob Cummings is well-remembered for his role as a cheerfully lecherous photographer surrounded by beautiful models in *The Bob Cummings Show* (seen in reruns as *Love That Bob!*). Prior to that successful series, though, Cummings made his first major foray into TV with this 1952-53 sitcom that's rarely seen today.

Robert Beanblossom is a haplessly incompetent real estate salesman employed by the firm of Thackery Real Estate in Southern California. At the end of a week, while other salesmen have racked up impressive commissions, Bob is likely to owe the firm money. (Later episodes, however, will show Bob as the small firm's only salesman.) Low man on the totem pole, he is at first given an office that seems to be a converted closet. His cramped workspace is decorated with motivational signs—"Never take no for an answer"; "Never be late."

Beanblossom is, in fact, such an incompetent salesman that it fairly begs the question of how he obtained, and keeps, his job. His grouchy boss, Willis Thackery, explains that, when he was in the hospital three years earlier, he needed a transfusion, and the only person who had the blood type needed was Bob Beanblossom. Sighs Mr. Thackery, "I've Beanblossom blood running in my veins." Another episode hints at a different explanation. Thackery, a 27-year veteran of the real estate field, chastises his incompetent salesman:

> THACKERY: Your father, Hiram Beanblossom, was one of the finest real estate men I've ever known. But you ... you ... how do you explain it?

BOB: Well, sir, Mr. Thackery, I try to do everything just the way you tell me. I usually get the customer just to the point where they're ready to say yes.
THACKERY: Then what happens?
BOB: Well, frankly, sir ... they say no.

Bob's girlfriend, who's considerably smarter than he, is Julie Marshall, secretary to Mr. Thackery, who terms her "the most efficient secretary in Southern California." It is often Julie who intercedes and saves the day when Thackery's short fuse, combined with Bob's incompetence, leads to the boss' cry, "Beanblossom, you're fired!"

In a typical early episode, "The Movie Star" (11/22/52), Mr. Thackery's latest client is film actor Reginald Denny (playing himself). Thackery and Denny have a golf date, and need a third player, so Julie sends Bob. Bob, who's more accustomed to playing miniature golf, nevertheless shows up in some ridiculous vintage sportswear that belonged to his father, and an instruction book written by the late Mr. Beanblossom, Sr. (*How to Play Golf in Spite of the Weather*). Though he's been warned by his boss that Denny hates to lose, and

Bob Cummings and wife Mary are surrounded by their children. As co-owner of *My Hero*, he kept a tight rein on costs, saying, "Whenever we go over the budget, it comes out of my baby's food."

despite Bob's own ineptitude as a golfer (he shatters the windshield of a nearby car, and beans the workman mowing the greens with an errant ball), he somehow wins the game. Trying to make amends with the angered client, Julie agrees to a lunch date with Denny, who has the reputation of being a wolf. Jealous Bob disguises himself as a fellow diner, hiding behind his newspaper which has had holes cut in the pages so that he can spy on his girlfriend (and feed himself). Denny retaliates by lighting the newspaper on fire, leaving hapless Bob to be doused by a waiter with a seltzer bottle. And that's only the first half of the episode....

Most of the episodes called for Cummings' character to interact with a beautiful woman or two (actress Mary Beth Hughes guested in the series opener). As an NBC press release explained it, "It seems that lovable charm boy Robert S. Beanblossom (who doesn't seem wholly possessed of all his buttons) has an unusual effect on almost all of the feminine gender. Exotic and various ladies fight for his smiles, swoon for his caresses, but leave Beanblossom merely embarrassed and confused."[1]

At the end of each episode, when things unexpectedly come out all right, Julie embraces Bob and exclaims, "My hero!" He usually responds, at least in the early episodes, with steam coming out of his ears. Said Cummings, "Beanblossom is a sort of lovable jerk who muddles through life sublimely unaware of reality, who seems always to land out of trouble through some kind of strange luck."[2]

Born June 10, 1908, as Charles Clarence Robert Orville Cummings, the actor began his career in New York. Since British actors were all the rage at the time, Cummings promptly dubbed himself Blade Stanhope Conway, with accent to match. He made his Broadway debut in a short-lived 1931 show called *The Roof*. Later, when Hollywood casting directors wanted Texans, he obligingly converted himself into Brice Hutchens, claiming a Texan upbringing. He broke into films in the early 1930s, and had racked up more than 50 film credits by the time he turned to television work in the early 1950s. Never a top-rank star, Cummings nevertheless appeared in some genuine film classics, like Alfred Hitchcock's *Saboteur* (1942), though he readily admitted that he was often cast in roles that someone else had turned down. He interrupted his career only for his World War II service as an Army flight instructor.

Cummings' agent Don Sharpe was instrumental in placing the star on television. Having previously helped Lucille Ball get a TV berth, and launched several of his TV-wary clients into *Four Star Playhouse* (CBS, 1952–56), Sharpe made a savvy deal for Cummings. The star would own a substantial piece of his television show.

Before the weekly series got underway, however, there were adjustments made to the concept as originally developed. The pilot episode, "El Toro," written by Mitchell Lindemann and directed by Fred Guiol, cast the star as Donald Sherlock Holmes, bumbling real estate agent ("Holmes Homes Are Happy

Homes"), who doubles as an amateur detective. Julie Bishop appeared as Julie Marshall, with Chick Chandler as Don's rival Conrad. Though the series format and the star's character were different, the pilot nonetheless aired as the ninth episode of *My Hero.*

NBC placed *My Hero* on its Saturday evening schedule, where its main competition was CBS's popular stunt game show *Beat the Clock* (1950–58). Critic Bob Foster, an admirer of Cummings' work in films, was dismayed by the first two episodes of *My Hero*: "[F]or the present, there is a lot of room for improvement."[3] *Time* (11/24/52) was kinder, saying, "The gags are broad ... and so is the acting, but there are plenty of simple-minded laughs."

Said critic John Crosby, "*My Hero* is really a very funny and engaging light comedy, largely because of Cummings, who not only acts the role of Robert S. Beanblossom but also helps write and produce it.... The plots of these wingdings are outrageously implausible but they are written pretty much tongue in cheek so it doesn't matter greatly."[4] Crosby, in one of his less astute professional judgments, thought the show could give *I Love Lucy* a run for its money.

"A Beanblossom," the star told Crosby, "is an amateur inventor who turns out such useful items as a supersonic ray gun cigarette lighter that you can depend upon to explode during a demonstration. This fellow has a father who was perfect at everything and his son never stood a chance—even if he were normal—which he is not. He has phenomenal luck, most of it bad. While he loses every battle, he manages to win the last, but not because of any herculean effort on his part."

The character's unusual moniker, according to Cummings, belonged to a real-life Chicago businessman and his wife, whom he had met shortly before the series got underway. The real-life Mr. Beanblossom had found a silver pencil that the star lost, and held on to it for many years until he had an opportunity to return it personally. "Right then and there," Cummings claimed, "I knew I had the name for my character in *My Hero.*"

Cummings was billed above the title in *My Hero.* He told a journalist he'd been intrigued with the possibilities of television for almost twenty years, since appearing in a number of experimental video broadcasts in the early 1930s. He claimed to find little difference between motion picture work and TV, though he admitted budgets were tighter in the latter, a particular concern to him as a profit participant. "There's very little margin for error and no room for a lot of retakes. Whenever we go over the budget, it comes out of my baby's food."[5]

Born August 30, 1914, leading lady Julie Bishop began acting in films as a child in the mid–1920s, originally using her given name, Jacqueline Wells. In the 1930s, she appeared in films like Universal's *The Black Cat* (1934). In 1941, she was signed to a Warner Brothers contract, and, at the insistence of studio boss Jack Warner was rechristened Julie Bishop. She spent much of the decade acting opposite some of the biggest male stars of the era—Humphrey Bogart,

Alan Ladd, and John Wayne, among others. She is the mother of actress Pamela Susan Shoop.

Featured as Bob's boss was veteran actor John Litel (1892–1972), also a longtime Warners player with more than 200 films on his résumé, dating back to the late 1920s. Normally a featured player, his credits included a recurring role as lawyer-father Carson Drew in Warners' *Nancy Drew* series of the late 1930s, and another paternal role in Paramount's *Henry Aldrich* series a few years later. After *My Hero*, he had a recurring role in the Western *Stagecoach West* (ABC, 1960-61) prior to his retirement in the late 1960s.

Not a three-camera, studio audience show like *I Love Lucy*, *My Hero* was filmed using motion picture techniques more akin to what Cummings knew. The show went into the NBC schedule in November 1952, after most other new fall shows had already premiered, occupying a time slot most recently held by *My Little Margie* (CBS and NBC, 1952–55). Sponsor Philip Morris used Cummings' show to promote its Dunhill cigarettes. The company forbade the use of the words "lucky" and "cool" in the series, as those alluded to rival cigarettes.

Cummings claimed that his television series not only increased his fan mail, and brought him greater recognition when he went out in public, but also bolstered interest in his movie work. Schedule conflicts, however, caused him to decline a co-starring role in MGM's *Latin Lovers* (1953), opposite Lana Turner. Cummings' deal allowed him a substantial measure of creative control on *My Hero*, and he contributed to most of the show's early scripts, as well as taking a producer credit. Later in the season, his duties were lessened and he confined himself to acting in the show. Most of the later scripts were the work of the team of Maurice Richlin and Rik Vollaerts.

While all was lighthearted on-screen, off camera there were indications that *My Hero* was a troubled show. In December, syndicated columnist Peg Simpson blasted the show with both barrels, saying, "How such a talented actor can adjust his professional pride enough to accept a starring role in such an absurd series is beyond me. Yet Cummings and his good supporting cast are making fools of themselves in this morass of stupidity each week."[6] Simpson reported that Hollywood rumor predicted changes were in the wind for Cummings' show.

A few days later, the *Los Angeles Times* reported that series producer Mort Greene had filed a breach of contract suit against Cummings and his wife and manager Sharpe. "Greene alleges that Sharpe, at the behest of the Cummingses, stripped him of all authority as the show's producer, yet held him responsible for the 'derisive commentary' on the show by reviewers," which Greene's lawyer charged had damaged his client's reputation. The matter was further inflamed when the sheriff's deputy charged with serving Cummings legal papers filed assault charges against the actor. The deputy, who'd tried to hand over the papers through a car window as the star left the RKO studio, said Cummings put the vehicle into gear and dragged him down the street, resulting in a wrenched arm and bruises. "I thought at the time he was an autograph seeker," Cummings told the *Times*.[7] Though the assault charges were dismissed, Cummings still went to court in January 1953, where Greene was asking for reimbursement of his $600-a-week salary, plus punitive damages. After dragging on for several months, the suit was ultimately settled out of court with what was reported to be a sizable payoff for the show's former writer-producer.

Defending his desire to have creative input on *My Hero*, Cummings told a journalist, "We started out with eight writers and none of them had ever seen me act before. Now in the past 20 years I've made 72 movies, and I think in that time I've come to know the kind of a guy my public expects to see."[8] He said he had particularly resisted the scriptwriters' tendency to place him in unmotivated comedy scenes. Various scripts called for the actor to be doused with mud, sprayed with water, knocked on the head with a vase, and coated in soot. Cummings claimed that the animal performers seen occasionally on the show were treated more humanely than he was; at least they had on-set welfare workers looking out for their interests.

Despite efforts to improve the show, *My Hero* ceased production after its first season, with 33 episodes in the can. The show promptly went into syndication with Official Films, while the star, freed of his TV commitment, was scooped up by movie producers for roles in *Lucky Me* and *Dial M for Murder*, both released in 1954. New stations continued to be launched in television markets, and a number of them signed up to show the reruns. Though the show had hardly been a success, the need for programs, plus the kid appeal of *My Hero*'s slapstick comedy, made it viable for at least a few years to come. Cummings, who owned a 40 percent share of *My Hero*, bragged to columnist James Bacon that he had declined a buyout offer of $250,000 for his rights in the show's syndication. His profit participation left him in a considerably more comfortable position than some other stars of early sitcoms being seen in reruns. Cummings, dining out one evening, had his car parked by actor Alvin Childress, better known as Amos of the *Amos 'n' Andy* series. Though that show had ceased production in 1953, it was still widely syndicated, making it difficult for Childress to get other work.

Some predicted that the failure of *My Hero* meant that Cummings' career as a TV sitcom star was over as well. At that time, few performers were given a second chance if their initial series was a failure. However, he received good notices for his performance in *Studio One*'s production of "Twelve Angry Men" in the fall of 1954, and ultimately won an Emmy for it. Shortly afterwards, he was launching a more substantial television comeback.

In the summer of 1954, Cummings signed a deal with Paul Henning and George Burns to develop a new series, this time wisely leaving the creation of the series concept to his partners. Burns' McCadden Productions provided major funding for the project, for which Henning, a longtime *Burns and Allen* writer, would serve as producer and head writer. In January 1955, Cummings returned to weekly TV with the starring role in NBC's *The Bob Cummings Show*, casting him as a lecherous but likable bachelor photographer living in a dream world of feminine beauty. Supporting him were Rosemary DeCamp, Ann B. Davis, and Dwayne Hickman. The show enjoyed a healthy run through 1959 and later went into syndication as *Love That Bob!* Cummings was Emmy-nominated as Best Actor every year the show was in production.

Though none of his later efforts would match the popularity of this series, Cummings continued to work in series television through much of the 1960s. A second *The Bob Cummings Show*, also known as *The New Bob Cummings Show*, struggled through its first season on CBS in 1961-62 and was not renewed. The CBS fantasy sitcom *My Living Doll*, co-starring Julie Newmar, showed promise upon its premiere in 1964, but fell apart rapidly, not helped by the chilly relationship that developed between its two stars. Cummings walked off the show before filming was complete for its first (and only) season. Though that was his last series role, the actor would continue to work steadily in television guest appearances throughout the 1970s. Cummings died of kidney failure and complications from pneumonia on December 2, 1990, at the age of 82.

When *The Bob Cummings Show* was in the planning stages, the star was determined to take a lesson from the failure of his first series. "The trouble with Beanblossom," Cummings said in retrospect, "was that the show had too much plot improbably presented. I was playing an idiot, which made all the other characters in the show idiots and the audience idiotic for watching it. Even the wildest of comedy must have believability or you can't suck an audience in long enough to get them interested."[9]

O.K. Crackerby!

Burl Ives (*O.K. Crackerby*), Hal Buckley (*St. John Quincy*), Brooke Adams (*Cynthia Crackerby*), Brian Corcoran (*O.K. Crackerby, Jr.*), Joel Davison (*Hobart Crackerby*), Laraine Stephens (*Susan Wentworth*), Dick Foran (*Slim*)
    Executive Producer: Rod Amateau. *Creators*: Cleveland Amory, Abe Burrows. *Producers*: Elliott Lewis, Charles Stewart. *Writers*: Tom Adair, James Allardice, Richard Baer, George Balzer, Earl Barret, Abe Burrows, Phil Davis, Robert C. Dennis, Rich Eustis, Arnold Margolin, Bill O'Hallaren, Jim Parker, Al Rogers, Terry Ryan, Tony Webster. *Directors*: Rod Amateau, Abe Burrows, Claudio Guzman, Leonard Horn, Thomas Montgomery, David Nelson, Gary Nelson, Seymour Robbie, Jack Shea, Ezra Stone. *Script Consultant*: Abe Burrows. *Story Editor*: Phil Davis. *Technical Consultant*: Cleveland Amory. *Creative Consultant*: Sid Dorfman. *Associate Producers*: David Davis, Ron Silverman. *Directors of Photography*: Brick Marquard, Charles Van Enger, James Van Trees. *Film Editors*: Santo L. Bernardo, Richard Brockway, Jim Faris, Leon Selditz. *Assistant Directors*: Wesley E. Barry, William Owens, Lou Place. *Production Manager*: W.A. Porter. *Art Director*: Jan Van Tamelen. *Supervising Music Editor*: Robert H. Raff. *Supervising Sound Editor*: Jim Bullock. *Theme Song*: Robert Emmett Dolan, Abe Burrows. *Production Coordinator*: Ray Summers. *Casting*: Tom Jennings. *Production Mixers*: Stan Cooley, Earl Snyder. *Dialogue Coach*: Jim Burrows. *Post-Production Supervisor*: Larry Heath. *Set Decorator*: Victor A. Gangelin, Dave Love, Charles Vassar. *Programmer Furnished by* Ampex. Beresford Productions, Inc., in association with United Artists Television.
    Aired Thursdays at 8:30 P.M. on ABC-TV. First aired September 16, 1965; last aired January 6, 1966. 17 episodes (1 in black-and-white, 16 in color).

    QUINCY (explaining to his boss the proper way to host a party for a viscount): There should be a written invitation.
    CRACKERBY: All right, you write him a letter and tell him O.K. Crackerby is giving a party a week from Saturday night, and wants him to come put on the feedbag.

An Oklahoma billionaire's efforts to break into high society were the subject of this short-lived ABC sitcom. Actor-singer Burl Ives would be given above-the-title billing in his first series, which was widely expected to be a sizable hit given the pedigrees not only in front of but behind the camera.
    In the pilot episode, Crackerby and his three children have just arrived in Palm Beach and are looking for lodging at the exclusive Hotel Havenhurst. When the hotel staff initially snubs Crackerby and his family, refusing to rent him the entire penthouse floor, he simply picks up the phone and in five minutes has purchased the hotel lock, stock, and penthouse. The Havenhurst-

O.K. Crackerby!

Crackerby, as it is quickly renamed, becomes the family's home away from home.

A widower, O.K. (given name Omar) has three children: 16-year-old Cynthia and her younger brothers O.K., Jr., 13, and Hobart, 9. His previous home base was Stillwater, Oklahoma. O.K. balks at being described as the richest man

The family that smiles together stays together, or so the Crackerbys seem to believe. Pictured are (left to right): Brian Corcoran (O.K., Jr.), Burl Ives (O.K., Sr.), Joel Davison (Hobart), and Brooke Adams (Cynthia).

in the world, but thinks calling him the richest man in America may be understating a little.

Deciding that his children need a tutor-companion, O.K. settles on St. John Quincy, a socially well-connected but impoverished young man. A gifted athlete and presentable young-man-around-town, Quincy is nonetheless at loose ends, employed on the sales staff at a sporting goods store. O.K.'s investigators at the Pinkerton Agency look into Quincy, and describe him as "a man who is very good at weekends, but not very good in the middle of the week."

Crackerby explains to his prospective employee that he needs help integrating himself and his family into Palm Beach society, where they are looked down upon as *nouveau riche*:

> CRACKERBY: You bring in oil wells with a drill, not a fish fork. See, I haven't had time for all the little finer things. But my kids, somebody's gotta teach them all the stupid little niceties to help 'em get in.
> QUINCY: In where?
> CRACKERBY: Society, high society.
> QUINCY: Mr. Crackerby, how do you define "high society"?
> CRACKERBY: I define it as something I'm out of, and I don't like being out of anything unless I'm the one who wants out.

Disliking Crackerby's high-handedness, St. John initially refuses the job offer, telling the billionaire he can't be bought. O.K. proceeds to sweeten the deal by providing a chauffeur-driven limousine for the young man's use, depositing $5,000 in his previously meager checking account, and buying out the sportswear store where he's employed.

St. John has a lady friend from his own social class, beautiful Susan Wentworth, technically his third cousin ("my mother was a Quincy") but whom St. John hopes to make his girlfriend. At least, that is their relationship in the pilot episode; later scriptwriters will depict it differently.

Ultimately, St. John Quincy decides to accept the job as tutor to the Crackerby kids. St. John soon learns that he has his work cut out for him helping them adjust to the world around them. Having grown up with tremendous wealth, O.K.'s boys enjoy playing the stock market for recreation, and keeping tabs on the lucrative oil wells their father leased them. In "Crackerby for Treasurer" (10/7/65), O.K., Jr., campaigns for a grammar school office by hiring a skywriter to emblazon his campaign slogan across the skies of Palm Beach, and throwing a rally for which he books Willie Mays, Sandra Dee, and the Beatles to entertain. (None of the above actually appears in the episode.)

Back at the Crackerby ranch in Oklahoma, O.K.'s loyal employee Slim occupies an office (equipped with a bed and refrigerator) where he's on 24-hour-a-day call to do whatever his wealthy employer needs done at a moment's notice. He does so with the help of a massive computer that can instantly provide almost any type of information his boss needs to carry out his schemes.

O.K. Crackerby! was the invention of two well-known names, playwright-director Abe Burrows and author and longtime *TV Guide* reviewer Cleveland Amory. Amory was considered to be something of an expert on affluent society, having penned books such as *The Last Resorts,* a nonfiction account of the wealthy at play in Palm Springs, Palm Beach, and elsewhere.

Born June 14, 1909, series star Burl Ives said he earned his first dollar for singing at the age of four. Ives had initially enrolled in Eastern Illinois State Teachers College with the intent of becoming a professional educator. Making a living any way he could during the Great Depression, he roamed the country. At various times, he played football professionally, and was a lead singer in an evangelistic show. In the 1940s, Ives became known to audiences as a folk singer, heard on the radio and in films.

In 1955, he was a Broadway smash as Big Daddy in Tennessee Williams' drama *Cat on a Hot Tin Roof,* for which he was chosen by Williams and Elia Kazan despite others' misgivings about his acting chops. He was lured to Hollywood for roles in films such as *East of Eden* (1955) and *Desire Under the Elms* (1958), and won a Best Supporting Actor Oscar for his role in *The Big Country* (1958). At the time *Crackerby* began, he'd recorded more than forty albums, and had recently been seen playing a genie in *The Brass Bottle* (1964).

"Funny thing about the singing," Ives remarked in 1965. "I started out with folk songs across the country, got my reputation that way. But when I began to act, the public forgot I could sing, particularly if the show was a success. Then I go back singing a while — and they never think of me as anything else."[1] So as not to destroy the illusion of his new character, Ives decreed that he would not sing in his sitcom.

Also off-limits for the show's writers were references to Ives' weight, variously estimated at between 275 and 300 pounds. "I never tell it," he informed one interviewer forward enough to broach the subject. "In fact, I usually don't allow anyone to ever mention it. My talent has nothing to do with weight. I'm known as a large man and that's it. I'm an actor, not a comedian. The minute you permit someone to discuss your weight you become a buffoon."[2]

At the time he was approached about *Crackerby*, Ives had been considering a different series, but hesitated. He'd just read Merle Miller's scathing *Only You, Dick Daring,* depicting the ugly politics and senseless decision-making that Miller experienced working in television. After reading the pilot script sent to him by Amory, however, Ives allowed himself to be won over by the prospect of the talent behind the scenes, and the promise that he would be allowed some creative say-so in the series.

"I had another television project all set to go," Ives said. "It was a big, hour-long dramatic show set in the Caribbean, and doing it would have taken much more out of me than this one."[3] The finished pilot for *Crackerby* was in the can by late January, and by February 1 sold to ABC. The sample episode was filmed in black-and-white and the weekly series in color.

The actor-singer took up residence in a luxurious apartment at the Chateau

Marmont when shooting for *O.K. Crackerby!* began in the summer of 1965. Though he numbered a boat and a trailer among his possessions, Ives claimed he didn't share his character's fascination with wealth. "I was pretty poor once, but I was just as happy being poor as I am now.... I remember losing a farm in Pennsylvania, and friends commiserated with me. But I couldn't feel sad about it. 'I was just passing through,' I said. The land is still there for someone else. You really don't own anything."[4]

Featured as young St. John Quincy was 28-year-old Hal Buckley, a veteran of several Off Broadway shows including one called *Driftwood*, which co-starred two other newcomers, Joan Rivers and Barbra Streisand. In Hollywood, he mostly supported himself as a model and with roles in television commercials. It was one of the latter that brought him to the attention of ABC president Tom Moore. Buckley claimed he was the last in a long line of young actors to vie for the role. "There was no one left," he said. "I think it was the wives of the producers that finally decided that I came across on the screen with what the series needed."[5] He was, in fact, a former Harvard man himself, though he had transferred to another school before graduation.

The series also provided the first major television exposure for 16-year-old Brooke Adams, more than a decade before she attracted the notice of moviegoers in films like *Invasion of the Body Snatchers* and *Days of Heaven* (both 1978). Child actor Brian Corcoran was one of several acting kids in his family, among them his older sister Noreen, the co-star of *Bachelor Father* (CBS, NBC and ABC, 1957–62). Actor-singer Dick Foran (1910–79), seen as Slim, racked up numerous film credits in the 1930s and 1940s, going from a singing cowboy at Warner Brothers to roles in Universal horror films like *The Mummy's Hand* (1940).

O.K. Crackerby! was given a cozy hammock of a time slot between two other well-known ABC sitcoms: the fading *The Donna Reed Show* (1958–66), going into its eighth and final season, and *Bewitched*, a Top Ten hit during its first season. Opposite Ives' new show on CBS was *My Three Sons*, making its debut on that network after a profitable five-year run on ABC. *Sons* was shrewdly slotted by CBS executives to air in the same time slot it had occupied to solid ratings on ABC the previous two years. Meanwhile, NBC would go after a different audience with the Western *Laredo* (1965–67).

The Associated Press' Cynthia Lowry, having screened the pilot episode of *Crackerby*, was dubious, saying, "Ives is a persuasive performer and may be able to convert this into a silk purse, although the opening show looked like pigskin."[6] A reviewer for the syndicated *TV Scout* column (9/15/65) was a little more enthusiastic: "The dialogue is smart and snappy and Buckley is ingratiating as St. John Quincy."

Within weeks, there were cracks visible beneath the surface of Ives' show, which ABC executives had fully expected to be a smash. Interviewed in September, the star admitted they'd seen little in recent weeks of creator Abe Burrows, who had not contributed to the show's scripts since co-authoring the second episode. "Or at least he's supposed to be overseeing scripts," Ives said tartly.[7] In fact, despite their prominent "created by" credit in *Crackerby*'s opening titles, Burrows was largely occupied with his Broadway comedy *Cactus Flower*, which opened that December, and Amory's involvement with the show also appeared to be at an end. Rod Amateau, whose credits included production stints on *The George Burns and Gracie Allen Show* (CBS, 1950–58) and *The Many Loves of Dobie Gillis* (CBS, 1959–63), served as executive producer on *Crackerby*, with veteran comedy writer Charles Stewart as producer. With only a handful of episodes in the can, veteran producer Elliott Lewis (*The Lucy Show*) replaced Stewart, and comedy writer Sid Dorfman was brought on board as a consultant, but improvements in the show were minimal. In November 1965, Ives himself saw the handwriting on the wall and sent a letter to a number of newspaper columnists, announcing that *O.K. Crackerby* was a goner, beating ABC to the punch.

In January 1966, with ratings falling, *Crackerby* was unceremoniously yanked from ABC's Thursday night lineup, after only seventeen episodes had aired. The show's final aired episode, "Operation Susan" (1/6/66) finds St. John and Susan acting as best man and maid of honor at the wedding of friends, and thus contemplating the future of their own relationship. By this point, Susan says that she has been "chasing" St. John for five years, unsuccessfully trying to elicit a marriage proposal. Only when they have an argument that causes Susan to accept another man's proposal on the rebound does St. John acknowledge how much he cares for her, and tell her that he loves her.

Taking *Crackerby*'s place was *The Double Life of Henry Phyfe*, a spy sitcom starring Red Buttons, which would fare no better and be dropped by the summer of 1966.

The failure of a sitcom created by Abe Burrows and starring Burl Ives came as a surprise to many. Invited to do a post-mortem on his just-canceled show, Ives said, "The show had no boss. It's as simple as that. Abe Burrows was supposed to be it. He wrote the first show and he visited us once and we never saw him again."[8] Amateau, who stepped in as show runner, was also involved with NBC's *My Mother the Car* (1965-66), leaving him overburdened.

Ives returned to series television when he accepted a lead role in *The Lawyers*, an hour-long drama that rotated with two other shows to form NBC's *The Bold Ones*. Co-starring with Joseph Campanella and James Farentino, Ives enjoyed a three-year run, from 1969 to 1972, before the show wore out its welcome. During the run of that show, Ives married Dorothy Koster, 44, an interior decorator, and continued to act through the late 1980s. Upon his 80th birthday in 1989, he declared himself officially retired. By the time of his death from cancer in 1995, Ives was less remembered for his series work on television than he was for narrating a perennial holiday special, Rankin-Bass' *Rudolph the Red-Nosed Reindeer*, which had been seen yearly since its debut in 1964.

Of *O.K. Crackerby!*, Ives would acknowledge in retrospect that the show's format had limitations that did not play out well over the course of multiple episodes. "It was a thing about me breaking into society with my kids. How many times can you do that? After three or four attempts, something's got to give."[9]

Occasional Wife

Michael Callan (*Peter Christopher*), Patricia Harty (*Greta Patterson*), Jack Collins (*Max Brahms*), Joan Tompkins (*Mrs. Brahms*), Sara Seegar (*Mrs. Christopher*), Bryan O'Byrne (*Man in the Middle*), Stuart Margolin (*Bernie Kramer*), Jack B. Riley (*Wally Frick*), Vin Scully (*Narrator*)

Executive Producer: Harry Ackerman. *Producer*: Bob Claver. *Creators*: Lawrence J. Cohen, Fred Freeman. *Writers*: Richard Baer, Lawrence J. Cohen, Robert Riley Crutcher, Stan Cutler, William Davenport, Peggy Chantler Dick, Martin Donovan, Fred Freeman, Lila Garrett, Bernie Kahn, Martin A. Ragaway, Gene Thompson. *Directors*: Jerry Bernstein, Bob Claver, Danny Dayton, Richard Kinon, Russ Mayberry, Gary Nelson, Ernest Pintoff, Gene Reynolds, Paul Junger Witt. *Script Consultants*: Stan Cutler, Martin Donovan. *Associate Producer*: Paul Junger Witt. *Music Consultant*: Don Kirshner. *Post-Production Supervisor*: Lawrence Werner. *Music Supervisor*: Ed Forsyth. *Music*: Shorty Rogers. *Title Song*: Howard Greenfield, Ernie Pintoff. *Director of Photography*: Lloyd Ahern. *Art Directors*: Ross Bellah, Robert Purcell. *Film Editors*: Asa Clark, Howard Kunin, Leon Selditz. *Set Decorator*: Sidney Clifford. *Hair Stylist*: Faith Schmein. *Assistant Directors*: Jon C. Andersen, George R. Batcheller, Jerrold Bernstein. *Makeup Supervisor*: Ben Lane. *Sound Effects*: Fred J. Brown. Screen Gems.

Aired Tuesdays at 8:30 P.M. on NBC-TV. First aired September 13, 1966; last aired August 29, 1967. 30 color episodes.

PETER: Greta, be a good wife, will you, and don't interfere with my love life!

A provocative title for its time was designed to intrigue viewers of this standard-issue Screen Gems sitcom. *Occasional Wife* was a romantic comedy centering on a phony marriage-for-convenience that threatens to turn into a genuine love match — if boy and girl can stop fighting long enough.

Protagonist Peter Christopher works at the Brahms Baby Food Company (slogan: "Every meal is a lullaby"). Wanting to climb the corporate ladder, Peter is frustrated by company founder and president Max Brahms, who after 27 years of marriage and a company founded on procreation, believes firmly that married men make the best executives. Accordingly, the other ambitious young men who work for Brahms have photos of their wives and children prominently displayed on their desks. Peter, meanwhile, is known to his boss as "the company bachelor."

Peter wants to advance his career, but not at the expense of giving up his freewheeling bachelorhood. Mostly his evenings consist of wining and dining bimbos like blonde, ditzy Ginger Snap and Cookie Carruthers, or the twin sisters Rennie and Reenie. But when he's left out of interviews for a promotion, Peter decides it's time to take action.

Pretty blonde Greta Patterson, who's employed as a hatcheck girl in the bar where Peter goes to drown his sorrows, inadvertently suggests a solution. Greta, a would-be dress designer, tells Peter that the wedding ring she wears on the job is a phony designed to help her avoid romantic entanglements with the customers while saving up money for art school. Peter and Greta cut a deal: She will pose as his wife, attending business functions, in exchange for his renting and furnishing an apartment for her in his building (a brownstone on East 64th Street), financing three art lessons a week, and buying her contact lenses. As Peter says in a clip seen weekly in the show's opening titles, "Greta, I want you to be my wife — occasionally."

They invent a history for themselves: They had their first meeting at the Huntington Yacht Club, where their eyes met; she gave up her career in Boston (Peter says she was "a librarian"; Greta: "a dancer") to marry Peter. Peter's long-term plan is to keep up the pretense of being married to Greta just long enough to achieve a vice-presidency at the Brahms company, after which his "wife" will suffer "a tragic boating accident."

The scheme works initially, as Mr. and Mrs. Brahms approve of Greta, and Peter is accordingly awarded with a promotion to a junior executive position (with his own office and a secretary). Over the next several months, however,

 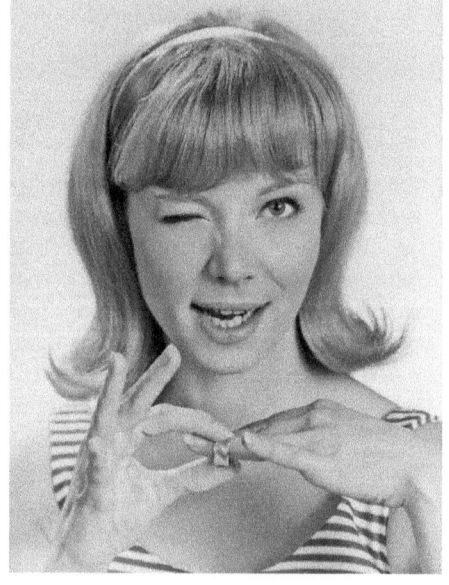

Michael Callan (left) and Patricia Harty (right) are the mismatched couple in NBC's *Occasional Wife.*

the strain of pretending to be married proves more complicated than Peter or Greta anticipated. Peter's mother also believes that he and Greta are truly married.

His chief rival at work is another aspiring young executive, Wally Frick (an early role for character actor Jack Riley, best known as neurotic therapy patient Elliott Carlin on CBS's 1972–78 *The Bob Newhart Show*). Wally, described by the show's narrator as "a gifted tattletale and dangerous backstabber," is constantly vying with Peter to see who can shine the brightest in their boss' eyes. Luckily for Peter, Wally, whose grasping and aggressive wife Vera (Susan Silo) describes him as "a klutz," usually shoots himself in the foot.

Baseball announcer Vin Scully, the voice of the Los Angeles Dodgers since 1950, took on a new role here as the sitcom's narrator, who opens each show by intoning, "This is a modern fable of the big city." Scully gives the play-by-play as each episode progresses. Most episodes revolve around a misunderstanding or circumstance that threatens to expose the truth about Peter and Greta's "marriage." When Mr. Brahms sees Greta dancing with another man in a club, or Greta's parents pay an unexpected visit, there's always a last-minute shuffle of quick answers. In "GP Loves UU" (12/13/66), Greta accepts another man's marriage proposal, and Peter must devise a plan that will explain her departure from his life. In "I Do, We Don't" (10/18/66), Peter's mother demands that Peter and Greta renew their vows in a second ceremony, since she didn't get to attend the first one.

In addition to her *faux* marriage to Peter, Greta also goes out occasionally with timid, hangdog Bernie Kramer. Last-minute summonses from Peter often cause Greta to break dates with Bernie, so much so that his mother doesn't believe Greta exists. Bernie thinks Peter is Greta's brother; his own sister Bernice has the hots for Peter. Periodically, Greta and Peter renegotiate their deal when something above and beyond is required of her charade, such as accompanying Peter on a business trip, or missing a class so as to volunteer with Mrs. Brahms' charity.

When quick action is needed, Peter and Greta travel back and forth from his apartment (714) on the seventh floor to hers on the ninth floor via the fire escape, much to the bafflement of the nebbishy-looking man who lives in the apartment in between. Eventually, he takes to sitting at his window with a bowl of popcorn, finding it more interesting than the movies he used to watch on TV.

As the months pass, however, it's clear that Peter and Greta's constant companionship is developing into a mutual attraction that neither is ready to admit. Though Peter isn't ready to give up his freewheeling bachelorhood, and tells Greta they could never really be married, because "you know too much about me," he's impressed by this woman who's clever and witty as well as beautiful. For her part, Greta professes to be uninterested in Peter, and insists that they keep their relationship platonic, but can't resist giving him the eye when she barges into his apartment while he's changing clothes.

The series was created by Fred Freeman and Lawrence J. Cohen, who contributed scripts to a varied list of popular sitcoms, including *The Andy Griffith Show, Bewitched,* and *Gilligan's Island*. It was in some ways the flipside of another recent sitcom, *The Cara Williams Show* (CBS, 1964-65), which took as its premise a married couple who pretend *not* to be because they work for a company that forbids employing both spouses.

In an interview published only days after the show's premiere, star Michael Callan said that he found his first starring role demanding enough to wonder just how much fame he wanted. "If this is a sample of what it's like, I don't know. The demands are rough. The phone never stops ringing. Somebody is always after you to do something. Maybe I've grown past wanting this."[1]

Born Michael Calinoff (another source says Martin Harris Calininff) in Chester, Pennsylvania, on November 22, 1935, the future Michael Callan was taking singing and dancing lessons at the age of eleven. He came to the attention of the industry with his featured role as Riff in the original Broadway production of *West Side Story* (under his then-professional name, Mickey Calin). Signing a contract with Columbia Pictures, he made his film debut in *They Came to Cordura* (1959), playing a wounded soldier, and was soon being groomed for full-fledged leading man status. The studio built up his experience with guest roles in Screen Gems shows like *Hazel* (NBC and CBS, 1961–66) and second-tier films like *Gidget Goes Hawaiian* (1961). Though his film and television work made little use of his dancing skills, aside from the film *Pepe* (1960), Callan felt that the sense of timing he'd developed as a dancer was an asset to his acting as well. Some observers described him as a young Jack Lemmon, a comparison made especially after he did a funny drag sequence in *The New Interns* (1963). Renewing his Columbia deal in 1964, Callan had yet to attain top stardom, but was enough of a known entity to movie audiences that his new arrangement called for a sizable role in one movie per year. Callan, predicted syndicated columnist Erskine Johnson (5/12/64), "is building up to a box office explosion."

Some were surprised by Callan's willingness to go into a sitcom while he was still getting movie roles (most notably a co-starring role in the critically acclaimed *Cat Ballou*). "I'm tired of working only four or five months a year," he explained. "I can't stand the inactivity any more.... These are the good years for me and I want to work every week if I can."[2] His contract for *Wife* included some "outs" that would permit him to take occasional singing gigs in nightclubs, and perhaps squeeze in a movie during the show's hiatus period.

Occasional Wife would be only the latest in a long string of sitcoms from Columbia's Screen Gems unit. Callan's new bosses had also had a hand in hit shows ranging from *Hazel* to *Bewitched*, and it was former sitcom star Jackie Cooper, now running the studio, who signed Callan on the dotted line for the series.

Executive producer Harry Ackerman discovered leading lady Patricia Harty in a low-budget film called *Harvey Middleman, Fireman* (1965). The onscreen rapport that producers hoped she would have with Callan would go a long way toward making *Occasional Wife* a success with viewers. As one critic noted, "Of course, the idea is to tantalize the public with the attractive couple who are too busy worming their way out of embarrassing situations to take a second off and let chemistry go to work."[3]

Of her screen performances, Harty said, "I always play girls a little sexy, a little cute and a little shrewd."[4] In real life, she'd been married for the past three years to her manager, Tom Kearney, and when not working lived with him in a New Hampshire farmhouse. Callan, meanwhile, was married to Carlyn, a former dancer, and was father to two young daughters. At first, there had been absolutely no chemistry off-screen between Callan and Harty, but that would change. "I couldn't bear him," Harty said, describing her first impression of her co-star. "However, there was something about him. It was rare when you saw a dancer who looked so virile."[5]

By the standards of mid–1960s television, the premise was just sufficiently risqué that NBC thought *Occasional Wife* might attract viewers who found the long-running *The Red Skelton Show* on CBS old-hat. "The networks would never have bought the show five years ago," admitted producer Bob Claver. The scripts occasionally touched on matters not usually covered in 1960s television. In the pilot episode, when Peter's mother is bemoaning his single status, she tells him "it's just not normal" to be unmarried at his age, and suddenly has a disquieting thought:

"Peter, I really don't know how to say this," his mother quavers, "but are you ... are you ... eccentric?" Peter indignantly denies being anything of the sort, and storms out of his mother's apartment while clutching her purse (which he picked up in lieu of his briefcase).

"Of course, it tickles people's fantasies," Claver acknowledged of the show's premise.[6] The show also offered an urban New York City setting that was, at the time, still fairly unusual, though ABC would score a hit the same year with Marlo Thomas' *That Girl* (1966–71), which also depicted a young woman pursuing her career dreams in the Big Apple.

Jack Collins, cast as Peter Christopher's fatherly boss, was a veteran character actor seen often in other Screen Gems sitcoms like *Bewitched*. He'd previously made numerous appearances on *The Milton Berle Show* and acted in more than two dozen Broadway shows. Cast as Brahms' patrician but sensible wife was Joan Tompkins (1915–2005), whose long list of credits included a 1940s Broadway run in the original *My Sister Eileen* as well as some radio work. Tompkins had previously been a regular on the courtroom drama *Sam Benedict* (NBC, 1962-63), and was married to another prolific radio actor, Karl Swenson.

Seen occasionally as Greta's date was actor Stuart Margolin, best-remembered for his later work with James Garner, co-starring in *Nichols* (NBC,

1971-72) and subsequently as the hero's former cellmate, Angel Martin, on *The Rockford Files* (NBC, 1974–80). Sara Seegar, already a veteran of another Screen Gems sitcom, *Dennis the Menace* (CBS, 1959–63), played Peter's mother, though her appearances were infrequent as the season progressed.

Two possible concerns with the show were identified: one, that the premise was basically a one-joke idea that would wear out quickly; the other, that some viewers, especially women, wouldn't sympathize with Peter Christopher's eagerness to avoid matrimony.

In January, Screen Gems announced a viewer contest to give a name to the anonymous "Man in the Middle" played by Bryan O'Byrne. The winner would receive a trip to Hollywood and a guest appearance on *Wife*. Viewers sent more than 75,000 contest entries, though no name was unveiled onscreen in subsequent episodes.

NBC declined to renew the show for a second season. *The Girl from U.N.C.L.E.*, which gave Callan and Harty's sitcom its lead-in, had failed to draw strong ratings, and in March it was reported that *Occasional Wife* would be replaced by *The Jerry Lewis Show* that fall. It's difficult to imagine that the writers could have sustained the show much longer without introducing a new storyline.

As it happened, both stars were experiencing some of the downsides of marriage. Though both Callan and Harty were married when the series began, they would soon separate from their respective spouses. In March 1968, newspapers reported that the one-time *Occasional Wife* to Michael Callan would be landing the role full-time, when the former co-stars announced their real-life engagement. They were married in June, at their home in Coldwater Canyon.

Harty landed two subsequent sitcom roles, both as full-fledged wives. She played the title character in yet another adaptation of the comic strip *Blondie* (CBS, 1968-69), opposite Will Hutchins as Dagwood. Though it would seem that the actress had it all, both professionally and personally, the truth was more complicated. "All my life I'd been planning and working toward marriage and a series of my own," she later said. "Finally I had all the material things I wanted, including a house in Beverly Hills. But when I had it all I was never unhappier. I was miserable every morning when I woke up."[7]

When *Blondie* was canceled, Harty divorced Callan and disappeared from Hollywood for several years. In 1975, her hair back to its natural brunette color and her name changed to Trisha Hart, she resurfaced for a brief run as co-star of NBC's short-lived *The Bob Crane Show*. The show was not a success, but Hart came away from the experience with a new husband — the series' associate producer Les Sheldon.

Callan, though shying away from series roles after *Occasional Wife*, remained a busy film and TV actor throughout the mid–1990s, accepting an occasional gig even into the early 2000s. He was seen as a guest star on shows ranging from *Medical Center* (CBS, 1969–76) to *Funny Face* (CBS, 1971), and appeared in the inaugural episode of *Love, American Style* (ABC, 1969–74).

In 1995, Fox unveiled *Ned and Stacey*, which used a similar premise of a man who wants a phony wife for the sake of his career. Thomas Haden Church (*Wings*) and Debra Messing (*Will and Grace*) played the sham married couple, who in this instance actually went through with the ceremony and shared an apartment, but pledged to live platonically. Little more successful than its 1960s counterpart, it was canceled midway through its second season.

The People's Choice

Jackie Cooper (*Socrates "Sock" Miller*), Patricia Breslin (*Amanda Peoples Miller*), Margaret Irving (*Augusta "Gus" Bennett*), Paul Maxey (*Mayor John Peoples*), Leonid Kinskey (*Pierre*), John Stephenson (*Roger Crutcher*), Dick Wesson (*Rollo*), Mary Jane Croft (*Voice of Cleo*)

Creator-Producer: Irving Brecher. *Producer*: E.J. Rosenberg. *Writers*: G. Carleton Brown, Bob Fisher, Morris Freedman, Frank Gill, Jr., Joel Kane, Alan Lipscott, Milton Pascal. *Directors*: Irving Brecher, Jackie Cooper, Robert S. Finkel, Leigh Jason, Peter Tewksbury. *Associate Producers*: G. Carleton Brown, Frank Gill, Jr. *Production Supervisor*: Al Simon. *Directors of Photography*: Phillip Tannura, James Van Trees. *Assistant Directors*: Joseph Depew, George King. *Unit Manager*: Herbert Browar. *Supervising Editor*: Stanley Frazen. *Editors*: Henry DeMond, Edward Mann, Thomas Neff, Howard Smith, Aaron Stell. *Sound Editor*: Bernard F. Pincus. *Casting*: Kerwin Coughlin. *Music*: Lou Kosloff, Mahlon Merrick. *Art Directors*: Lewis Creber, Stephen Goosson, George Van Marter. *Set Decorators*: Claude Carpenter, Dorcy Howard. *Wardrobe*: Myrtle Logan. *Makeup*: Gene Roemer. *Hair Stylist*: Bertha French. *Sock Miller's Trailer*: Airfloat. *Cleo's Coach*: Frank Inn. Norden Productions; filmed by McCadden Productions.

Aired Thursdays at 8:30 P.M. (through December 1955), then Thursdays at 9 P.M. on NBC-TV. Premiered October 6, 1955; last aired September 25, 1958. 104 black-and-white episodes.

This is New City ... people — laughter — romance — heartbreak. I work here. My name's Cleo. I'm a dog. — Cleo the basset hound, taking a page from the book of *Dragnet*'s Sergeant Friday

One of NBC's relatively few sitcom successes of the 1950s, *The People's Choice* is usually described not as a romantic comedy about the developing relationship between a young city councilman and the mayor's daughter, or as a vehicle for Oscar-nominated former child star Jackie Cooper, but as "the show with the talking dog." That gimmick, combined with the chemistry of its human players, worked well enough to give the show a three-year run.

Socrates ("Sock") Miller (Cooper) is a young man working as a field ornithologist with the U.S. Fish and Wildlife Service. Since his job entails tracking migratory birds, Sock travels the country in a trailer, accompanied by his pragmatic, dry-witted Aunt Augusta, who raised him after his parents died, and his basset hound Cleo. A Korean War veteran, Sock has put more than 80,000 miles on his trailer since leaving the service and starting his career. His boss, the district supervisor, is tough-talking Hilda Larson (Elvia Allman), who in turn reports to Chief Inspector Sidney Baxter (Richard Deacon), her fiancé of eight years' duration.

As the series opens, Sock has been staying for the past few months in the aptly named New City, a small suburban community in the San Fernando Valley near Los Angeles. As the narrator notes, "New City was built in a hurry," and consequently some of its residents lack basic services like streetlights and sewers. Sock has been spending time with Mandy Peoples, the pretty daughter of New City's mayor, but considers himself a confirmed bachelor, due primarily to his nomadic life.

He's living temporarily in the Paradise Trailer Park, where his best friend is Pierre, an aspiring artist who shows up nightly to mooch dinner at the Miller trailer, much to the disgust of Aunt Gus. Mandy, while attracted to Sock, has also been seeing another man her father considers far more suitable—Roger Crutcher, a stuffy, ambitious young man who's up for reelection to his post as city councilman, and who doesn't think much of "the riffraff in those trailers."

The show's most noteworthy gimmick is introduced in the first scene, when Sock calls his dog Cleo. The camera cuts to a close-up of the dog, and we hear a voiceover of Cleo thinking, "Who were you expecting, Grace Kelly?" Like most of the amusing lines in the pilot, this is received with raucous laughter on the soundtrack. (Though many commentators, then and later, described *The People's Choice* as a show with a talking dog, there are no special effects used to depict Cleo actually speaking, as there would later be on CBS's *Mister Ed*, and no suggestion that Sock or anyone else is aware of his dog's unusual gift.)

Later, when Sock

"You're a ham!" says Sock Miller (Jackie Cooper) to his lady friend Mandy Peoples (Patricia Breslin) as they prepare for a TV fundraiser in *The People's Choice*.

and Mandy are getting romantic, Cleo borrows a phrase associated with producer-creator Irving Brecher's hit series *The Life of Riley*: "What a revoltin' development *this* is!" When Mandy purposely drops the ignition key to her car, so that she can have Sock to herself a little longer, Cleo, who seems to be jealous of her human competition, promptly fetches it and returns it.

Unable to find the rare nuthatch he's been tracking in New City, Sock is ready to move on, but Mandy is determined to keep him close by a little longer. Having previously been booked to deliver a TV commercial for Roger's reelection campaign, Mandy instead uses her on-camera time to tell viewers they should vote for a write-in candidate, Sock Miller. Unlike the incumbent, who mostly acts as a yes man for the mayor, Mandy promises Sock won't be "a rubber stamp for the mayor." After all, she points out, he just refused to marry the mayor's daughter.

Thanks to Aunt Gus, who sets his clock back, Sock sleeps through Election Day, but is awakened that evening by news photographers who inform him he has just been elected. Angered, Sock fires up his trailer and prepares to leave New City in the dust. Instead, he allows himself to be persuaded to return to town and assume the responsibilities of councilman.

The second segment, "How Sock Met Mandy" (10/13/55), offers a flashback (through Cleo's eyes) of the sparring couple's first meeting. Just as Sock is about to trap the rare bird he's been chasing, the sound of a tire blowout scares off his prey. The driver of the car is Mandy, who catches Sock's eye, but clearly leaves Cleo unimpressed. ("She's nothing! She's only got two legs.") In weeks to come, Sock will raise the mayor's blood pressure with such stunts as his proposal to reroute a local freeway so that some trees housing rare birds will be undisturbed, and so as to avoid the park where New City's symphony orchestra offers its outdoor concerts.

A running plot throughout the first season is Sock's rivalry with Roger Crutcher. In "The Unseating of Councilman Sock" (10/20/55), Roger conspires to disqualify Sock from serving as councilman, by demonstrating that he has lived in New City for one day less than the 90 days required to hold office. When Sock remembers that he tagged a rare bird on his first day in town, Mandy and the men go scouting in the woods to find the dated avian evidence that will make or break Councilman Miller's political career.

For much of that season, Sock only reluctantly acknowledged his attraction to Mandy, who blatantly sets her cap for the happy bachelor. Aunt Gus is sympathetic to Mandy's goal, and occasionally even a co-conspirator in carrying out one of her schemes, but warns her that she's not the first young lady who's wanted to get Sock to settle down. In "Sock and the Syrene" (3/22/56), a Marine colonel and his aide visit New City to decide whether it is the best site for a new training depot. Sock volunteers to house the aide in his trailer before learning that the sergeant is a beautiful blonde woman, one he dated while he was in the service, and nicknamed "Honey Lips." Sgt. Joan Dooley (played by Doris Singleton) is actually in love with her superior officer, the colonel, and decides that a little harmless flirtation with Sock might elicit a marriage proposal from her reluctant beau.

The show's second season finds two key romances coming to fruition in New City. Not only does Sock's Aunt Gus marry Mayor Peoples, but in "Sock Takes the Plunge" (12/13/56), our hero finally elopes with Mandy. The producers' decision to allow Sock to marry Mandy was made with some trepidation. Earlier shows like Wally Cox's popular *Mr. Peepers* (NBC, 1952–55) had kept viewers on the hook with the hope that someday the lead characters would get married; yet, when they did, viewers lost interest and ratings fell.

The People's Choice devised a gimmick to maintain interest after the nuptials. Rather than face the disapproval of her father, who does not believe Sock is an appropriate match for Mandy, the newlyweds decide to keep their union a secret for the time being. Not until the beginning of the show's third and final season do Sock and Mandy reveal to her father that they've actually been married for some time. By then, Sock has also given up his work as a naturalist and completed a law degree.

Other changes during the second season included the addition of Sock's old Marine buddy Rollo, played by Dick Wesson (who would spend a number of years as the narrator of Walt Disney's weekly television shows). Like Sock's friend Pierre, whom he replaced, Rollo, who lives rent-free with Sock, is a champion freeloader, so much so that, when Sock packs his best clothes for a trip out of town, Rollo is left behind in his underwear.

After their marriage, Sock and Mandy (with Rollo in tow) relocate to Oklahoma, where he gets a job selling houses in a newly established development, Barkerville. The job with Barker Amalgamated allows him and Mandy to move into their own new home, though he struggles under the pressure of selling suburban tract homes in an area that's off the beaten path. Both Mandy's father and Sock's aunt continue to be frequent visitors, though the characters are no longer seen every week. As the series comes to a close, Sock and Mandy are expecting the arrival of their first child.

Through it all, as Cleo comments in one of her asides to viewers, "The director cuts to me when he wants a dash of sex appeal!"

The People's Choice would be the second popular NBC sitcom to come from the pen of writer-producer Irving Brecher. In 1949, Brecher adapted his hit radio series *The Life of Riley* to TV, but that first version, which starred Jackie Gleason, did not catch on. Revived in 1953, with William Bendix playing the lead role, *The Life of Riley* enjoyed a profitable five-year run on NBC. Previously, Brecher had written the screenplays of the Marx Brothers films *At the Circus* (1939) and *Go West* (1940), as well as winning an Oscar nomination for his script contributions to *Meet Me in St. Louis* (1944).

This was the first regular series role for actor Jackie Cooper; he was given one-third ownership of the property, partnering with George Burns and

Brecher. Burns, thanks to the success of his filmed version of *The George Burns and Gracie Allen Show* (CBS, 1950–58), had become something of a TV mogul at that time, with his McCadden Productions also responsible for the popular *The Bob Cummings Show* (NBC and CBS, 1955–59).

Born John Cooperman, Jr., the future Jackie Cooper began his career early, making several appearances in "Our Gang" comedies. At the age of nine, he was a Best Actor Oscar nominee for his lead role in *Skippy* (Paramount, 1931), losing out to Lionel Barrymore. He is probably the only nominee who ever waited until the next day to find out whether he won or lost, because he had long ago dozed off by the time the announcement was made. He remains to this date the youngest nominee ever in that category. A highly paid star for much of his childhood, Cooper would nonetheless see his career come to a screeching halt when he hit puberty. Offered the chance to stick around at MGM playing bit parts until he outgrew what Louis B. Mayer considered his awkward teen years, with his pay cut accordingly, Cooper declined.

After serving in the Navy during World War II, Cooper struggled to resuscitate his career. At one point, he changed his name to Jack Cooper, which he considered more befitting a leading man, and hired a press agent to sell this "new" star. The gimmick didn't work, and was quickly abandoned.

"When I was younger and insecure," Cooper admitted to reporter Vernon Scott, "I resented people saying they remembered me when I was a little boy. I thought I'd never outgrow my childhood. But now I know they mean it as a compliment. At least a dozen times a day I'm reminded of my kid pictures. It doesn't bother me now."[1]

Off camera, Cooper didn't share his character's reluctance to settle down, and had in fact been to the altar three times. Bringing a welcome stability to the actor's home life was his marriage to Barbara Kraus on April 29, 1954. That same year, his Broadway comedy *King of Hearts* ran for 279 performances, earning him the attention and respect of New York producers, and Cooper began to feel that his adult life was settling into place for the first time.

After beginning to establish his credentials as an adult actor with his Broadway work, Cooper won roles in live television shows in New York, where he soon carved out a thriving career. "Now that I've gotten into television, I intend to stick with it," he said in 1954. "It is much harder work than the movies or the stage, but I enjoy it. It's just that you have to know your parts better. You can't improve them the next night like on the stage, or do it over as in the movies. Once you are on the air, things must run like clockwork."[2]

In reality, though, the type of television work that Cooper was doing — mostly New York–based, live anthology shows — was living on borrowed time. Meanwhile, film series work, usually based in California, was booming. Reluctantly, he told his agents to pursue a sitcom for him, and *The People's Choice* was the result. He later claimed that he took the job on the basis of a talk with Brecher, declining to read the script once he'd heard the concept explained.

Having completed the pilot, he had doubts as to whether it would sell, and didn't know whether to be pleased or dismayed when it did.

His leading lady in the series was twenty-five-year-old Patricia Breslin, who'd made her television debut while still a teenager, playing Juliet in a 1949 episode of TV's *Philco Television Playhouse*. After *The People's Choice*, Breslin would be Mickey Rooney's leading lady in the film *Andy Hardy Comes Home* (1958) and later became a regular on the ABC soap opera *General Hospital* (1963–).

Moving out to Los Angeles from New York to film the series pilot, Breslin almost lost the job before she got started. Days before shooting commenced, the actress suffered an injury. "It was one of those silly things," Breslin told a reporter. "I was clowning around, practicing ballet steps in my New York apartment. Suddenly my tour didn't jete and — zing — a broken foot."[3] Luckily for Breslin, producer Brecher agreed to work around her injury rather than replace her, having every scene in the pilot blocked so as to disguise her inability to walk.

Cast as Mandy's father, Mayor John Peoples, was veteran character Paul Maxey (1907–63). Maxey, for many years a mainstay of the Pasadena Playhouse, had more than 100 movie roles to his credit, and also appeared in several early episodes of *Lassie* (CBS, 1954–71) as the father of Jeff Miller's buddy Porky.

Margaret Irving (1898–1988), seen as Aunt Gus, had a résumé that varied from her early years as a Ziegfeld girl, to a featured role opposite the Marx Brothers in Broadway's *Animal Crackers* (1928–29). In recent years, she'd had a lengthy stage run in the hit musical comedy *Happy Birthday*, starring Helen Hayes. In her late fifties, Irving brought a wealth of experience to her work in *The People's Choice*, becoming one of the show's most valuable featured players.

One of Brecher's most important casting sessions for the series involved the selection of a dog to play the role of Cleo. He paid a visit to Dorothy Shula, a breeder who specialized in basset hounds. Brecher met a number of the breeder's puppies, and was particularly taken with the dog who would become Cleo. Shula readily admitted that this particular dog had been adopted twice, but returned by the prospective owners; both times, she'd gotten carsick on the ride to her new home, and then proved to be less than fully housetrained. Hedging his bets, Brecher took along five other dogs as possible understudies for Cleo, but Cooper was instantly taken with the shy puppy and declared her his co-star. Serving as Cleo's trainer would be a young Frank Inn, later to become one of Hollywood's best-known animal wranglers. Radio and TV actress Mary Jane Croft, familiar from her many featured roles in Lucille Ball's shows, voiced Cleo. (Another voice was used in the pilot episode.)

"It was a lucky thing that Cleo was susceptible to training," Inn said in 1957. "Each film gives Cleo something different to do and I only have three or four days in which to train her. By now, she knows over one hundred different tricks which she performs on command."[4] Inn claimed that more than 35,000 fans had written in requesting photos of the canine leading lady of *The People's Choice*.

Variety's review of the show's September 1955 premiere termed it "a superficially gimmicked concoction.... [T]he writing and the characterization just wasn't there to give the farce any lasting rest. A pedestrian effort from practically every angle." Added *The New York Times* (10/7/55), "When ... *The People's Choice* was conceived, its originators must have proclaimed that it was an 'off beat' show. This, in the broadcasting business, has come to constitute an accolade. If a production is 'off beat,' it should follow that it is refreshing and appealing. But *The People's Choice* [is] one of the weirdest attempts at situation comedy since the invention of the hotfoot.... [E]ven a talking dog can't carry a show without some support from her writers."

During the show's first season, it was placed on NBC's Thursday night schedule, to follow Groucho Marx's popular *You Bet Your Life* (1950–61). After a few months, *The People's Choice* swapped time slots with Jack Webb's *Dragnet*, which had taken a hit in the ratings at 9 P.M., opposite CBS's *Climax*.

Though *The People's Choice* became a moderately successful sitcom, running three seasons before its reruns went into syndication, it was regarded with minimal fondness by star Cooper, who considered it a gimmick show and resented playing second fiddle to a wisecracking canine. Stripped of the running commentary by Cleo, *The People's Choice* would actually have been, for its time, a relatively adult comedy about male-female relationships. Unusually for the sitcoms of the day, there were no major child characters to be seen, and there was little or no slapstick comedy. (Unfortunately, as Cooper no doubt realized, *The People's Choice* without Cleo would also have been a rather dull and talky show.) Cooper later claimed that appearing in the show had, quite literally, made him sick, causing him to develop ulcers: "[F]ilmed television in general and *The People's Choice* in particular gave me a pain in the duodenum ... I had to go home every night and face the prospect of learning scenes which were written for your average, or below-average, twelve-year-old mentality."[5]

By the time *The People's Choice* ended its run, Cooper was learning that he enjoyed working behind the camera as much as, if not more than, acting. Since the second season, he had been the most frequent director of the show, ultimately helming more than two-thirds of the episodes filmed. As creator-producer Brecher's day-to-day involvement in the show lessened, Cooper increasingly took the reins. Beyond his work as an actor, he took an interest in activities such as redesigning the show's opening titles. Conscious about the show's budget as a part owner, he took pride in bringing it in under cost as often as possible.

Cooper also began developing outside projects. He told reporters that he had bought the rights to *Skippy* and would produce a new version. "I don't want to do *People's Choice* much longer," he said in 1957.⁶ He soon got his wish, as the show was canceled at the end of its third season.

Near the end of the show's run, Sock and Mandy were expecting their first child. In "The First Anniversary" (5/8/58), Sock's old Marine buddy Louie arrives in Barkerville and invites Sock to go on a week-long fishing trip. Sock wants to go, but is hesitant to tell Mandy, since it will mean being away on their anniversary, and leaving her during her pregnancy. Unbeknownst to Sock, his wife wishes he would go on the trip, so that he will feel guilty enough to buy her the $100 sack dress she wants.

Only a year after the demise of his first sitcom, Cooper returned with his second TV venture, the military comedy *Hennesey* (q.v.), which would also enjoy a three-year run. This show was more to the actor's liking than *The People's Choice*. In the mid–1960s, with acting opportunities not that impressive, Cooper took a position as head of production at Screen Gems, the television arm of Columbia Pictures, where his duties involved overseeing the production of other sitcoms like NBC's *I Dream of Jeannie* (1965–70).

The same basic gimmick that worked for *The People's Choice* resurfaced a few years later in *Happy* (q.v.)., substituting a talking baby for a talking dog. Not long afterwards, George Burns also invested money in *Mister Ed* (CBS, 1961–66), the profitable and long-running sitcom centering on a talking horse.

Pete and Gladys

Harry Morgan (*Pete Porter*), Cara Williams (*Gladys Porter*), Verna Felton (*Hilda Crocker*), Gale Gordon (*Uncle Paul Barton*), Frances Rafferty (*Nancy*), Shirley Mitchell (*Janet Colton*), Peter Leeds (*George Colton*), Mina Kolb (*Peggy Briggs*), Joe Mantell (*Ernie Briggs*), Bill Hinnant (*Bruce Carter*), Ernest Truex (*Pops*)

Executive Producer–Creator: Parke Levy. *Producer*: Devery Freeman. *Writers*: Arthur Alsberg, Nathaniel Curtis, Stan Dreben, Bob Fisher, Bill Freedman, Devery Freeman, Jim Fritzell, Everett Greenbaum, Louis M. Heyward, Walter Kempley, Parke Levy, Alan Lipscott, Samuel Locke, Bill Manhoff, Arthur Marx, Bobby O'Brien, Milton Pascal, Joel Rapp, Larry Rhine, Jack Roche, Bob Schiller, Henry Sharp, Phil Sharp, Danny Simon, Bob Weiskopf. *Directors*: Norman Abbott, Jack Arnold, Earl Bellamy, David Butler, Leslie Goodwins, James V. Kern, Sidney Lanfield, Sidney Miller, Gene Reynolds, William D. Russell. *Associate Producers*: James V. Kern, Bill Manhoff. *Story Consultant*: Arthur Alsberg. *Music Composed and Conducted by* Wilbur Hatch. *Directors of Photography*: Fred Bentley, Lester Shorr. *Assistant Directors*: Frank Mayer, Gordon McLean. *Unit Manager*: Frank Mayer. *Production Supervisor*: Gordon McLean. *Art Directors*: Albert Heschong, Stan Jolley, Hal Pereira. *Set Decorators*: Robert R. Benton, Sam Comer. *Casting*: Kerwin Coughlin. *Film Editors*: Ralph Davis, Jr., Everett Dodd, Fred Maguire, Dick Wormell. *Sound Effects Editor*: Gene Eliot. *Music Editor*: Gene Feldman. *Script Supervisors*: Jean Downing, Frances Steens. *Makeup*: Harry Ray, Roland Ray. *Property Masters*: Ross Burke, Irving Sindler. *Hair Stylist*: Lillian Shore. *Costumers*: Bill Edwards, Grace Harris, Marie Harris, Kenneth Harvey, Sylvia Liggett. *Production Sound Mixers*: Frederick A. Kessler, Harry Lindgren, Harold Lewis. Rerecording: Joel Moss. *Mr. Morgan's Wardrobe*: Kuppenheimer, Petrocelli. *Titles and Opticals*: Pacific Title. El Camino Productions, in association with CBS-TV.

Aired Mondays at 8 P.M. on CBS-TV. First aired September 19, 1960; last aired September 10, 1962. 72 black-and-white episodes.

GLADYS: Pete, why are you so suspicious?
PETE: Because I asked you to do something, and you did it!

One of television's earliest sitcom spinoffs was this early 1960s CBS show derived from supporting characters in the long-running Desilu comedy *December Bride* (1954–59). In that popular series, Spring Byington starred as Lily Ruskin, a charming and fun-loving woman in her sixties who moves in with her daughter and son-in-law, and proceeds to challenge the familiar TV stereotype of the nagging, interfering mother-in-law. Aired for several years in the 9:30 P.M. Monday slot directly after *I Love Lucy*, *December Bride* became an audience favorite.

Pete and Gladys

A key character in *December Bride*, Pete Porter (played by Harry Morgan), was the next-door neighbor and friend of the Henshaw family. Pete's cynical wisecracks provided some welcome balance to the sweetness and light that permeated much of *December Bride,* and his favorite target for insults was his never-seen wife, Gladys. The part won Morgan an Emmy nomination in 1959,

Just another average day *chez* Porter: Cara Williams and Harry Morgan are *Pete and Gladys*; or, in this case, Gladys and Pete.

just as the show was winding down after a five-year run. Morgan later said that the role of Pete Porter "spoke for all men with latent hostility to wives and mothers-in-law. Guys used to stop me in the street and congratulate me."[1]

According to his creator, veteran radio and TV comedy writer Parke Levy, Pete was an extension of the writer himself. "Call it my weird sense of humor," Levy noted, "but I've never gotten out of the habit of deflating my wife Beatrice. Particularly, when friends praise her, I tear her down, jokingly, of course. It's really a game that Beatrice, thank goodness, understands, or I wouldn't be here to tell the tale."[2]

When *December Bride* had run its course, Levy sold CBS on the idea of a follow-up show that would explore the home lives of the Porters—reportedly the idea of his much-maligned wife. CBS executives saw this as an opportunity to give America what it had clearly missed since Lucille Ball left weekly TV—a zany, impulsive redheaded housewife. In 1960, Ball relocated to New York City and signed a deal to make her Broadway debut in *Wildcat*. She was telling reporters that she intended to pursue her stage career for the next five years or so, and wouldn't be back on television any time soon. Her decision left the TV sitcom field wide open for *Pete and Gladys,* which would even air on Monday nights, long the home of Lucy on CBS.

The series opener, "For Pete's Sake" (9/19/60), scripted by Levy and his longtime associate Bill Manheim, shows Pete and Gladys Porter settling into their newly purchased home in Westwood, California. Pete takes a dislike at first glance to their new next-door neighbor Phil Martin (played by Bill Heyer), who responds in kind. Gladys, on the other hand, quickly makes friends with Phil's French-born wife Michele (Delphine Seyrig) when they meet at the beauty shop. Michele, who's used to being subservient to her husband, is intrigued by Gladys' explanation that, in America, "The men run the country, we run the men." When Michele, after Gladys' coaching, tries out a new technique on her husband—crying and saying she will go home to Mother when she doesn't get her way—Phil's feud with Pete kicks into high gear. In the end, of course, it's the women who set their men straight and bring things to a happy understanding. Also along for the ride is another favorite character from *December Bride,* the Porters' wisecracking older friend Hilda Crocker.

Though Pete's sarcastic sense of humor is alive and well, much of it here is expended on women other than Gladys. In the opening scene, when Gladys makes her first entrance carrying a moose head, Pete cracks, "Gladys! You've decapitated your mother!" Later, he tells Hilda, "Haven't I always said you'd have made a wonderful Miss America?" Knowing the rest by heart, Hilda chimes in with him as he adds, "...only they hadn't discovered it yet!"

Later episodes showed Pete working as an insurance salesman for the firm of Springer, Slocum and Klibber, Insurance Brokers, while Gladys becomes the typical *Lucy*-esque housewife with plenty of time on her hands and a never-ending variety of schemes.

Born April 10, 1915, Harry Morgan entered movies in the early 1940s, and played dozens of supporting roles before making the switch to TV with *December Bride* in 1954. Though most of his film credits were as Henry Morgan, he took to using "Harry" instead after people began to confuse him with the radio and TV comedian Henry Morgan. A solid utility player and a reliable professional, Morgan can be spotted in genuine film classics like *High Noon* (1952), but also accumulated his share of credits in more mundane fare like *Crime Doctor's Man Hunt* (1946) and *Boots Malone* (1952).

Called in to read for the part of Gladys, Cara Williams quickly showed herself to be not the typical up-and-coming actress. When Parke Levy remarked, "I've never heard of you, young lady," Williams snapped back at the veteran comedy writer, "I never heard of you either!"[3] By all indications, Williams, who also reputedly walked out on a job interview with George Cukor once when he kept her waiting too long in the outer office, and spurned an opportunity to appear in the stage musical *Goodbye Charlie* when she couldn't get along with star Lauren Bacall, was not one to stand on ceremony, or to refrain from speaking her mind.

Born Bernice Kamiat on June 29, 1925, in Brooklyn, Williams grew up poor during the early years of the Depression. In the early 1940s, while still a teenager, she and her mother relocated to California. The talented and attractive teen was signed to a contract at 20th Century–Fox, where she originally played bit roles under the stage name Bernice Kay. In 1952, she became the wife of 20-year-old aspiring actor John Barrymore, Jr., in a ceremony held in Las Vegas. Her featured role in Stanley Kramer's critically acclaimed *The Defiant Ones* (1958), opposite Tony Curtis and Sidney Poitier, won her the admiration of her leading man and, more importantly, a Best Supporting Actress nomination. That nomination perhaps explained why Williams took exception when her soon-to-be-employer Levy professed himself ignorant of her career. Tony Curtis later told a *TV Guide* reporter, "She's a complete original. There's nobody like her. She's a very sexy girl, but she's also like a man. I tell you what she's like: She's like having a best friend you'd like to kiss."[4]

Also reprising her role from *December Bride* in *Pete and Gladys* was the veteran character actress Verna Felton (1890–1966), as Hilda. Hilda served as the best friend of heroine Lily on *December Bride* and would do the same with the female star of *Pete and Gladys*. Felton received co-star billing in the show's opening titles that first year.

Aside from Felton, there were an unusual number of additional recurring characters during the show's two-year run. Seen in multiple episodes were three distinct sets of married couples who were friends and neighbors of the Porters—the Coltons, the Briggses, and the Browns. Gladys' father and nephew, as well as Pete's uncle, were seen on a recurring basis as well.

Variety's reviewer (9/21/60) seemed a bit nonplussed by the opener, which left him rather cold. "It's a comedy about a man and a wife who move into a new neighborhood, period. Nothing on which to hang the comedy ... a story line or anything resembling it was completely absent." The reviewer did feel, however, that Cara Williams was a find, praising her comedic instincts. *TV Guide* (2/10/61) thought the show "trite" and Williams "a mail-order Lucille Ball."

One of the disadvantages of a spinoff, of course, was the inconvenience of trying to remain true to what the audience already knew about the show's established characters. From the beginning, viewers could see that, despite what Pete had implied on *December Bride,* Gladys was not ugly, sloppily dressed, a lousy cook, or a nagging harridan. Those comments could be attributed to humorous exaggeration on Pete's part. However, there also remained the bothersome fact that, in the original series, Pete and Gladys had become parents. During the final season of *December Bride,* the Porter family had expanded to include baby Linda, a move the current show's writers quickly came to regret.

As Harry Morgan explained, "Even at the beginning of the new series, the baby presented plot problems. We solved it temporarily by explaining that the baby was staying with Gladys' mother until Pete and Gladys got settled into their new home."⁵ A few weeks later, however, a more drastic and permanent solution was found, and suddenly Pete and Gladys were childless. For the remainder of the series, there would be no further mention of Linda.

Initial ratings for *Pete and Gladys* were fair-to-middling. Halfway through the 1960-61 season, it was ranked among the top 40 shows on TV, enough to keep it alive in an era when, as *Time* magazine commented, "the top ten shows were once again practically the private preserve of gunslingers." *Dennis the Menace* (1959–63) and *The Andy Griffith Show* (1960–68) were among the few sitcoms really ringing the ratings bell for CBS that season. Renewed for 1961-62, the series underwent some staffing changes both in front of and behind the camera.

For the second season, *I Love Lucy* veteran Jim Kern was signed to serve as principal director and associate producer. *Lucy* writers Bob Schiller and Bob Weiskopf contributed a number of the second-year scripts as well. Verna Felton was dropped from the cast and Frances Rafferty, another *December Bride* veteran (she'd played Lily's daughter Ruth), was signed to play a recurring role as yet another friend-of-Gladys, this one named Nancy. Another recurring character added for the second season was Gladys' young nephew Bruce, a psychology student at UCLA.

Gale Gordon (1906–95) continued to appear occasionally as Pete's Uncle Paul, who'd raised him. Practical to the core, Paul took a dim view of Pete's marriage to scatterbrain Gladys since first meeting her seven years earlier, especially since disaster tended to befall him in her presence. Invited to the house in "Uncle Paul's Insurance" (10/26/61), he politely declines, saying, "I'm in no mood to have a bowling ball dropped on my toe, a drink spilled on my tie, or a banana cream pie pushed in my face." Not to mention the time Uncle Paul, an antique collector, purchased an $1,800 vintage chair, which Gladys promptly sat in and broke. Or the time she sprayed him with the garden hose, or burned a hole in his slacks while ironing his favorite suit.

Instead, persuaded to visit on a night he's told Gladys won't be home, he finds himself accidentally hypnotized and reverted to childhood, as Gladys has been. Paul and Gladys have finger-painted on the living room wall and had a mud fight before they are brought out of their trance. Off-screen, Gordon was a mild-mannered man who was once quoted as saying, "People who exhibit temper are very disagreeable. I don't like to be disagreeable."[6]

Perhaps because there were so many *Lucy* veterans on staff, the character of Gladys grew more to resemble Lucy Ricardo with the passing of time. In "The Hoarder and the Boarder" (9/21/61), Pete insists that Gladys clean out the garage, which is full of priceless treasures like the dented back fender of his wife's old car, a memento of the time she collided with Cary Grant's car.

One of the better episodes of the second season was "Who Was That Man?" (1/15/62), written by Bob Fisher and the show's story consultant, Arthur Alsberg. It begins at the breakfast table, with Pete reading aloud from a newspaper column:

> PETE: According to Dr. James F. Sorensen, there are five points that contribute to a successful marriage.
> GLADYS: Oh, go on, Pete. He's a very bright man.
> PETE: "Point one. A husband and wife should tell the truth to each other at all times."
> GLADYS: We do that, all right.
> PETE: According to points two, three, four, and five, we should now be total strangers.

Though we never learn what those other four points were, the writers have now reiterated the importance of honesty and communication between husbands and wives. So when Gladys' old boyfriend Hal Stevens calls and asks her to lunch, she tells Pete about the invitation, and declines when he shows some signs of being jealous of his old rival. Of course, she inadvertently meets up with him anyway, at a downtown hotel, and then tries to make a hasty escape when Pete unexpectedly arrives on the scene.

Not long afterwards, Gladys is hauled in by a policeman who finds her in front of the hotel, wearing a makeshift dress assembled from window treatments in Hal's room, and purposely deflating the tire of her parked car. She tries to give the police sergeant what strikes her as a perfectly logical explanation:

"Sergeant, please, you've got to hear my story! I'm a victim of circumstances. It all started when I was having coffee in this coffee shop. They spilled the coffee on me. Well, then I telephoned my husband; he was in this other booth. So naturally I hid behind the dessert cart. And I didn't want to get caught in these drapes, so I let the air out of the tire. But my husband's expecting a flat tire...."

This fast-paced episode, which really gives Williams a chance to shine, also points up the factors that perhaps doomed *Pete and Gladys* from the outset. She's given a funny script, and makes the most of it, but the specter of Lucy is everywhere. At first, the show seems to be doing a remake of one *I Love Lucy* episode ("Lucy Is a Matchmaker"), then takes a few unexpected turns and winds up reminiscent of another *Lucy* segment ("Ricky and Fred Are TV Fans"), with its climax in which Lucy and Ethel are taken into custody by the police in the midst of trying to sabotage their husbands' TV antenna. *Pete and Gladys* even uses the same character actor, Frank Nelson, as the exasperated policeman. And, of course, Gale Gordon, who would be increasingly important to Ball's career in years to come, was a semi-regular on *Gladys*, as Lucy stock player Shirley Mitchell ("Marion Strong") had been during the first season.

Though she'd previously said she had no intention of doing another TV series, Lucille Ball ultimately found herself disillusioned with Broadway. In the spring of 1962, with Desilu's fortunes on the downswing, co-owner Lucy signed a lucrative deal to return to CBS with *The Lucy Show*. Coincidentally or not, it was at about the same time that the network canceled *Pete and Gladys* after a two-year run. Still, there seemed to be faith that Cara Williams, still under long-term contract to CBS, had a future as a television star. Reruns of *Pete and Gladys* joined CBS's daytime lineup in the fall of 1962, replacing the canceled soap opera *The Brighter Day,* and would play for the next two years.

As for Morgan, he still had another twenty years of steady television work ahead of him, though he would rarely be the top-billed star in his subsequent efforts. With two series roles behind him, he rang up an amazing nine more, most of them on NBC, being a cast member of *The Richard Boone Show* (1963-64), *Kentucky Jones* (1964-65), *Dragnet* (1967-70), *The D.A.* (1971-72), *Hec Ramsey* (1972-74), *Blacke's Magic* (1986), and finally the syndicated sitcom *You Can't Take It With You* (1987-88). His most famous role, of course, was his Emmy-winning turn as Col. Sherman Potter in *M*A*S*H*. Morgan joined the show in 1975 and continued through its finale in 1983, after which he reprised his role in the unsuccessful spinoff *AfterMASH* (CBS, 1983-84).

As late as 1975, however, as he was just beginning his long run as Colonel Potter, Morgan told a journalist that he still counted *Pete and Gladys* among his best TV experiences. "My favorite [character] was Pete in *Pete and Gladys* because I just played myself."[7]

Creator–executive producer Parke Levy returned to CBS one last time with *Many Happy Returns* (1964-65), a sitcom lucky enough to be slotted in the 9:30 P.M. Monday berth following *The Lucy Show.* This series, which dealt with the staff of a department store's complaint counter, he also attributed to his wife, whom he claimed was well-known to the staff of the Los Angeles retailer Ohrbach's. But when his dealings with network executives over that show turned into an ugly power struggle over creative control, Levy, already a wealthy man from *December Bride* and other projects, walked away, allowing *Returns* to die after 26 segments.

Following her co-starring role in the Danny Kaye comedy *The Man from the Diner's Club* (1963), Cara Williams returned to prime TV with star billing in *The Cara Williams Show*. That highly touted show, which co-starred Frank Aletter, was one of the major flops of the 1964-65 season, and from that point forward Williams' TV career slowed. Absent from screens (except in reruns) for almost a decade, she resurfaced in a recurring role in the early years of *Rhoda* (CBS, 1974–78). Otherwise, Williams did little TV work, racked up a few more film credits, and retired from acting in the late 1970s.

Always somewhat ambivalent about her career, the leading lady of *Pete and Gladys* once said, "I'm not out to prove anything. I'm not about to give it all up to do a play on Broadway ... I know some people will say I'm not a good actress for saying this, but anyone who plays a heavy drama night after night — well, it's got to be for the money. There's nothing worse than yesterday's lines."[8]

Peter Loves Mary

Peter Lind Hayes (*Peter Lindsey*), Mary Healy (*Mary Lindsey*), Bea Benaderet (*Wilma*), Merry Martin (*Leslie Lindsey*), Gil Smith (*Stevie Lindsey*), Sarah Marshall (*Gloria Watkins*), Ronny Graham (*Barry Watkins*), Joan Tompkins (*Claire Rogers*), David Lewis (*Bill Rogers*), Herb Ellis (*Lou Porter*), Howard Smith (*Horace Gibney*)

Producer: Billy Friedberg. *Format Created by* Danny Simon. *Writers*: Norman Barasch, Mel Diamond, Billy Friedberg, Sam Locke, Carrol Moore, Joel Rapp, Terry Ryan, David Schwartz, Mel Tolkin. *Writing Supervisor*: Billy Friedberg. *Directors*: Robert Butler, Sidney Miller. *Associate Producer*: Edward Rissien. *Directors of Photography*: Frank Carson, Carl Guthrie, Harry Wild. *Production Manager*: Barry Crane. *Art Director*: George Renne. *Supervising Art Director*: Richard Berres. *Assistant Director*: Bob Vreeland. *Set Decorators*: Carl Biddiscombe, James Roach. *Production Supervisor*: Jack Sonntag. *Music*: Buddy Bregman. *Music Supervisor*: Herschel Burke Gilbert. *Editorial Supervisor*: Bernard Burton. *Editors*: Dick Heermance, Thomas Neff. *Sound*: Stephen Bass, Woodruff H. Clarke, Earl Snyder, Jack Solomon. *Sound Effects*: Norval Crutcher, Jr. *Assistant to Producer*: Thelda Victor. *Makeup*: Burris Grimwood, Nick Marcellino, Carlie Taylor. *Casting*: Stalmaster-Lister Company. Four Star–Mirisch–Mount Tom Productions in association with Mirisch Telefilms, Inc.

Aired Wednesdays at 10 P.M. on NBC-TV. First aired October 12, 1960; last aired May 31, 1961. 32 black-and-white episodes.

PETER (*with wife Mary, at the breakfast table*): Where are Leslie and Stevie?
MARY: Out in the yard playing, since eight o'clock.
PETER: Oh? Is it good for anybody to be outdoors so long?

This single-season NBC sitcom cast its husband-and-wife stars in somewhat autobiographical roles—as married entertainers who decide to move out of New York City and into a peaceful Connecticut suburb. Familiar faces to television audiences since the late 1940s, Peter Lind Hayes and Mary Healy were known mostly for their work on live variety and talk shows. This was their only venture into a filmed situation comedy.

The second episode, "High Society" (10/19/60), began with a brief explanation of the show's premise, for viewers who had missed the previous week's show. In the episode's opening moments, over an aerial view of Connecticut, an off-screen narrator reports, "This is Suburbia, U.S.A., a phenomenon of the twentieth century." As Peter, Mary and their children appear onscreen, he continues, "And here are four pioneers to the new land of the PTA, the shopping center, and the crabgrass. Welcome, noble settlers, to the modern community of Oakdell!"

Their longtime live-in housekeeper, who has made the move with them from city apartment to suburban home, is Wilma, who refers to Peter as "Squire Lindsey." The two children, Leslie and Stevie, would be relatively minor characters in the series, not even appearing in some episodes.

The show's opening titles showed animated figures of Peter and Mary first

Peter Lind Hayes (right) kisses real-life wife Mary Healy, as their juvenile co-stars from *Peter Loves Mary,* Gil Smith and Merry Martin, look on.

performing before a TV camera, then being whisked away by taxi to the train station, where they board a train, cross the bridge from New York, and finally take a station wagon from the train station to their home in the Connecticut suburbs. Like *Mrs. G. Goes to College* (q.v.), *Peter Loves Mary* originated from Four Star Productions. The company, responsible for the popular shows *The Rifleman* (ABC, 1958–63) and *Wanted: Dead or Alive* (CBS, 1958–61), also sold another sitcom, *The Tom Ewell Show* (q.v.), to CBS that year.

In "High Society," Peter and Mary are newly arrived in their suburban home of Oakdell, and the local newspaper has reported the arrival of this celebrity couple "of stage and television." Mary is craving an invitation to a society party being thrown by Mr. and Mrs. Phillip Haggermeyer, but their only social invitation is to get together with an old show business chum, "Peanuts" Hagen (played by guest star Paul Hartman), who's delighted to learn they've settled in Oakdell. In a series of misunderstandings, the Lindseys decline an invitation from Hagen in hopes that an invitation from the Haggermeyers for the same evening will materialize, not knowing that Phillip Hagermeyer and "Peanuts" Hagen are in fact the same person. Meanwhile, Mary, having her hair done, makes friends with the Haggermeyers' maid, whom she mistakes for the mistress of the house, and is puzzled when she's invited to a stock car race.

In "A Star Is Born" (11/23/60), Peter and Mary's eight-year-old daughter Leslie is cast as the lead in the school play, but proves to have absolutely no talent for singing, dancing, or acting. Offering to direct the show, Peter tries to prevent Leslie from being embarrassed by cutting as many of her scenes as he can. But the parents of other children whose roles were reduced or eliminated by Peter's rewrites take offense, and since they are also some of the town's main merchants and workers, suddenly the Lindseys have no telephone or electrical service, their garbage is left at their curb, and inedible meat is served for dinner.

Though the show revolves primarily around their home life, it's made clear that Peter and Mary continue a busy performing career as well. In one episode, they mention being home in Oakdell for the first time in a month. Others tell the stories of what happens when Peter decides to write his memoirs, as well as his efforts to obtain the starring role in a new television sitcom called *Depend on Daddy.*

Hayes thought the show business angle set *Peter Loves Mary* apart from the glut of other family-based TV sitcoms. Pointing out that no one ever saw *The Adventures of Ozzie and Harriet*'s Ozzie Nelson in his work life, Hayes added, "I think we've got a good situation because you know what I do. I'm an entertainer, and so is Mary. The conflict comes because I like the show biz life, and Mary goes for the garden club, PTA bit."[1] To Mary's disapproving father, Peter is "a simple, well-meaning, bumbling knucklehead," even more so after an IQ test gives him a 97 score.

Of course, there had been a little sitcom called *I Love Lucy* that covered somewhat similar territory, and Hayes joked that the working title for their new series had been *I Hate Desi*. There was something of a role reversal, however, since Hayes undertook the bulk of the comedic work in the series, while wife Mary Healy primarily served as his down-to-earth straight woman. Another prospective title, *Peter and Mary*, was vetoed when someone took note of CBS's new sitcom *Pete and Gladys* (q.v.) and decided the two titles could be confusing. Unlike *I Love Lucy*, though, *Peter Loves Mary* would allude to its stars' nightclub act, but seldom actually show them at work. The episode "Peter Takes Stock" (3/29/61), in which Peter, Mary and her father Horace help out at a friend's struggling nightclub, provides the most extensive look at what their act might have been like, with Hayes performing several impersonations in costume, and Healy revealing a lovely singing voice.

Other episodes were largely standard-issue sitcom. In "The Best Women" (12/7/60), Mary and her friends Gloria and Claire have all been nominated for the presidency of the Oakdell Garden Club. None of the women especially wants to be elected, but their husbands' competitive nature is aroused, and in short order Mary's and Claire's candidacy is the subject of full-page campaign ads in the local newspaper, the *Oakdell Chronicle*, while the Lindseys' neighbor Barry Watkins sends a car down the main street of town with a loudspeaker urging passersby to elect his wife Gloria.

Born June 25, 1915, as Joseph Conrad Lind, Peter Lind Hayes was the son of a vaudeville performer, actress-singer Grace Hayes, and was indoctrinated into the show business life practically from birth. While still a teenager, he was onstage at the famed Palace Theater, doing a featured comedy routine in his mother's act. In 1940, he met and married Mary Healy, a Hollywood newcomer under contract to 20th Century–Fox who'd previously been named Miss New Orleans of 1935. Hayes soon became aware that his new wife was a fine singer. Professionally, they became a team in 1947, not long after Hayes' discharge from the Air Force, and seldom performed separately from that point on.

Hayes and Healy were early converts to the television industry. Still in demand for nightclub work, Mr. and Mrs. Peter Lind Hayes nonetheless pursued a steady gig in television, in the hopes of having a steadier home life. In 1949, they'd adopted a baby boy, Michael, and had plans to add a daughter to the family as well.

That same year, Hayes and Healy starred in their first regular series, *Inside U.S.A. with Chevrolet*, a musical revue seen Thursday nights on CBS. (This show afforded Lucille Ball one of her first television appearances, prior to *I Love Lucy*.) That show lasted only one season, but Hayes and Healy were back in the fall of 1950 in NBC's *The Peter and Mary Show*. Retitled *The Peter Lind Hayes Show* after a few weeks on the air, this hybrid sitcom-sketch show had the stars playing themselves, in the format of hosts who each week presented as their dinner guest a well-known singer, comedian, or actor. The show's set was built to resemble the stars' real home. The supporting cast included character actress

Mary Wickes, who played their housekeeper in early segments. A contemporary critic said the guest star lineup wasn't bad, and enjoyed some of the singing, but thought the show's format flawed. "We can't quite see a home couple hanging about the house in evening clothes and bursting into song at the drop of a cue line."[2]

Not so widely known to modern audiences, Hayes and Healy were familiar faces and voices to most viewers of the 1950s and early 1960s. For much of the 1950s, they were under contract to CBS to serve as substitute hosts for Arthur Godfrey's radio and television shows whenever he was ill or on vacation. Their 1953 movie, *The 5,000 Fingers of Dr. T.*, a Dr. Seuss–devised fantasy co-starring Hans Conried, was a notorious bomb in its day, but has since become something of a cult film. In 1958, Hayes and Healy teamed for the Broadway comedy *Who Was That Lady I Saw You With?* by Norman Krasna, which ran for just over 200 performances. That fall, Hayes began a daily 60-minute talk-variety show on ABC television, but the morning show was not a success and ended after a brief run. Profiling them in *The Saturday Evening Post* in 1958, journalist Pete Martin noted, "The rapport between Peter and Mary ... is rare and special. It's more than husband-and-wife rapport—it's vaudeville-team understanding—a talent for anticipating each other's thoughts and actions as well as words. An audience is aware of the magic between the two."[3]

Though the routines of suburban life were new to their *Peter Loves Mary* characters, Hayes and Healy were in fact longtime residents of New Rochelle, which would soon become well-known as the home of the fictional characters of *The Dick Van Dyke Show* (CBS, 1961–66). In the early 1950s, they saved their money to buy a home, a commitment that held particular meaning for the couple. "My father died when I was two years old," Hayes explained. "Mary's father died when she was very young, too. Neither of us knew what it was to have a complete home life when we were young, and I think that's given us a drive to make sure our own kids have a chance for full happiness—a nice home in a nice town, and a full set of parents."[4]

Prior to launching their sitcom, Hayes and Healy had been going through a period of relative inactivity, taking time off from their usual TV chores for travel and leisure. Hayes admitted, however, that he was ill-suited to downtime. "How did I bear up, doing nothing? Badly. It wasn't so bad when the weather was good and I could play golf or go on the boat. But when winter fell, I had nothing to do but stay indoors and stare at the walls."[5]

While Hayes readily admitted that the potential financial windfall from reruns of a hit series had tempted him and his wife, he said there was another impetus for their desire to switch from live TV to film. "For ten years Mary and I did some of our best things on live television. And after they were over there was no record of what we had done, and no residual payments. When I get to be 65 years old and my kids ask me what we did in show business I want to be able to run off some films for them — and also have some money in the bank from residuals."⁶ They were encouraged by the success of their former New Rochelle neighbor John Forsythe, going into his fourth year as the well-remunerated star of *Bachelor Father* (NBC, CBS and ABC, 1957–62). Also encouraging was their friend Lucille Ball, who told Mr. and Mrs. Hayes that working in a weekly series opposite husband Desi Arnaz in *I Love Lucy* had given them some of the happiest times of their marriage.

Featured in the series as housekeeper Wilma was character actress Bea Benaderet (1906–68). Benaderet said she felt fortunate to be offered the job after her long affiliation with the Burns and Allen television shows. "I am so lucky to be able to jump from one series to another," she said. "So many people in this business wouldn't take a chance — they'd be afraid I'd be too closely associated with Burns and Allen. Others like the people connected with *Peter Loves Mary* do you the courtesy of assuming you can act. I've never been a one-faceted person and I don't intend to start now."⁷ Benaderet employs a slightly more stylized speaking voice in this role than she did as Blanche Morton on *The George Burns and Gracie Allen Show* (CBS, 1950–58). Roughly simultaneous with her debut on *Peter Loves Mary* was the beginning of Benaderet's long-lasting gig as the voice of Betty Rubble on *The Flintstones* (ABC, 1960–66).

Serving as the program's principal director was Sid Miller, best-known for his work with actor-dancer Donald O'Connor. Prior to assuming the helm of *Peter Loves Mary*, Miller had recently completed directing Lou Costello in *The 30-Foot Bride of Candy Rock* (1959), and had also had a stint with Walt Disney Productions. Potential sponsor Procter and Gamble reportedly viewed only about half of the pilot episode before making a firm offer for a season's worth of shows on NBC, with 32 original segments to be followed by seven repeats.

Once the pilot sold, Mr. and Mrs. Hayes took up temporary residence in California. Ironically, *Peter Loves Mary* caused them to do exactly the opposite of what their TV characters were experiencing. The Hayes' real-life children, similar in age to their sitcom counterparts, were left at home in New Rochelle, in the care of their grandmother, while Peter and Mary worked on the West Coast.

"Tell you the truth," Hayes said, "Mary isn't going into this series wholeheartedly. She'd rather be home in New Rochelle than go trotting off to California to make the shows. But people keep telling her she'll change her mind. Lucille Ball, for one. Lucy's assured Mary that after she sees herself in a few shows, she'll flip."⁸ By mid–July, they had relocated to California and rehearsals for the new series were underway.

Though it wasn't widely discussed at the time, there was another reason why Healy was uncertain about taking on the full-time job of starring in *Peter Loves Mary*. Only weeks before Hayes and Healy moved to the West Coast to begin the series, she had undergone a mastectomy. Much later, she admitted that she "was physically and psychologically shook up"⁹ by her bout with breast cancer. It was on the advice of her doctor that she resumed a regular work schedule so quickly after her surgery.

Initial critical reaction to the show was mixed. *Variety* (10/19/60), after giving the season opener a look, thought Mr. and Mrs. Hayes were not yet adjusted to filmed sitcom work, citing "their joint inability to deliver dialog in a natural or fluid manner." More to the critic's liking was the part of the segment that allowed the stars to present a portion of their nightclub act. *Time*'s reviewer (10/24/60) disliked the sitcom; he thought Hayes and Healy "charming and civilized performers. But the show is brainless." The Associated Press' Cynthia Lowry (10/13/60) was dubious as well: "Maybe subsequent shows will improve and the first episode was merely an effort to get the situation and the characters established...." A more favorable reaction came from *The New York Times* (10/13/60), whose reviewer termed the series opener "a light-hearted fast moving affair" that ably showcased Hayes' "skillful horseplay."

Though Benaderet and the child actors who played the younger Lindseys were the only performers given regular featured billing in the show's closing titles, a variety of recurring characters were established during the first season's 32 shows. Howard Smith made several appearances as Mary's father Horace Gibney, owner of a plastics manufacturing company, while Peter's agent Lou was seen as well. Smith's role was much like the one he would play as the overbearing industrialist Harvey Griffin on *Hazel* (NBC and CBS, 1961–66), which premiered one year later. Seasoned radio actress Betty Garde made a few appearances as Gladys, the sour maid next door who was Wilma's friend. Alan Reed's guest appearance in the pilot has led some TV historians to wrongly credit him as a regular in the series.

With time, network executives and sponsors learned that 10 P.M. was an inauspicious time slot in which to air a situation comedy. The 1960-61 network schedules were heavily populated with new sitcoms, among them a few that would make television history. ABC launched *My Three Sons,* starring Fred MacMurray, which enjoyed an unprecedented twelve-year run there and later on CBS, while CBS' *The Andy Griffith Show* (1960–68) achieved both critical acclaim and popularity. However, on the whole the networks' track record that year was discouraging. By late March (3/31/61), *Time* tabbed the 1960-61 season "the worst in the 13-year history of U.S. network television." They reported that some thirty shows were destined for the scrap heap, among them *Peter Loves Mary.*

Peter Loves Mary proved to be the final major television exposure for Mr. and Mrs. Hayes. By the time of its cancellation in the spring of 1961, New York City, from where most of their television and radio programs had originated, was rapidly losing its position as the primary television production center. Most filmed programs, by then, originated in California. In 1963, they began a stint hosting a daily morning talk show for New York City's WOR radio, broadcast live from their New Rochelle home. Mary, in particular, accepted few jobs from that point forward that required her to be away from home, and Hayes began to perform solo more than he ever had in the past fifteen years. He continued to make occasional TV or movie appearances into the first half of the 1980s.

A year or so after *Peter Loves Mary* was junked, its star admitted that he had been disappointed with his own show, calling the experience "a complete waste of time. The pressures of getting out a show a week were too much — no time to fix up scripts, edit lines to make them sharper. Out of 32 shows we did, I would only want to look at six again."[10] One of Mary's most enduring memories of the series was the offstage friendship that developed between Mr. and Mrs. Hayes and young actor Steve McQueen, shooting *Wanted: Dead or Alive* on an adjoining soundstage.

Hayes died on April 22, 1998, in Las Vegas, at a hospice where he had been a resident. He was survived by Mary and by their two children. Though *Peter Loves Mary* may not have left behind the legacy that Mr. and Mrs. Hayes had hoped, there is a living, breathing reminder of the couple and their stardom. The family tradition is carried on by their actress daughter Cathy Lind Hayes, who was a regular on the sitcom *Chicken Soup* (ABC, 1989), and more recently had a recurring role on *Grey's Anatomy* (ABC, 2005–).

The Tom Ewell Show

Tom Ewell (*Tom Potter*), Marilyn Erskine (*Fran Potter*), Mabel Albertson (*Irene Brady*), Cindy Robbins (*Carol Potter*), Sherry Alberoni (*Debbie Potter*), Eileen Chesis (*Sissy Potter*), Norman Fell (*Howie Fletcher*)
Producer: Hy Averback. *Creators*: Bob Carroll, Jr., Madelyn Martin. *Writers*: Bob Carroll, Jr., Iz Elinson, Fred S. Fox, Howard Leeds, Madelyn Martin, Michael Morris, Milton Pascal, Larry Rhine, Max Wilk. *Script Consultants*: Bob Carroll, Jr., Madelyn Martin. *Directors*: Hy Averback, Bill Harmon, Richard Kinon, James Sheldon. *Writing Supervisor*: Billy Friedberg. *Associate Producer*: Bill Harmon. *Music*: Jerry Fielding. *Music Scoring*: Rudy Schrager. *Music Supervisor*: Herschel Burke Gilbert. *Production Supervisor*: Jack Sonntag. *Editorial Supervisor*: Bernard Burton. *Supervising Art Director*: Bill Ross. *Art Directors*: Gibson A. Holley, George Renne. *Directors of Photography*: Chas E. Burke, Frank Carson, Carl Guthrie, Harry Wild. *Production Managers*: Barry Crane, Bruce Fowler, Jr. *Assistant Directors*: Don Torpin, Bob Vreeland. *Editors*: Chandler House, Thomas Scott, Sherman Todd. *Music Editor*: Aubrey Lind. *Set Decorators*: Chester Bayhi, Pat Delaney, James E. Roach. *Makeup*: Burris Grimwood, Paul Malcolm, Phillip Rhodes, Carlie Taylor. *Sound*: Frank Sarver, Earl Snyder. *Sound Effects*: Verna Fields. *Wardrobe*: Robert B. Harris. *Casting*: Phil Benjamin, Marjory McKay. *Mr. Ewell's Suits*: Kuppenheimer Clothes. Four Star Productions.
Aired Tuesdays at 9 P.M. on CBS-TV. First aired September 27, 1960; last aired July 18, 1961. 32 black-and-white episodes.

CAROL (with her sisters in tow): Daddy, we'd like to talk to you.
TOM (puzzled): They can't have spent that money already.

Best known for his comic turn opposite Marilyn Monroe in *The Seven Year Itch* (1955), actor Tom Ewell made his television series debut with this CBS sitcom casting him as a hapless suburban husband and father bedeviled by the women in his life. *The Tom Ewell Show* was the first major post–*I Love Lucy* project for writers Bob Carroll, Jr., and Madelyn Pugh (renamed Madelyn Martin since her marriage to up-and-coming TV producer Quinn Martin). Martin said the series concept was inspired by her father's life; the original title of the show was *David's Harem*.

Ewell played real estate salesman Tom Potter, living in Las Palmas, California, with his wife of twenty years and three daughters—17-year-old Carol, 11-year-old Debbie, and six-year-old Sissy. Given the frequency of their assaults on his wallet, Tom sometimes refers to them as "three short gold diggers." In the pilot, "Tom Takes Over," written by Carroll and Martin, Tom is feeling crowded by the women in his life. After a frustrating morning in which he can't shave because all the hot water is gone, is pestered by teenage daughter Carol to lend her his car, and shells out money for her younger sister's new dress, Tom complains to his buddy Fletch (played by Frank Nelson) about what he terms "that harem of mine."

In addition to wife Fran, mother-in-law Irene, and his three daughters, Tom also shares his home with a dog named Mitzi and a cockatiel, Phoebe. "Do you have any idea what it's like to live in a house with wall-to-wall women?" Tom confesses to Fletch that he has a recurring dream in which he's able, for once, to spend a quiet evening alone by himself. Not knowing that his mother-in-law is listening, Tom says gloomily that it'll never happen, especially with Mother Brady, who's been visiting for the past five years, "stuck to us like a poultice."

Upon realizing he's been overheard, a shamefaced Tom tries bringing home gifts for his women to make amends. But Fran coolly informs him that her mother took a bus out of town that afternoon, and that she and the girls will go to the movies so as to give him his precious evening alone.

Tom soon misses his family, even more so when he learns that Fran had an attack of appendicitis while at the movies and was rushed to the hospital for surgery. He assures his wife that he can readily assume responsibility for their daughters during her hospital stay and convalescence, but his self-confidence proves misplaced.

The episode's slapstick climax, reminiscent of the famed "Job Switching" episode of *I Love Lucy*, finds Tom throwing the house into chaos with his attempts to make breakfast for his daughters. After burning a pan of sweet rolls, letting a pot of oatmeal overflow onto the floor, and destroying his necktie in the garbage disposal, the hapless homemaker finally throws in the towel. When his mother-in-law returns, he gratefully accepts her help, saying, "It takes a heap of women to make a house a home."

Film and Broadway actor Tom Ewell came to series television with *The Tom Ewell Show,* a program he would later describe as "stupid."

Aired as the show's fourth episode on October 18, 1960, the pilot was produced and directed by Jerry Thorpe, who'd previously helmed *December Bride* (CBS, 1954–59) for Desilu. Set to produce the weekly series was actor-turned-producer Hy Averback, who'd recently been working on *The Real McCoys* (ABC and CBS, 1957–63). Averback also served as the series' principal director.

Born April 29, 1909, in Owensboro, Kentucky, as Yewell Tompkins, Ewell was a student at the University of Wisconsin, headed for a career as a lawyer, when he confessed his longing for show business to a similarly inclined school friend, Don Ameche. Both men got their feet wet as actors in stock companies in the late 1920s. After making his Broadway debut in 1934, playing a small role in *They Shall Not Die,* Ewell carved out a solid New York acting career over the next dozen years. His early years were difficult, playing roles in more than 20 shows that opened and closed quickly. His career was interrupted only by his wartime service in the Navy. In 1947, the stage comedy *John Loves Mary* became one of his first major hits.

Though he'd played a small film role as early as 1940, it was his featured role in *Adam's Rib* (1949) that made him a known entity in Hollywood. When his Broadway hit comedy *The Seven Year Itch,* for which he won a Best Actor Tony, was adapted to film in 1955, Ewell reprised his stage role opposite Marilyn Monroe. The role solidified his typecasting as an average Joe, middle-class husband, but follow-up roles of similar quality and popularity were limited. At the age of fifty, Ewell was open to the idea of starring in his own television show.

"I've really been looking for a series for a long time," he said shortly before his show's September 1960 debut. "I was so anxious to find a series that for the past few years I've been restricting my [television] appearances to one or two a season. I didn't want to be in the position of having worn out my welcome before I had a show of my own."[1] Before signing up for *The Tom Ewell Show,* he'd had a development deal with NBC, but that network had been unable to come up with a vehicle that Ewell liked.

The quick sale of the pilot forced Ewell to resign from the cast of *A Thurber Carnival,* a Broadway comedy in which his co-stars included Alice Ghostley, Paul Ford, and Peggy Cass. Ewell had long wanted to do the Thurber show, and regretted leaving it once it had been successfully launched, but also had high hopes for his new TV venture. The 51-year-old star's proceeds from *The Tom Ewell Show* were intended to insure a reliable financial future for his wife and young son. His work schedule for the sitcom, however, which found him waking at 5:30 A.M., and returning home some 14 or 15 hours later, left him little time to spend with his five-year-old son Taylor.

Marilyn Erskine, signed to play Tom's wife Fran in the show, was only in her mid-thirties but already boasted a long list of film and television credits, including appearances in most of the prestige video anthologies of the 1950s (*Studio One, Robert Montgomery Presents,* etc.). Born April 24, 1926, Erskine was an actress from early childhood. She made her Broadway debut co-starring with Shirley Booth in *Excursion* (1937), appeared in radio dramas like *Life Can Be Beautiful* and *Road of Life,* and went on to be an original cast member of *Our Town*. It was in New York that she first made friends with Ewell. She relocated to California in 1950, touring with a show she'd done on Broadway, and never left. In 1954, she teamed with Keefe Brasselle for *The Eddie Cantor Story,* in which she played wife Ida. After a brief, early marriage to film producer-director Stanley Kramer was annulled, Erskine married an insurance executive and had two children.

Said Ewell of his leading lady, "She's one of the easiest people in the world to work with. Of course I'd tell you that anyway, but it happens to be true. And talented."[2]

Cast as Tom's mother-in-law was the gifted character actress Mabel Albertson (1901–82), best known for her later role as neurotic mother-in-law Phyllis Stephens on *Bewitched* (ABC, 1964–72). The sister of actor Jack Albertson, she was already a veteran of the Desilu sitcom *Those Whiting Girls* (CBS, 1955–57). Former Mouseketeer Sherry Alberoni, who'd earlier appeared in another family-based sitcom, *The Ed Wynn Show* (NBC, 1958-59), was cast as middle daughter Debbie. Pretty Cindy Robbins, who played eldest daughter Carol, had been the subject of a studio promotional campaign that dubbed the blonde newcomer "The Champagne Girl." She later became the wife of actor-singer Tommy Leonetti.

Actor Norman Fell, years before his memorable stint as Stanley Roper on *Three's Company* (ABC, 1977–84), had a recurring role as Tom's best friend Howie Fletcher (known to all as Fletch), the proprietor of Fletcher's Pharmacy. He replaced longtime Jack Benny collaborator Frank Nelson, who'd essayed the same role in the series pilot. Though not a regular, Alice Ghostley, Ewell's stage co-star from *A Thurber Carnival,* turned up twice in the series with Special Guest Star billing. Initially cast as one of Tom's real estate clients, Ghostley resurfaced a few weeks later to play his eccentric, widowed sister Polly.

CBS placed the show on its Tuesday night schedule, with a lead-in from the popular *The Many Loves of Dobie Gillis* (1959–63). Ewell's competition on NBC was the Boris Karloff–hosted horror-mystery anthology *Thriller* (1960–62). Ad agency executives and other industry observers fully expected Ewell's show to emerge as a sizable hit amidst a boatload of other sitcom newcomers.

Critic Bill Fiset professed himself a longtime admirer of Ewell's comic gifts, but hated the show nonetheless. "The half hour series is a situation comedy of the sofa school. The TV family sits on a sofa in the living room and tries to be funny. I think it's the same sofa used by *Danny Thomas, Father Knows Best, My Three Sons, Fibber McGee* and dozens of others. I think the jokes have been used by dozens of others, too."[3] *Time* magazine (10/10/60), similarly unimpressed, dryly suggested an alternate title for the show: *Father Knows Nothing.*

Even after several episodes of his show were in the can, Ewell was uncertain how things were going. Used to playing his comedy before a live audience on Broadway, and to being able to work out the kinks during out-of-town previews, he felt unable to gauge whether or not the show was funny. Initial viewership was high, but Ewell had concerns nonetheless. After watching the first aired episode of his show, and reading the initial reviews, which were mixed, Ewell decided the show needed some retooling. In particular, he felt that the emphasis on broad physical comedy had been a mistake.

"The ideal family in TV consists of three children and a dog," he postulated in a December 1960 interview. "And when you get in that situation, it must be played realistically. But farce is not realistic, it is not to be believed. And because it is artificial, the tempo is different and you defeat it if you try to play it in a realistic atmosphere."[4] He also felt vindicated by the reviews in his own concern that his character had been written as a typical bumbling sitcom dad.

Ewell told reporters that future episodes of *The Tom Ewell Show* would strike out on a different path. However, his desire to see the show become subtler and more believable inevitably put him at odds with writer-creators Carroll and Martin. According to Carroll, he and his writing partner had seen a similarity between Ewell and Lucille Ball, both of them able to register funny reactions to bizarre situations. The former *Lucy* writers had told interviewers unapologetically during the early days of *The Tom Ewell Show* that comedy akin to what they had written for Lucy would be the order of the day. "Time to get out the fright wigs and the cream pies," Martin had said a few months earlier. Carroll concurred: "We're going broad again. It's wild time."[5]

Though initially the star had bowed to his writers' successful sitcom experience, by the time a handful of episodes had aired, Ewell was determined to chart a different course. In late October, Carroll and Martin were relieved of their responsibilities as head writers of *The Tom Ewell Show*. They retained their ownership stake in the series, but would have no day-to-day involvement with subsequent episodes. Billy Friedberg assumed the task of supervising the show's scripts.

The basic premise, however, was largely unchanged. In "No Fun in the Sun" (1/17/61), Tom has been advised by his doctor to slow down and take a little time for relaxation. Tom and Fran make reservations for a long weekend at a resort hotel, planning to leave the girls behind in the care of Fran's mother. Once the Potters' vacation is underway, though, Tom finds himself unable to put the girls out of his mind, despite the best efforts of the resort's overbearing social director to involve him in games, hikes, sports, etc. Eventually, Tom and Fran cut their weekend short and spend the rest of their vacation at home with their family.

Like most sitcom dads, Tom Potter seems to be more capable and functional at the office than he is at home. Confident in his sales technique as a real estate man, Tom explains his philosophy to a young protégé in "The Salesmanship Lesson" (12/27/60). Gesturing to the street map of Las Palmas he keeps over his desk at work, Tom says of his community, "It looks placid. But under the surface, it's seething with unrest. The people with little places want big places. The people with big places want bigger places. And the people with bigger places are crying taxes, and want to get back to the little places."

He even numbers a celebrity or two among his client list. In "Site Unseen" (12/6/60), Dick Powell, head of Four Star Television, made a cameo appearance as himself. The plot involves Tom's efforts to lease some open land outside Las Palmas to Powell's production company for location shoots, only to have second thoughts when it appears that the profitable deal will disturb the quality of life in Tom's community.

In the spring of 1961, CBS canceled *The Tom Ewell Show*. The decision came as a surprise to some, including the star himself, who had recently purchased a house in California. The show's ratings were in fact pretty decent, outpacing *Thriller* and ABC's *Stagecoach West*, and above the 30 share usually cited as the benchmark for renewal, but the ax was dropped nonetheless.

Making plans to return to the stage that summer, Ewell took a philosophical view of the cancellation. "When I start a show, I'm always aware there'll be a closing time," he told columnist Hedda Hopper. "Sometimes it comes too soon and you end regretfully; again it comes too late and you suffer from the strain of an overlong run."[6] Over the next few years, his television work was limited, with the actor preferring to concentrate his energies on theater. For a time during the 1960s, his sitcom would be revived in syndication under the title *The Trouble with Tom*.

Though his TV sitcom had not been a success, it appeared that Ewell would be given a second try. In late 1962, *TV Guide* columnist Dan Jenkins reported that Four Star Productions was at work on a new show for the actor, with the working title *The Little World of Tom Springer*. The format of the show called for Ewell to play what another journalist termed "the philosophying [sic] proprietor of a small town general store."[7] No such show appeared on network schedules, however.

Ewell returned to television in the 1970s, accepting a co-star role on the popular cop show *Baretta* (ABC, 1975–78) with Robert Blake. He later spent a year playing an inebriated Old West doctor in the ABC sitcom *Best of the West* (1981-82), which drew nice reviews but limited audiences. The veteran actor died on September 12, 1994, at the age of 85, at the Motion Picture Country House and Hospital in Woodland Hills, California, after a series of illnesses.

Of the sitcom that had borne his name, he said dismissively in 1969, "It was a stupid series. I'd just as soon forget about it."[8]

Wendy and Me

Connie Stevens (*Wendy Conway*), George Burns (*Himself*), Ron Harper (*Jeff Conway*), James Callahan (*Danny Adams*), J. Pat O'Malley (*Mr. Bundy*), Bartlett Robinson (*Willard Norton*)
Executive Producer: William T. Orr. Producer: George Burns. Writers: William Burns, Elon Packard, Norman Paul. Director: Gene Reynolds. Associate Producer: Herm Saunders. Director of Photography: Louis Jennings. Art Directors: Art Loel, Carl Macauley. Film Editors: George R. Rohrs, Noel L. Scott, Bill Wiard. Music: George Duning. Music Editor: Erma E. Levin. Sound: Samuel F. Goode, Stanley Jones, Francis E. Stahl. Assistant Director: Phil Rawlins. Set Decorators: Theodore Driscoll, William L. Kuehl. Makeup Supervisor: Gordon Bau. Supervising Hair Stylist: Jean Burt Reilly. Wardrobe for Connie Stevens: Très Gay. Wardrobe for George Burns: Tavelman of Beverly Hills. Warner Brothers Pictures, in association with Natwil Productions.
Aired Mondays at 9 P.M. on ABC-TV. First aired September 14, 1964; last aired September 6, 1965. 34 black-and-white episodes.

The 1958 retirement of Gracie Allen brought to a close the record-breaking career of one of show business' most popular and beloved comedy teams, Burns and Allen. Over the course of more than 30 years, George Burns and wife Gracie found favor with audiences in vaudeville, radio, films, and finally their hit television series *The George Burns and Gracie Allen Show* (CBS, 1950–58). Not ready to retire when his wife did so, George continued his career in television, films, and concerts, but was at a loss as to how to proceed without a kooky dame on his arm. *Wendy and Me*, which Burns produced and starred in, was his attempt to reconstruct the Burns and Allen magic with a new generation of performers. Actress-singer Connie Stevens, who had co-starred in the successful detective show *Hawaiian Eye* (ABC, 1959–63), was the woman on whom Burns bestowed the mantle of taking Gracie's place.

The show cast Stevens and Ron Harper as a young married couple, Wendy and Jeff Conway, who take up residence in Apartment 217 of the Sunset de Ville apartments in Southern California. Jeff is employed as a pilot with Trans-Globe Airlines, as is his best buddy Danny. As George explains, "When Wendy met Jeff, she was an airline stewardess. And in order to be an airline stewardess, you have to take an intelligence test. So Wendy took one — and kept it."

The apartment building is owned by George Burns, who lives one floor down from the Conways in Apartment 104, and casts an amused eye on the complications that ensue each week from Wendy's confused brain. As George tells us, "This building is real funny. I don't even have to watch television." Using some of the same gimmicks he had employed so effectively in his original series, George serves both as the show's on-camera narrator, looking into the camera and addressing viewers directly, and a character who takes part in the weekly stories. He also leads into the commercial breaks, frequently by looking into the camera and saying, "Do it."

George's apartment has a grand piano in the living room, and his accompanist, Bob Fisher, is usually near at hand. Since his singing is not universally loved, he bought the building so as to have a rehearsal space, and stipulates that the tenants cannot evict the landlord. He is careful to sign his new tenants to a lease before they have an opportunity to hear him sing.

Mr. Bundy, the building maintenance man, lives in the basement. Though befuddled by Wendy, he often serves as helper in carrying out her little schemes. In fact, his role in the series is roughly a cross between Harry Von Zell, who served so often as George's stooge in the original series, and Blanche Morton, Gracie's best friend.

Jeff's best friend and fellow pilot, Danny Adams, lives across the hall from the Conways in Apartment 219. Danny is a relentless girl-chaser, though his advances come to a screeching halt if a woman mentions marriage. Almost every morning, Danny walks into the Conway apartment and sits down to breakfast, often helping himself to whatever is there before Jeff makes it to the table. Given the complications of Danny's busy romantic life, Jeff refers to his buddy as "a one-man *Peyton Place*."

As for Wendy, many of her lines and actions could certainly have come from Gracie's mouth. When she visits the grocery store, she's apt to come home with a dozen cans of dog food, though the Conways don't have a pet. But, as Wendy says, with a sale that good, she can afford to rent one. When Mr. Bundy commis-

Connie Stevens is no threat to Martha Stewart as the addled leading lady of ABC's *Wendy and Me*.

erates, saying he too sometimes buys items that weren't on his shopping list, Wendy has a ready solution — "I always do my shopping and then make a list out to fit it." She is, however, a bit more emotional than Gracie, and cries when things go wrong.

Though he doesn't use a magic TV set, as he did in the later episodes of *Burns and Allen,* George is the omniscient narrator who somehow always knows what's going on upstairs in the Conways' apartment. When not seen in his apartment, Mr. Burns, as all the other characters call him, is usually out in the lobby. Occasionally, when the situation calls for it, he either throws an additional complication into the plot, or acts as *deux ex machina.* In "Wendy's Private Eye" (11/2/64), she hires a private detective to tail Jeff, wrongly believing that he's seeing another woman. When the problem hasn't been resolved near the end of the 30-minute show, George tells us, "This thing is getting out of hand. I better straighten this out." He proceeds to step into the hallway, explain the mix-up to Wendy, and bring about a happy ending just in time for the fade-out.

On the other hand, in "Wendy the Waitress" (11/23/64), when Wendy offers to fill in for a waitress one night so that the stranger can attend her sister's wedding, George takes matters into his own hands upon realizing that Jeff won't catch her in the act of doing this. Talking Jeff and his boss out of going to another restaurant for dinner, George makes sure they visit the one where Wendy is working, saying with a smile, "Ask for Booth Three."

ABC slotted *Wendy and Me* in a Monday night berth that brought with it some heavy-duty competition. On CBS was a funny lady with her own track record — Lucille Ball, returning for the third year of her highly rated *The Lucy Show* (1962–68), which had been in television's Top Ten the previous season. NBC, not conceding the time slot, placed its popular, long-running musical variety hour *The Andy Williams Show* (1962–67) there. The result caused Stevens to refer to the 9 P.M. Monday time slot, with little exaggeration, as the roughest on that year's schedule.

Still, ABC was not without its own firepower. Aside from *Wendy and Me,* the perennial runner-up network filled the remainder of the 9–10 P.M. hour with *The Bing Crosby Show* (1964-65), another new series that represented the popular crooner's sitcom debut.

Midway through the season, Stevens said, "It's fun to be carrying a show, but boy, is it work! I know now what Laurence Olivier meant when he said the most important factor for success was not talent but energy. They had to move my dressing room next door to the stage so I could save the walk."[1]

Heading the supporting cast was actor Ron Harper (born January 12, 1936), previously one of the stars of the police drama *87th Precinct* (NBC, 1961-62), as Jeff Conway. Pretty young actresses could often find a role on *Wendy and Me* as well, and among the aspiring starlets who made an early appearance in the series were Brenda Benet and Raquel Welch.

Many of the episodes find Wendy trying to help out a friend or even a stranger, solving their problems with her own unique logic. When she learns that Danny's old girlfriend Edna needs a job, Wendy accompanies her to an interview at a doctor's office, and lends some helpful advice:

WENDY: It's easy to be a receptionist. Now, all you have to remember is when the people come in, you say, "Next, please," "Step in here," and "Take your clothes off."
EDNA: Wendy, there's more to it than that.
WENDY: Well, if it turns out to be a mailman, just apologize, and give him an aspirin.

Though not every man might have wanted to tolerate the confusion that Wendy's mind could produce, Jeff confides in one episode, "I'll tell you a little secret. I love every minute of it."

Born January 20, 1896, as Nathan Birnbaum, Burns dropped out of school and entered vaudeville at a young age, but had little success until he met his performing partner Gracie Allen in 1923. Following their marriage in 1926, Burns and Allen became a top comedy act. Their act translated ably to radio, where they first headlined their own show in 1932, to films, and ultimately to television with the fall 1950 debut of CBS's *The George Burns and Gracie Allen Show*.

Gracie's retirement in 1958 left George at loose ends. He wasn't ready to stop working, claiming that he'd been taking it easy the whole time he'd been his wife's partner. But after thirty-odd years as half of the Burns and Allen team, he had difficulty adapting to a new style of comedy. His solo show, *The George Burns Show*, which featured most of the supporting cast from *The George Burns and Gracie Allen Show*, debuted in the fall of 1958 on NBC, but was canceled after its first year. For a time, he'd adapted some of his Burns and Allen routines into a nightclub act with Carol Channing, playing the 1962 World's Fair, among other venues.

In the early 1960s, his television work consisted of occasional specials and some behind-the-scenes work. He owned a substantial piece of the hit comedy *Mister Ed* (CBS, 1961–66), lending the show some of his former writers as well as *Burns and Allen* featured player Larry Keating. When he took note of the comedic potential of Connie Stevens, he saw an actress he thought could be a younger version of Gracie, and put into place the concept that emerged as *Wendy and Me*.

Born Concetta Rosalie Anna Ingoglia on August 8, 1938, the daughter of a professional musician, Connie originally trained as a singer. She had her first big break with a featured role in the Jerry Lewis comedy *Rock-a-Bye Baby* (1958), but came to national attention co-starring as Cricket Blake in the popular ABC detective show *Hawaiian Eye*, which premiered in 1959 and enjoyed a four-year run. Not long prior to launching *Wendy and Me*, Stevens had married actor James Stacy (later the star of the Western series *Lancer*).

According to Stevens, no one at Warner Brothers knew what to do with her in the wake of *Hawaiian Eye*'s cancellation, though she was still under contract, and doubted her acting abilities. She clamored for substantial roles—she would later pursue the role of the young wife in the film version of *Who's Afraid of Virginia Woolf?*—but largely in vain. She filmed a routine horror movie, *Two on a Guillotine*, in 1964, before being approached about the starring role in *Wendy and Me*.

Stevens found herself surprised by the energy and stamina of her 68-year-old co-star. "When we made the pilot, he was on the set for every scene, even those he wasn't in. Of course, as the producer, he's got a hand in everything."[2] Though he didn't take a writing credit on *Wendy and Me*, the scripts were prepared under Burns' supervision by his longtime writers Norman Paul, Elon Packard, and his younger brother Willy.

As it turned out, George's production company landed not one but two time slots on ABC's Monday night schedule. Seen at 8:30 P.M. was *No Time for Sergeants*, adapted from the hit Broadway play and 1958 film, both of which had starred Andy Griffith. Immediately following that show was *Wendy and Me*. Burns explained to columnist Margaret McManus, "I came to Warner Brothers to get Connie Stevens, and when I got Connie, they got me. They liked what I did with *Wendy* and gave me *Sergeants*."[3]

Inevitably, there were comparisons between the role of Wendy Conway and the Gracie Allen persona, even before the show's premiere. "It's the same general type," George conceded to McManus that summer. "Wendy's just a little off center." As he had so often said about his wife, Burns insisted that Stevens was more than a comedienne. "It takes an actress—a real actress, not just a comedienne—to do this kind of role. She has to believe what she's saying and doing, and not think it's funny. If she plays it as if it were funny—she's dead."[4]

One or two observers asked whether it was possible Gracie might appear in *Wendy and Me*, but Burns quickly dismissed the idea, saying that she was happy in retirement. Not widely known at the time was the fact that Allen, in poor health, had retired on doctor's orders, and her heart problems had only grown worse in the last several years.

Only days before the scheduled premiere of *Wendy and Me*, tragedy struck when Gracie Allen died of a heart attack. Believed to be only in her late fifties, she was in fact nearly seventy years old at the time of her death. Because he had asked her not to see his new show until it aired on television, Gracie never saw *Wendy and Me*.

Though critical reviews for *Wendy and Me* were mixed, Stevens drew praise for her starring performance. In 1965, a critic for the syndicated *TV Key* column praised Stevens, saying she "has sharpened her comedy timing to such a point, she holds her own even opposite a seasoned pro like George Burns."[5] Stevens enjoyed *Wendy and Me*, but was uncertain she wanted to make a long-term commitment to the role. "A while back," the star said, "a lady told me:

'You're so wonderful in that show, you're gonna be on the air for 15 years.' My reaction to that was—my eyes widened and I panicked. I just don't have the emotional capacity to stick with something for that long."[6]

As it turned out, she needn't have worried about getting tied down. In the spring of 1965, when *Wendy and Me* completed its first season, ABC did not renew the show for a second year. Burns' longtime best friend Jack Benny was also shown the door that season, his NBC sitcom canceled after losing its time slot to the new *Gomer Pyle, U.S.M.C.* (1964–68).

Burns continued to pursue television work in the wake of *Wendy*'s cancellation, on both sides of the camera. In 1965, his production company sold NBC *Mona McCluskey*, starring Juliet Prowse as a movie star married to an Army man, but that too failed to catch on, lasting only one season.

Co-star Ron Harper had even worse luck with his 1966 series *The Jean Arthur Show*, which CBS canceled after three months. In 1967, he was cast in a lead role in the ABC wartime drama *Garrison's Gorillas*, but this too was short-lived, lasting for only a year. After yet another unsuccessful prime time series, CBS's *Planet of the Apes* (CBS, 1974), Harper spent much of the late 1970s and 1980s in daytime TV, with ongoing roles in the CBS soap operas *Love of Life* and *Capitol* and the first-run syndication version of *Charles in Charge*.

Burns made a spectacular comeback in 1975 with the release of *The Sunshine Boys*, for which he won a Best Supporting Actor Oscar (the oldest actor ever to do so). Stevens' only series role after *Wendy and Me* found her playing Helen, the ex-wife of Bill Daily, in the sitcom *Starting from Scratch*, which played in first-run syndication during the 1988-89 season. In 1974, she played a Marilyn Monroe–type doomed starlet in the well-received ABC TV-movie *The Sex Symbol*, but other worthy roles proved scarce. In later years, Stevens founded a very successful cosmetics company, and in 2005 was elected to the position of secretary-treasurer with the Screen Actors Guild.

For some Burns and Allen purists, the very idea of Connie Stevens—or anyone else—stepping into Gracie's shoes makes *Wendy and Me* a lost cause from the get-go. But those who can put aside their skepticism may just find this ABC sitcom a surprisingly enjoyable riff on one of America's best-loved comedy acts.

Appendix: Chronological List of Shows

The 30 sitcoms covered in this book are listed below chronologically, by their premiere dates. For those shows sold in first-run syndication (*The Great Gildersleeve, How to Marry a Millionaire, The Jim Backus Show*), the date shown is simply fall of their year (1955, 1957, 1960), as each individual station that bought the shows chose different days, dates and times at which to broadcast them.

November 8, 1952	My Hero	NBC
September 17, 1953	Meet Mr. McNutley/ The Ray Milland Show	CBS
September 4, 1954	The Mickey Rooney Show: Hey Mulligan	NBC
September 7, 1954	It's a Great Life	NBC
Fall 1955	The Great Gildersleeve	Syndicated
October 6, 1955	The People's Choice	NBC
September 8, 1956	Hey, Jeannie!/The Jeannie Carson Show	CBS
January 4, 1957	Mr. Adams and Eve	CBS
Fall 1957	How to Marry a Millionaire	Syndicated
September 28, 1959	Hennesey	CBS
June 8, 1960	Happy	NBC
Fall 1960	The Jim Backus Show: Hot Off the Wire	Syndicated
September 19, 1960	Pete and Gladys	CBS
September 27, 1960	The Tom Ewell Show	CBS
October 6, 1960	Angel	CBS
October 12, 1960	Peter Loves Mary	NBC
September 26, 1961	Ichabod and Me	CBS
October 4, 1961	Mrs. G. Goes to College/ The Gertrude Berg Show	CBS
October 12, 1961	Margie	ABC
September 23, 1962	McKeever and the Colonel	NBC

September 28, 1962	*I'm Dickens ... He's Fenster*	ABC
September 15, 1963	*Grindl*	NBC
September 22, 1963	*The Bill Dana Show*	NBC
September 14, 1964	*Wendy and Me*	ABC
September 16, 1965	*O.K. Crackerby!*	ABC
September 8, 1966	*Love on a Rooftop*	ABC
September 11, 1966	*It's About Time*	CBS
September 13, 1966	*Occasional Wife*	NBC
January 9, 1967	*Mr. Terrific*	CBS
September 23, 1969	*The Governor and J.J.*	CBS

Chapter Notes

Angel

1. Erskine Johnson, "Hollywood Today," Kingsport (TN) Times, September 23, 1960.
2. Joe St. Amant, "Oppenheimer Unknown," Hayward (CA) Daily Review, February 6, 1961.
3. "Angel from Paris," San Antonio Light, August 14, 1960.
4. Gregg Oppenheimer, interview with author, March 10, 2009.
5. Harriet Van Horne, "New French Comedienne Enchanting in Angel," El Paso (TX) Herald-Post, October 7, 1960.
6. Oppenheimer interview.
7. "Annie of Angel Has Two Problems," Madison (WI) Capital Times, January 14, 1961.
8. Arnold Hano, "The 'Little Fellow' of Daktari," TV Guide, August 6, 1966.
9. Charles Witbeck, "Comedy Show Angel Not Ordinary Series," Charleston (WV) Gazette, July 18, 1960.

The Bill Dana Show

1. Alan Ward, "Bill (Jose Jimenez) Is Two Wonderful People," Oakland Tribune, May 3, 1964.
2. Edgar Penton, "Up, Jose, Up!" Oxnard (CA) Press-Courier, February 22, 1964.
3. Hal Humphrey, "Dana Not Nearly So Funny as Jose," Los Angeles Times, September 4, 1963.
4. Penton, "Up, Jose, Up!"
5. Cynthia Lowry, "Bill Dana Works Hard at Comedy," Pasadena Independent Star-News, May 17, 1964.
6. Cecil Smith, "Why Bill Dana Quit Jose Jimenez Role," Los Angeles Times, July 1, 1970.

The Governor and J.J.

1. "The Governor and J.J. Tackles Generation Gap," Muscatine (IO) Journal, September 11, 1969.
2. Bob MacKenzie, "No More Dancing," Oakland Tribune, July 10, 1969.
3. Vernon Scott, "Dan Dailey Sees No Surprises in New TV Series," Lebanon (PA) Daily News, September 24, 1969.
4. Leslie Raddatz, "Dailey for Governor," TV Guide, November 15, 1969.
5. Norma Lee Browning, "Luck Shines on Julie as Personable J.J.," Abilene Reporter-News, July 5, 1970.
6. Rick Du Brow, "J.J. Series is Tops on CBS," Fresno (CA) Bee, January 12, 1970.
7. Charles Whitbeck, "Easy for Governor and J.J. to Be Current in Election Year," Madison (WI) State Journal, July 12, 1970.
8. Vernon Scott, "Incumbent TV Governor Admits His TV Election 'Fixed,'" Las Cruces (NM) Sun-News, October 25, 1970.
9. "Dan Dailey Dies at Age 62," Jefferson City (Missouri) Post-Tribune, October 17, 1978.

The Great Gildersleeve

1. Bob Foster, "Great Gildersleeve Proves Fine Comedy," San Mateo Times, August 18, 1955.
2. "The Great Gildersleeve on WIBA Today at 4:30," Capital Times (Madison, WI), August 31, 1941.
3. Dick Kleiner, "The Marquee," Chillicothe (MO) Constitution-Tribune, September 29, 1955.
4. Hal Humphrey, "Gildersleeve on TV May Add to Confusion," Oakland Tribune, October 5, 1955.
5. Steven H. Scheuer, "Gildersleeve Is Click in Pilot Film," Syracuse Herald Journal, September 16, 1955.
6. Kleiner, "The Marquee."
7. Burt A. Folkart, "Willard Waterman, Actor on Radio, Screen, and Stage," Los Angeles Times, February 4, 1995.
8. Walter Ames, "Gildersleeve Goes TV Tonight; Video Theater Grabs New Properties," Los Angeles Times, October 16, 1955.

Grindl

1. "Imogene Coca Comes Home," Oxnard (CA) Press-Courier, August 10, 1963.

2. Ibid.
3. Ibid.
4. Lydia Lane, "Individuality, Not Looks, Paid Off for Imogene Coca," *Madison* (WI) *State Journal*, March 15, 1964.
5. "Rumors of Imogene Coca's Retirement Are Exaggerated," *Jefferson City Post-Tribune*, November 30, 1962.
6. "That Nut, Imogene Coca, Returns in 'Grindl': Sid Caesar's 'Ex-Wife' Has Her Own Show," *Hammond* (IN) *Times*, September 8, 1963.
7. Cecil Smith, "Swift Comes Back for Loot, Not Art," *Los Angeles Times*, November 29, 1963.
8. Hal Humphrey, "Imogene May Score," *Victoria* (TX) *Advocate*, August 25, 1963.
9. Earl Wilson, "Imogene Coca Victim of Gremlins," *Long Beach* (CA) *Press-Telegram*, September 17, 1963.
10. Alan Gill, "The Wibble Wobbles," *Cedar Rapids* (IO) *Gazette*, October 9, 1963.
11. Vernon Scott, "Imogene Rare in California; a Non-Driver," *Great Bend* (KS) *Tribune*, January 13, 1964.
12. Ed Misurell, "Imogene Coca: The Return of an Early Native to Video," *McKean County* (PA) *Democrat*, November 14, 1963.
13. Harvey Pack, "'Ex-Grindl' Imogene Coca Plans Appearances on Danny Kaye Program," *Charleston* (WV) *Gazette-Mail*, October 11, 1964.
14. Ibid.

Happy

1. "George Sees Son as Actor," *Los Angeles Times*, May 11, 1958.
2. Aleene Barnes, "Happy Is Word for Ronnie Burns Series," *Los Angeles Times*, June 5, 1960.
3. Vernon Scott, "Young Ronnie Burns Making TV Debut in *Happy* Tonight," *Kittanning* (PA) *Simpson's Leader-Times*, June 8, 1960.
4. Sally Latham, "TV's Richest Woman in Town," *Fort Pierce* (FL) *News Tribune*, April 14, 1961.
5. Cecil Smith, "Silver Lining in Cloud of Reruns," *Los Angeles Times*, June 8, 1960.
6. Bill Fiset, "These Forgettable Evenings," *Oakland Tribune*, August 17, 1960.
7. Jay Fredericks, "TV 'Repeats' Welcomed After Seeing New Shows," *Charleston* (WV) *Gazette-Mail*, June 19, 1960.
8. "Out of the Mouths of Babes," *TV Guide*, July 16, 1961.
9. Cynthia Lowry, "Yvonne Lime to Return to Husband, Home," *Gettysburg* (PA) *Times*, December 30, 1960.

10. Ibid.
11. Hedda Hopper, "Teen-Agers Vote for Yvonne and She Zooms to the Top," *Los Angeles Times*, August 7, 1960.

Hennesey

1. "Birth of a Show," *TV Guide*, September 26, 1959.
2. Jackie Cooper, "No One Can Laugh All the Time, Cooper Says," *Jefferson City* (MO) *Post-Tribune*, July 7, 1961.
3. Harvey Pack, "ABC Moves in Public Affairs Race," *Hammond* (IN) *Times*, May 9, 1961.
4. "Birth of a Show."
5. "Outdoor Abby Is In With *Hennesey*," *TV Guide*, November 26, 1959.
6. "No Wonder He Can Act!" *TV Guide*, May 7, 1960.
7. Bob Thomas, "Hennesey Will Wed Miss Hale," *Las Cruces* (NM) *Sun-News*, April 1, 1962.

Hey, Jeannie / The Jeannie Carson Show

1. Dorothy Roe, "Fashionable Glamour Girl Needs Soft Voice, Wardrobe of Accents," *Jefferson City* (MO) *Post-Tribune*, March 14, 1957.
2. Faye Emerson, "English TV Star in U.S. Is Good Will Ambassador," *El Paso* (TX) *Herald-Post*, April 11, 1957.
3. Fred Danzig, "Jeannie is a Girl Who Likes Work," *Chicago Tribune*, February 1, 1959.
4. Cecil Smith, "KTTV Gets Fox Films; 'Hey, Jeannie!' to Debut," *Los Angeles Times*, September 8, 1956.
5. "Jenkins: Actor, Cab Drivers' 'Buff,'" *Jefferson City* (MO) *Daily Capital News*, July 2, 1960.
6. Emerson, "English TV Star."
7. "Taking a Fling in TV," *TV Guide*, December 29, 1956.
8. Ibid.
9. Bob Foster, "TV Filmers Find Things Pretty Risky," *San Mateo Times*, October 3, 1956.
10. Bob Thomas, "*Hey, Jeannie* Must Wait Until March to Learn Fate," *Corpus Christi Times*, January 26, 1957.
11. Robert L. Sokolsky, "Looking and Listening," *Syracuse* (NY) *Herald Journal*, February 8, 1957.
12. Thomas, "*Hey, Jeannie* Must Wait."
13. Hal Humphrey, "Powell on Rampage," *Waterloo* (Iowa) *Daily Courier*, May 2, 1957.

14. Eve Starr, "Inside TV," *Pasadena* (CA) *Star-News*, August 13, 1957.
15. Charles Denton, "Elfin Jeannie Carson Plans Try Again to Hit Sweepstakes," *Bridgeport* (CT) *Post*, January 19, 1958.

How to Marry a Millionaire

1. Lydia Lane, "Takes Care, Money to Keep Hair Dyed," *Big Spring* (TX) *Daily Herald*, November 4, 1959.
2. Harold Heffernan, "TV's 'Loco' Not So Dumb," *Charleston* (WV) *Gazette*, December 10, 1958.
3. Charles Mercer, "Hold On to Your Bankbook," *Tucson Daily Citizen*, December 6, 1958.
4. Charles Denton, "Glamor Girls Have Rough Way to Go on Television," *Charleston* (WV) *Gazette-Mail*, July 12, 1959.
5. Faye Emerson, "Millionaires Interest Them — Only on TV Show," *Albuquerque Tribune*, November 28, 1957.
6. Marty Baumann, *The Astounding B Monster* (New York: Dinoship, 2004), p. 159.

Ichabod and Me

1. Harold Stern, "*Ichabod and Me* One of a Kind," *Hammond* (IN) *Times*, August 30, 1961.
2. Vernon Scott, "Reta Shaw: Sexless and Very Delighted," *Coshocton Tribune*, January 9, 1969.
3. "She Remembers Jimmy Dean," *TV Guide*, January 13, 1962.
4. Rick du Brow, "Television in Review," *Redlands* (CA) *Daily Press*, March 21, 1962.
5. Hank Grant, "Sterling Unable to Figure TV Bosses," *Hayward* (CA) *Daily Review*, April 29, 1962.
6. Dina-Marie Kulzer, *Television Series Regulars of the Fifties and Sixties in Interview* (Jefferson, NC: McFarland, 1992), p. 72.

I'm Dickens ... He's Fenster

1. Harold Hefferman, "Two Comedians in New Series," *San Antonio Express*, September 3, 1962.
2. Hank Grant, "John Astin Vet in Show Biz Circles," *Hayward* (CA) *Daily Review*, October 14, 1962.
3. Dick Kleiner, "Bridges Eyes His New Show As a 'Heyday for a Ham,'" *Austin* (MN) *Daily Herald*, October 6, 1962.
4. "Emmaline Has Changed," *Gastonia* (NC) *Gazette*, May 5, 1968.
5. Joan Crosby, "They're Mr. and Mrs., But Only on Television," *San Antonio Express*, May 13, 1963.
6. Ruth E. Thompson, "Emmaline Henry Stays in Demand," *Simpson's Leader-Times*, August 22, 1964.
7. Cynthia Lowry, "New Comedy Series on Television in September," *Gettysburg* (PA) *Times*, August 10, 1962.
8. Joan Crosby, "They're Mr. and Mrs."
9. Joe Finnigan, "Sorry — Your Sandwich Has Been Canceled," *TV Guide*, September 6, 1980.

It's a Great Life

1. Walter Ames, "Bill Bishop Using TV Role for Screen Test; Medics Honoring Miner," *Los Angeles Times*, March 30, 1955.
2. Vernon Scott, "They Shine as Biggest TV 'Bums,'" *Long Beach* (CA) *Independent*, December 20, 1954.
3. "James Dunn Convinced That an Oscar Can Sometimes Be a Jinx," *Indiana* (PA) *Evening Gazette*, March 5, 1955.
4. "TV Writers Are Little Known," *Galveston Daily News*, April 23, 1955.
5. Ellis Walker, "Video Notes," *Hayward* (CA) *Daily Review*, February 20, 1956.
6. Walter Ames, "O'Shea Notes Peril in Being Funnier Than Week Before," *Los Angeles Times*, March 18, 1956.
7. "Film and Video Stars Retiring," *Corpus Christi Times*, January 31, 1957.

It's About Time

1. Charles Witbeck, "Acting Couple Ready for Cues in New Fall Television Programs," *Charleston* (WV) *Gazette-Mail*, July 10, 1966.
2. Joan Crosby, "*Star Trek*: Science Fiction 'For Real,'" *Chillicothe* (MO) *Constitution-Tribune*, October 11, 1966.
3. Vernon Scott, "Veteran Video Stars in *It's About Time*," *Long Beach* (CA) *Independent Press-Telegram*, September 11, 1966.
4. Dick Kleiner, "Hollywood Today!" *Benton Harbor* (MI) *News-Palladium*, September 7, 1966.
5. Bob MacKenzie, "Bob MacKenzie on Television," *Oakland Tribune*, September 19, 1966.
6. "*It's About Time* Goes Modern," *Long Beach* (CA) *Independent Press-Telegram*, January 22, 1967.

The Jim Backus Show

1. John Crosby, "Comedian Answers Call to Radio, Fears TV Series," *Pasadena Independent Star-News*, November 3, 1957.
2. Dick Kleiner, "Como Has Surprises," *Waterloo* (IA) *Daily Courier*, September 8, 1955.
3. Vernon Scott, "Actress Nita Talbot is the Kiss of Death in Hollywood," *San Mateo Times*, November 24, 1961.
4. Hal Humphrey, "Jim Backus' Wife Gets a Job," *Portsmouth Times*, April 21, 1961.
5. Bernice Ashby, "Backstage," *Hagerstown* (MD) *Daily Mail*, February 18, 1961.
6. Vernon Scott, "Backus Holds TV Record," *Oakland Tribune*, March 22, 1969.

Love on a Rooftop

1. Bill Byers, "All the Makings for a Knockout," *Abilene Reporter-News*, August 15, 1966.
2. Melvin Durslag, "Judy Carne — Brash, Confident, Scared!" *TV Guide*, October 15, 1966.
3. Dick Kleiner, "Show Beat," *Danville* (VA) *Register*, November 1, 1968.
4. Rick du Brow, "ABC Hints Some Hope for 66–67," *Tucson Daily Citizen*, September 7, 1966.
5. Jack Gould, "TV Season Debuts Oh So Weakly," *Des Moines Register*, September 8, 1966.
6. Durslag, "Judy Carne — Brash, Confident, Scared!"
7. Judy Stone, "He's Alias Smith or Alias Jones," *TV Guide*, May 15, 1971.

Margie

1. "No Machine Guns on New Series," *Kittanning* (PA) *Simpson's Leader-Times*, October 21, 1961.
2. "Today's Cover — Meet Cynthia Pepper — TV's *Margie*," *Oakland Tribune*, February 11, 1962.
3. "Memories of *Margie*: Songwriter Says TV Series Takes Him Back 41 Years," *Corpus Christi Caller-Times*, January 14, 1962.
4. "New Series, *Margie*, is Set in 1920s," *Fresno Bee*, June 25, 1961.
5. Stan Maays, "Whatever Became of Margie?" *Bucks County* (PA) *Courier Times*, October 26, 1968.

McKeever and the Colonel

1. "*McKeever and the Colonel* Premieres Saturday Night," *Jefferson City* (MO) *Post-Tribune*, October 5, 1962.
2. "Allyn Joslyn Feels TV Series Role Big Break," *Jefferson City* (MO) *Post-Tribune*, August 17, 1962.
3. Hal Humphrey, "Tic Tac TV," *Hayward* (CA) *Daily Review*, October 7, 1962.
4. John Eimen, telephone interview with the author, July 29, 2009. All subsequent quotes from Eimen are from this interview.
5. Bert Resnik, "TV Dietician Afflicted with Inaccurate Scales," *Long Beach* (CA) *Independent Press-Telegram*, March 3, 1963.

Meet Mr. McNutley / The Ray Milland Show

1. Bob Thomas, "Ray Milland Reluctant TV Performer; Success Weird Story," *Danville* (VA) *Bee*, October 5, 1953.
2. "Milland Plays TV Professor," *Kalispell* (MT) *Daily Inter Lake*, February 28, 1954.
3. Peg Simpson, "Ray Bolger Show Bows in Tonight on WSYR Video," *Syracuse* (NY) *Post-Standard*, October 8, 1953.
4. "Milland Show Returns to TV," *Williamsport* (PA) *Gazette and Bulletin*, September 15, 1954.
5. Wayne Oliver, "TV Not Hurting Ray Milland's Movie Career," *Danville* (VA) *Bee*, November 23, 1954.

The Mickey Rooney Show

1. Aline Mosby, "Rooney, Settled Down Now, Returns in New TV Series," *Stars and Stripes*, August 11, 1954.
2. Erskine Johnson, "Hollywood," *Kingsport* (TN) *Times*, June 28, 1954.
3. "Mrs. Rooney Takes Care of Family Funds: Clearing Up Financial Mess," *Danville* (VA) *Bee*, July 1, 1954.
4. Mosby, "Rooney, Settled Down."
5. Hal Humphrey, *Oakland Tribune*, August 11, 1954.
6. John Crosby, "TV Notes: 'Salute to the Press,'" *Waterloo* (IA) *Courier*, December 17, 1954.

---

7. Wesley Hyatt, *Short-Lived Television Series, 1948–1978: Thirty Years of More Than 1,000 Flops* (Jefferson, NC: McFarland, 2003), p. 169.
8. Bob Thomas, "Imogene Coca Has Knack for Disaster," *Corpus Christi Times*, March 16, 1967.

7. Laurence Laurent, "10 Programs the New Year Might Be Happier Without," *Washington Post*, December 26, 1954.
8. Arthur Marx, *The Nine Lives of Mickey Rooney* (New York: Stein and Day, 1986), p. 201.

Mr. Adams and Eve

1. "A Fourth for TV," *TV Guide*, December 3, 1955.
2. Erskine Johnson, "Erskine Johnson in Hollywood," *Blytheville (AR) Courier-News*, January 4, 1957.
3. Cecil Smith, "Mr. Adams, Eve Bows Out on TV," *Los Angeles Times*, August 3, 1958.
4. "At Home on TV," *San Antonio Express-News*, January 12, 1958.
5. Steven H. Scheuer, "Ida Lupino, Duff Switch to Comedy," *Hammond (IN) Times*, February 15, 1957.
6. Walter Ames, "Ida, Howard Enact True-to-Life Parts on TV," *Los Angeles Times*, May 19, 1957.
7. Fred de Cordova, *Johnny Came Lately: An Autobiography* (New York: Simon & Schuster, 1988), p. 109.
8. Hal Humphrey, "Ida Lupino Bids for Fame on TV," *Oakland (CA) Tribune*, January 10, 1957.
9. Eve Starr, "Inside TV," *Pasadena Star-News*, January 9, 1957.
10. Marie Torre, "Then Came the Dawn..." *Cedar Rapids (IA) Gazette*, March 11, 1958.
11. William Ewald, "Television in Review," *Kittanning (PA) Simpson's Leader-Times*, February 12, 1958.
12. Smith, "Mr. Adams, Eve Bows Out."
13. Erskine Johnson, "Hollywood Today," *Ironwood (MI) Daily Globe*, March 8, 1958.

Mr. Terrific

1. Dick Kleiner, "TV Battle: Nice, Terrific," *Lima (OH) News*, January 6, 1967.
2. "*Mr. Terrific* Isn't Easily Convinced It's No Good," *Jefferson City (MO) Daily Capital News*, February 11, 1967.
3. Dwight Whitney, "What's a Nice Kid Like You Doing in a Place Like This?" *TV Guide*, May 27, 1967.
4. Kleiner, "TV Battle."
5. Walt Dutton, "Dick Gautier: A Mechanical Genius," *Los Angeles Times*, January 6, 1967.
6. Hal Humphrey, "Supermen Strain the Eye Muscles," *Los Angeles Times*, January 10, 1967.
7. Hal Humphrey, "Awards Time for 10-Worst Shows," *Los Angeles Times*, December 28, 1967.
8. Mark Phillips, "The Amazing, Astounding, Typically Inane, Hollywood Saga of the Rise and Fall of Mr. Terrific," *Outré*, #29, 2002.

Mrs. G. Goes to College / The Gertrude Berg Show

1. Erskine Johnson, "Gertrude Berg Still Popular After 30 Years," *Eau Claire (WI) Daily Telegram*, February 23, 1962.
2. "The Unsinkable Molly Goldberg," *TV Guide*, November 25, 1961.
3. Ibid.
4. Cynthia Lowry, "Lowry Says Mollie Goldberg to Be Hit in New TV Program," *Hagerstown (MD) Daily Mail*, October 5, 1961.
5. Margaret McManus, "Gertrude Berg Loves Life," *Syracuse (NY) Post-Standard*, October 15, 1961.

My Hero

1. "Comes Now Robert Cummings as New TV Comedy Actor," *Ogden (UT) Standard-Examiner*, November 12, 1952.
2. Dick Long, "Looking and Listening," *Syracuse Herald-Journal*, November 8, 1952.
3. Bob Foster, "*My Hero* Show Fails to Do Justice to Cummings," *San Mateo Times*, November 21, 1952.
4. John Crosby, "Radio and TV Comments," *Reno Evening Gazette*, February 14, 1953.
5. Charles Denton, "Robert Cummings an Old 'Hand' in a New Medium," *San Mateo Times*, November 7, 1952.
6. Peg Simpson, "Cummings Seen Hurting Career in Poor Production," *Syracuse (NY) Post-Standard*, December 13, 1952.
7. "Sheriff's Aid Lays Assault to Film Actor," *Los Angeles Times*, December 19, 1952.
8. Hal Humphrey, "Stars Demanding More Voice in Own Programs," *Oakland Tribune*, December 30, 1952.
9. "Up-and-Coming Cummings," *TV Guide*, April 9, 1955.

O.K. Crackerby!

1. Harold Heffernan, "TV Anchors Vagabond Burl Ives," *Berkshire (MS) Eagle*, August 21, 1965.
2. Kay Gardella, "Burl Ives is Imposing Figure," *Corpus Christi Caller-Times*, September 26, 1965.

3. Joan Crosby, "Ives Happy with TV Role," *Lima* (OH) *News*, September 1, 1965.
4. Charles Witbeck, "Ives to Star in New TV Series," *Winona* (MN) *Daily News*, August 1, 1965.
5. Nevart Apikian, "Buckley's 'Zing' Wins New Series Role," *Syracuse* (NY) *Post-Standard*, September 18, 1965.
6. Cynthia Lowry, "New Shows Continue," *Hobbs* (NM) *Daily News-Sun*, September 17, 1965.
7. Joan E. Vadeboncoeur, "Ives Has a New Role," *Syracuse* (NY) *Post-Standard*, September 19, 1965.
8. "Irish, British Hospitality Help Ives Recover from Show's Demise," *Bristol* (PA) *Daily Courier*, January 15, 1966.
9. Ibid.

Occasional Wife

1. Margaret McManus, "Callan Unsure He Enjoys Fame," *Syracuse* (NY) *Post-Standard*, September 17, 1966.
2. Vernon Scott, "Callan Has a New Angle on Career," *Long Beach* (CA) *Independent*, July 1, 1966.
3. "*Occasional Wife*: Luscious," *Ogden* (UT) *Standard-Examiner*, October 23, 1966.
4. Bill Byers, "Make Believe Wife Says She's Square," *Abilene Reporter-News*, September 14, 1966.
5. Marian Dern, "*Occasional Wife* Wouldn't Have Made It Five Years Ago," *San Mateo Times*, October 15, 1966.
6. Earl Wilson, "Pat Harty Chalks Up into Pool Hall Set," *Lowell Sunday Sun*, November 29, 1968.
7. "Same Girl, New Look," *Hagerstown* (MD) *Morning Herald*, March 11, 1975.

The People's Choice

1. Erskine Johnson, "Hollywood," *Kingsport* (TN) *Times*, June 28, 1954.
2. "Jackie Cooper's Sold on TV Despite the Quick Changes," *Washington Post*, March 7, 1954.
3. Walter Ames, "Actress Does TV Film with Broken Leg; Cheer Leader Is Benny Star," *Los Angeles Times*, October 6, 1955.
4. "Dog Star, Cleo, Is Tired Hound," *Hammond* (IN) *Times*, April 7, 1957.
5. Jackie Cooper with Dick Kleiner, *Please Don't Shoot My Dog: The Autobiography of Jackie Cooper* (New York: Morrow, 1981), p. 181.
6. Bill Fiset, "Cleo Yawns Back at Jackie Cooper," *Oakland Tribune*, October 9, 1957.

Pete and Gladys

1. Vernon Scott, "Pete, Gladys Branch from *Bride* Show," *Pasadena* (CA) *Independent*, August 24, 1960.
2. Hank Grant, "Daily Experiences Create Show Themes," *Troy* (NY) *Record*, September 11, 1964.
3. Erskine Johnson, "Hollywood," *Kingsport* (TN) *Times*, December 6, 1960.
4. Richard Gehman, "The Wild, Wild World of Cara Williams," *TV Guide*, July 8, 1961.
5. Cynthia Lowry, "Pete and Gladys Quietly Abandon Baby in Series," *Anderson* (IN) *Daily Bulletin*, December 15, 1960.
6. Bert Resnik, "Bert's Eye View," *Long Beach* (CA) *Independent Press-Telegram*, December 19, 1965.
7. Vernon Scott, "Harry Morgan Joins *M-A-S-H* Cast," *Salina* (KS) *Journal*, August 10, 1975.
8. Joan Crosby, "Cara Wants 'The Girls' to Like Her," *Madison* (WI) *Capital Times*, October 29, 1964.

Peter Loves Mary

1. Bob Thomas, "Peter, Mary Like TV Series But Won't Settle in Hollywood," *Idaho State Journal*, November 4, 1960.
2. Peg Simpson, "Article Reveals How Not to Wreck Your Video Set," *Syracuse* (NY) *Post-Standard*, March 22, 1951.
3. Pete Martin, "I Call on Peter Lind Hayes and Mary Healy," *Saturday Evening Post*, December 27, 1958.
4. Charles D. Rice, "The Double Life of Peter and Mary," *Los Angeles Times*, August 3, 1958.
5. Thomas, "Peter, Mary Like TV Series."
6. Vernon Scott, "*Peter Loves Mary* and the Money," *Lowell* (MA) *Sun*, November 28, 1960.
7. Steven Scheuer, "Bea Benaderet Is Reduced to Housekeeper in Series," *Modesto Bee*, May 7, 1961.
8. Marie Torre, "Comedy for Peter and Mary," *Cedar Rapids Gazette*, March 28, 1960.
9. Peter Lind Hayes and Mary Healy, *Moments to Remember with Peter and Mary: Our Life in Show Business from Vaudeville to Video* (New York: Vantage Press, 2004), p. 262.
10. Cynthia Lowry, "Peter Lind Hayes Urges 'Viewing Diets' to Create TV Hunger," *Long Beach* (CA) *Independent Press-Telegram*, March 4, 1962.

The Tom Ewell Show

1. Harold Stern, "Tom Names His Show for Better or Worse," *Salina* (KS) *Journal*, August 19, 1960.
2. "One Little Word—And That'll Be the End of 'Marilyn Erskine, Girl TV Player,'" *TV Guide*, March 10, 1961.
3. Bill Fiset, "About Television," *Oakland Tribune*, October 11, 1960.
4. Cynthia Lowry, "Over the Airwaves," *Hobbs* (NM) *Daily News-Sun*, December 5, 1960.
5. Charles Witbeck, "Funny Lines, Funny Faces Make Good Comedy," *Troy* (NY) *Record*, August 27, 1960.
6. Hedda Hopper, "Tom Ewell Planning One-Man Stage Show," *Los Angeles Times*, July 11, 1961.
7. Hank Grant, "Consider 90 Minute *Ben Casey* Program," *Troy* (NY) *Record*, November 12, 1962.
8. Margaret McManus, "Tom Ewell Seeking Perfection," *Syracuse* (NY) *Post-Standard*, July 2, 1966.

Wendy and Me

1. Bob Thomas, "Connie Stevens Always Displays Sunny Confidence While Working," *Cumberland* (MD) *Evening Times*, December 9, 1964.
2. "Old Pro Still Burn-Ing Up the Networks," *Oxnard* (CA) *Press-Courier*, August 1, 1964.
3. Margaret McManus, "George Burns Returning to TV," *Syracuse* (NY) *Post-Standard*, June 7, 1964.
4. Alan Gill, "Connie Stevens Has Great Potential, Says George Burns," *Kokomo* (IN) *Morning Times*, August 11, 1964.
5. *TV Key Previews*, February 22, 1965.
6. Richard Warren Lewis, "'An Apple Blossom with the Wham of a Bulldozer,'" *TV Guide*, May 1, 1965.

Bibliography

Adir, Karin. *The Great Clowns of American Television.* Jefferson, NC: McFarland, 1988.
Baumann, Marty. *The Astounding B Monster.* New York: Dinoship, 2004.
Brooks, Tim. *The Complete Directory to Prime Time TV Stars.* New York: Ballantine, 1987.
_____, and Earle Marsh. *The Complete Directory to Prime Time Network and Cable TV Shows.* 9th ed. New York: Ballantine, 2007.
Bubbeo, Daniel. *The Women of Warner Brothers: The Lives and Careers of 15 Leading Ladies, with Filmographies for Each.* Jefferson, NC: McFarland, 2002.
Caesar, Sid, with Eddy Friedfeld. *Caesar's Hours: My Life in Comedy with Love and Laughter.* New York: Public Affairs, 2003.
Carne, Judy. *Laughing on the Outside, Crying on the Inside: The Bittersweet Saga of the Sock-It-to-Me Girl.* New York: Rawson, 1985.
Castleman, Harry, and Walter J. Podrazik. *Harry and Wally's Favorite TV Shows.* New York: Prentice Hall, 1989.
Cooper, Jackie, with Dick Kleiner. *Please Don't Shoot My Dog: The Autobiography of Jackie Cooper.* New York: Morrow, 1981.
Cox, Jim. *The Great Radio Sitcoms.* Jefferson, NC: McFarland, 2007.
de Cordova, Fred. *Johnny Came Lately: An Autobiography.* New York: Simon & Schuster, 1988.
Fernandes, David, and Dale Robinson. *A Guide to Television's Mayberry R.F.D.* Jefferson, NC: McFarland, 1999.
Green, Paul. *Pete Duel: A Biography.* Jefferson, NC: McFarland, 2007.
Hayes, Peter Lind, and Mary Healy. *Moments to Remember with Peter and Mary: Our Life in Show Business from Vaudeville to Video.* New York: Vantage Press, 2004.
Hyatt, Wesley. *Short-Lived Television Series, 1948–1978: Thirty Years of More Than 1,000 Flops.* Jefferson, NC: McFarland, 2003.
Kulzer, Dina-Marie. *Television Series Regulars of the Fifties and Sixties in Interview.* Jefferson, NC: McFarland, 1992.
Leigh, Wendy. *True Grace: The Life and Death of an American Princess.* New York: Thomas Dunne Books, 2007.
Maltin, Leonard, ed. *Leonard Maltin's Movie Encyclopedia.* New York: Plume, 1994.
Mank, Gregory William. *Women in Horror Films, 1930s.* Jefferson, NC: McFarland, 1999.
Marill, Alvin H. *Mickey Rooney: His Films, Television Appearances, Radio Work, Stage Shows, and Recordings.* Jefferson, NC: McFarland, 2005.
Marx, Arthur. *The Nine Lives of Mickey Rooney.* New York: Stein and Day, 1986.
Mitz, Rick. *The Great TV Sitcom Book.* New York: Perigee, 1988.
O'Neil, Thomas. *The Emmys: Star Wars, Showdowns, and the Supreme Test of TV's Best.* New York: Penguin, 1992.

Prouty, Howard H., ed. *Variety Television Reviews*. 15 vols. New York: Garland, 1989–1991.

Terrace, Vincent. *Encyclopedia of Television Subjects, Themes, and Settings.* Jefferson, NC: McFarland, 2007.

_____. *Television Character and Story Facts: Over 110,000 Details from 1,008 Shows, 1945–1992.* Jefferson, NC: McFarland, 1993.

Tucker, David C. *The Women Who Made Television Funny: Ten Stars of 1950s Sitcoms.* Jefferson, NC: McFarland, 2007.

In addition to the sources listed above, the following websites were consulted:

The Classic TV Archive (www.ctva.biz)
The Internet Broadway Database (www.ibdb.com)
Newspaperarchive.com

Index

Numbers in *bold italics* indicate pages with photographs.

Abbott, Norman 67, 74, 113, 186
Abbott and Costello 65
The Abbott and Costello Show 123, 131
About Mrs. Leslie 122
Ace of Clubs 56
Ackerman, Harry 33, 100, 102, 104, 171
Acton, Ralph 94
Adair, Tom 164
Adam-12 97
Adams, Brooke 164, *165*, 168
Adams, Don 12, *13*, 16, 17
Adams' Apples 70
Adam's Rib 204
The Addams Family 79, 116, 119, 143
Adelman, Jerry 87
The Admiral Broadway Revue 34
Adventures in Paradise 51, 109
The Adventures of Ozzie and Harriet 111, 196
The Adventures of Sam Spade 139
The Adventures of Tugboat Annie 123
AfterMASH 192
Ahern, Lloyd 61, 171
Alberoni, Sherry 202, 205
Albert, Katherine 61, 62
Albertson, Jack 54
Albertson, Mabel 202, 205
Aldrin, Dorothy 128
Aldworth, Jack 5
Aletter, Frank 87, 89, 193
Alexander, Van 128
Alfred of the Amazon 148
Alias Smith and Jones 105
All About Eve 84, 136
All Ashore 131
All in the Family 23, 99
Allardice, James 164
Allen, Barbara Jo *see* Vague, Vera
Allen, Gracie 42, 43, 208, 212
Allen, Irwin 89
Allen, Lloyd 149
Allen, Ray 113, 115, 143

Allen, Steve 14, 74
Alley, Kirstie 45
Allman, Elvia 178
Alsberg, Arthur 5, 74, 186, 191
Amateau, Rod 107, 120, 164, 169
Ameche, Don 204
American Federation of Television and Radio Artists 30
The Americanization of Emily 77
Ames, Leon 70
Amigo Productions
Amory, Cleveland 164, 167
The Amos 'n' Andy Show 30, 83, 122, 162
Anatomy of a Psycho 42
"And the World Begat the Bleep" 24
"And Then I Wrote Happy Birthday to You" 88
Anders, Merry 61, 63, *65*, 66
Andersen, Jon C. 171
Anderson, James 136
Andrews, Edward 145
Andriot, Lucien 80
The Andy Griffith Show 15, 16, 38, 56, 70, 73, 82, 85, 115, 153, 155, 174, 190, 200
Andy Hardy Comes Home 183
The Andy Williams Show 210
Angel 5–11, 12
Animal Crackers 183
The Ann Sothern Show 71, 89
Annabel 61
"The Annapolis Man" 51
Annie McGuire 53
Anniversary Waltz 111
Another World 22
Ansara, Michael 64
Anthony, Lon 128
Appel, Victor B. 40
Applegate, Eddie 61
Arden, Eve 123
Are You with It? 57
Arnaz, Desi 5, 139, 199
Arnold, Jack 87, 143, 147, 186
Arquette, Cliff 110
Arsenic and Old Lace 115

Arthur, Beatrice 66
Arthur, Jean 135
Astin, John 74, *75*–79
Astor, Burt 143
At the Circus 181
Ates, Roscoe 133
Atwater, Edith 100, 104
Aubrey, James 52
August, Helen 100
August, Tom 100
Austin, Charlotte 64
Austin, Gene 64
Avedon, Barbara 20, 100; *see also* Hammer, Barbara
Avedon, Doe 64
Avedon, Richard 64
"The Average Man" 130
Averback, Hy 40, 47, 149, 202, 204
Avery, Phyllis 120, *121*, 123
Avery, Steven Morehouse 123

"B-Day for Earl" 82
Babes in Arms 22
Baby Take a Bow 83
Baby Talk 40, 45–46
Bacall, Lauren 61, 189
Bachelor Father 168, 199
The Bachelors 86
Backus, Henny 98
Backus, Jim 94, *95*, 97, 98–99, 118
Bacon, Archie 47
Bad Girl 83
Badiyi, Reza S. 20
Baer, Richard 27, 47, 100, 164, 171
Bailey, Raymond 111
The Baileys of Balboa 103
Baker, Harrison A. 80
Bakewell, William 130
Baldridge, Frank 27
Balenda, Carla 128, 131, 134
Balkan, Adele 107
Ball, Lucille 5, 58, 64, 77, 128, 139, 159, 188, 190, 192, 197, 199, 206, 210
Balzer, George 145, 164
Bangert, Johnny 107
Banks, Cherie 136

227

Index

Barasch, Norman 194
Barefoot in the Park 104
Baretta 207
Barker, Warren 107
Barret, Earl 20, 24, 164
Barron, Jack 67, 120
Barry, Patricia 98
Barry, Wesley E. 164
Barrymore, John, Jr. 189
Barrymore, Lionel 182
"The Barter System" 69
Barton, Charles 27, 33, 120
Bass, Stephen 194
Bast, William 71
Batcheller, George R. 171
Bates, Barbara 80, 83–84
Batman 145
Bau, Gordon 208
Bauer, Frank 128
Baur, Frank 54, 136
Bavier, Frances 80, 82, 85
Bayhi, Chester 107, 202
Beat the Clock 160
Beckman, Henry 74
Beckner, Neal 87
Beetley, Samuel E. 54, 136, 157
Beir, Fred 70
Belding, Richard 143
Bellah, Ross 33, 100, 171
Bellamy, Earl 186
Belles on Their Toes 110
Bells Are Ringing 89
Beloin, Edmund 157
Belson, Jerry 12
Ben Casey 86
Benaderet, Bea 194, 199
Bender, Russell 120
Bendix, William 181
Benet, Brenda 210
Benjamin, Phil 202
Benny, Jack 70, 104, 205, 213
Benson 22
Benson, Frank Red 20
Bentley, Fred 186
Bentley, Len 20
Benton, Robert R. 186
Beresford Productions, Inc. 164
Berg, Cherney 149, 151, 153
Berg, Gertrude 149–155, **151**
Bergen, Jerry 34
Berger, Ralph 5, 94, 157
Berke, Les 67
Berle, Milton 18, 130
Bernardine 42
Bernardo, Santo L. 164
Bernay, Josef 128
Berns, Mel 61, 149
Bernstein, Jerrold (Jerry) 100, 171
Berres, Richard 194

Berry, Ken 98
Berryman, June 57
Best of the West 207
"The Best Women" 197
The Best Years of Our Lives 80
"The Bet" 78
Beulah 30
The Beverly Hillbillies 25, 111
Bewitched 38, 71, 102, 104, 118, 139, 168, 174, 175, 205
Biddiscombe, Carl 149, 194
The Big Country 167
Bigelow, Joe 33
The Bill Cosby Show 31
Bill Dana Productions 15
The Bill Dana Show 12–19, 37–38
Bing, Mack 100
The Bing Crosby Show 210
Binyon, Claude, Jr. 87
Birnbaum, Nathan *see* Burns, George
Birnie, Richard 120
Biroc, Joseph F. (Joe) 54, 128
Bishop, Julie 157, 160
Bishop, William 80, **81**, 82, 85, 86
Black, Ralph 128
Black, William 5
The Black Cat 160
Blacke's Magic 192
Blake, Robert 207
Bliss, Sally *see* Balenda, Carla
Blitzer, Barry 74, 113
Blondie 32, 99, 176
Blyden, Larry 97
The Bob Crane Show 176
The Bob Cummings Show 66, 157, 163, 182
The Bob Newhart Show 77, 173
Bobbikins 42
Bobrick, Sam 12
Bogart, Humphrey 160
The Bold Ones 169
Bonanza 25
Boone, Pat 42
Booth, Shirley 36, 111, 122, 154, 205
Boots Malone 189
Born, David 40, 43
Born, Steven 40, 43
Bostock, Barbara 100
Botteller, Joyce *see* Carne, Judy
Bouchey, Willis 27, **95**
Bowman, John Clarke 67
Boyer, Charles 137
Boys Town 98
Bradford, John 107, 113

The Brady Bunch 23, 26, 38, 77, 87
Bransten, Richard 109
The Brass Bottle 167
Brasselle, Keefe 205
Brebner, Ardelle 120
Brecher, Irving 178, 180, 181–182
Bregman, Buddy 194
Brenner, Ray 107
Breslin, Patricia 178, **179**, 183
Breslow, Lou 120
Bricken, Jules 120
The Bride and the Beast 64
Bridget Productions 136
Bright Eyes 83
The Brighter Day 192
Bringing Up Buddy 44–45, 89
Broadside 145
Brockway, Richard 164
Brooke, Hillary 131
Brooks, Mel 17, 147
Brooks, Rolland M. 40, 74
Brooks, Stanley J. 12
Broughton, Bruce 20
Browar, Herbert 178
Brower, Robert 143
Brown, Fred J. 100
Brown, G. Carleton 40, 41–42, 44, 178
Brown, James H. 67
Browning, Elizabeth Barrett 28
Bruzlin, Alfred 61
Buckley, Hal 164
Buckner, Sara 45
Buhler, Kitty 120
Bullock, Harvey 113, 115, 143
Bullock, Jim 164
Bundle of Joy 98
Burch, Ruth 12
Burke, Chas E. 113, 202
Burke, Ross 186
Burke, Sonny 47, 51
Burlingame Productions 5
Burnett, Carol 24
Burns, George 42, 43, 162–163, 181–182, 185, 208–213
Burns, Ronnie 40, **41**–45
Burns, William (Willy) 208, 212
Burr, Raymond 137
Burrows, Abe 164, 167, 168–169
Burrows, Jim 164
Burton, Bernard 54, 113, 136, 149, 194, 202
Burton, Robert 34
Bus Stop 109
Bush, Florence 67

Index

Butch Cassidy and the Sundance Kid 105
Butler, David 186
Butler, Robert 40, 47, 149, 194
Butler, Rudy 27, 80
Buttons, Red 146, 169
Buzzy Wuzzy 34
Bye Bye Birdie 9, 147
Bygraves, Max 42
Byington, Spring 186

Cactus Flower 169
Caesar, Sid 34, 38, 58, 59, 93, 97
Cahan, George 87
Cahoon, Richard 61
Calhoun 52
California National Productions 94
Calin, Mickey *see* Callan, Michael
Calinoff, Michael *see* Callan, Michael
"A Call to Arms" 63
Callahan, James 20, 26, 208, 213
Callan, Michael 171, *172*, 174, 175, 176
Calvelli, Joseph 27
Cambern, Donn 107
Camel Cigarettes 141
Camp Runamuck 36
Campanella, Joseph 169
Canfield, Mary Grace 36
Cannon, Dyan 142
Cantor, Eddie 111
Capacchione, Frank 80, 87
Capitol 213
Capps, McClure 27, 80
Capra, Frank 110
Captain Nice 143, 145, 146–147, 148
Car 54, Where Are You? 37, 90
The Cara Williams Show 89, 174, 193
Cardi, Pat 87, 90
Carleton, Claire 128
Carne, Judy 100, *102*–105
Carnegie, Andrew 54
Carneol, Jess 61
Caron, Leslie 11
Carpenter, Claude 178
"Carpenters Four" 77
Carroll, Bob, Jr. 5, 11, 202, 206
Carson, Frank 194, 202
Carson, Jack 110
Carson, Jean 56
Carson, Jeannie 54–55, *56*–60

Carvey, Dana 135
Cass, Peggy 204
Castle, William 104
Cat Ballou 77, 174
Cat on a Hot Tin Roof 167
Chaloupka, Hugh 33
Chandler, Chick 160
Chandler, George 67, *68*, 70, 71
Channing, Carol 211
Charles in Charge 26
Charley's Aunt 123
Chase 17
Cheaper by the Dozen 84
Cheers 155
"Cherchez la Roommate" 66
Cherry, Budd 20
Cherry, Stanley Z. (Stan) 12, 113
Chesis, Eileen 202
Chevillat, Dick 12, 33, 74, 80, 83, 94, 96
The Chicago Teddy Bears 90
Chicken Soup 201
Chico and the Man 50
ChildHelp USA 45
Childress, Alvin 162
Chudnow, Byron 143
Chulay, John C. 61
Church, Thomas Haden 177
Cinader, Robert A. 94, 96–97
Clark, Asa 171
Clark, Candy 71
Clark, Dane 132
Clarke, Charles 54
Clarke, Robert 130
Clarke, Woodruff H. 61, 113, 194
Clasen, Gil 20
Claver, Bob 149, 171, 175
Clifford, Sidney 171
Cline, Wilfrid M. 40, 113
Cline, William T. 20
Coca, Imogene 33–39, *35*, 87, 89, 90, 93
Coe, Fred 89
Cohen, Lawrence J. 171, 173
Coil, Marvin J. 128
Colasanto, Nicholas 20
Colbert, Norman 113
Colean, Chuck 67
Coleman, Leroy 94
Collins, Gary 23
Collins, Jack 171, 175
Collins, Joan 126
Comer, Sam 186
Como, Perry 44, 97
Compinsky, Alec 61
Congress of Mexican-American Unity 18

Connelly, Joe 67, 120, 121–122, 123
Conrad, Con 111
Conried, Hans 198
Conservatoire Nationale 8
Conte, Richard 22
Conway, Dick 40, 61, 157
Coogan, Jackie 113, 116, 117, 119
Cooley, Stan 94, 164
Coon, Gene L. 67
Cooper, Barbara Kraus 182
Cooper, Jackie 47, *48*–53, 174, 178, *179*, 181–183, 184–185
Cooperman, Alvin 40, 43
Cooperman, John, Jr. *see* Cooper, Jackie
Corby, Ellen 133
Corcoran, Brian 164, *165*, 168
Corcoran, Noreen 168
Corman, Roger 63
Corrick, Jack 120
Corrigan, Lloyd 40, 42
Corsaut, Aneta 149, 152, 155
Costello, Lou 199
Coughlin, Kerwin 178, 186
"Country Club Dance" 64
"The Court Jester" 17
Courtney, Chuck 147
The Courtship of Eddie's Father 50
Coward, Noël 56
Cox, Wally 36, 134, 181
"Crackerby for Treasurer" 166
Crain, Earl, Sr. 120
Crain, Jeanne 108
Cramer, Duncan 54, 136
Crane, Barry 113, 194, 202
Crawford, Joan 85, 104
Creature from the Black Lagoon 147
Creber, Lewis 61, 178
Crime Doctor's Man Hunt 189
Croft, Mary Jane 178, 183
Cronjager, Henry 12, 94
Crosby, Gary 12, 16, 17
Cross, James 61
Crowe, James M. 33, 128
The Crusader 189
Crutcher, Norval, Jr. 54, 194
Crutcher, Robert Riley 171
Las Cuatro Noches de la Luna Llena 22
La Cucaracha 42
Cukor, George 189
Cult of the Cobra 9
Cummings, Charles Clarence Robert *see* Cummings, Robert (Bob)

Cummings, Mary **158**, 161
Cummings, Robert (Bob) 122, 157, **158**
Currier, Richard 120
Curtis, Nathaniel 120, 186
Curtis, Tony 189
Cutler, Stan 171

The D.A. 192
Dailey, Dan 20–24
Dailey, Irene 22
Daily, Bill 213
Daktari 9
Dallas 99
Dalton, Abby 47, **48**
Dan Raven 45
Dana, Bill 12, **13**
Daniel, Eliot 5
Daniels, Glen 157
Daniels, Harold 157
Daniels, Marc 149
Daniels, William 145, 147
The Danny Kaye Show 18, 38
The Danny Thomas Show 12, 15, 110–111, 205
Dante 141
Darby, Kim 105
D'Arcy, Wilbur L. 87, 107
Dare, Danny 61
Darley, Dick 87
Date Line Tokyo 132
Dattelbaum, Archie 40
Dave and Charley 110
Davenport, William (Bill) 5, 33, 149, 171
David, Paul 33
David Swift Productions 33
David's Harem 202
Davis, Ann B. 118, 163
Davis, Benny 111
Davis, David 164
Davis, George W. 94
Davis, Jerry 33, 74
Davis, Madelyn Pugh *see* Martin, Madelyn Pugh
Davis, Phil 164
Davis, Ralph, Jr. 186
Davis, Roger 105
Davis, Sammy, Jr. 50
Davis, Stanley 94
Davison, Joel 164, **165**
Dawn, Robert 67
Dawson, Robert 47
Day, Doris 116
Days of Heaven 168
Dayton, Danny 171
Deacon, Richard 179
Dean, James 71, 97
Dear Me, The Sky Is Falling 155
The Debbie Reynolds Show 11

DeCamp, Rosemary 163
December Bride 49, 186, 187–188, 189, 190, 193, 204
de Cordova, Frederick 136, 140
Dee, Sandra 166
Dee, Vincent 67
Deep Valley 123
The Defiant Ones 189
de Grasse, Robert 5
Delaney, Pat 202
DeMond, Henry 178
Dennis, Robert C. 164
Dennis the Menace 32, 147, 176, 190
Denny, Reginald 158–159
Depew, Joseph 47, 178
Derman, Bill 61
Derman, Lou 61, 113
de Sica, Vittorio 22
Desilu Playhouse 5, 141
Desire Under the Elms 167
Deuel, Peter 100, **102**–106
DeVol, Frank 33, 54, 74, 77
DeWitt, Alan 87, 91
Dewlow, Bernice *see* Dulo, Jane
De Wolf, Karen 61
Diage, Louis 100
Dial M for Murder 122, 162
Diamond, Mel 74, 194
Dick, Peggy Chantler 171
The Dick Van Dyke Show 16, 32, 38, 134, 154, 198
Diller, Phyllis 105
Dinehart, Alan 87
Dinosaurus! 91
Diskant, George E. 54, 136, 157
Disney's Wonderful World of Color 17
Dobie Gillis see The Many Loves of Dobie Gillis
Doc 155
Dodd, Everett 186
Dolan, Robert Emmett 164
Don Sharpe Enterprises 157
The Donna Reed Show 104, 105, 111, 168
Donnell, Jeff 126
Donner, Richard 87
Donohue, Jack 107
Donovan, King 33, 35, 37, 38
Donovan, Martin 171
Dorfman, Sid 164, 169
The Doris Day Show 147
Dorsey, Rosemary 12
The Double Life of Henry Phyfe 169
Dowd, Ross 94
Downing, Jean 186

Doyle, Frank 157
Dozier, William 35
Dragnet 184, 192
Dreben, Stan 186
Drew, Bernard 61
Driftwood 168
Driscoll, Theodore 208
Du Brow, Rick 24
Duel, Pete *see* Deuel, Peter
Duet 46
Duff, Bridget 140
Duff, Howard 136, **137**, 139–142
Duffy, Julia 46
Duffy's Tavern 27
Duggan, Andrew 25
The Duke 57
Duke, Maurice 128, 132, 133, 134
Duke, Patty 79
Dulo, Jane 54, 57
Dumbell People in a Barbell World 146
Duncan, *Be Careful* 79
Duning, George 208
Dunn, James 80, 82–83, 85, 86

East of Eden 167
The Ed Sullivan Show 58, 91
The Ed Wynn Show 205
The Eddie Cantor Story 205
Edelstein, Tillie *see* Berg, Gertrude
Eden, Barbara 61, 62, 63–64, **65**, 66
Ederer, Bernard 80, 136
The Edge of Night 22
Edwards, Bill 186
Edwards, Blake 128, 131
Edwards, Mervyn (Buck) 110
Edwards, Ralph 137
Edwards, Rowland 43
"The Egg and Ray" 124
87th Precinct 210
Eimen, John 113, **114**, 116, 118, 119
El Camino Productions 186
Elinson, Iz 12, 40, 202
Elinson, Jack 5, 12, 54, 157
Eliot, Gene 61, 186
Ellenson, Robert 100
Elliotte, John 27, 31
Ellis, Herb 194
Elmer Gantry 42
Ensign O'Toole 17, 89, 117, 118
Erskine, Marilyn 202, 204–205
Eunson, Dale 61–62
Eunson, Katherine Albert *see* Albert, Katherine

Index

Eustis, Rich 164
The Eve Arden Show 85, 115, 141
Ewell, Tom 202, **203**
Excursion 205
The Exhaustion of Our Son's Love 146

Fabian **151**, 155
Fair Exchange 103
Falcon Crest 52
Family Affair 45
The Famous Adventures of Mr. Magoo 98–99
Faraday and Company 26
Farentino, James 169
Fargé, Annie 5, **6**, 8–11
Faris, Jim 164
Farrell, Charles 130
The Father Dowling Mysteries 155
Father Knows Best 43, 70, 141, 205
"Fawcett Is Running" 25
Faye, Alice 83
Fedderson, Don 45
Fedderson, Yvonne Lime *see* Lime, Yvonne
Feiner, Ben, Jr. 61
Feldman, Edward H. 5
Feldman, Gene 20, 186
Fell, Norman 202
The Felony Squad 141
Felton, Verna 186, 189, 190
Ferguson, Perry II 20
Fibber McGee and Molly (radio) 27, 28
Fibber McGee and Molly (TV) 32, 205
Ficker, Jane 136
"Field Trip" 125
Fielding, Jerry 20, 23, 202
Fields, Verna 202
Filmakers, Inc. 137
Finian's Rainbow 60
Finkel, Robert S. 27, 178
Finn, Herbert 87
"The First Anniversary" 185
"The First Day" 151
Fisher, Bob (accompanist) 208
Fisher, Eddie 141
Fisher, Robert (Bob, writer) 5, 74, 107, 113, 178, 186, 191
Fitts, Margaret 40
Fitzgerald, Ed 140
The 5,000 Fingers of Dr. T 198
"Flaming Youth" 108
Flamingo Road 141
Flicker, Theodore J. 12

The Flintstones 89, 199
Florea, Johnny 94
Fontaine, Joan 137
Fools Rush In 34
Foote, Dorothy Cooper 100
"For Pete's Sake" 188
Foran, Dick 164, 168
Ford, Glenn 135
Ford, Paul 204
Forman, Joey 128, 131, 132, 134
Forrest, Russell 149
Forsyth, Ed 33, 100, 171
Forsythe, John 199
Forte, Fabian *see* Fabian
40 Carats 86
Four Just Men 22
Four Star Playhouse 137–138, 141, 159
Four Star Productions 54, 59, 113, 117, 136, 149, 151, 157, 194, 196, 202, 207
Fowler, Bruce, Jr. 149, 202
Fowler, Keith 33
Fox, Della 5
Fox, Frank 74
Fox, Fred S. 40, 54, 202
Francis, Arlene 155
Franciscus, James 51
Frankenstein 1970 64
Franklin, Elbert W. 143
Fraser, Elisabeth 113, 116–117
Frazen, Stanley 178
Freedman, Benedict 107, 128
Freedman, Bill 87, 186
Freedman, Morris 120, 178
Freeman, Devery 186
Freeman, Fred 74, 171, 174
Freeman, Kathleen 90
French, Bertha 178
Fried, Gerald 87, 143
Friedberg, Billy 117, 194, 202, 206
Friedman, Irving 40
Friedman, Seymour 33
Friend, Budd S. 54, 94, 136
"Friendship" 81
Frito-Lay 18
Fritzell, James (Jim) 136, 149, 186
"From Here to Maternity" 23
Funny Face 176

Gabriel, John 117
The Gale Storm Show: Oh! Susanna 58
Gangelin, Victor A. 164
Garde, Betty 200
Gardner, Ava 131
Garland, Judy 38

Garner, James 26, 175
Garrett, Lila 171
Garrett, William R. 54
Garrison's Gorillas 213
Garst, Bill 47
Gausman, Hal 27
Gautier, Dick 143, 147, 148
Gaye, Lisa 61, 66
Gaynor, Janet 137
General Electric 122, 125
General Electric Theater 70, 122
General Foods 9
General Hospital 99, 118, 183
Generation 105
Gentlemen Prefer Blondes 77
The George Burns and Gracie Allen Show 42, 140, 162, 169, 181, 199, 208, 211
The George Burns Show 42, 211
The George Gobel Show 126
The George Lopez Show 19
Gering, Richard 107
Germain, Larry 143
Gershe, Leonard 80
Gershman, Ben 87
The Gertrude Berg Show 154–156; see also *Mrs. G. Goes to College*
Gertsman, Maury 74
Get Smart 16, 17, 145, 147
Ghostley, Alice 145, 204, 205
"The Ghosts of Consolidated" 140
Gidget 103
Gidget Goes Hawaiian 174
Gifford, Frances 83
Gilbert, Herschel Burke 113, 149, 194, 202
Gildersleeve on Broadway 29
Gildersleeve's Bad Day 29
Gildersleeve's Ghost 29
Gill, Frank, Jr. 40, 41–42, 44, 178
Gilligan's Island 87, 89, 90, 92, 94, 99, 141, 147, 148, 174
The Girl from U.N.C.L.E. 176
The Girl in the Red Velvet Swing 126
The Girls in 509 35
Gladysa Productions 87, 89
Glass, Gaston 107
Glass, Jack R. 27, 80
Gleason, Jack 33
Gleason, Jackie 74, 97, 132, 133
Glynis 11
Go West 181
Gobel, George 98, 126, 141
Godfrey, Arthur 98, 198

Goetten, Armor E. 54
Going My Own Way 17
Gold, Donald 33
The Goldbergs 149, 152
Golden Earrings 125
The Golden Girls 19, 66
Golden Globe Awards 24
Goldfarb, Annie *see* Fargé, Annie
Goldman, Hal 145
Gomer Pyle, U.S.M.C. 213
Gonzalez, Jose Luis 18
Goodbye Charlie 189
Goode, Samuel F. 208
Goodman, Al 54
Goodman, Hal 107, 110
Goodman, Ralph 107
Goodrich, Jack 27
Goodwins, Leslie 87, 157, 186
Goosson, Stephen 128, 178
Gordon, Al 145
Gordon, Gale 9, 186, 190–191
Gordon, Ruth 150
Gosfield, Maurice 98
Gossert, Gene 12
The Governor and J.J. 20–26, 213
"GP Loves UU" 173
Grable, Betty 22, 61
Grace, Henry 94
Grace, Mary 87, 90
Graham, Ronny 194
Grant, Cary 76, 142
Grant, Jennifer 142
Great Day in the Morning 116
The Great Gildersleeve 27–32
The Great Gildersleeve (film) 29
The Great Gildersleeve (radio) 28–29, 31
"The Great Schultz" 34
The Greeks Had a Word for Them 61
Green Acres 36, 83
Greenbaum, Everett 61, 149, 186
Greene, John L. 33, 61, 94
Greene, Mort 157, 161–162
Greenfield, Howard 100, 171
Greenhow, Thomas 80
Greenway, Lee 5
Grey's Anatomy 201
Grier, Rosey 126
Griffin, Stephanie 27
Griffith, Andy 212
Grimwood, Burris 149, 194, 202
Grindl 17, 33–39, 90
"Grindl, She-Wolf of Wall Street" 34
Gross, Roland 54

Grossman, Budd 87, 143, 147
Guess Who's Coming to Dinner 77
Guest, Don 87
Guiol, Fred 159
Gunsmoke 92, 103
Gurasich, Lynda 20
Guthrie, Carl 194, 202
Guzman, Claudio 74, 100, 164
Guzman, Patricio 5

Hagen, Earle 12, 16
Hagman, Larry 99
"Hail to the Chief" 51
Hal Roach Studios 27, 83
Hall, John 12
Hamilton, Kipp 117
Hamilton, Richard 61
Hamlin, Harry 142
Hammer, Barbara 5, 107; *see also* Avedon, Barbara
Hanna-Barbera 89
Hansen, Peter 118
Happy 40–46, 185
Happy Birthday 183
Happy Days 107, 112
"Happy Marriage" 7
Hardwicke, Cedric 149, 150, 151–153
The Hardy Boys Mysteries 104
Harlen Productions 113
Harmon, David P. 87, 88, 143
Harmon, William (Bill) 54, 113, 149, 202
Harper, Ron 208, 210, 213
Harper Valley P.T.A. 66
Harrington, Pat, Jr. 111
Harris, Bob, Jr. 20
Harris, Grace 186
Harris, Jack H. 87, 91
Harris, Jonathan 12, *13*, 16, 17
Harris, Julie 109
Harris, Marie 186
Harris, Phil 83
Harris, Robert B. 54, 113, 136, 149, 202
Harrison, Joseph 67
Hart, Trisha *see* Harty, Patricia
Hart, William Sterling *see* Sterling, Robert
Hartman, Paul 124, 196
Harty, Patricia 171, *172*, 174–175, 176
Harvey, Kenneth 186
Harvey Middleman, Fireman 175
Hatch, Wilbur 136, 186
A Hatful of Rain 71
Hawaiian Eye 208, 211–212

Hawk 103
Hawkins, Jack 22
Hawkins, Jimmy 67
Hayden, Jeffrey 113
Hayes, Cathy Lind 201
Hayes, Helen 183
Hayes, Peter Lind 194, **195**, 196–199, 200–201
Hayward, Chris 20
Hazel 36, 104, 111, 116, 154, 174, 200
Healy, Mary 194, **195**, 197–201
Heath, Bill 40, 74, 94
Heath, Larry 47, 164
Heaven Can Wait 115
Hec Ramsey 192
Heermance, Dick 194
Heidi 56
Helm, Harvey 113
Henerson, James 100
Hennesey 36, 47–53, 185
The Hennesey Company 47
"Hennesey Meets Harvey Spencer Blair III" 50
"Hennesey Meets Honeyboy" 50–51
Henning, Paul 162
Henry, Agnes 54, 136
Henry, Buck 17, 145, 146
Henry, Emmaline 74, 76, 78
Henry, Maxwell 61
Henry Aldrich series 161
Herbert, F. Hugh 109
Here Come the Brides 77
Here We Go Again 99
Here's Lucy 23
Herlinger, Karl 54, 157
Herzig, Siegfried 120
Heschong, Albert 186
Hester Street 148
Hey, Jeannie! 12, 54–60
Heyday Productions 74
Heyer, Bill 188
Heyward, Louis M. 186
Hickman, Dwayne 163
High, Perzy 74
High Noon 189
High School Confidential! 116
"High Society" 194, 196
Hiller, Arthur 74, 77
Hilton, Arthur D. 54, 149
Hinkley, Don 15, 74
Hinnant, Bill 186
"The Hiring of Jose" 14
Hitchcock, Alfred 122, 127
"The Hoarder and the Boarder" 191
Hoffman, Charles 120
Hoffman, Joseph 67
Hogan, James 120

Index 233

Hogan's Heroes 99
Hokom, Lillian 47
Holley, Gibson A. 202
Hollywood House 97
The Hollywood Palace 18
The Hollywood Squares 52
Homeier, Skip 45
Honest Harold 29
The Honeymooners 74
Hooperman 53
Hopper, Hedda 44, 45
Hopper, Jerry 87, 94
Hormel, George 11
Horn, Leonard 164
Horwitt, Arnold 107
Hotaling, Frank 149
Hotel 46
House, Chandler 149, 202
"How Sock Met Mandy" 180
How to Marry a Millionaire 61–66
How to Marry a Millionaire (film) 61, 66
Howard, Bruce 87
Howard, Cy 103
Howard, Dorcy 47, 178
Howard, Ron 112
Howells, J. Harvey 70
Hubbard, John 128
Huggins, Roy 109
Hughes, Bonnie 143, 147
Hughes, Mary Beth 159
Hunnicutt, Gayle 101
Hurst, Ralph 54
Huston, Lou 33
Hutchins, Will 176

"I Do, We Don't" 173
I Dream of Jeannie 64, 66, 77, 92, 140, 148, 185
I Love Lucy 5, 7, 11, 64, 124, 133, 139, 141, 160, 161, 186, 190, 196–197, 199, 202, 203
I Married a Monster from Outer Space 136
I Married a Woman 98
I Married Joan 97, 99
I Remember Mama 110
I Was a Teenage Werewolf 43
Ichabod and Me 67–73
Idelson, Bill 12
Ilou, Edward 40, 61, 107
I'm Dickens ... He's Fenster 74
The Imogene Coca Show 35
The Incredible Shrinking Man 147
Ingels, Marty 74, **75**–79
Ingerman, Martin *see* Ingels, Marty
Ingoglia, Concetta Rosalie *see* Stevens, Connie

Inn, Frank 178, 183–184
Inside U.S.A. with Chevrolet 197
Inspecting Carol 60
Invasion of the Body Snatchers 168
The Iron Horse 147
Ironside 137
Irving, Hollis 107
Irving, Margaret 178, 183
Isaacs, Bud S. 67
Isaacs, Charles 54, 56
It! The Terror from Beyond Space 9
It's a Gift 109
It's a Great Life 80–86, 96
It's About Time 38–39, 87–93, 118
It's Always Jan 63
Ivano, Paul 94
Ives, Burl 164, **165**, 167–170
Ivo, Tommy 107

J & M Productions 67
Jack London 82
Jackie Cooper Productions 47
The Jackie Gleason Show 18, 131, 132, 133
Jacobs, Jack 120
Jacobs, Ronald 12
Jacobs, Seaman 33, 61
Jahfa Productions 149
James, Dick 61
James, Richard 40
James Dean 71
Janiss, Vivi 80
Jason, Leigh 178
"The Jazz Band" 110
The Jean Arthur Show 213
The Jeannie Carson Show 59–60; *see also Hey, Jeannie!*
Jeannie Productions 54
"Jeannie's Here" 54
"Jeannie's Income Tax" 54
Jeffreys, Anne 71, 72, 73
Jell-O 51
Jenkins, Allen 54, 57
Jennings, Louis 208
Jennings, Tom 164
The Jerry Lewis Show 176
The Jim Backus Show (radio) 97
The Jim Backus Show: Hot Off the Wire 67, 83, 94–99
The Jimmy Stewart Show 147
"Job Switching" 203
Joe and Mabel 97
The Joey Bishop Show 52
John Loves Mary 204

The Johnny Carson Show 64
Johns, Glynis 11
Johnson, Arte 47, 50
Johnson, Lamont 5
Johnson, Nunnally 61
Johnson, Stanley E. 113
Johnson Wax 8
Jolley, Stan 186
The Jonathan Winters Show 52
Jones, Dean 117
Jones, Gana 61
Jones, Gordon 120, **121**, 123, 125
Jones, Paul 61
Jones, Shirley 42, 79
Jones, Stanley 208
Jose Jimenez in Jollywood 15
Jose Jimenez in Orbit 15
Joslyn, Allyn 113, 115–116, 118
The Judy Garland Show 104
Julia 112, 155
June, Ray 128
Jurist, Ed 33

Kahn, Bernie 171
Kalish, Austin 113
Kamiat, Bernice *see* Williams, Cara
Kane, Joel 80, 87, 145, 178
Kanin, Garson 150
Kanter, Hal 112
Kantor, Igo 40
Karloff, Boris 42, 205
Karns, Roscoe 47, 49
"Kathy Goes to New York" 84
Katzman, Leonard 128
Kay, Bernice *see* Williams, Cara
Kaye, Danny 33
Kayro Productions 67
Kazan, Elia 167
Kearney, Tom 175
Kearns, Joseph 137
Keating, Larry 43, 211
Keays, Vernon 40
Keefer, Don 5, **6**, 9
Keith, Brian 140
Keith, Ronald 27, 31
Keller, Jack 100
Keller, Mary Page 46
Keller, Sheldon 12, 74
Kellino, Roy 137
Kelly, Grace 122, 124
Kelly, Thomas F. 80
Kelly, Tom 94
Kempley, Walter 74, 186
Kenney, Marie 40
Kent, David 117
Kent Cigarettes 51

Index

Kentucky Jones 192
Kenyon, Sandy 100
Kern, James V. 186, 190
Kerner, Jacqueline Francine *see* Parker, Penney
Kessler, Frederick A. 186
Ketchum, Dave 74
The Kid 116
Kilgallen, Dorothy 146
Kimlin, Newell P. 80
King, George 47, 178
King, Harry 54, 113, 149
King, Hugh 47
King of Hearts 182
King Production Service 47
Kingston Trio 155
Kinon, Richard 100, 136, 149, 171, 202
Kinskey, Leonid 178
Kirgo, George 20
Kirkwood, Jack 54, 59
Kirshner, Don 100, 171
Kirshner, William 96
Kissin' Cousins 112
Klatzkin, Leon 61, 157
Klein, Larry 107, 109
Kline, Henry 143
Knapp, Harry 94
Knight, Ted 63
Knotts, Don 15, 19
Kohn, John 61
Kojak 31, 36
Kolb, Mina 186
Komack, James 47, 50
Kosloff, Lou 178
Koster, Dorothy 169
Kowalski, Frank 47
Kraft Foods 44
Kraft Television Theatre 147
Kramer, Stanley 189, 205
Krasna, Norman 198
Kuehl, William L. 208
Kufel, Stan 12
Kulkovich, Henry *see* Kulky, Henry
Kulky, Henry 36, 47
Kulp, Nancy *81*
Kunin, Howard 100, 171
Kupcinet, Irv 155
Kupcinet, Karyn 149, 152, 155
Kusely, Irma 5

L.A. Law 142
Ladd, Alan 161
Lady of Burlesque 82
Lamphear, John 87
Lancer 25, 211
Land of the Giants 119
Landis, Jessie Royce 23
Landres, Paul 54

Lane, Ben 33, 100, 171
Lane, Ivan 116
Lane, Nathan 135
Lane, Scott 113, *114*, 116, 118, 119
Lanfield, Sidney 67, 186
Langan, Glenn 109
La Plante, Laura 85
Laredo 168
Larsen, Dottie 5
Larson, Richard A. 94
Lassie 17, 71, 85, 91, 183
The Last Resorts 167
Latin Lovers 161
The Lawyers 169
Leader, Tony 143
Leave It to Beaver 67, 71, 117, 122
Lederer, Charles 136, 137
Ledoux, Leone 40, 43
Lee, Joanna 67
Lee, Peggy 51
Leeds, Howard 12, 61, 202
Leeds, Peter 186
LeGrand, Richard 12
Leigh, Vivien 57
Lemmon, Jack 174
Lenard, Kay 61
Leonard, Sheldon 12, 15, 38
Leonetti, Tommy 205
Leslie, Phil 33
A Letter to Loretta 120
Levin, Erma E. 208
Levy, David 119
Levy, Parke 186, 188, 189, 192–193
Lewin, Albert E. 33, 87, 107, 113, 120
Lewine, Robert 9
Lewis, Al 12
Lewis, Bill 94
Lewis, David 194
Lewis, Elliott 164, 169
Lewis, Forrest 27, 31, 67
Lewis, Harold 186
Lewis, Jerry 38, 61, 211
Liebman, Max 56
Life Can Be Beautiful 205
The Life of Riley 50, 180, 181
Life with Father 31
Life with Luigi 12, 27
Liggett, Sylvia 186
Lili 8
Lime, Yvonne 40, *41*–45
Lind, Aubrey 149, 202
Lind, Joseph Conrad *see* Hayes, Peter Lind
Lindemann, Mitchell 159
The Lineup 152
Link, Robert 80
"Lion Hunt" 129

Lipscott, Alan 5, 107, 178, 186
Litel, John 157, 161
Little, Rich 100, 104
The Little World of Tom Springer 207
Livingston, Roy V. 61
Lloyd, Harold 33
The Lloyd Bridges Show 119
Locke, Samuel (Sam) 87, 113, 186, 194
Loco 62
Loeb, Lee 33
Loeb, Philip 150
Loel, Art 208
Logan, Barbara 83
Logan, Joshua 8
Logan, Myrtle 178
Lombardi, Joe 94
Look Who's Talking 40, 45
Loomis, Diana 61
The Loretta Young Show 31
Lorre, Peter 152
Los Angeles Dodgers 173
Lost in Space 16, 17, 119, 130
The Lost Weekend 120, 123
The Love Boat 115
"Love Comes to Westfield" 118
Love, Dave 164
Love, American Style 115, 176
Love of Life 213
Love on a Rooftop 100–106, 112
Love Story 77, 126
Love That Bob! 157, 163
Love That Jill 71
Lowe, Mundell 100
Lubin, Arthur 143
Lubow, Sid 33
Luciano, Michael 107
Lucky Me 77, 162
"Lucy Is a Matchmaker" 192
The Lucy Show 32, 77, 83, 169, 192, 210
Lueker, Arthur 80
Lunt, Alfred 116
Lupino, Ida 136, *137*–142
Lupino, Stanley 137
Lynch, William 67, 120
Lynde, Paul 38

M Squad 140
MacArthur, Charles 86
Macauley, Carl 208
MacBurnie, John 120
MacFarlane, Louella 136
Mack, Dotty 131
MacKenzie, Jack 67
MacLane, Roland 40, 61, 87, 157

Index   235

MacMurray, Fred 10, 200
The Magic Lantern 132
Maguire, Fred 186
A Majority of One 150
Make Room for Daddy 124
Malcolm, Paul 202
The Male Animal 123
Malin, Anna 40
Mame 32
The Man from the Diner's Club 193
The Man from U.N.C.L.E. 23, 36
Man Without a Gun 64
Mandelik, Gil 40
Manheim, Mannie 94
Manhoff, William (Bill) 54, 61, 186, 188
Manings, Allan 67, 113
Mann, Edward 178
Mannheim, Het 100
Manoff, Bill 20
Mantell, Joe 186
Many Happy Returns 147, 192–193
The Many Loves of Dobie Gillis 43, 109, 111, 115, 169, 205
Manzanares, Mercedes 5, 74
Marcellino, Nick 194
March, Hal 87
Marcus, Bob 113
Margie 107–112, 154
Margie (film) 109
"Margie" (song) 111
Margolin, Arnold 164
Margolin, Stuart 171, 175–176
Margulies, William 54
Markham 126
Marks, Laurence (Larry) 61, 120
Marks, Sherman 33
Marlowe, Nora 20
Marmon, Ben 87
Marquard, Brick 164
Marquette, Desmond 54, 136
Marshall, Garry 12, 74
Marshall, Sarah 194
The Martha Raye Show 14
Martin, Betty 54, 113
Martin, Gene F. 5
Martin, Madelyn Pugh 5, 11, 202, 206
Martin, Mary 60
Martin, Merry 194, 195
Martin, Quinn 26, 202
Martin, William 47
Martinelli, Tony 143
Martinson, Leslie H. 128
Marvin, Lee 140

Marx, Arthur 94, 113, 134, 186
Marx, Groucho 123, 154, 184
Marx Brothers 64, 181, 183
Mary Poppins 71
M*A*S*H 47, 52, 192
Massen, Osa 126
Mathers, Jerry 71
Mathers, Jimmy 67, 68
Matheson, Tim 115
Matlock 26
Maverick 49, 109
Maxey, Paul 178, 183
"Maxie's Silent Partner" 154
Mayberry, Russell 100, 171
Mayberry R.F.D. 25, 73, 86
Mayer, Frank 186
Mayer, Louis B. 182
Mayo, Virginia 82, 86
Mays, Willie 166
Mazurki, Mike 87, 88, 90, 91, 118
McAdam, Michael R. 120
McCadden Productions 162, 178, 182
McCallon, Lynn 47
McCarthy, John 67, 143
McClanahan, Rue 66
McCulloch, Cameron (Cam) 5, 12, 20
McDearmon, David 87
McDonald, Ray 116
McDonough, Donna 12
McDowell, Hugh 47, 128
McDowell, Malcolm 156
McFarland, Jerry 12
McGiver, John 143, 147, 148
McGovern, George 26
McGreevey, John 33
McGuire, Biff 60
McGuire, Don 47, 48–50, 52, 53
McHale's Navy 145
McKay, Marjory 54, 149, 202
McKeegan, Walter 47, 74
McKeever and the Colonel 113–119
McKenney, Ruth 109
McKnight, Tom 113, 117
McLean, Gordon 186
McLean, William 94, 95
McLeod, Norman 40
McNear, Howard 41
McQueen, Steve 201
McWhorter, Frank 27
Me and Molly 150
Meadows, Roy 61
Medical Center 176
Meehan, John 67
Meet Me in St. Louis 181
Meet Mr. McNutley 120–125

Melnick, Al 26
Meriwether, Lee 89
Merrick, David 8, 77
Merrick, Mahlon 178
Merrill, Howard 12, 74, 149, 153
Mesa of Lost Women 116
Messing, Debra 177
Messinger, Marie 128
Metcalfe, Burt 45
Meyer, Otto W. 61
Michaels, Richard 47
Mick, John 40
Mickey 77, 134
Mickey Rooney Enterprises 128
The Mickey Rooney Show: Hey Mulligan 128–135
The Midnight Rounders 111
Milland, Ray 120, 121, 122–123, 124, 125–127
Miller, James M. 107
Miller, Marvin 100
Miller, Merle 52, 167
Miller, Sidney (Sid) 143, 186, 194, 199
Millhollin, James 33, 34
Mills, Jack 128
Milton, Franklyn 94
The Milton Berle Show 175
Mr. Adams and Eve 136–142
Mister Ed 32, 117, 145, 179, 185, 211
Mr. Magoo 94
Mr. Mort 61
Mr. Novak 126
Mr. Peepers 36, 37, 71, 90, 134, 152, 181
Mr. Smith Goes to Washington 110
Mr. Terrific 143–148
Mitchell, Shirley 31, 186, 192
Mockridge, Cyril J. 107
Mohr, Mai 61
Molin, Bud 5
Molly and Me 151
Mona McCluskey 213
Monaster, Nate 5, 54
Mondello, Anthony 100
Monroe, Marilyn 61, 202, 204, 212
Montagne, Edward J. 145
Montenaro, Joe 47
Montgomery, Thomas 164
The Moon Is Blue 109
"Moon or Bust" 133
Moore, Carrol 194
Moore, James 107
Moore, Mary Tyler 53, 78
Moore, Robert 12
Moore, Tom 168

236 Index

Moorhead, Barbara Jean *see* Eden, Barbara
Morgan, Gloria 12, 128
Morgan, Harry 186, **187**–188, 189, 190
Morgan, Henry 189
Morris, Howard 12, 93
Morris, Michael 87, 202
Morriss, Frank E., Jr. 67
Morrow, Douglas 20
Mosher, Bob 67, 120, 121–122, 123
Moss, Joel 27, 80, 186
Moss, Marty 27
"The Mother Affair" 155
Mother Is a Freshman 151
Mother Was a Freshman 151
Mother Wore Tights 22
Motion Picture and Television Country Home and Hospital 119, 207
Mount Tom Productions 194
"The Movie Star" (*It's a Great Life* episode) 85
"The Movie Star" (*My Hero* episode) 158
Movie Stars 142
Mowbray, Alan 130
Mrs. G. Goes to College 147, 149–156, 196
Mulcahy, Mac 40, 61
Mullaney, Jack 87, 89
The Mummy's Hand 168
The Munsters 67, 122, 143
Murder, My Sweet 90
Murphy, Ben 105
Murray, John Fenton 128
Mustin, Burt 67
Musuraca, Nicholas (Nick) 54, 80
My Favorite Martian 91
My Hero 157–163
My Little Margie 41, 83, 130, 131, 161
My Living Doll 89, 163
My Man Godfrey 139
My Mother the Car 169
My Name Jose Jimenez: A Photographic Interview 15
My Sister Eileen 109, 175
My Three Sons 10, 26, 45, 110, 111, 168, 200, 205
Myers, Frank 12

The NBC Wednesday Mystery Movie 26
Nabors, Jim 77
The Nancy Drew Mysteries 59
Nathan, Daniel A. (Dan) 40, 107, 120

National Lampoon's Vacation 39
National Telefilm Associates 61, 64
Natwil Productions 208
Nealis, Andy 113, 149
Ned and Stacey 177
Neff, Thomas 149, 178, 194
"The Neighbor" 118
Neilan, Marshall, Jr. 74
Neilson, James 120
Nelson, David 164
Nelson, Frank 192, 202, 205
Nelson, Gary 164, 171
Nelson, Gene 117
Nelson, James 40
Nelson, Lori 61, 63, 64, **65**–66
Nelson, Ozzie 196
Nelson, W. Argyle 5, 40, 94
Neptune's Daughter 83
Neumann, Dorothy 70
Never Too Young 90
The New Bob Cummings Show 163
New Faces of 1934 34
The New Interns 174
The New Loretta Young Show 52
The New Phil Silvers Show 89
Newhart 46
Newman, Lionel 107
Newmar, Julie 163
Nibley, Aaron 33
Nichols 26, 175
Night and the City 90
Night Key 42
Niven, David 137
Niver, James 5
Nixon, Richard M. 26
No Time for Sergeants 212
Nodella, Burt 40
Norden Productions 178
Norton Simon, Inc. 20
Norton, Cliff 87, **88**, 91
Not Wanted 137
Nothing Sacred 139
Novarro, Ramon 107
The Nude Bomb 19
Nuyen, France 8
Nyby, Christian (Chris) 33, 54, 80, 83, 113
Nye, Bud 33
Nye, Louis 15

O.K. Crackerby! 164–170
"Objective: Moon" 83
O'Brien, Bobby 186
O'Byrne, Bryan 171, 176
Obzina, Martin 120
Occasional Wife 171–177
O'Connell, David J. 67

O'Connor, Carroll 23
O'Connor, Donald 199
The Odd Couple 22
Official Films, Inc. 162
O'Halleren, Bill 164
Ohanian, George 67
O'Hanlon, James 33
O'Keefe, Winston 33
"The Old Grad" 118
"The Old Stowe Road" 69
Olivier, Laurence 210
O'Malley, J. Pat 208
Once Upon a Horse... 98
One Happy Family 45, 116
One of the Boys 135
"One Smart Apple" 70
Onionhead 49
Only You, Dick Daring! 52, 167
Operation Petticoat 79
"Operation Susan" 169
Oppenheimer, Gregg 9, 10
Oppenheimer, Jess 5–11
The Oregon Trail 86
Orkin, Harvey 61
Orlebeck, Les 113
Orr, William E. 40
Orr, William T. 208
O'Shea, Michael 80, **81**–86
Ostroff, Howard 12, 17
Otto, Bud 113
"Our Brothers' Keepers" 92
Our Miss Brooks 123
Our Town 205
Outrage 137
Outrageous Fortune 77
Owens, William 164

Packard, Elon 94, 208, 212
Packer, Doris 40, 43–44
Paget, Debra 66
Paige, Janis 63
Paisley, James 5, 94
The Pajama Game 71
Paley, Irving 67
Paley, William 25, 92, 150
Panic in Year Zero! 126
The Parent Trap 36
Paris, Jerry 12
Parker, Jim 164
Parker, Penney 107, 110–111
Parrish, Helene 61
Pasadena Playhouse 42, 183
Pascal, Milton 61, 107, 120, 178, 186, 202
Patrick, Lee 136, 140
Patterson, Neva 20, 26
The Patty Duke Show 59, 105, 112
Paul, Norman 12, 157, 208, 212

Index

Pearce, Monty 149
Pearl 155–156
Pearl Harbor Survivors Association 51
Peary, Harold (Hal) 29–30, 32
Peck's Bad Boy 116
Pelletier, Louis 5
Penn, Leo 149
"The Penthouse" 62
The People's Choice 41–42, 47, 51, 178–185
Pepe 174
Pepper, Cynthia 107, **108**
Pepper, Jack 109
Pereira, Hal 186
Perlman, Rhea 155–156
Perrin, Nat 61, 64
Perry Mason 11, 36
Pete and Gladys 5, 186–193, 197
The Peter and Mary Show 197
Peter Gunn 123
The Peter Lind Hayes Show 197
Peter Loves Mary 194–201
"Peter Takes Stock" 197
Peterson, Maggie 12, **13**, 17
Petticoat Junction 25, 104
The Phil Silvers Show 51, 98, 116, 141
Philco Television Playhouse 183
Philip Morris, Inc. 161
Philips, Lee 20
Phillips, Irving 120
Phillips, Webster 149
The Phyllis Diller Show 79
Picnic 42
The Pill Caper 148
Pillow Talk 77
Pillsbury 134
Pincus, Bernard F. 47, 178
Pintoff, Ernest 171
Place, Lou 164
Planet of the Apes 213
Platt, Ed 20, 23
Plaza Suite 22
Plymouth Adventure 110
Poitier, Sidney 189
Polifroni, Pam 87
Pollyanna 36, 71
Pommer, John 157
Porter, W.A. 164
Post, Ted 120
Poston, Tom 15
Powell, Dick 57, 59, 117, 137, 140, 150, 207
Powell, Norman 149
Powell, Richard 20
Powers, Mala 137

Prager, Stanley 33
Prelude 79
Prelutsky, Burt 20
Prentiss, Ann 145
Presley, Elvis 90, 112
Price, Roger 20
Pride of the Family 124
Priestley, Robert 5
Private Secretary 120
Procter & Gamble 38, 199
Prowse, Juliet 213
The Pruitts of Southampton 105
The Public Life of Cliff Norton 90
Pugh, Madelyn *see* Martin, Madelyn Pugh
Purcell, Robert 100, 171
Pycha, Jerome, Jr. 128
Pyke, Charles F. 40

Queen of Outer Space 110
Questel, Mae 154
Quillan, Joe 5, 94
Quine, Richard 128, 131
Quinn, Anthony 135

Radnitz, Brad 87
Raff, Robert H. 164
Rafferty, Frances 186, 190
Rafkin, Alan 20
Ragaway, Martin 61, 171
Raguse, Elmer 80
Rames, Neva 40
Randall, Tony 76
Randolph, Amanda 30
Randolph, Lillian 27, 30
Rank, J. Arthur 57
Rapf, Matthew 27
Rapp, Joel 87, 113, 187, 194
Rase, Betty Jane 131
Rawlings, Richard L. 87, 107, 143
Rawlins, Phil 208
Rawson, Ron 83
Ray, Harry 186
Ray, Roland 186
The Ray Milland Show 125–127; *see also Meet Mr. McNutley*
Raydic Productions 80
Raye, Martha 58
Raymond, Guy 67
Raynor, William 143
Reagan, Ronald 24
The Real McCoys 111, 204
Rebel Without a Cause 97
Red Channels 139
The Red Skelton Show 25, 71–72, 175
Redd, James S. 67, 120

Redmond, William 54, 57, 58
Redwood Productions 87
Reed, Alan 136, 140, 200
Reed, Robert 23
Reeve, Robert 12
Reid, Kenneth A. 12
Reilly, Jean Burt 208
Reiner, Carl 93
Reiss, Stuart 74
"Remember Pearl Harbor" 51
Renne, George 194, 202
Revenge of the Creature 63
Revue Productions 120
Reynolds, Burt 103
Reynolds, Gene 47, 52, 94, 100, 107, 171, 186, 208
Rhine, Larry 107, 186, 202
Rhoda 193
Rhodes, Phillip 202
Rich, Theodore (Ted) 12, 20, 74
The Richard Boone Show 192
Richards, Lloyd 54
Richardson, Don 107
Richlin, Maurice 54, 157, 161
"Ricky and Fred Are TV Fans" 192
Riesner, Dean 113
Rifkin, Leo 67, 107, 113
The Rifleman 11, 196
Riley, Jack B. 171, 173
The Rise of the Goldbergs 149
Rissien, Edward 194
Ritter, John 53
Ritter, Thelma 150
Rivers, Joan 168
Roach, James E. 194, 202
Road of Life 205
The Roaring Twenties 108
Robbie, Seymour 164
Robbins, Cindy 202, 205
Robert Montgomery Presents 70, 204
Roberts, Tony 128
Robinson, Bartlett 208
Robinson, J. Russel 111
Roche, Jack 186
Rock-a-Bye Baby 211
The Rockford Files 176
Rocky King, Inside Detective 49
Roe, Guy 54
Roemer, Gene 40, 178
Rogers, Al 164
Rogers, Dorothy 20
Rogers, Ginger 109
Rogers, Grayson 54
Rogers, Roswell 5
Rogers, Shorty 171
Rogne, Mandine 113

Index

Romantic Comedy 102
Roncom Video Films, Inc. 40, 44
The Roof 159
Room 222 26
Rooney, Mickey 77, 128, **129**–135
Roots 31
Rorke, Hayden 136, 139–140
Rose, David 80, 94, 96, 136
Rose, Kay 113, 149
Rose, Si 61
Rosen, Robert L. 87
Rosenbaum, R. Robert 33, 100
Rosenberg, E.J. 40, 178
Rosenberg, Ruby 157
Ross, Bill 54, 113, 136, 149, 202
Ross, Bob 67, 73
Ross, Earle 27
Ross, Joe E. 87, 89, 90
Ross, Marion 149, 154
Roth, Marty 74, 87, 100
Roup, Major 87
Route 66 78
Rowan and Martin's Laugh-In 50, 105
Royal Academy of Dramatic Arts 137
Rudolph the Red-Nosed Reindeer 169
Rudolph, Oscar 157
Ruggles, Charlie 98
Rugolo, Pete 67
Run, Buddy, Run 147, 148
The Runaways 26
Ruskin, Coby 12
Russell, John L. 120
Russell, Rosalind 141, 150
Russell, William 80
Russell, William D. 33, 186
Ryan, Meg 135
Ryan, Terry 164, 194

S.C. Johnson 9
Saboteur 159
Sabu 132
Saeta, Eddie 128
Saffian, R. Allen 113
The Saga of the Viking Women and Their Voyage to the Waters of the Great Sea Serpent 49
Saks, Sol 136, 139
Sales, Soupy 51, 118
Salkow, Sidney 120
Sally and Sam 112
Sam Benedict 175
Same Time, Next Year 102
Sanders, Dirk 8

Sandrich, Jay 12, 20
Santley, Joseph 128
Sargent, Dick 45
Sarver, Frank 202
Saunders, Herm 208
Savage, George 120
Savalas, Telly 36
Schallert, William 54, 59
Schiffer, Robert 128
Schiller, Bob 186, 190
Schlitz Playhouse 49
Schmeir, Faith 171
Schneider, Margaret 61
Schneider, Paul 61
Schoenbrun, Herman 87
Schrager, Rudy 149, 202
Schwartz, David 194
Schwartz, Elroy 87, 88, 91, 113
Schwartz, Howard 149
Schwartz, Sherwood 38, 87, 88, 89, 90, 99
Scott, Noel L. 208
Scott, Thomas 202
Scott, Walter M. 61, 107
Screen Actors Guild 71, 131, 213
Screen Gems 17, 33, 35, 36, 52, 100, 104, 171, 185
Scully, Vin 171, 173
The Sealtest Village Store 83
Search for Tomorrow 60, 97
Seattle Repertory Theatre 60
Seegar, Sara 171, 176
Seelin, Jerry 113
Seid, Art 61
Seiter, William 120
Seldes, Gilbert 78
Selditz, Leon 164, 171
Self, William 107
Sellecca, Connie 46
"Senior Citizen Charlie" 78
Serling, Rod 72
Seuss, Dr. 198
"Seven Days to Live" 130
The Seven Year Itch 202, 204
Seventh Heaven 137
Sex Kittens Go to College 116
The Sex Symbol 213
Seyrig, Delphine 188
The Shanghai Gesture 90
Shannon, Wanda 45
Shapiro, Stanley 54
Sharp, Henry 5, 186
Sharp, Phil 186
Sharpe, Don 159, 161
Shaw, Reta 67, 71
Shea, Jack 87, 164
Shea, William 47
Shear, Barry 33
Sheldon, James 5, 107, 202

Sheldon, Les 176
Sheldon, Willard 120
Sher, Jack 107
Sherman, Harry T. 20
Shoop, Pamela Susan 161
Shore, Lillian 186
Shorr, Lester 186
A Shot in the Dark 11
Shufflebottom, Jean *see* Carson, Jeannie
Shuken, Phillip 94
Shula, Dorothy 183
Sid Caesar Presents 35
Siegel, Roy 40
Sillman, Leonard 34
Silo, Susan 173
Silver, Dave 33
Silverman, Ron 164
Silvers, Phil 38, 89, 113
Simon, Al 178
Simon, Danny 186, 194
Simon, Neil 22, 104
Sinatra, Frank 140
Sindler, Irving 186
Sing Along with Mitch 78
Singer, Ray 12, 33, 74, 80, 83, 94, 96
Singer, Sidney A. 80
Singleton, Doris 5, **6**, 9, 27, 31, 181
Siodmak, Curt 54
"Site Unseen" 207
The $64,000 Question 62
Skelton, Red 65, 76
Skiles, Marlin 94
Skippy 182, 184–185
Slade, Bernard 100, 102, 104
"A Small Matter of Being Fired" 74
Smith, Cecil 18, 38
Smith, Craig 87
Smith, Frank 54
Smith, Gil 194, **195**
Smith, Howard (editor) 178
Smith, Howard (actor) 194, 200
Smith, Jack Martin 107
Smith, James E. 157
Smith, Kent 23
Smith, Paul 143, 148, 149, 152
"Smog Gets in Your Eyes" 85
Snyder, Earl 164, 194, 202
"Sock and the Syrene" 180
"Sock Takes the Plunge" 181
Solomon, Jack 149, 194
Solomon, Leo 61
Sommars, Julie 20, **21**, 22–24
Sommers, Jay 33, 36
Sonntag, Jack 54, 113, 149, 194, 202
Sothern, Ann 71, 120

Index

The Sound of Music 60
Sound Off 131
Sousa, Robert 12
Spigelgass, Leonard 150
Spin City 22
Spinout 90
Stacy, James 211
Stagecoach West 161, 207
Stahl, Francis E. 208
Stalmaster-Lister Company 47, 194
Stand Up and Cheer 83
Stander, Arthur 149, 152
Stanford, Don 67
"Stanley the Fighter" 145
"Stanley the Jailbreaker" 145
Stanwyck, Barbara 82
"A Star Is Born" 196
Star Trek 119
Starkey, Dewey 128
Starr, Belle 49
Starr, Ben 120, 157
Starting from Scratch 99, 213
Steens, Frances 186
Stell, Aaron 178
Stephens, Laraine 164
Stephenson, John 178
Sterling, Robert 67, **68**, 70–73
Stern, Leonard 20, 23, 24, 74, 75
The Steve Allen Show 15
Stevens, Connie 208, ***209***, 211–213
Stevens, Craig ***21***
Stewart, Charles 5, 12, 164, 169
Stewart, James 135
Stone, Ezra 5, 164
Storefront Lawyers 26
Storm, Gale 41, 58, 130
Strait-Jacket 104
Streisand, Barbra 168
Strenge, Walter 143
Strickland, Amzie 16
Strimpell, Stephen 143, ***144***, 146–148
The Stu Erwin Show 63
Stuart, Barbara 27, 31
Studio One 162, 204
Styler, Burt 33, 87, 107, 113, 120
The Subject Was Roses 22
"Subletting the Apartment" 63
Suddenly, Last Summer 42–43
Sugar Babies 134
Sugarfoot 141
Sullivan, Don 20
Sullivan, Frank 27

Sultan, Arne 20, 21, 24
Summers, Ray 164
The Sunday Man 146
The Sunshine Boys 213
Superman 52
Supertrain 99
Swackhamer, E.W. 47, 100, 102
Swartz, Kenneth (Ken) 12, 40
Sweet Sixteen 110
Swenson, Karl 175
Swift, David 33, 35, 36, 37
Sylos, Ralph 143
Szathmary, Irving 12, 74
Szathmary, William *see* Dana, Bill

The Tab Hunter Show 71
Tackitt, Wesley Marie 107, 110
Take Her, She's Mine 112
Talbot, Nita 94, 97–98, 99
Talbott, Gloria 136
Talent Associates 20, 23
Talent Scouts 98
Tannen, Charles 33
Tannura, Phillip 178
Tartikoff, Brandon 66
Tarzan 148
Tate 44
Taub, Warner, Jr. 136
Taylor, Carlie 113, 194, 202
Taylor, Don 124
Taylor, Keith 113, ***114***, 117, 118, 119
Tell It to Groucho 154
Ten from Your Show of Shows 38
Terry, Jay 20
Tewksbury, Peter 178
That Girl 36, 105, 175
That Touch of Mink 76
That's My Boy 61
There Shall Be No Night 116
"There's Got to Be Something Wrong with Her" 101
"There's No Such Thing as a Bad Barracuda" 37
They Came to Cordura 174
They Shall Not Die 204
They Won't Forget 115
The Thin Man 98
The Thing from Another World 83
The Thing with Two Heads 127
The Third Man 16
The 30-Foot Bride of Candy Rock 199
This Is Alice 64

This Is Your Life 82, 137
Thomas, Danny 12, 15, 19, 38, 78, 124
Thomas, Dean 27
Thomas, Harry 74
Thomas, Marlo 105, 175
Thompson, D.J. 123
Thompson, Gene 20, 171
Thompson, Marshall 5, ***6***, 8–11
Thorpe, Jerry 204
Those Websters 29
Those Whiting Girls 205
Three Coins in the Fountain 112
Three's Company 77, 205
Thriller 141, 205, 207
A Thurber Carnival 35, 204, 205
Tibbles, George 70
Tickle Me 90
"Tight Quarters" 51
The Time Tunnel 89
Titanic 115
Tobacco Road 82
Tobin, George 40, 74
Todd, Sherman 157, 202
Tolkin, Mel 67, 74, 107, 194
The Tom Ewell Show 5, 11, 196, 202–207
"Tom Takes Over" 202–203
Tompkins, Joan 171, 194
Tompkins, Yewell *see* Ewell, Tom
The Tonight Show 140
"Too Many Secretaries" 27
"Too Many Sergeants" 118
Toomey, Regis 128, 131
Top Banana 77
Topper 71, 140
"El Toro" 159
Torpin, Don 12, 149, 202
Townsend, Perc 120
Tracy, Spencer 98
Trager, Milt 94
Travolta, John 45
"The Tree" 125
A Tree Grows in Brooklyn 83
Trepeck, James 40
The Trouble with Angels 141
The Trouble with Tom 207
Truex, Ernest 186
Truscott-Jones, Reginald *see* Milland, Ray
"The Trusting Wife" 8
Tuesday Night at the Movies 24
Tugend, Harry 120, 125
The Tunnel of Love 116
Turk, Fred 40
Turner, Lana 161

Index

Tuttle, Frank 74
Tuttle, Tom 12
"Twelve Angry Men" 162
20th Century–Fox Television Productions 61, 107
"20th Century, Here We Come" 91
The Twilight Zone 36, 72, 117
The Twinkle in God's Eye 134
Two on a Guillotine 212
Tyne, George 20

"Uncle Paul's Insurance" 190
Under the Yum Yum Tree 35–36
United Artists Television 164
Universal Studios 143
"The Unseating of Councilman Sock" 180
The Untouchables 108
Urecal, Minerva 120, 123, 125
U.S. Fish and Wildlife Service 178
"The Utterly Perfect Man" 63

Vaccarino, Maurice 94
Vague, Vera 54, 59
Vail, Lester 61
"The Vamp" 111
Van Dyke, Dick 9, 78
Van Enger, Charles 164
Van Horne, Harriet 10
Van Keuren, Sidney 27, 80
Van Marter, George 178
Van Scoyk, Robert 107
Van Tamelin, Jan M. 54, 113, 164
Van Trees, James 128, 164, 178
Vassar, Charles Q. 61, 164
Vickers, Martha 131
Victor, Thelda 194
Vintage '60 77
The Virginian 86, 141
"A Visit from Steve's Mother" 82
Voland, Herbert 100, 104
Volcano Pictures, Inc. 128
Vollaerts, Rik 120, 157, 161
Voyage to the Bottom of the Sea 50, 91
Vreeland, Bob 194, 202

Wald, Malvin 120
Walker, Pat 131
Walt Disney Productions 199
Walt Disney's Wonderful World of Color 91
Walter of the Jungle 148
Walters, Charles 20

Wanted: Dead or Alive 196, 201
Ward, Skip 149, 152
Warner, Jack 160
Warner, Jody 45
Warner Brothers Pictures 208, 212
Warren, Eda 100
Wasden, Marlene *see* Dalton, Abby
Waterman, Willard 27, **28**, 29
Watkins, Linda 23
Watson, Bobs 94, 98
Wayne, John 161
Weatherwax, Paul 61
Webb, Donald E. 87
Webb, Jack 17, 97, 184
Webster, Frank 74
Webster, Tony 164
"The Wedding" 6
"Wedding Anniversary" 40
Weis, Don 113, 136, 145
Weiskopf, Bob 186, 190
Weiss, Joseph 33
Welch, Raquel 210
Welcome Back, Kotter 50
Welk, Lawrence 58, 59
Welles, Sheilah 145
Wells, Jacqueline *see* Bishop, Julie
Wendy and Me 22, 208–213
"Wendy the Waitress" 210
"Wendy's Private Eye" 210
Werner, Lawrence 33, 171
Werner, Mort 15
Wessel, Richard 80
Wesson, Dick 178, 181
West Side Story 174
Weyman, Hap 20
"What Elephant?" 17
Wheeler, Lyle 61
When My Baby Smiles at Me 22
When Things Were Rotten 147
Where's Raymond? 115
White, Andy 27, 31
White, Betty 66
White, Christine 67, 70, 71
White, David 118
White, Jesse 145
White, Robert (Bob) 80, 113, 136
White, Stanford 126
The White Shadow 52
Who Was That Lady I Saw You With? 198
"Who Was That Man?" 191
Who's Afraid of Virginia Woolf? 212

Wiard, Bill 208
Wickes, Mary 149, 152–153, 155, 198
Widrig, Clem W. 61
Wiesen, Bernard 61
Wilcox, Frank 87, 91
Wild, Harry J. 149, 194, 202
Wildcat 188
Wilder, Myles 143
Wildley, Lou 94
Wiler, Lloyd 47
Wilk, Max 113, 202
Will and Grace 177
Williams, Cara 5, 186, **187**, 189, 190, 192, 193
Williams, Guy 130
Williams, Hope 20
Williams, Tennessee 167
Willock, Dave 107, 110
Wilson, Gerard J. 107
Wilson, Stanley 67, 120, 143
Window on Main Street 70
Winged Victory 116, 123
Winkler, Harry 20
Witt, Paul Junger 171
Wolf, Harry 47
Wolpert, Roland 20
"The Woman's Touch" 96
Wood, Bob 25
Wood, Edward D., Jr. 64
Wooden, Arvard 47
Woods, Alan 107
World of Giants 9
The World of Suzie Wong 8
Wormell, Dick 186
Worth, Lothrop 27
Wostak, Ray 47
Wray, Richard G. 120
Wurtzel, Paul 74
Wyatt, Jane 141
Wyckoff, Robert 33
Wyle, George 87

You Asked for It 85
You Bet Your Life 123, 130, 154, 184
You Can't Take It with You 192
Young, Alan 109, 145, 146, 148
Young, Collier 136, 137
Young, Ernie 47
Young, Loretta 120, 151
Your Show of Shows 33, 37, 56

Zimmer, Jon 67
Zorro 130
Zorro and Son 19
Zugsmith, Albert 116

www.ingramcontent.com/pod-product-compliance
Ingram Content Group UK Ltd.
Pitfield, Milton Keynes, MK11 3LW, UK
UKHW041940140426
5217IPUK00014B/575